CZARTORYSKI

AND EUROPEAN UNITY

1770-1861

POLAND'S MILLENNIUM SERIES

OF THE

KOŚCIUSZKO FOUNDATION

Czartoryski

AND EUROPEAN UNITY

1770-1861

BY M. KUKIEL

If we wish to progress
we must have an object we have not yet attained.
And in order to be always in progress
we must be capable of conceiving an object
which will never be attained.

—CZARTORYSKI, *1803*.

PRINCETON NEW JERSEY

PRINCETON UNIVERSITY PRESS

1955

Printed in the United States of America
by Princeton University Press, Princeton, New Jersey

PREFACE

IT WAS A VERY LONG LIFE—it lasted more than ninety years—and from Czartoryski's early youth until his death it was constantly devoted to the cause of his country and to the still greater cause of the freedom and unity of Europe. It was continuously connected with the most important events of 19th century European history.

Czartoryski was born before the First Partition of Poland, when the Commonwealth was still intact and, despite its weaknesses and ordeals, still a great power. He appeared on the political scene at the time of Poland's internal regeneration and the constitutional reform of the Great Diet. After Poland's catastrophe he was a hostage at the court of Catherine II; a Russian dignitary, he became a friend of the Grand Duke Alexander and, after some dramatic adventures, the young Emperor's mentor and closest confidant. He was a member of the "Secret Committee" (the real government of Russia), Acting Minister of Foreign Affairs, responsible for an entirely new policy of the Empire and for plans for the reshaping of Europe that would ensure to its nations freedom and security and lay the foundation-stones of a European union. He obstinately championed the idea of rebuilding Poland in dynastic or personal union with Russia. He was Curator of the University of Vilna and of the educational district covering the Polish eastern provinces annexed by Russia in all the three partitions, and was therefore responsible for the momentous progress Polish civilization achieved in those territories during the first three decades of the 19th century, progress which strengthened the Polish national consciousness in Lithuania and Ruthenia for generations. He was Tsar Alexander's closest collaborator at the Congress of Vienna, and together with him the founder of the Kingdom of Poland—the so-called Congress-Kingdom—as well as the organizer of the new state. Shortly after, he became a defender of its constitution and of the rights of its people against arbitrary acts of violence and autocracy.

Preface

After the outbreak of the revolution of 1830, it was Czartoryski who became the president of the Polish national government. He was largely responsible for the stubborn perseverance of fighting Poland as well as for the extension of the struggle beyond the frontier of the Kingdom to the provinces of Lithuania and Ruthenia. Afterwards, as outlaw and exile for the next thirty years, he ceaselessly championed not only the rights of his people, whose spokesman he became, but also the freedom of Europe. Very many of his countrymen recognized him as their "chief," as did many Serbs and Bulgars; the Circassian insurgents looked to him as their leader and the protector of their cause. He was recognized as king *de facto* by a strong political faction in exile and by many people in Poland. He survived Tsar Nicholas and defied his successor's *point de rêveries*. After thirty years of inexorable struggle against the Russian impact on Europe, when new hopes for Poland were stirred, his own life was nearing its end. Still, his were the instructions which determined the political attitude of most of the Poles. He fought as a soldier in 1792, in the first of the series of wars for his country's independence; then, when the period of armed struggle was nearing its close, he gave his last blessing to his people.

He was the contemporary of five Russian sovereigns. His partners and adversaries included Vorontsov, Rumiantsev, Nesselrode, and Gorchakov; Talleyrand, Guizot, Thiers, Lamartine, Walewski, and Drouyn de Lhuys; Pitt, Fox, Castlereagh, Grey, Palmerston, and Russell; Cobenzl, Metternich, Buol, and Goluchowski. He was an adversary of the great Napoleon and became a friend of Napoleon III. His activities as statesman started at the time of Jefferson's presidency and ended at the time of Lincoln's.

Czartoryski's political life was a long and difficult one; and it is not easy to write his biography. More than a thousand volumes and portfolios of his records were carefully preserved by his son and transferred from his Paris residence, the Hôtel Lambert, to the Czartoryski Museum at Cracow where—for fifty years —they were freely accessible for historical research. The selection of his correspondence with Emperor Alexander I was published shortly after his death by his son, and a more extensive volume, together with his French memoirs in 1887, by Charles

Preface

de Mazade; an English edition (not quite identical) was published a year later. But until recently there was no detailed historical monograph on Czartoryski. The large biography by B. Zaleski (1881) remained unfinished; it ended with the beginning of the Prince's political career. In the first two decades of this century, monographs and essays by the great historian Szymon Askenazy helped considerably to elucidate Czartoryski's activities up to the November revolution of 1830, and some other historians, mostly of Askenazy's school, supplemented his research with their detailed studies. But no one undertook the task of writing a complete biography of Czartoryski, and the second half of his political life (1830-1861) remained largely neglected by historians; even Askenazy saw it as a period of unrealistic political romanticism.

The facts of Czartoryski's policy in exile were elucidated only after the First World War by Marceli Handelsman and his school, and many of its problems were analyzed in a series of detailed studies. Handelsman became more and more impressed by the immense scope of Czartoryski's diplomatic activities in exile, by the diversity and continuity of his efforts, by the fertility of his ideas and his tenacity in adversity. He became aware that Czartoryski's policy was a constant challenge to Russian pressure on Europe and that it prepared the ground for future anti-Russian coalitions; that its aims were not negative, but directed at the integration of Europe. He strove for better understanding and more solidarity among the nations of Western Europe; for the liberation of the countries of the Middle Zone of Europe between Germany and Russia; for bringing them closer together by allaying their mutual hostilities; for uniting efforts and paving the way towards a future federation of free peoples.

Shortly before the Second World War, Handelsman published a short biographical essay on Czartoryski, and started to write a comprehensive biography. In wartime, under German occupation, he continued that work in ever-present danger of arrest, often in hiding to avoid prison or death; he interrupted it later in order to write a detailed monograph of Czartoryski's policy during the revolution of 1848 and the Crimean War. This he managed to finish before he was arrested by the Gestapo in 1944; he died in a concentration camp shortly before the liberation.

The typescript of his work was preserved, and the first volume containing the biography of Czartoryski up to 1846 was published in Warsaw in 1948. A second followed in 1949. It contains a detailed study of Czartoryski's policy in the crucial period 1847-1849. The third, published in 1950 in two parts, gives a full political history of the Crimean War and brings the biography to its conclusion. But the whole work was written under appalling conditions, and the author's profound knowledge of Czartoryski's papers and his great learning could not appear at their best, in complete scholarly form. There remain many points open to controversy or demanding further elucidation; nor is it possible to endorse all the author's judgments.

The present book was written under very different circumstances, in the liberty and security of exile on friendly British soil; I enjoyed the hospitality of the British Museum, of the Public Record Office, of the Polish Research Centre in London, and also of the Bibliothèque Polonaise in Paris. The Polish correspondence of Lord Dudley Coutts Stuart in the Collection of Harrowby Manuscripts at Sandon Hall proved of paramount value, the more so because the Polish collections, and especially the archives from the Hôtel Lambert, well known to me from my long period of work in the Czartoryski Museum at Cracow, remained at the time beyond my reach. This book is therefore but an essay, a sketch of a historical portrait of the statesman as I perceive him after having lived several years among his relics and his papers, and after a study of his political ideas and activities.

Czartoryski was an ardent patriot, but he never confined himself and his activities to Polish affairs. His outlook was that of a European and a Westerner, his views were worldwide and extended far beyond his own generation. In many respects he seems nearer to us now than ever before. There was a great deal of foresight in his ideas and deeds, and many of the problems he dealt with have reappeared in this century. His ideas on European freedom and unity would in these days meet with more understanding than they did a hundred years ago, and his various political concepts present answers even to essential problems of today.

During his entire political life he was an Anglophile, connected by bonds of friendship and collaboration with British statesmen and the British people. There is much understanding and admiration for Britain in his letters, speeches, and writings, as well as much bitter criticism of British policy. But he never lost his faith in the greatness of the British nation; he accurately foresaw the future evolution of the British Empire for some generations to come, and, like many a Continental liberal statesman, sometimes dreamed of a Pax Britannica in Europe—a peace of liberty, justice, and the rule of law. He inspired many motions and debates in the British Parliament; and from the last of them a message of hope was brought to his bedside as he lay dying.

From his early years until the last hours of his life, Czartoryski's hopes for the future of Europe and of Poland were based on a deep-rooted trust in the providential part to be played by British liberalism in the history of mankind. He did not anticipate that that role would in time be assumed by the young democratic power of the New World. *Lux ex Occidente*, which he expected, was to appear only fifty-six years after his death, in President Wilson's message and in his Fourteen Points which so strangely coincided with the conceptions and claims of the Polish statesman.

May this book introduce him once more after many decades to the English-speaking world.

The author wishes to acknowledge his debt of deepest gratitude to the late Prince Adam Louis Czartoryski and to Princess Marie Louise Czartoryska, whose generous kindness and unstinted confidence allowed him to study the life and deeds of their ancestor under the most favorable conditions; to the Right Honorable the Earl of Harrowby and the Right Honorable the Viscount Sandon, who kindly granted him access to the Harrowby Manuscripts at Sandon Hall and especially to the papers of Lord Dudley Coutts Stuart and allowed him every facility for studying them; to Count Joseph Michałowski in Rome for having lent him a copy of the Memorandum of 1803 and for his most valuable comments and remarks; to Count Stefan Zamoyski, whose collection provided the iconographic material; to Doctor Czesław Chowaniec, the Chief Librarian of the Bibliothèque Polonaise in Paris, for his most valuable help; and to all those who assisted him in his research by their friendly advice.

He is most gratefully obliged to Sir Lewis Namier, F.B.A.,

who encouraged him to write the present volume and took much interest in its progress; to Professor Alexander Bruce Boswell for his friendly observations; to Professor Samuel Harrison Thompson of Colorado University for his invaluable support and advice; to Professor Stephen Mizwa, the President of the Kościuszko Foundation for having sponsored the book.

He also feels greatly indebted to Mrs. Marian Carr, who revised and corrected the first English draft, and to Miss R. Miriam Brokaw of Princeton University Press, who gave the finishing touch to the text.

Acknowledgement is also due to Major S. Gruca, who has designed the maps, for that most valuable contribution.

M.K.

ABBREVIATIONS USED IN NOTES

MANUSCRIPTS

Cz.Mss. Manuscripts of the Czartoryski Museum, Cracow

H.Mss. Harrowby Manuscripts at Sandon Hall

B.P.Mss. Manuscripts of the Bibliothèque Polonaise, Paris

F.O.65 Public Record Office, Foreign Office, Correspondence with Russia

PRINTED

Angeberg *Angeberg. Recueil des traités, conventions, etc. concernant la Pologne.* (1862)

Brit. Diplomacy C. Webster, *British Diplomacy: 1813-1815.* (1921)

Cz.M.(E) *Memoirs of Prince Adam Czartoryski and His Correspondence with Alexandre I, with documents relative to the Prince's negotiations with Pitt, Fox, and Brougham, and an account of his conversations with Lord Palmerston and other English statesmen.* Edited by Adam Gielgud. 2 vols. (London, 1888)

Cz.M.(F) *Mémoires du Prince Adam Czartoryski et sa correspondance avec l'Empereur Alexandre I.* Publiés par Charles de Mazade. 2 vols. (Paris, 1887)

Despatches J. H. Rose, *Despatches relating to the Third Coalition.* (1904)

Gleason, *Russophobia* H. Gleason, *The Genesis of Russophobia in Great Britain* (1950)

Handelsman M. Handelsman, *Adam Czartoryski.* 3 vols. (1948-1950)

Martens T. T. Martens, *Recueil des traités conclus par la Russie avec les puissances étrangères.* 14 vols. (1875ff.)

Nicholas Mikhailovich, *Alexandre I* Grand Duc Nicholas Mikhailovich, *L'Empereur Alexandre I.* 2 vols. (1912)

Nicholas Mikhailovich, *Stroganov* Grand Duc Nicholas Mikhailovich, *Le Comte Paul Stroganov.* 3 vols. (1905)

Sbornik *Sbornik Russkago Istoricheskago Obshchestva* (Magazine of the Russian Historical Society).

Abbreviations

Webster, *Castlereagh*   C. Webster, *The Foreign Policy of Castle-reagh*, 1812-1815. (1931)

Webster, *Palmerston*   C. Webster, *The Foreign Policy of Palmerston*. (1951)

Zamoyski   Jenerał Zamoyski (Ladislas Zamoyski's notes and papers). 6 vols. (1910ff.)

CONTENTS

Contents

Contents

Contents

ILLUSTRATIONS

CZARTORYSKI

AND EUROPEAN UNITY

1770-1861

CZARTORYSKI
By Paul Delaroche, ca 1850

THE STATESMAN
By de Antoni, 1831

THE YOUNG DIPLOMAT
By Joseph Abel, 1798

CHAPTER 1

FAMILY, PARENTS, EARLY YEARS

THE CZARTORYSKIS are princes of a dynastic Lithuanian extraction; they are descendants of Gedymin, Grand Duke of Lithuania, and of his son and successor, Olgerd. The founder of their family, *dux Constantinus felicis memoriae*, has been identified by modern historians with Olgerd's son, a brother of the founder of the Jagellon dynasty of Polish kings. In any case the Jagellons shared with the Czartoryskis their coat of arms and in two royal diplomas they were referred to as *fratres, consanguinei nostri*, or *sanguinis vinculo coniuncti*.[1]

For three consecutive centuries the Czartoryskis played a part in the Commonwealth's politics, but their influence was somewhat eclipsed by the rise of great new families, of less elevated descent but possessing immense fortunes. In the first decades of the 18th century the political exertions of Prince Casimir, Vice-Chancellor of Lithuania, his clever and energetic wife Isabella, nee Morstin, and their highly gifted sons, August and Michael, enhanced their position, as did his connection with the dynamic, gallant, and influential parvenu, Stanislas Poniatowski, who became his son-in-law. The marriage in 1731 of August Czartoryski to the heiress of the enormous fortune of the Sieniawski ensured the so-called "Family"[2] an extremely powerful position.

In the last centuries the Commonwealth had elected its kings

[1] The diplomas of Vladislaus III (1442) and Sigismundus Augustus (1569) in Cz. Family Papers in Cracow. For the descent of the Czartoryskis, see A. Boniecki, *Herbarz polski* (Polish Armorial), 1900, III, 319-321; and S. M. Kuczyński, *Ziemie Czernichowsko-Siewierskie pod rządami Litwy* (The Territories of Czernichow and Siewierz under Lithuanian Sovereignty), 1936, pp. 53, 170-171, 185. Constantine Olgerdovich appears in contemporary sources as having the territories of Czernichov (on the east of the Dnieper) and Czartorysk (in Volhynia) as fiefs.

[2] The term "Family" was commonly applied to them; it was used for a powerful family group with a policy of its own and a strong political influence.

freely and *viritim*; in fact they had already been imposed three times by armed violence and foreign intervention. (This had happened in the case of the two Saxon kings.) Loyalty to the sovereigns could not grow strong: their prestige was low, the parliamentary system was doomed to complete paralysis by the use of the *liberum veto*, the governmental functions were dying out, the treasury scarcely existed, the army was a mere skeleton. It was not to be wondered at that the Family's policy aimed at a revolutionary change: to seize power in order to rebuild the state and its institutions and to establish a hereditary monarchy on the English pattern. Their dynastic consciousness revived; aspirations restrained for centuries again came to the fore.

Towards the end of the reign of Augustus III (1733-1763) the situation was ripe for change. The party of the Family was led at this time by two brothers: August, the Voyvode of Ruthenia, and Michael, the Chancellor of Lithuania. It was predominant though bitterly opposed. The necessity of fundamental reforms was largely recognized. The mighty brain of Stanislas Konarski, a great political writer, founder of the Collegium Nobilium and reformer of the Piarists' schools, associated himself with their policy. The Family looked for foreign support and secured it in St. Petersburg. With Russia's help they prepared a coup designed to set aside the Saxon King and to gain unlimited control of the Commonwealth. The King's death simplified the problem, but it also necessitated the designation of his presumptive successor. The Family's candidate had been Prince August Czartoryski, a strong personality with great influence, but he was excluded by the Empress Catherine II when she ascended the throne. She herself had hinted at first at his son, the young general of Podolia, Prince Adam Casimir, a brilliant cavalier of unusual charm, but he declined the offer. So the new Empress's choice then fell upon their nephew and her favorite, the young Stanislas Poniatowski, who, although an intelligent, versatile, highly educated, and good-natured man, was without a strong personality or standing of his own, and was considered by the Empress to be a *sujet convenable*. He became, by her will, Poland's last king.

In spite of this disappointment, the Family's policy seemed to be a success. They were in control of the 1764 convocational diet preceding the election; Prince Adam Casimir was its marshal (i.e., president); the armed resistance of the Patriotic Party was broken, important reforms were voted, and the government was placed firmly in their hands. The subsequent election of Poniatowski—King Stanislas Augustus—was a mere formality. But almost immediately serious complications arose as a result of a fundamental miscalculation in the Family's political plans. What they wanted was permanent control of the government in an independent Poland; they were willing to follow a policy of friendship with Russia and to conclude a defensive alliance with her, but as an equal partner and without abandoning their own policy. The Russian attitude, however, despite some differences of opinion in Catherine's counsels regarding Poland's internal problems and territorial integrity, was one of complete control of Polish policy. In particular, Russia demanded control of Poland's foreign policy and would not tolerate any separate links between Poland and other powers. The Czartoryskis could, perhaps, have remained masters of Poland's domestic policy, but only at the price of her independence. That price they were not prepared to pay. They were sharply criticized by some historians and political writers for not having been more compliant to Catherine's will, but they regarded themselves as representatives of a great country and of a proud people.

A series of new Russian interventions in Poland resulted in Catherine's support for the reactionary opposition and its revolt under the form of the Radom Confederation, the breaking of the political power of the Family and the abolition of most of their reforms. The Family's work was completely destroyed, and they had to advise the King to submit to Russian dictation. Prince Adam Casimir and his wife, the charming Princess Isabella, tried to save the political position of the Family by using their close friendship with the omnipotent, authoritarian, rash, and violent Prince Repnin, the Russian Ambassador, in an attempt to tame him. A sentimental romance between the Russian proconsul and the young Princess unexpectedly followed; it survived Repnin's mission to Warsaw, and lasted several years, though not without dramatic entanglements.

Family, Parents, Early Years

The country was split by a prolonged armed revolt against the King and the Russian control, the Confederation of Bar. Four years of embittered struggle followed, which was conducted with more self-sacrifice and tenacity than political wisdom, efficiency, or military skill. The old Czartoryskis strove in vain for a reconciliation between the nation and the King, and for an understanding between him and France, which supported the Confederates. The struggle ended with the catastrophe of the First Partition. The Family's policy was a complete failure. Both the old leaders retired from the political scene.[3]

In the period between the First and the Third Partitions (1773-1795) the Family, deprived of strong leadership, was represented by their common heirs, Adam Casimir and Isabella. Prince Adam Casimir, the General of Podolia, entered the political stage in 1764. He was for twenty-five years in command of the Warsaw Military School (Cadet Corps) and he succeeded in inculcating in his many pupils a strong sense of duty and a wholehearted devotion to their country. Openminded, an intellectual with a passion for learning, a writer with an extensive knowledge of world literature, eager to promote intellectual and artistic activities and progress in every field, he was an inspiring leader. Among the pupils of his school were Kościuszko, the great revolutionary leader; Niemcewicz, long the most outstanding Polish writer; scores of future generals whose names resounded later in the Kościuszko revolution and in the period of the Napoleonic wars. All of them remained bound by grateful memories to their commander.

When, after the abolition of the Jesuit order, the Committee for National Education, an early ministry of education, was founded, Czartoryski became one of its most zealous and useful workers. The Prince General was in fact much more of a prince philosopher and was largely responsible for the intellectual regeneration of his country in the last three decades of the Polish Commonwealth.

His personal and public life was not without some anomalies.

---

[3] On the history of the Czartoryskis, see B. Zaleski, *Żywot A. J. Czartoryskiego*, 1881, I; and the 36 biographies of the Czartoryskis in *Polski Słownik Biograficzny*, IV; and L. Dębicki, *Puławy*, 1887-1888, 4 vols.

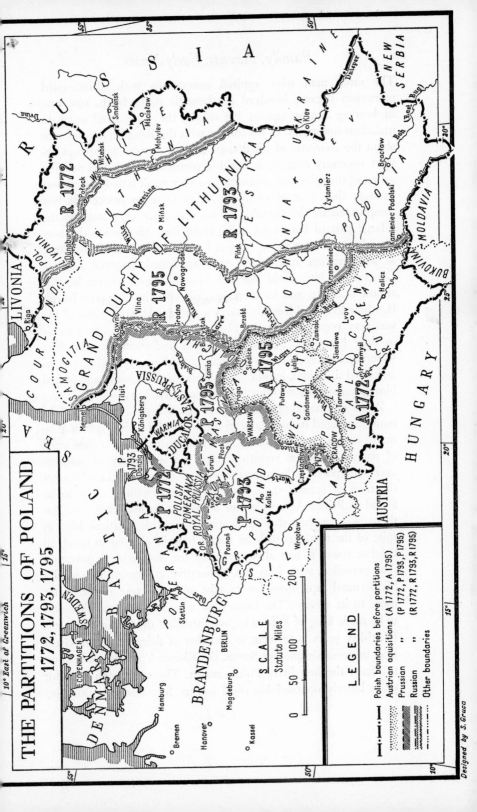

Family, Parents, Early Years

The same man who inspired generations with disinterested patriotism became involved in domestic party feuds, obstinate in bearing rancor against his cousin the King, and open to malicious influences. In his contest with the King he did not care about the character of his domestic allies, nor did he always observe necessary restraint in seeking partners abroad. His position —that of the mightiest aristocrat in a very weak state—was almost stronger than that of many sovereign German princes. It was complicated by the fact that he became, after 1773, *sujet mixte,* a large part of his estates being from then on outside the new boundaries, so that he was obliged to take the oath of allegiance as an Austrian subject. He was appointed Imperial Cavalry General and later Field Marshal. His links with Vienna became almost intimate, and he corresponded with the Emperor Joseph II, whose long and friendly letters were signed "Abbé Sartori." He was very popular with the Hungarians and was invited to sit in their House of Magnates. Divided and conflicting loyalties were the inescapable consequences, and these, by giving rise to awkward situations, handicapped his political activities and forced him to pursue a somewhat tortuous political line.

When emphasizing these aspects of his life, Marceli Handelsman discovered in his character a certain Hamletism common to many of his contemporaries. If Hamletism means a deficiency of energy in action resulting from the supremacy of intellect over will power—the supremacy of the man of thought over the man of action—there certainly was something of it to be found in Prince Adam Casimir as well as in his eldest son. But there was another striking feature about his political life: in spite of the tortuous path he found himself obliged to tread, in the last resort it was always anxiety for his country's salvation that prevailed with him—an imperative command to sacrifice his personal aspirations for its sake and to devote himself once more to its service. The same man who as young cavalier was to be made king of Poland by overthrowing the Saxon, Augustus III, thirty years later went to Dresden as delegate of the Great Diet to persuade another Saxon, the Elector Frederick Augustus, to accept the hereditary Polish crown. The same man who for years bitterly opposed his royal cousin, Stanislas Augustus, became his ardent collaborator in the great task of laying the foundations of a new political structure for the Commonwealth and of introducing the new Constitution of May 3, 1791. That brilliant representative of the *ancien régime*, who was treated by Joseph II as a personal friend and related by his daughter's marriage to the three dynastic partners in Poland's partition, was involved in the initial planning of the national revolution of 1794 and later, in 1812, joined the French revolutionary Caesar, became Marshal of the General Confederation of the kingdom of Poland, and sponsored the offer of the Polish throne to Bonaparte. A marked feature of his political temper—be it called Hamletism or not—was the absence of any longing for power and even a certain revulsion against striving for it. Another feature—manifested in his later years—was his dislike of any kind of extremism in politics, his preference for moderation and restraint, and his inclination towards a middle way. Some of these characteristics were inherited by his eldest son and namesake.

His political life was undoubtedly influenced by the strong personality of his wife, Princess Isabella, who was an emotional, sentimental woman, versatile, of inexhaustible vivacity and restless activity, ambitious and eager to play a part on the historical stage. Their ways parted for a time. At the beginning theirs was a *mariage de raison* made in order to combine the inheritance of the Czartoryskis with that of the Flemming family.[4] But after a period of sentimental adventures, they became united by a sincere friendship which lasted for the rest of their very long lives. Princess Isabella's ambitions became more and more centered on the salvation of her country, and on her children's part in its destinies. She found happiness in living for her children and for the Polish cause, and was in constant readiness to sacrifice everything for her country's sake, like the Spartan mother in the play by Kniaźnin, the poet, her admirer and friend. When her children grew up and left their parents' home, she found

---

[4] When in London (1764, or 1772?) the Princess suffered from "nostalgia"; so her husband introduced her to Franklin, whose very serious but kind and suave personality had a salutary influence upon her, and his wonderful playing of the harmonium gave her immense relief; he offered to give her lessons in playing the instrument. (See her own notes in extracts, B. Zaleski, I, 153, and L. Dębicki, *Puławy*, 1887, I, 97.)

another source of inner gratification in her passionate love for her country's past and for historical relics. In later years she founded at their residence Pulawy, the first Polish museum, the "Temple of Sibyl." She regarded herself as a second Sibyl, a guardian of the books of destiny of her people.

Earlier, however, she had undoubtedly helped to embitter her husband's relations with the King and to stimulate his rather slumbering aspirations to the crown. If he were not to have it, then one of his children should; if not Adam, then their elder daughter Maria, married to Prince Louis of Württemberg, a Prussian general, brother-in-law of the Grand Duke Paul (the future tsar), and of the Archduke Francis (the future emperor), and a nephew of a Hohenzollern. This unhappy marriage of her daughter was Princess Isabella's achievement, and was favored by Frederick the Great. It connected the Czartoryskis with several European dynasties, especially with Potsdam and Gatchina. But the unfortunate Princess Maria paid the price of these powerful connections with terrible personal experiences, Prince Louis being a debauched and brutal sadist. In 1792, while in the Polish service as lieutenant-general commanding the army of Lithuania, he betrayed his adopted country and tried to give it up without opposition to the Russian invader. The marriage broke up, and Princess Maria divorced her husband. The shock was formidable and it did not encourage the old prince to follow his wife's dynastic aspirations further.

By 1792, however, she was heart and soul with the nation in its struggle, and after defeat was one of the first to stir up a national revolution and to encourage Kościuszko in his plans. Ardent patriotism and a spirit of self-sacrifice were from then on the guiding motives of her life, and if her political thought and action sometimes conflicted with her husband's inclinations toward a more cautious policy, they contributed to the creation of a special atmosphere at Puławy, young Adam's family home, renowned as the mecca of Polish patriotism, and made that home the more dear to him.[5]

[5] L. Dębicki, *Puławy*, 1887-1888, 4 vols., esp. vol. I; Zaleski, *op.cit.*; Duc de Broglie, *Souvenirs*, I, 188-192; L. Dembowski, *Moje wspomnienia*, 1898, I; K. Koźmian, *Pamiętniki 1780-1815*, 1858, pp. 191-205, 255-259; J. U. Niemcewicz,

Family, Parents, Early Years

Prince Adam George Czartoryski was born on January 14, 1770, in Warsaw. As a child he was left to his nurse's care since his parents spent those years mostly in traveling abroad, together or apart. As a young boy he started his education under his father's intelligent and careful supervision, with a number of Polish and foreign teachers, one of whom, for a short time, was the physiocrat, Dupont de Nemours. The latter remembered after many years his pupil's extreme seriousness and the elevation of his mind as being unusual for that early age. Prince Adam's mother, who loved him passionately, reproached him for his taciturnity and reserve, and warned him not to appear cold, misanthropic, or egoistic. Actually there was in young Prince Adam something of a *figure de bronze*, a nickname which stuck to him and later became his pseudonym in his family's confidential letters.

His most recent biographer has put forward the theory that his personality was strongly affected by his mother's overwhelming and lasting influence and that the real clue to his character lay in a psychological complex arising from his submission to her will. But neither Prince Adam's correspondence with his mother nor his diaries and memoirs contain any enigmas to be elucidated by psychoanalysis. Undoubtedly his mother had a great influence on his education when he was a boy. She is known, for instance, to have made him learn by heart and recite from Racine's tragedy Mithridates' long harangue to his sons, in which he expounded his plan of a struggle for liberation from the Roman invader. Certainly she wanted to train her son as leader of his nation, its liberator, or even, perhaps, its ruler. Prince Adam's letters to her are warm and confident, and her letters to him are full of maternal solicitude and longing for his happiness and success. Nor did her will determine any of his action after the fateful year 1795.

There were certainly serious cases of interference by both parents in his life before that date. Instead of volunteering in a foreign army in order to learn the military art so that he might later serve his own country as a regular soldier, he was, much

Pamiętniki czasów moich, 1868, pp. 272-275. Cf. J. Fabre, *Stanislas Auguste et l'Europe des Lumières*, 1952, pp. 453-456

against his will, obliged to study political problems, to write political treatises, and even to take an active part in domestic party
politics. For a short time his tutor was the versatile Italian
diplomatic free lance, Abbé Scipione Piattoli, who was later to
play a part in the drafting of the Constitution of May 3. In 1788
Prince Adam attended the opening phase of the proceedings of
the Great Diet. He was one of the enthusiastic witnesses of the
session of November 3 when the Diet made, on a majority of
votes, the important decision to take military affairs into their
own hands by transferring the powers of the military department of the permanent council to a military committee to be
appointed by the parliament. "It is difficult to imagine"—he wrote
many years later—"the joy with which that victory was greeted.
. . . For the first time for many years the Polish national representation acted by its own will and not under Moscow's pressure,
not yielding to the orders of the Russian Ambassador. . . . Right
or wrong, they acted at last as a free people. . . ."[6]

Early in 1789 he left Poland with his mother for a long
sojourn abroad. His father, Prince Adam Casimir, wanted him
to visit Great Britain and to learn as much as possible about her
history, her institutions, and her political, cultural, and economic
life. In London he was given guidance and advice by the Lord
Chief Justice, Lord Mansfield, who more than thirty years before had been his father's friend and tutor in his studies of
English political law. The young Prince attended Warren Hasting's trial and was much impressed by the speeches of Burke,
Fox, Sheridan, and Grey. He listened with delight to Pitt's and
Wilberforce's parliamentary speeches against the slave trade. He
paid visits with his mother to several of the great English and
Scottish houses and tried to see as much as possible of British
industry. In Scotland he was introduced to Robertson and Hume.
A letter of one of his English acquaintances of that period, Dr.
Currie of Liverpool, written several years later to a British
politician, gives the following picture of the young Polish Prince:[7]
"He was then about twenty or twenty one, and a very fine young
man indeed, full of great expectations of happy changes in so-

[6] A. Czartoryski, *Żywot Niemcewicza*, 1860, pp. 59-60.
[7] Cz.M.(E), I, 50-51.

ciety, full of ardor, benevolence, and adventure. . . . He was very fond of comparing the statesmen and orators of France and England. Mirabeau and Fox were his heroes—but he preferred the latter. . . . He is an English-looking man, a black fellow, very tall and handsome—spoke our language and loved our country. . . ."

Czartoryski, the "great idolater of Fox," probably did not expect that his Whig heroes would before long have a rather disastrous influence on Poland's fate by their successful opposition to the policy of Pitt, who wished to save Turkey's integrity and Poland's political existence by building up a powerful coalition against Russia.[8]

Most probably Prince Adam left for his own home before the memorable Ochakov debate of March 29, 1791. The Princess on her way home paid a visit to Emperor Leopold II and was terrified by his sinister warning: "The Prussians betray you, they are plotting with Russia. I have proof of it in my pocket. Tell it to your husband and to the Marshals Potocki and Malachowski."

They arrived home shortly before the memorable day of May 3, 1791, when the new constitution of Poland was proclaimed. In Burke's view it was "a happy wonder," a victory of a "glorious conspiracy in favor of the true and genuine rights and interests of man," and it could be considered "as in regular progress, because founded on similar principles towards the stable excellence of the British constitution."[9] That was exactly the feeling of the Czartoryskis; Prince Adam was one of the many to whom that day remained the brightest in their lives.

A few months after that "happy revolution" Poland was politically isolated and abandoned to the Tsarina's vengeance. As the probability of a Russian invasion grew stronger, Prince Adam's fighting spirit prevailed over his parents' political ambitions concerning his career. He joined the army of Lithuania under the command of his brother-in-law, Prince Louis of

---

[8] See R. H. Lord, *The Second Partition of Poland*, 1915, pp. 162-191; J. H. Rose, *Life of Pitt*, 1923, pp. 385-389, 626, 631; S. Askenazy, *Przymierze polsko-pruskie* (The Polish-Prussian Alliance), 3rd. ed., 1919, pp. 132-140.

[9] E. Burke, *An Appeal from the New to the Old Whigs*, 1791, pp. 102-104.

Württemberg. He had already been, for a long time, titular chief of a company of national cavalry.

We have no information about Princess Isabella's farewell when they parted before the outbreak of the war of 1792; we only know what she wrote in her diary twenty years later, when her younger son, Prince Constantine, left for another war against Russia: "May God lead him and may his mother's blessings protect him from any danger. May the blood of the Jagellons in his veins incite him to glorious deeds and his devotion to his country show him the path on which he will proceed with good luck and distinction."

Before the invasion began, Prince Adam was fully aware of the catastrophic breakdown of the alliance with Prussia because of the latter's treason and he was cured for at least two decades of any illusions as to her policy. It would have been surprising if he had not understood the sad disappointments of his mother's political dreams. He witnessed the disastrous events connected with Prince Louis' treacherous desertion, and shared his sister's and his parents' humiliation and despair. During the short and hopeless campaign of his army he served as a gallant soldier and won the military cross. After the disastrous event of the war and the political capitulation of the King he left the army and, following the example of most of the patriotic leaders, went abroad.

Once more he made a long stay in England. We lack more ample information as to his whereabouts and his contacts in that country; there is some evidence that he had letters of recommendation to Lord Lansdowne, "a friend of his family," and established personal acquaintance with Fox, Charles Grey, Wilberforce, and other liberal leaders for whom he already felt a great admiration.[10] He certainly provided materials to Charles Grey's speech of February 21, 1793 against the new partition of Poland.

In 1794 the Austrians prevented his returning home in time to join Kościuszko's national forces in their desperate struggle; and his failure to do so seriously injured his feelings of patriotism

[10] Viel-Castel (Louis de), "Le P-ce Adam Czartoryski," *Le Correspondant*, 1862, xix, 692.

and was a source of self-reproach. But he had before him a much more painful trial. After the collapse of the insurrection, his parents, who had already been denounced for their support of Kościuszko's activities, had their estates confiscated or sequestrated by the Russians and faced material ruin. They decided to appeal to the old now almost forgotten friendship of Prince Repnin, who was then commander-in-chief in Lithuania. After having sounded out his Empress, Repnin urged them to send their two sons immediately to her court as a pledge of the Family's future behavior. The brothers yielded to their parents' will and left in despair for Grodno and St. Petersburg. Their education "had been entirely Polish and republican." Their minds "were full of Greeks and Romans." "With regard to political liberty more recent examples taken from the history of England and France had up to a certain point corrected our ideas without in any way diminishing their energy. . . . I should add"—Prince Adam admits—"that this feeling which penetrated the whole of our moral nature, was accompanied by an invincible aversion for all those who had contributed to the ruin of the fatherland we loved so much. . . ." For some time he was unable to meet a Russian either in Poland or elsewhere without feeling the blood rush to his head.

We do not know what he was told by his parents when they parted. Before they even reached St. Petersburg, Repnin received a note from the Tsarina accusing the young Czartoryskis of having, at their mother's request, taken the oath of young Hannibal and sworn eternal hatred to Russia and her sovereign.[11] It was certainly untrue; in any case, the oath would have been one which Prince Adams was not to keep. When he became acquainted with Russia and the Russians he felt much understanding and friendliness for them, and although he was later to lead an embittered struggle against Russia for his country's freedom, he was never able to hate the Russian people; national hatred was a feeling unknown to him. It seems quite probable, however, that he promised his mother that he would never betray his loyalty to Poland and would dedicate his life to his country.

[11] See Cz.M.(E), I, 55-57.

Family, Parents, Early Years

What he himself felt at that painful period (1795) he expressed in a poem, "Bard Polski" (The Polish Bard) which was an expression of the feelings of his generation at the very moment when Poland was to be suppressed as a state and nation:

"Now I have to endure baseness, to live among crimes. How unfortunate are those whom death has spared! How I abhor the degrading and ignominious protection! Oh, horror of slavery, which chains feelings in fetters and strangles thought. . . . Why did I not perish with my brothers on the battlefield with honor? . . ."

CHAPTER 2

EARLY EXPERIENCES IN
RUSSIA

MUCH HAS BEEN TOLD by Prince Adam in his Memoirs about the
first years of the young Czartoryskis' stay in the capital of the
Tsars; about their protracted penitence for the Family's political
sins; about their visits paid to the omnipotent favorite, Prince
Plato Zubov, and also to his brother, Count Valerian; about
their attendance at the favorite's *levées*; the several months of
waiting for an introduction to the Empress; about her gracious
reception and the favors she granted to the Polish exiles, who
were commissioned in the Guards and appointed Gentlemen of
the Court.[1] They flew into a golden cage and found a friendly
and sympathetic reception in Russian aristocratic homes. The
atmosphere, nevertheless, was tense and laden with potential
tragedies.

Czartoryski had much to tell; yet he did not reveal all, and
there were things which he never learned. Both Poles noticed
with surprise Catherine's hatred of the Grand Duke Paul and his
terror in meeting his mother. They did not understand why she
separated her newborn grandchildren from their parents and
especially from their father. They heard rumors about her design of depriving Paul of his rights as heir to the imperial
crown and of transferring the succession to his first-born son,
the Grand Duke Alexander.[2] They knew about the oath enforced
on the latter by his father to recognize him as his sovereign,
whatever might happen. But there seems to have been a dramatic
entanglement, of which a tradition, preserved in two families,
the Russian Shuvalovs and the Polish Branickis, is supposed to
be the only clue. It was alleged that the Grand Duke Paul was

---

[1] See Cz.M.(E), 1, 58-100.

[2] Cz.M.(E), 237. T. Schiemann, *Geschichte Russlands unter Nikolaus I*, Berlin,
1904 ff., 1, 12-14.

not Catherine's son. On the day of his official birth, October 1, 1754, she was delivered of a girl who, under the name of Alexandra Engelhardt, was to be educated by Potemkin's sister and to become the wife of the Polish Hetman Xavier Branicki. Incidentally, she was in fact Catherine's living portrait and her cherished protégée. Paul was alleged to be the son of a Karelian girl. By order of the Empress Elisabeth he had been substituted by the powerful and dreaded chief of her Secret Office, Alexander Shuvalov, for the newborn girl. The Empress wanted a boy as future tsar and she managed to have one. The boy was attractive, healthy, and strong, but Catherine knew the truth, and never forgot it.[3] A long time later, she spoke of Shuvalov as "having spread terror and horror over the whole of Russia." Until the very end of her life she meditated on how to eliminate her unfortunate successor, whose mind, it must be added, broke under the burden of the heavy responsibilities imposed upon him; he began to manifest symptoms of mental derangement.

Catherine's firstborn grandson, Alexander, had more of his mother's (a Württemberg princess) than of his father's traits, and the German race prevailed in his features and character. This young, fair, and charming boy was now the Empress' and Russia's hope. Catherine tried to educate him to be an enlightened sovereign in line with the Century of Enlightenment. "Monsieur de La Harpe inspired him with the love of Mankind, justice and even of liberty and equality for all." Being a stranger and confined, like many of his contemporary thinkers, to the realm of general ideas and far from the realities of Russian life, he was unable to prepare his pupil for his real tasks. Alexander had the most generous intentions, but La Harpe's noble ideas remained for him what they were: just *des phrases générales*. Moreover his real official tutor was Nicholas Soltykov, a courtier who knew perfectly well how to tread earthly, tortuous, and muddy paths: his achievement was the introduction to the Tsarina of Zubov, her last favorite.

[3] That tradition was kept in secrecy by both the families concerned until quite recently; the details were known to S. Askenazy. See H. Moscicki's article on "Branicka Alexandra" in the *Polski Słownik Biograficzny* (Polish Biographical Dictionary), II.

The Grand Duke Paul himself was also eager to contribute to the education of his two elder sons by teaching them the business of drill-sergeant, which he adored. They became fond of it, particularly the younger brother, Constantine, whose character was more influenced by his father's unfortunate heritage. On the drilling grounds of Gatchina they learned the dull and inhuman method of training troops and became accustomed to a cruel and tyrannical military discipline. Alexander had now two different lives: he had to assume one mask for his father, and another for his grandmother. He learned histrionic dissimulation, which was always to remain a trait of his character.

A long time after Alexander's death, Prince Adam, paying a warm tribute to the generous intentions of his former friend, attributed his frequently following tortuous paths to a "noble vanity": "He liked always to conquer hearts, to impress people, to overawe cabinets, to please generals, writers and the ladies— to be admired in the most brilliant salons and in the most confidential assemblies, as well as at the head of his armies."[4]

In those early years, one of his conquests was the young, gloomy, and mysterious Polish exile. He told him of his indignation at the crime committed by his grandmother against Poland. He assured him that he considered the reparation of that injury the great aim of his life. They revealed to each other their common ideals of liberty, justice, and brotherhood among nations. "It was a kind of freemasonry but the Grand-Duchess was let into the secret."[5] Czartoryski believed in Alexander's sincerity, and in spite of many disappointments and disasters he never lost this faith in his genuine good will.

Several Polish historians were inclined to discover in Czartoryski's Russian friendship a weakness, a new "complex" hampering his will and obscuring his thoughts; Handelsman's view is that

[4] A. Czartoryski, *Essai sur la diplomatie*, 1864, p. 85. See Alexander's confidence in his letter to La Harpe, Dec. 4, 1790, *Sbornik*, v, 7. For an explanation of Alexander's supposed "duplicity or affection" see also H. Nicolson, *The Congress of Vienna*, 1946, pp. 9-11. Alexander's vanity seems responsible for his running after romantic conquests, which later degenerated into erotomania; Cf. Melgunov, *Dela i ludi Alexandrovskogo vremeni* (Events and People of the Alexandrian Age), 1923, pp. 98-105.

[5] Cz.M.(E), i, 115.

Alexander's influence predominated over him for many years; and that that dependence lasted until the latter's death and the first contest with his successor, Nicholas I.[6]

This seems to be a rather controversial matter. In his relations with Alexander, Czartoryski was neither blindly infatuated nor complying. His political friendship with Alexander and several young liberal Russians was based on their common liberal creed and on the assumption that Poland would regain her independence and that she would recover the provinces annexed by Russia. It was not based on his resignation of the rights of his country but rather on their recognition by his Russian friends.

Moreover, it seems evident that in this partnership Czartoryski was, originally at least, the stronger partner. He dominated his imperial friend by the strength of his character and of his political beliefs, by his maturity and experience, by his knowledge of European affairs and even of Russian life. For years Alexander placed unlimited reliance on his friend and instinctively longed for his advice and support. When in 1797 Prince Adam obtained a leave to see his parents, his departure greatly alarmed the Grand Duke, who asked him to leave him a draft proclamation expressing his intentions in case he should be called to the throne during his friend's absence; and he put an offhand statement from Czartoryski with manifest comfort in his pocket. Alexander's confidential letters followed Prince Adam to Puławy; they were sent by various persons, among others by the Archduke Palatine, Alexander's brother-in-law.[7] Thus Czartoryski was Alexander's recognized mentor and he repaid his young friend's confidence with gratitude and sincere devotion; his feelings were deeper than Alexander's because such was the man.

After Paul's succession to the throne, Alexander's relations with Czartoryski became hampered by the latter's fear of his father. So after the release of Kościuszko, Czartoryski did not succeed in bringing his young Russian and his old Polish friend together. In his Memoirs he attributed this failure to Paul's aversion to any liberal ideas. Obviously there were many good reasons for the Emperor's suspicions. There is a letter written at

[6] Handelsman, I, Ch. 3.
[7] Cz.M.(E), I, 161-162, 171.

that time by the Grand Duke Alexander to La Harpe, in which the future Tsar confided to his preceptor his intention of giving freedom and a constitution to his country and of emancipating the peasants; he himself called it a legal revolution and added that he had agreed upon it with some people who had the courage to think. "We are but four: Mr. Novosiltsov, Count Stroganov, the young Prince Czartoryski, my A.D.C. who is a rare man, and myself."[8] Incidentally, both Novosiltsov and Stroganov had been admitted to Alexander's secret on Czartoryski's recommendation.[9]

However Paul's suspicions of the jacobin tendencies of his elder son and his three friends were not the only reasons for his hatred of Czartoryski. There was also a dramatic personal conflict between the autocrat and the young exile. Prince Adam's friendship with Alexander was shared by the latter's young, charming, and noble-minded wife, Elisabeth (born a Princess of Baden). However, she fell in love with their common friend. For Czartoryski it was the first great love of his life, and probably the only one. The romance was to last for a long time; it languished for years only to revive again, and its melancholy reminiscences remained alive to the end. We find ample information about this love affair in the memoirs of Countess Golovin, Countess de Lieven, the Duchess of Dino, Baron de Barante, and others, and a confirmation of it in some passages from Czartoryski's diary which were published by Askenazy when discussing the writings of the late Grand Duke Nicholas.[10] Handelsman's recent book gives us further evidence from Prince Adam's correspondence with his mother. She knew all about it; at Puławy the family feared for the fate of the lovers and of the little baby, the Grand Duchess Maria, whose dark hair revealed to the Tsar the identity of her father.[11]

[8] The letter of Sept. 27 (Oct. 8), 1797 from Gatchina, omitted in the publication of Alexander's letters to La Harpe (*Sbornik*, v), appeared in full text in N. K. Shilder's *Imperator Alexander I*, I, 280-282.

[9] Cz.M.(E), pp. 163-170. Early in 1797 he was appointed A.D.C. to the Grand Duke Alexander, and his brother A.D.C. to the Grand Duke Constantine.

[10] In *Uwagi*, 1924. Cf. Countess Golovin, *Memoirs*, London, 1910, pp. 99-104, 198-202. Also see S. Melgunov, *Dela i ludi Alexandrovskogo vremeni*, 1923, pp. 101-104.

[11] Handelsman, I, 34-36.

The Baron de Barante and the Duchess of Dino have told of the origin of the romance. According to Barante, Alexander grew tired of his wife very soon after they were married; however, he regarded it as unjust to demand of her a fidelity which he himself was not prepared to observe. Thus he had a written agreement with her permitting freedom to them both.[12] According to the Duchess of Dino, Elisabeth, depressed by her husband's indifference, confided her sorrow to their common friend. "Prince Adam felt much honored by this touching proof of confidence and with an eagerness inspired by genuine affection he tried to reestablish union in a family which was so dear to him. But"— the Duchess hardly dared to write it, although she knew it for certain—"Alexander not only did not follow his suggestions but he even told him many times that it was his duty as a friend to console Elisabeth, and the Grand Duchess herself displayed so much favor for Prince Adam that before long all St. Petersburg was satisfied that his friendly suggestions had succeeded. Taciturn and rather gloomy, he forgot his country's ordeal only when with Elisabeth. . . . In the meantime Catherine died and Paul I, who succeeded her, enamored as he was himself of his daughter-in-law, got rid of his more fortunate rival by giving him a mock political mission to Italy. . . ."[13]

The crisis was indeed dangerous for Czartoryski, Elisabeth, and Alexander as well; Paul's anger was terrible; the child's early death was even attributed by some contemporaries to the compliance of some person eager to anticipate the Emperor's wishes. There arose the danger of Czartoryski's deportation. It ended with his appointment as minister plenipotentiary to the court of Sardinia—an exile as envoy to a king in exile.

Most probably the origin of the Empress Maria's hatred for Czartoryski, as well as of that of the Grand Duke Constantine and some other Russians, was to be found in this romance. Not only did the dreams of personal happiness vanish for Prince Adam, but his hopes based upon Alexander's friendship were also badly shaken.

His enforced sojourn in Italy lasted two years. It enabled him

---

[12] Baron de Barante, *Souvenirs*, 1892, II, 201.
[13] Souvenirs de la Duchesse de Dino, 4e édition, pp. 159-162.

to become acquainted with Italian problems, to realize their gravity, and to perceive the possibility of the Kingdom of Sardinia playing a leading part in Italian politics.[14]

He did not return to St. Petersburg before Paul's assassination. When he came back, Elisabeth's feelings had already changed. Later on came her dramatic romance with Okhotnikov, the young officer who was assassinated—there were rumors that the Grand Duke Constantine had a hand in this murder. Her love for Czartoryski revived at the time of the Congress of Vienna. Alexander was asked to agree to a divorce in order to allow Elisabeth to marry Prince Adam. But the Emperor's attitude to the romance was now by no means favorable. He refused his consent, and it appears that the episode resulted in an estrangement from his friend. There remained only the bitterness of her broken life and Prince Adam's deep sorrow, yearning, and melancholy.

Many years later, when Alexander and Elisabeth were both dead, Czartoryski heard from the Grand Duke Constantine in a confidential talk in the Warsaw Belvedere the cruel words pronounced with apparent bonhomie: "I have your letters. I have the little ones. . . . The Emperor did very silly things. So did you. But one is young for a time. Now, when more than fifty, you should not do them any more. I did silly things too—who does not? I have put certain letters aside to be disposed of if something happens to me. . . ."[15] Thus, at that time, in 1827, the reminiscence of the dramatic romance provided the Grand Duke with a moment's superiority over Czartoryski.

[14] Early in 1799 he was released from his post of Alexander's A.D.C. and appointed Court Marshal to Grand Duchess Helena. On Aug. 12, 1799 he was appointed Minister at the court of Sardinia. He joined the court in Florence at the end of the year, and followed it to Rome in the summer of 1800. Early in 1801 he was directed to leave his post and to join the Russian legation in Naples. Details in Cz.M.(E), 1, 205-218.

[15] S. Askenazy, "Dwie rozmowy w Belwederze" (Two Talks in Belvedere), Nowe Wczasy, 1910, pp. 450-451.

CHAPTER 3

CZARTORYSKI A RUSSIAN
STATESMAN

IT WAS FORTUNATE for Czartoryski that he was far from St. Petersburg on the terrible night when his young friend was elevated to the imperial throne over his unfortunate father's mutilated and trampled body, and that he did not take any part in that grim tragedy. In his Memoirs he has related all that he learned about those events, showing a tendency to lighten his friend's guilt and in particular to eliminate his responsibility for the assassination itself; he did not, however, try to explain away Alexander's part in the plot nor to minimize the gravity of Alexander's moral anguish. "This ineffaceable stain . . . settled like a vulture on his conscience, paralyzed his best faculties at the commencement of his reign and plunged him in a mysticism sometimes degenerating into superstition at its close."[1]

On the first news of Paul's death, Princess Maria wrote to her brother from Puławy: "I write you in joy, in delight; you certainly know already about Wappy's [A nickname for Paul?] death. . . . Our dear and adored Grand Duke is Emperor. . . . I am mad from exultation. . . ."[2] Alexander called him to St. Petersburg: "I do not need to say how impatiently I am waiting for you."[3]

Thus began Czartoryski's career as a Russian statesman. For several years he was to play a leading part in Russia's foreign policy, as well as an important one in her domestic affairs, and for a further nine years he was to remain one of the outstanding figures in her political life.

How this could have happened was an enigma to many contemporaries and to some historians as well: young Hannibal

[1] Cz.M.(E), I, 231-232.
[2] Quoted by Askenazy, *Napoleon a Polska*, III, 423.
[3] Letter of Mar. 17, 1801, Cz.M.(E), I, 222-223.

invested in Rome with *consulari potestate*. L. B. Namier was right in saying on another occasion that a great many profound secrets are lying hidden somewhere in print, but are most easily detected when one knows what to seek. Almost everything concerning Czartoryski's adventure as a Russian statesman was in print sixty years ago: his correspondence with Alexander I. Several documents omitted in the publications of Charles de Mazade and of A. Gielgud were later published by the Grand Duke Nicholas Mikhailovich in his books on Alexander I and on Paul Stroganov. The large series of volumes of Vorontsov's Papers (*Archiv Vorontsova*) brought to light further evidence, especially Czartoryski's correspondence with both Vorontsovs: Alexander, the old Chancellor, and Simon, the Ambassador in London. There remain a great many of Czartoryski's unpublished papers of that period, and although many of them have been studied by several historians, there is still much to be done if a detailed study of his work as minister, state counsellor, and curator is to be made. But the answer to all questions concerning his partnership with Alexander is to be found in print in their letters and notes of their conversations, and Prince Adam himself gave a reliable and outspoken commentary in his Memoirs.

Back in St. Petersburg he became a member of the Secret Committee founded by Alexander in order to reorganize the Empire and to achieve the "legal revolution" which he had meditated upon for many years. He called it jokingly his "Comité de Salut Public." It was composed of the same few friends whom he had named in 1797 in his letter to La Harpe: Stroganov, who was the *spiritus movens*, his cousin Nicholas Novosiltsov, and Prince Adam; the three were already bound together by mutual understanding and devoted friendship. They were joined now by Victor Kochubey, but the triumviri still held a special position as Alexander's confidential advisers and companions.[4]

In the first period, their common effort was concentrated on the problem of modernizing the Russian Empire. Prince Adam's primary task was to plan a new organization of the central authorities. He proposed the abolition of the collective govern-

[4] For the Secret Committee, see Nicholas Mikhailovich, *Stroganov*, 1, Introduction and pp. 53-78.

ing bodies, the Collegia, and the establishment instead of responsible ministers. The decree reorganizing the government on those lines was his work; it was published in September 1802. Then, on Alexander's request, after some hesitation and delay in giving his decision, he accepted the post of Deputy Minister of Foreign Affairs under the nominal authority of the very old Chancellor Alexander Vorontsov, a noble-minded elder statesman with broad views, but hampered in his work by age and sickness; Prince Adam enjoyed his full confidence and warm friendship. A year later, in January 1804, he was given the full control of this department, with the rank of minister. At the same time he was a member of the Council for Educational Affairs and of the committee for the reform of the Jews, and from February 1803 he had, as Curator of the University of Vilna, the control of all the schools in the eight western provinces (i.e., the former Polish provinces annexed in 1772, 1793, and 1795). From January 1805 he had a seat in the senate and in the state council. From the beginning he was the principal adviser to the Emperor; in 1805 Alexander called him his mentor, and in some instances his position was almost as important as it would have been had he been Russia's prime minister.

It is understandable that the Russian reaction to the amazing fact of a Pole playing a decisive role in their country's affairs was rather hostile. As early as 1803 both of the Princes Dolgoruki, Alexander's aides-de-camp, boasted that they would get rid of the stranger by violence if necessary. They were backed by the Empress-Dowager, Maria Teodorovna, whose influence on Alexander became very great after the sinister night of Paul's assassination, when she had tried in vain to avenge her husband's death and to seize power for herself. The young Emperor, already disarmed by the consciousness of his guilt, hardly found the moral courage to oppose his mother's requests. M. Handelsman advanced the theory that Alexander's idea in appointing Czartoryski was to have a scapegoat for his personal foreign policy, with the secret aim of being able to victimize him if necessary.[5] That conjecture seems rather improbable, for by appointing this

[5] Handelsman, I, 60.

stranger, Alexander exposed himself. By the very fact of being a Pole, Czartoryski as Russian minister was bound to become the object of suspicion and slander, and both he and the Tsar were inevitably subjected to bitter criticism and hostile attacks. "What people most objected to in the case of Alexander"—so read Czartoryski's Memoirs—"was my presence at his court and my appointment as assistant to the Minister of Foreign Affairs. . . . They could not get used to seeing me at the head of the department: a Pole enjoying the confidence of the Emperor and initiated into all secrets of the state was to them an intolerable innovation." There could not be a more convincing testimony that Czartoryski's appointment could in no way make things easier for the young sovereign; in fact, it was a serious liability. Alexander had appointed him because he trusted Prince Adam more than anyone else, and because he considered his collaboration indispensable to his own work as emperor and regenerator of Russia.[6]

Shortly after Prince Adam's appointment, the British Ambassador wrote to the Foreign Office: "Prince Czartoryski, for some years past the intimate and most confidential friend of the present Emperor of Russia . . . is now second in point of precedency, but perhaps first in point of influence in the Foreign Department."[7] A year later Josef de Maistre, the Sardinian envoy, wrote to his King: "Czartoryski is haughty and reticent. . . . I have some doubts whether a Pole who had himself dreamed of a royal crown can sincerely become a good Russian. . . ." De Maistre was closely associated with the Jesuits, who—after the dissolution of their order—found sanctuary in Russia, and Czartoryski's liberal tendencies in politics and education did not meet with his approval. But De Maistre's dislike of Czartoryski was shared by many Russians, and Prince Adam made no efforts to gain popularity. The Austrian envoys reported on his personality: "cold to the bones, taciturn, avoiding society."[8] A Russian diplomat, old Morkov, complained that he had seen the Minister

---

[6] Cf. Czartoryski's letter of Mar. 22, 1806, Cz.M.(F), II, 102.

[7] Withworth to Hawkesbury, Jan. 4, 1803.

[8] Hudelist and Stadion quoted by Wertheimer, *Geschichte Oesterreichs und Ungarns*, Leipzig, 1889, I, 209. J. de Maistre, *Mémoires et Correspondance*, 1858, 268.

for a very short time and as the latter did not speak when not questioned, and Morkov's "discretion does not allow to put questions," the talk did not contribute to mutual understanding. Since Prince Adam's ideas were known only to a few friends, the wildest rumors were circulated in both Russian capitals and he was frequently accused of Jacobinism. Such was also the opinion brought by the Duke of Gloucester from his northern journey in 1803 about that "idolater of Fox," and one of the most Anglophile of the Continental politicians.[9] At the same time Napoleon warned the Markgraf von Baden, the father of Empress Elisabeth: "Your son-in-law is surrounded by Poles, his minister and his mistress are of that nationality, and the latter (Countess Marie Naryshkin, nee Princess Czetwertyńska) is a mischievous woman."[10] Simon Vorontsov sent a warning from Berlin that Czartoryski was particularly hated there, and for that there were of course good reasons.

When Prince Adam came back to St. Petersburg in 1801 he had to face an important *fait accompli* in Alexander's foreign policy: his peace treaty with France. The Paris treaty had been concluded against his strong conviction. By ratifying it, the young Emperor lost the opportunity of having a say as to the future of Europe and of reaching a lasting settlement of European problems on a basis of equilibrium and stability. The treaty—Czartoryski reproached the Tsar—contained only one important stipulation, and that one was directed against Poland: it bound the contracting parties to refrain from supporting any external or internal adversary of the other. It was undoubtedly directed against the Polish legions serving with the French armies as well as against the French Royalists.[11]

According to what Prince Adam writes in his Memoirs, in those early months of his reign Alexander was not inclined to commit Russia in European affairs: "He had seen with equal aversion the wars of Catherine and the despotic follies of Paul." He rather favored a policy of generous isolation and of concentration on internal reforms. Such was the idea of Count

[9] Cz.M.(E), I, 50-51.
[10] Nicholas Mikhailovich, *L'Impératrice Elisabeth*, 1908, II, 195.
[11] See T. Martens, XII, Nr. 448.

Kochubey, Czartoryski's predecessor at the Foreign Ministry. In Czartoryski's eyes this policy if genuinely followed had the disadvantage of reducing the state to insignificance and humiliation, and it by no means conformed to the feelings of the Russians themselves.[12] The Emperor with his noble ideas was "an exotic plant among them and he felt estranged and unhappy."

In 1802, at his mother's instigation, he went to Memel to meet the royal Prussian couple, without confiding his plan to his companions of the Secret Committee; he became the friend of King Frederick William III, and even more so of Queen Louise, and although a little shocked by her obtrusive coquetry, he ever after felt some chivalrous sentiments for her. Four years later he was told with some sarcasm by his Polish friend: "Your Imperial Majesty has considered Prussia from that time not as a political state but as a cherished person towards whom you have felt you have contracted certain obligations."[13] In Czartoryski's eyes this "political state" was rather like a beast of prey. Little more than sixty years had then elapsed since the first conquest of Silesia, thirty years since the appropriation of Polish Pomerania, nine since the annexation of Danzig, Thorn, and Poznań, and only seven since the seizure of Warsaw; and at the time Prussia was busy robbing German territories in complicity with Buonaparte. Nevertheless the Emperor's Prussian friendship was a fact to be taken into account, and the Dowager Empress, assisted by the Dolgorukis, was preserving that precious link with her Potsdam cousins.[14]

No wonder that Czartoryski hesitated before taking the responsibility of a department burdened with such an inheritance. But on the other scale of the balance, there were numerous proofs of Alexander's affection for and confidence in him, of his liberal idealism and of his genuine good will towards the Polish nation: he not only granted the Poles a kind of cultural self-government under Prince Adam's control within Russia's boundaries, and restored Polish political prisoners in Russia to liberty,

---

[12] *Memoirs*, I, 280-283.

[13] Letter to the Emperor, Apr. 15, 1806, Cz.M.(E), II, 125; original text: Cz.M.(F), II, 113.

[14] See Nicholas Mikhailovich, *Alexandre I*, I, 25, 43.

but he also intervened successfully with the other two partitioning powers in favor of Polish prisoners and exiles. Though often
discouraged, Czartoryski considered it his duty to undertake that
difficult experiment, still hoping that there would be an opportunity of achieving great things simultaneously for Russia,
for Europe, and for his own country. "After having been placed
at the head of affairs I felt like a soldier who, being thrown by
chance and friendship into the ranks of a foreign army, fights
gallantly out of a sense of honor and in order not to abandon his
master and friend. Alexander's boundless confidence made me
feel it my duty to do my best to serve him and to add luster to
his policy as long as I had the direction of it. Moreover, I firmly
believed that it might be possible for me to reconcile the tendencies of the Russian nation with the generous ideas of its ruler
and to make use of the Russian craving for glory and supremacy
for the general benefit of mankind. . . ."[15]

Czartoryski's political ideas when entering the Ministry of
Foreign Affairs were set out in 1803 in an extensive memorandum on the "Political system to be adopted by Russia," and
obtained the Emperor's approval. Unfortunately, the document
has not up until now been printed; it is, however, preserved in
Prince Adam's records.[16] As he emphasized in his Memoirs, the
principles expounded in that memorandum were almost precisely
those contained in his comprehensive treatise *Essai sur la Diplomatie* written a quarter of a century later.

The memorandum sets forth a completely new program for
Russia's foreign policy as opposed to the previous one, Count
Kochubey's program of "passive policy" and isolation. As a child
of the "Siècle des Lumières" Czartoryski began by reasoning
about the nature of the mutual relations between nations. He
agreed with the prevailing view of the philosophers, that the
"state of nature" of human beings was one of mutual fear and

---

[15] Cz.M.(E), II, 9 ff.

[16] Cz.Mss. 5226, pp. 15-137. I had a copy rendered accessible by Count Joseph
Michalowski (Rome). The original manuscript is in a secretary's hand, corrected
by Prince Adam, with some minor alterations and remarks by his father, the Prince
General. D'Ancona, *Scipione Piattoli e la Polonia* (1915) attributed it, without any
foundation, to that politician; but Piattoli was at the time in Saxony, and made
personal contact with Czartoryski as late as towards the end of 1804.

suspicion, and that laws and institutions were created as necessary conditions of a peaceful social life. But, he reasoned, the nations were still in this "state of nature" because there were no institutions or laws to ensure their security from aggression and violence. Thus, self-preservation and self-defense remained the first principle of any foreign policy; but equity and reason demanded the recognition of a higher principle, of the general welfare of nations, of a "Society of States." Nations should strive for common prosperity by uniting in an "association." In order to achieve a union of nations, three conditions must be realized. First, the further progress of civilization and its growth among backward people. Czartoryski had confidence in the immense influence that the printed word and international trade would have in bringing nations closer to each other. Second, the redrawing of state frontiers in accordance with the nationality of the inhabitants and the natural boundaries between nations. Third, the adoption of liberal institutions and representative governments by most countries. Thus lasting peace would be achieved by means of gradual changes.

Several people had given this question consideration before Czartoryski, including Abbé de St. Pierre, Rousseau, and, more recently, Kant in his *Zum ewigen Frieden* (1795); but Czartoryski was the first to relate the problem of lasting peace to the principle of nationality, to the idea of a "natural equilibrium," and to political liberalism.

"If we wish to progress," he wrote, "we must have an object we have not yet attained. And in order to be always in progress, we must be capable of conceiving an object which will never be attained." He felt that one must remember the conditions of the time, stand firmly for one's country's security, have open eyes for all that happens abroad, and be ready to face any contingency. But at the same time one must be aware that the progress and well-being of other nations are by no means prejudicial to one's own, as they assist trade and international intercourse. "A government which goes beyond self-defense when dealing with other nations is guilty of injustice."

Here Czartoryski stigmatized the policy of the three partitioning powers with regard to Poland. He did not regard Russia as a naturally aggressive power. Her extension was already excessive. Her future should be founded on the development and exploitation of her immense territories rather than on further conquests. Thus he could agree with Count Kochubey's idea of "passive" policy, if passivity meant abstaining from aggression and conquest. But he did not admit the possibility of Russia's having no say in European affairs. Her policy must be "magnanimous, just and sober, worthy of her position and her power." She must avoid any appearance of weakness, for it was just this that had been the cause of the recent calamitous turn of events in the affair of the German indemnities.

In presenting his own plan for an active Russian foreign policy, Czartoryski first considered her position in relation to that of the other powers. He regarded England as the only one really dangerous to Russia; she had recently given proofs of this by the action of her navy on the Baltic Sea. At the same time, she was an invaluable, though too exclusive, partner in trade and a potential ally, because of her concern with peace and security in Europe and of her position as the last sanctuary of liberalism after it had been banished from the Continent. Czartoryski considered the need of building up Russia's sea power to check any renewed threat and to reduce the British monopoly of overseas trade by connections with secondary maritime powers; he insisted upon the importance of America. Nevertheless he emphasized the necessity of a close understanding and collaboration with Britain: "Any quarrel with England could bring ruin to this country." If England and Russia had an agreed policy with regard to the Continent of Europe, they could impose it as a law. Thus he considered an agreement with England the keystone of Russia's new policy and he suggested sending there a special envoy to sound out the government and test public opinion. This was the origin of Novosiltsov's mission to London a year later.

France appeared in the memorandum as Russia's natural ally. Czartoryski felt that their real interests did not collide. If France opposed Russia in the past century, she did so not in her own interest but only to protect her traditional allies: Sweden, Turkey, and Poland when threatened by Russia. The Revolution and

Bonaparte's policy of aggression and conquest had altered their mutual relations. Czartoryski suggested that Bonaparte should be met with calm firmness and a common stand on the part of the European powers. He rejected any temptation of appeasement based on a division of spoils. "France realizes that she has reached her natural frontiers; let her keep them but not push beyond them under any pretext." As to the spreading of French revolutionary ideas, he suggested that counteraction should be taken in the form of propaganda for liberalism and the rousing of French public opinion against Bonaparte's arbitrary rule, a program which was to be strictly followed by the Tsar several years later.

By Poland's partition, Austria and Prussia had become Russia's neighbors and a potential threat. Czartoryski hinted with remarkable foresight at the still distant danger of a common invasion of Russia by united German powers. He insisted upon the expediency of restoring a reunited Poland in the very interest of Russian security. The Poles would be grateful for liberation and therefore remain reliable friends and allies, the more so that they would have to face the possibility of renewed Prussian aggression. An independent Poland, even if separated from Russia, would give her greater security than the present situation with the Germans on the River Bug. But Russia should take the initiative and secure the Polish crown for the Grand Duke Constantine. As presumptive heir to the imperial throne, Constantine inspired horror in the Russian people; but if placed on the throne of a country with a liberal constitution and an inveterate sense of legal order, he would be compelled to exercise self-control and restraint. It was a fateful suggestion which Prince Adam was later to deplore. He also hinted at the possibility of a union of Poland with Russia, which would extend Russia's direct control to Danzig and to the Carpathian Mountains.

Turkey appears in these considerations as completely moribund. Her decay had gone too far to permit recovery, and any shock from the outside might precipitate the end. Russia must prevent any other European power from securing the inheritance, especially in European Turkey. She could not allow any power to gain control of the Straits. Czartoryski advocated the founding of a large Greek state and securing a protectorate over Balkan peoples. If necessary, the Slavs in the northwestern part of the peninsula could be united with their brethren under the Hungarian crown—a conception of greater Croatia. For the time being, he postulated an active policy in the Balkans, making contacts with Greeks and Slavs and checking French influence everywhere. Here was the starting point of Russia's long-term Balkan policy, which was pursued by her for generations to come.

Czartoryski considered the creation of a free union of Italian states and the building up in the north of the peninsula of an independent national state, comprising at least the Italian Republic, Piedmont, and Venezia.

A German national empire, independent of both Austria and Prussia, was to be created in Western Germany, organized on federal lines like the United States of America, or at least as had been the Dutch confederated provinces or the Swiss confederation before the French conquest. Czartoryski would have liked to foster the German national spirit, which he thought was completely dormant and which was bound to arise before long, but under the banners of Prussia. He was aware of the great difficulty of reorganizing Germany on the proposed lines, but he relied upon Russia's great influence in Germany to pave the way.

Czartoryski emphasized that such a reshaping of Europe would give the states more national homogeneity and more natural boundaries, which should result in a natural equilibrium. It would be the common task of Russia and Britain to ensure its stability. He spoke with bitter sarcasm of the policy of the participants in the late coalitions and of their complete disregard of the rights and welfare of nations. But he believed that the influence of public opinion was increasing immensely everywhere. "When somebody said fifteen years ago, that the English form of government was the best one, he was regarded as a dreamer; now, most honest and sensible people take the same view, and their numbers are growing every day." Thus he firmly believed in his vision of a new Europe, regenerated by the adoption of the principle of nationality, reorganized by means of linking minor states together in unions or federations, and united in an association of states. The division of Europe into two parts, with France and the countries which she controlled at one side, and the former coalition powers at the other, must disappear. Russia and England, backed by an unconquerable league of states, should make proper use of their joint power for establishing equilibrium and imposing real and durable peace.

The memorandum was given a favorable and even an enthusiastic welcome by the Emperor and his Secret Committee; it became the program of Czartoryski's foreign policy when he took over the portfolio of foreign affairs. The very immensity of the aims helped to make of it an article of common creed. The "République de Sully," as Stroganov called the plan of uniting Europe, appeared as a sacred cause, worthy of sacrifices and risks.[17] Prince Adam felt encouraged to transform this general idea into a more elaborated plan, which was to be expounded a year later in the instructions for Novosiltsov. But before long, disappointments followed. He was to discover, "too late and with great pain," that the young Emperor "had no deep or definite conviction as to the subjects which engaged the attention of his Cabinet." No strong decision followed his enthusiastic approval and Czartoryski's actions were often counterbalanced by outside interventions. Some historians even concluded that from the first moment Czartoryski was the dupe of Alexander's shrewdness; the Memel episode was quoted as a proof. It appears rather that Alexander's activities displayed more wavering and irresolution than dexterity or cunning. His Prussian imbroglio was to bring nothing but disasters upon him, upon Russia and Europe.

Nor does it seem justifiable to dismiss Czartoryski's conception of Russian policy as mere unrealistic phantasies. Though idealistic in their spirit, they were in accord with some of the traditional tendencies of the past and they contained the seeds of future developments. Czartoryski's policy revived Russia's ambition of hegemony in the Near East. It did even more: it was the first outline of a policy for emancipating and guiding the Slav peoples, of Russian Panslavism. Before long Czartoryski was not only

---

[17] Stroganov's attitude is reflected in his letter to his wife, London, Feb. 18, 1806 (Nicholas Mikhailovich, *Stroganov*, III, 218): he complains of the destruction of the "République de Sully" by the Emperor's errors; Prince Adam would explain to her what it meant.

in close collaboration with the Greek patriot Capo d' Istrias, and in close relation with the princes and politicians of Moldavia and Walachia; he was also the supporter of Kara George, the heroic Serbian leader, as well as a protector of the Montenegrins. While trying to avoid provoking Austrian hostility, he aimed at the emancipation of the Slavs within the frontiers of the Hapsburg monarchy. His plan has proved to be a precedent and an inspiration for many Russian political undertakings up to the present day. It differed from these later plans in its ideological, humanitarian, and liberal tendencies, in the spirit of European solidarity which permeated it, and in its principle of close cooperation with Great Britain. It also differed greatly in its approach to the Polish problem: the reintegration of Poland by the return of the provinces which Russia had annexed. Certainly it was not a policy that could easily be swallowed by the Russians, and this Czartoryski fully realized.

There had been no clearly defined Russian policy regarding the provinces of the former Polish Commonwealth annexed in the last partitions, and—R. H. Lord rightly emphasized—no one considered them otherwise than as Polish lands.[18] Catherine's boasting that she had restored to Russia what had once been separated from her was little more convincing than Maria Theresa's claims for her Hungarian crown to what was to be called Galicia. In actual fact there were in the annexed provinces no Russian elements other than officials, police, troops, and a few political or military dignitaries rewarded by the Tsarina with large donations of land. Not only were the landowners, the clergy, and the small gentry Polish—i.e., mostly but not exclusively polonized Lithuanians, White Ruthenians, or Ruthenians (Ukrainians), and many settlers from Central Poland—but there was also a large Polish element in the urban population and even among the peasants in some districts. There was no other national consciousness than the Polish. On the other hand, however, the peasant masses mostly spoke their ancient national tongues: Lithuanian (a smaller fraction) and White Ruthenian or Ruthenian (Ukrainian); and both Ruthenian dialects, although different, were kindred to the Russian language, and the Russians were

---

[18] See R. H. Lord, *The Second Partition*, pp. 41-43.

inclined to minimize the difference. A great part of the population were of the Orthodox faith or of Greek-Catholic rite; the latter were considered by the Russians as having been forcibly annexed by the Papacy and therefore liable to be reunited with the Orthodox Church. Both these factors, the ethnological and the religious, favored a policy of Russification of the newly acquired provinces. The new and influential Russian landowners were, of course, protagonists of such a policy, which appealed also to the interests of the bureaucrats and offered prospects of further donations and rewards. But such a policy could by no means be carried out with success without an appeal for the support of the peasant masses. It had been done before in 1768 in the Ukraine, and attempts of the same kind were made in 1789-1790, but these revolts, instigated by Russian agents, were directed against Poland as a foreign country; now a revolt of the peasants against their Polish overlords would mean a social revolution within Russia's boundaries, and thus a danger to the existing social order in Russia proper, where the slavery of the peasants was much worse *proof ?* than it had been in Poland.

Therefore a middle course was chosen: that of repressing all national activities and at the same time of winning over the upper classes by safeguarding their social privilege of exploiting the peasants and leaving them with some vestiges of their old institutions. The Poles were humiliated in their national and religious feelings, but at the same time the most influential among them had their particular interests favored. This policy met with some response, since many of the elder generations were inclined to accept things as they came and their national aspirations were restrained by the fear of social unrest. The Jesuits, who still had their stronghold at Polock, favored the acceptance of Russian domination. A kind of appeasement between the Russians and the Poles went on, founded upon the slavery of the peasants and on the subservience of a great part of the Polish gentry to the conquerors.]

Czartoryski's policy was bound to cause an almost revolutionary change in the situation. First of all, it aimed at returning those provinces to a restored Polish kingdom, and regenerating the Polish element in them in the spirit of the May 3 Constitution.

It meant the elimination of social unrest by the introduction of progressive and humanitarian ideas and a gradual emancipation of the peasant masses. It meant the quelling of religious strife by a policy of freedom of conscience and of tolerance, and was opposed to the Jesuit tendencies and influence. As for the national differences, Czartoryski felt no more embarrassed by them than a British statesman feels in having Welsh- or Gaelic-speaking countrymen.

Czartoryski laid the foundations of the future of those provinces by his great educational work, a continuation of that of the Polish Committee for National Education. He met with eager response and support in all parts of the dismembered Commonwealth and until 1806 he could reasonably expect to unite all Poles behind his policy. As to the advantages which he hoped to bring to Russia by the realization of his scheme, the most important was the prospect of a durable and free union with a strong Polish kingdom, with a common foreign policy, thus extending Russia's influence in the Vistula basin and strengthening it in Central and Eastern Europe. He could honestly pledge his compatriots' loyalty to such union inaugurated by a generous act of restitution, and he was assured of the best will of the Emperor, who called it *son idée favorite*.

Nevertheless, the difficulties arising on Russia's side were far from negligible: Russian opinion was divided on Polish problems, and most Russians shared the belief that what Catherine the Great had conquered must be kept as part of the Empire. Thus that part of the political plan had to be kept secret in order that Russian public opinion should not be prematurely alarmed. Czartoryski was fully aware that there was only one way of winning over Russian public opinion to his policy, namely its prompt and brilliant success. That could be achieved, he emphasized, only by carrying out the whole scheme with determination and firmness. Those virtues, however, were not characteristic of Alexander in the early years of his reign. He still hesitated to commit himself finally as to the line his foreign policy should follow; he still yielded to contradictory influences and pressures, though—as a well-informed person confidentially told a British friend—"they were not likely to prevail against the prepossession of the Emperor in favor of Prince Adam Czartoryski, Count Stroganov junior (adjoint in Mr. de Kochubey's department), and Mr. Novosiltsov. He said: 'Ils n'ont qu'une âme'; but their inexperience and their want of confidence in their own strength gave great advantage to their opponents. . . ." The informer realized the difficulties of Prince Adam's position as a Pole, and his extreme caution in expounding his opinions.[19]

The difficulties in carrying out the plan did not, however, center only on St. Petersburg. The solution of the Polish problem had to be forced on Prussia, and Czartoryski had to take into account Alexander's emotional ties and the Prussophile tendencies of many Russians as well as Maria Teodorovna's influence on her son. It may have been that he also underestimated the difficulty of securing an understanding with Great Britain on this question. It was certainly not easy to convince Downing Street of the advantages of such a tremendous extension of Russia's influence and power. In 1791 Pitt had been ready to oppose even by force Russia's extension to the Dniester and her impact on Poland; now, the British Cabinet was supposed to be more inclined to acquiesce in Russia's prospective control of a restored, reunited, and reconciled Poland and of the whole of the Balkan Peninsula with Constantinople and the Straits, Greece and the Ionian Islands.

In the early weeks of 1804 one of Prince Adam's Greek agents conveyed to a British friend "the Emperor's anxiety to concert measures with His Majesty [King George III] for the emancipation of the Greeks," and informed him that "His Imperial Majesty entertained strong doubts about the willingness of the British Cabinet to see a Russian Prince on the throne of Constantinople; that if these doubts were removed, His Imperial Majesty would go to any length to support the King in the present war. . . ." Thus the Greek patriot suggested that Sir John Warren, the British Ambassador, should write a letter to that effect in order to dissipate any doubts as to Britain's consent to such an arrangement.[20] The Ambassador was never approached on this matter, nor had any Russian Minister expressed such

19 B. Garlike to Warren, Jan. 3, 1804 (F.O.65/54).
20 Warren to Hawkesbury, Feb. 3, 1804 (F.O.65/54).

sentiments to him, but obviously it was far from reassuring as to the moderate character of Russia's political aims or ambitions. Ostensible instructions for Count Simon Vorontsov, the ultra-Anglophile Russian envoy in London, suggested only that the survival of a Turkish empire ought to depend on the improvement of the fate of its Greek and Slavonic subjects, as both humanity and sound policy demanded it. A Greek agent was sent to London to state the case of his people and Vorontsov felt compelled to present his objections against the idea of a Greek empire.[21] In fact Prince Adam's diplomacy did not confine itself to the problems of Greece, and he deserved to be considered as a precursor of the Balkan league (of 1912).[22] Czartoryski's idea was to redeem such a shifting of the balance of power by basing the Russian hegemony in eastern Europe on liberal and humanitarian principles, on a system of collective security and even on a supranational structure ensuring a lasting peace. London, however, could be reconciled with such ambitious Russian aims only under pressure of the necessity of looking for Russia's partnership in the renewed struggle against Bonaparte. Thus, in spite of Czartoryski's desire to see the Emperor in the role of a mediator and arbiter of Europe, the inevitable consequence of his plans was a rupture between Russia and France and the creation of a Third Coalition.

[21] See Martens, xi, 79-80.

[22] See H. Batowski, "Un precurseur polonais de l'Union balkanique," *Revue internationale des études balkaniques*, Beograd, 1936, pp. 114-116. Also see P. P. Panaitescu, *Correspondence lui Constantin Ypsilanti*, 1933, pp. 27-28; and S. Askenazy "Z przeszłości Czarnogórza" (From the Past of Montenegro), *Szkice i portrety*, 1937, pp. 81-87.

CHAPTER 4

PRINCE ADAM'S GRAND DESIGN
AND THE THIRD COALITION

THE RUPTURE of the peace treaty of Amiens seemed to open the road to Russian mediation together with a complete revision of the *status quo* of Europe, dislocated as it was by Bonaparte's conquests and his recent *faits accomplis* in Italy, Switzerland, and Germany. D'Antraigues, the chief of the royalist espionage network against France, now a correspondent of Czartoryski, provided information (partly faked as usual) on French preparations for an invasion of the Ionian Isles, Morea, and Albania. This warning gave Russian diplomacy an incentive for sounding the opinion of the cabinets of Europe as to concerted political action, backed by a display of force, with a view to preventing further French encroachments. In November 1803 the first Russian offer of an alliance was made to the British government.[1] As late as February 1804 Sir John Warren stated his government's readiness to cooperate. Czartoryski seemed rather reluctant to conclude a bilateral agreement on that particular problem; he emphasized the necessity of a prior arrangement with Austria and of a "distant insight into the conduct of Prussia." In his instructions to Vorontsov, the Russian Ambassador to the Court of St. James, he stated that Russia's only desire was to maintain the Ottoman Empire in its present state. But at the same time he hinted at the necessity of improving the situation of the Ottoman subjects of Greek Orthodox faith, as a condition *sine qua non* of the survival of Turkey. This stipulation aroused some suspicions in London as to Russia's real intentions. A joint action of a Russian force from Corfu and of British forces from Malta came under discussion, and before long another important matter was brought up,

[1] See J. H. Rose, *Napoleonic Studies*, App. IV.

namely the problem of financing the military action of the Continental Powers by means of British subsidies.[2]

In March 1804 the capture and execution of the Duc d'Enghien created a new situation. It was a flagrant violation of international law, because carried out on territory of the German Empire, and an offense to Russia, since the territory of Alexander's father-in-law, the Markgraf of Baden, had been the scene of the raid. Although the latter displayed much restraint in handling the incident, it provided a good starting point for a diplomatic offensive. Russia's intervention was justified by her rights—problematic though they were—as guarantor of the German Empire. Czartoryski's note protesting against and asking for an explanation of the incident was met, as was to be expected, by Talleyrand's venomous retort: "The complaint which Russia is raising today invites a question: if at the time when England plotted the assassination of Paul I the Russian government had known that the authors of the conspiracy were as near as a league from the frontier, would they not have hastened to seize them?" The allusion to the impunity of those responsible for Paul's assassination, and thus to Alexander's complicity, was obvious, and the young Emperor's reaction went further than Czartoryski had expected. He was still meditating on Russia's part as arbiter and mediator. Instead of committing her to a military alliance with Britain against Napoleon, he considered in the first instance "a system of defense to prevent any further advance or aggression on the part of France upon the territory or the independence of the rest of Europe." It was all that he thought feasible for the time being, neither Austria nor Prussia being ready to adopt "a more vigorous line of policy."[3] Only after the consolidation of such a defensive league and after having achieved its military preparedness was France to be invited to discuss with the united powers their plan for a general peace. Czartoryski even succeeded in bringing Prussia to sign a secret declaration on May 24, 1804 which amounted to a defensive alliance on similar lines.[4] But Austria's

[2] See Sir John Warren's correspondence with Hawkesbury and Harrowby (F.O.65/54-55). Martens, XI, 79 sq.

[3] See Warren to Hawkesbury, May 12, 1804 (*Despatches*, pp. 10-12).

[4] Martens, VI, 341 f.

attitude was even more cautious, and neither of the German powers was prepared to refuse recognition of Napoleon's title as emperor. There existed even serious divergencies of views between Russia and England, Pitt's war aims being the restoration as far as possible of the *status quo* before the war, while Alexander and Czartoryski did not consider the reestablishment of the *status quo* possible or even desirable, and insisted upon a complete revision of the map of Europe.

Before the exchange of views among St. Petersburg, London, and Vienna had advanced beyond cautious diplomatic soundings, the clash over the affair of the Duc d'Enghien precipitated further developments. The Tsar now urged a rupture with France. He even impressed Czartoryski by his ardor, buoyant energy, and defiance. In August a Russian note was sent to Paris demanding the evacuation of Naples, a complete rearrangement of the affairs of Italy, an adequate compensation for the King of Sardinia for his losses, the evacuation of Northern Germany (particularly of Hanover), and a pledge of complete neutrality for the German Empire. Weeks elapsed before the French answer came: it was a harsh rebuff. An ultimatum followed, and the Russian diplomatic agent, Oubril, had to ask for his passport. Now there could be no more delay in promoting Czartoryski's and Alexander's common plan of a new order in Europe. "We had to make England understand," writes Czartoryski in his Memoirs, "that the wish to fight Napoleon was not in itself sufficient to establish an indissoluble bond between her government and that of St. Petersburg, and that to be permanent such a bond must be based not on a common feeling of revenge but on the most elevated principles of justice and philanthropy."[5]

The main lines of the plan were laid down in the instructions for Novosiltsov, the deputy Minister of Justice and member of the Secret Committee; he was to be sent to London as special messenger of the Emperor in order to approach Pitt confidentially (as well as his opponent Fox) and to discuss the whole plan with them. No one was informed of the purpose of his journey; even the British Ambassador could only tell his Minister that the

[5] Cz.M.(E), II, 35-36.

visitor "is much in the confidence of the Emperor" and that one "cannot speak too highly of his talents and character."[6]

Novosiltsov was in fact capable, efficient, and versatile, but also cynical and unscrupulous, so this eulogy of his character was rather deceptive; nevertheless, at that time he enjoyed Czartoryski's warm friendship and confidence and was known to be an Anglophile well acquainted with British institutions and British political circles. A few years before, in 1800-1801, he had made a prolonged sojourn in London, and some evidence of the part he played in the conspiracy against Paul I is to be found in his correspondence with Count Simon Vorontsov, the Russian Ambassador.[7] Prince Adam now informed Vorontsov of the forthcoming visit of Novosiltsov, who "in one hour's talk would be able to say more than a hundred sheets of paper," and who enjoyed the full confidence of the Emperor. The journey was undertaken with the knowledge and approval of the Ambassador's brother, the Chancellor Alexander Vorontsov.[8]

The "Secret Instructions" to Novosiltsov were signed by the Emperor on September 11/23, 1804, and countersigned by Czartoryski.[9] They were to serve as "complement and commentary" to those received by the Russian Ambassador. The assumption was that "the most powerful weapon hitherto used by the French and one still threatening the other European states, was the general opinion which France managed to inculcate that her cause was that of national liberty and prosperity. The good of humanity, the true interest of the lawful authorities, and the success of the enterprise contemplated by the two powers demanded that France should be deprived of this formidable

[6] Warren to Harrowby, Sept. 23, 1804 (*Despatches*, p. 41).

[7] On Novosiltsov, see S. Smolka, *Polityka Lubeckiego*, 1907, II, 239 ff; S. Askenazy, *Łukasiński*, 1928, I, 387-389; *Arch. Vorontsova*, XI, 380-381; XVIII, 435-436.

[8] Czartoryski to S. Vorontsov Aug. 18-30, 1804 (*Arch. Vorontsova*, XV, 245-246).

[9] Piattoli's major part in drafting the plan was erroneously credited by Thiers, who had seen some of his memoranda after Novosiltsov's mission to England; see Cz.M.(E), II, 93-95. D'Ancona, *Scipione Piattoli*, 1915, simplified the problem by attributing without any proof to Piattoli the authorship of Czartoryski's basic memorandum "Sur le système politique que devrait suivre la Russie," 1803; and Dr. H. Schaeder, *Die Dritte Koalition und die Heilige Allianz*, 1934, went even further, without consulting either Czartoryski's or Piattoli's Mss.

weapon. . . ." Novosiltsov was ordered to point out "that it was an absolute condition of an intimate and cordial union between Russia and England."

The Emperor emphasized his repugnance toward any reactionary measures and to the reestablishment of the old abuses in the countries to be liberated from Napoleon's control; they should be "assured of liberties founded on a solid basis." The King of Sardinia should be restored to his throne and "his share of the territories recovered from France should be as large as possible," but he should be invited "to give his people a free and wise constitution." The political existence of Switzerland must be restored and strengthened by the improvement of its government "based on local requirements and on the wishes of the people" sufficiently to make its neutrality respected. The same principle was to guide the common policy with regard to Holland: the form of its government ought to conform to the national character and to the wishes of the population. As regards Germany, the instructions suggested the creation of a West German federal state independent of Austria or Prussia.

The same line of conduct should be followed with regard to France: "We should declare to the French nation that our efforts are directed not against her but only against her government . . . and that we now appeal to her not to preach revolt and disobedience to the law, but to urge all parties in France to trust the allied powers, whose only desire is to emancipate France . . . and to make her free to choose any government she may herself prefer. . . ." Russia did not consider restoration of the Bourbons as necessarily a solution. The choice of the person and the family to be called to reign over France was regarded as a secondary matter; the most essential condition was that the future sovereign should submit to the constitution adopted by the nation. That part of the instruction did not seem to exclude a negotiated peace with Napoleon as emperor.

Novosiltsov was ordered to discuss with the British ministers the problem of the different forms of government to be established in the various countries; but the principles should be everywhere the same: they could be summarized in the expression "reasonable freedom." By promoting this principle against despotism and anarchy, Russia and England would produce "a general enthusiasm for the good cause, the results of which would be incalculable," thus securing the true means of "restricting French power within its just limits." It would also assist in putting the future peace of Europe on a solid and permanent basis. "The object would be, first, to attach nations to their governments by making it possible for them to act only for the benefit of their subjects; and, secondly, to stabilize the relations between the various states by more precise rules which would be so drawn up as to make it in the interest of each state to respect them." Reasonable freedom seemed capable of consolidating governments and "of surrounding them with certain enclosures against the passions, undaunted ambitions, or moral insanity of some rulers." That fine tribute to the moderating influence of public opinion and to the value of constitutional regimes was the more striking, as being solemnly sponsored by the Lord and Autocrat of All the Russias.

There followed a long discussion of the problem of establishing the rule of law among nations. Little of this is to be found in the mutilated English text of the document, and it is necessary to refer to the French original.[10]

The instructions suggested that the enormous influence of the two powers would have to be used, if they succeeded in liberating Europe, for ensuring a lasting peace. Should there be general peace, nothing could possibly prevent the conclusion of a special treaty which would settle the mutual relations of the European states. Czartoryski recalled the Treaty of Westphalia, which had an almost similar aim; that work, though imperfect, was regarded for some generations as a code of modern diplomacy. However, more needed to be done; he suggested the inclusion in the general peace treaty of a statement of the principles of the rights of nations: "Why not subordinate to those principles the positive law of the various countries? Why not define the rights of the neutrals and impose an obligation not to wage war without having previously exhausted all means of mediation. . . ?" In order to safeguard the peace, a league could be founded and its stipulations

10 See Cz.M.(E), ii, 47-48, and Cz.M.(F), ii, 33-39.

would form something of a new code of international law which, being sanctioned by most of the European states, would become invariably valid for the cabinets, because any infraction would provoke the reaction of the united forces of the new league. Czartoryski did not doubt that after having experienced the dangers of a precarious or illusory independence, most governments would be eager to adhere to a league which could ensure their security. He supposed that the secondary states would attach themselves to that idea *de cœur et d'âme*, the more so because some of them would contain in their own constitutions the germs of tranquillity and a remedy against the violence of authoritarian regimes in political action. The stability of the whole structure, however, would repose on the intimate cooperation of the courts of St. Petersburg and London as guarantors of the new order, on their wisdom, example, and inspiration. "Both those powers can only ensure a durable union and prevent any trouble in the future, because for many years there has been no jealousy between them nor any conflict of interests." That optimistic view on Russo-British relations was to be tested before long.

Thus a supranational structure for collective security was proposed, and in the few pages of the document there were ideas which were due to be solemnly proclaimed a century later in President Wilson's first Point, in the Covenant, and in the Kellogg Pact. There was some future in those "chimerical fancies" which irritated Thiers while writing his *Histoire du Consulat et de l'Empire* and which, as the editors of the English version of Czartoryski's Memoirs probably thought, would appear somewhat shocking to the late Victorian politicians who were their prospective readers.

There followed a survey of the map of Europe as it was to be drawn anew. The most suitable frontiers for the different countries were to be drawn up, either as designed by nature herself in this form—for instance, by mountains or seas—or as indicated by the need of providing outlets for the natural and industrial output of each country. The ethnographic factor would be taken into consideration, and an attempt would be made to unite homogeneous peoples within the boundaries of a state as a necessary condition to harmony between peoples and government.

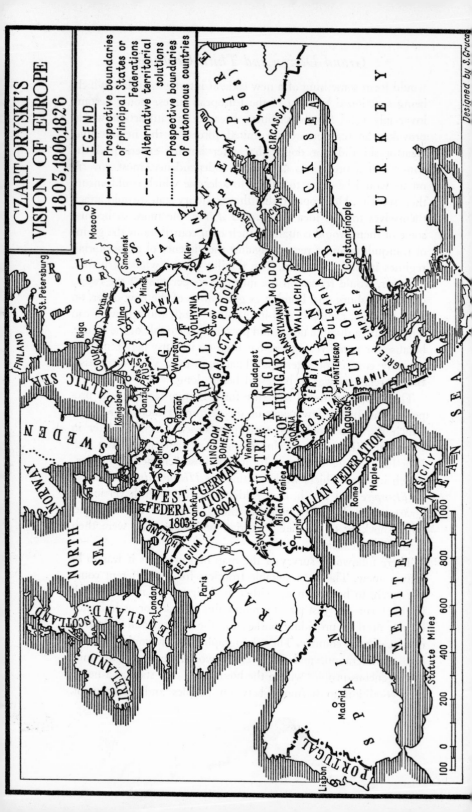

"The commotions from which Europe has continually suffered for some centuries were in most cases provoked by the total abandonment of that natural equilibrium." What Alexander and Czartoryski had in mind was very different from the traditional concept of the balance of power and much in advance of it in terms of the principle of nationality. Those articles of the instructions were, in principle if not literally, a prelude to President Wilson's Points Five to Thirteen.

Certainly—in contrast to President Wilson—his Russian and Polish precursors were aware of the danger of small separate states, too weak to ensure their own security and by this weakness provoking the rapacity of their powerful neighbors. The secondary states should be reinforced, the small ones agglomerated to the greater or amalgamated into federated unions. On those lines was to be found the solution of the problem of putting fetters on French rapacity, as well as of creating some counterbalance to Austria and Prussia by reconstructing Italy and Germany, which were not to be absorbed either by Austria or Prussia. A close union of the German states separated from both those powers was considered.

As to the prospective allies, Austria would almost certainly be persuaded by the fear of losing Russian support and British subsidies. The forecast as to Prussia was less sanguine; probably it would be necessary to force the decision upon her. As to Turkey, the instruction paid lip service to the principle of her integrity, but advocated an arrangement more in conformity with the principles of humanity and sound policy: before agreeing to the alliance which the Porte proposed to Great Britain and Russia, it would be their duty to ensure some better existence for the Christian populations now oppressed by Turkish domination. This provision of the instructions was bound to provoke concern in London as to the future of Turkey; but the problem was a serious one and its solution could not be indefinitely postponed. Once more the corresponding paragraph of the document reads like a prelude to President Wilson's Eleventh and Twelfth Points.

There was, further, a hint of the possibility of some advantages for Austria, Prussia, or Sweden; in this event Russia would claim equivalent acquisitions (e.g., in Poland). The preponderance of England and Russia was to be maintained to a certain degree as a safeguard for the future league of nations. Great Britain, however, was to be induced to make some concessions with regard to the maritime code "the only point where the British government is not exempt from reproach." This suggestion was not easily swallowed by the British partner. It recalled Emperor Paul's league of neutrals, but in the light of future developments which led to the second American war it is not deserving of dismissal as a tactless and unrealistic pretense. It is interesting to compare its wording with that of President Wilson's Second Point.[11]

Novosiltsov was instructed to act on those lines, taking care not to expose himself unnecessarily; he was given much freedom as to the priority of the various items and the way in which he would convince his partners. It was anticipated that the Russian Ambassador, Count Vorontsov, would not share the views expounded in the instructions—he was, indeed, a convinced partisan of Pitt's policy. Novosiltsov was directed to win him over by persuasion and to secure his cooperation. Finally, there was a proviso which by far exceeded the limits of the envoy's ability: he was to induce the British statesmen to desist from the one-party government and to appoint a government of all parties and all talents. There was also a warning at the end: if the British Cabinet was not able to agree with these broad and generous views, Russia's offers of cooperation with Britain were to be made with reserve.

The initiative of building up a league in order to check the French impact on Europe and to oppose any future aggression was certain to be welcomed at Downing Street. Pitt was sometimes upset by the secrecy of the new Russian policy, but at the same time he was certainly aware of Czartoryski's effort to stiffen

[11] See also P. Rain, *Un Tsar Idéologue, Alexandre I*, 1913, pp. 143-145; Charles Dupuis, *Les antécédents de la Société des Nations—le plan d'Adam Czartoryski et d'Alexandre I*, Séances et Travaux de l'Acad. des Sciences Morales et Pol., 1929, 2e Sem., pp. 25-44; Mirkine Guetzévich in the *Recueil des Travaux en l'honneur de P. M. Milioukov*, 1929. Ch. Morley, "Alexander I and Czartoryski," *Slavonic and East European Review*, 1947; and P. S. Wandycz, "The Polish Precursor of Federalism," *Journal of Central European Affairs*, Jan. 1953.

the attitude of both the German powers. He was informed of the secret declarations exchanged in November 1804 between Russia and Austria, and of Russia's later compact with Sweden. Foundations of a new coalition were finally laid, and Pitt, while facing the threat of a French invasion, could not be indifferent to this opportunity of putting an end to Britain's dangerous isolation by the diversion of the peril from his country and the carrying of the war into enemy-controlled western Europe. When asked sometime before by the Russian envoy not to make peace without Russia's participation, he had rather gloomily hinted at his country's increasing difficulties in waging war alone, and the danger of exhaustion and discouragement among the British people.[12]

But, in spite of Britain's paramount interest in concluding an alliance with Russia and inducing other Continental powers to adhere to it, the negotiation was not to be easy. A great divergence of opinion was necessarily presumed as to the general principles—the principle of the balance of power being in conflict with those of nationality and collective security. What mattered even more was the fact that the British Cabinet stood for *status quo ante bellum*, the Russian Emperor for a complete reconstruction of Europe. Pitt would have preferred to have France confined within her former frontiers; Alexander's and Czartoryski's instructions alluded with some preference to the *frontières naturelles*. As to the initial steps to be taken, the Tsar's idea was to force Bonaparte to negotiate with the united powers. In Pitt's view, the only reason for a mission to Paris was to demonstrate the adversary's responsibility for the general conflagration. While Czartoryski's intention was to give France at least a chance of reconciliation with Europe, for Pitt a victorious war was the only way of restoring peace.

Novosiltsov's mission apparently proved a success. The report on his talks with Lord Harrowby and Pitt emphatically claimed a complete agreement with the British government on the principles to be followed by the future coalition.[13] The agreement

---

12 S. Vorontsov to Czartoryski, Sept. 28, 1804 (*Arch. Vorontsova*, xv, 273-274).

13 Novosiltsov's report in Cz.M.(E), II, 59-68, undated; probably Dec. 31, 1804 (see *Arch. Vorontsova*, xviii, 455-456). Extracts of his correspondence with Alexander I and Czartoryski, Nov. 1804 to Feb. 1805: Martens, xi, 89-104.

was achieved in a somewhat unexpected manner, Novosiltsov having in fact dropped the program he should have imposed on his partners and accepted their own ideas as "approximate to those of H. M. the Emperor."[14] Thus they easily agreed, that a seizure of Constantinople by any foreign power should be *une lésion du droit de gens*. They agreed on the principles of balance of power, of forcing back France into her "ancient limits," and of establishing strong barriers against her future expansion. There also reappeared the design of firmly establishing Prussia on the left bank of the Rhine. The idea of conferring upon Prussia the guardianship of the lower Rhine and of Holland was not a new one at Downing Street; it was Pitt's traditional endeavor to enable Prussia to perform such a noble mission. He had expounded it with much emphasis in 1791 in the Ochakov debate,[15] and despite Prussia's behavior since 1794 he still adhered to this idea.

The new Foreign Secretary, Lord Mulgrave, while transmitting a draft of the treaty to Vorontsov, gave the British viewpoint, erroneously supposed to be "according to the sentiments" of the Russian Emperor, with much precision and clarity.[16] Three objects were to be achieved by the "concert": first, to rescue from the domination of France those countries which it had subjugated since the beginning of the Revolution, and to reduce France to its former limits as it stood before that time; second, to make such an arrangement with respect to the territories recovered from France as might provide for their security and happiness and at the same time constitute a more effective barrier against future encroachments on the part of France; third, to form at the restoration of peace a general agreement and guarantee for the mutual protection and security of different powers and

---

[14] The divergence between Novosiltsov's instructions and his interpretation of them in his report seems to have been overlooked by J. H. Rose, who denies the existence of any conflict of principles between British and Russian policies. The contrasting features of both these policies appear distinctly in Czartoryski's correspondence with Simon Vorontsov, *Arch. Vorontsova*, xv; P. Rain, *op.cit.*, p. 145; Ch. Dupuis, *op.cit.*, p. 44; Martens, *loc.cit.*

[15] See *The Parliamentary Register*, 1791, vol. 29, pp. 46-49.

[16] Note of Jan. 19, 1805 (F.O.65/60). Published by C. Webster, *British Diplomacy, 1813-1815*, App. 1, pp. 388-394, with omission of some paragraphs concerning Prussia.

for the reestablishment of a general system of public law in Europe.

The emphasis was laid on the first point: "Nothing short of it [of reducing France to the *status quo* before the Revolution] can completely satisfy the view which both sovereigns form for the deliverance and security of Europe." As we have seen before, this was neither Alexander's nor Czartoryski's view.

As this aim—the British state paper continued—and particularly the "entire recovery of the Netherlands and the countries occupied by France on the left bank of the Rhine" could not be achieved without the active participation of Prussia, the necessity of founding a sufficient inducement for her in order to neutralize French temptations (the bait of Hanover) was emphasized. Thus the restoration of the ancient rights of the liberated countries—such was the British interpretation of the second point—was to be subordinated to the security of Europe, which would best be served by giving the lands of the Italian Republic to Austria and the lands of the left bank of the Rhine to the river Maas to Prussia.

The Foreign Office realized that "some danger may possibly exist to Holland from the near and powerful neighborhood of Prussia surrounding her," but it estimated "that this and every other danger that can be stated will be of infinitely less magnitude when threatened on the side of Prussia, than if it were to be apprehended from France."[17] Thus, in order to match the present aggressor, the future one was to be invited to take over his "Wacht am Rhein," and on the Maas.

At the same time the note to Vorontsov suggested as "extremely desirable" "that the Emperor of Russia should immediately and distinctly notify the King of Prussia of his determination not to acquiesce in his obtaining by an arrangement with France any acquisition in any part of Germany and particularly that of Hanover. . . . All these considerations, however, may too probably be insufficient, unless enforced by the appearance of a powerful Russian army on his [Prussia's] frontiers." Thus the future guardian of the security of the Low Countries ought to be

---

[17] Mulgrave to Gower, Jan. 21, 1805 (*Despatches*, pp. 88-92).

first warned by the threat of armed invasion to desist from his bad habit of robbing his neighbor's lands.

Lord Mulgrave's dispatches paid warm tribute to Novosiltsov's "zeal, candor, and ability" and they expressed "the highest sentiments of the esteem and regard of any member of H. M. Government" for the Tsar's special envoy. Novosiltsov's successes were not limited to his negotiations with Mulgrave and Pitt. Old Vorontsov always refused to entertain any contact with the Prince of Wales (he thought it would be contrary to his loyalty to the King) and with the Whig opposition (he thought it an offence to Pitt); and Czartoryski's insistence could not surmount that obstacle. This time Novosiltsov, provided with a friendly letter from Czartoryski to Fox, had not only confidential talks with the latter, but also friendly and frequent contacts with Lord Moira and conversations with the Prince of Wales. "There was —as Stroganov mentioned after a year—some kind of treaty between them, Lord Moira was a witness."[18]

Novosiltsov's mission had apparently been a remarkable success; he himself reported that it was marvelous or even miraculous. He boasted that Pitt had designed him as the most suitable common delegate to Bonaparte.[19] Czartoryski had less reason to admire his friend's achievements when he read the British project of the treaty: Novosiltsov had given up the Russian viewpoint in most important matters and had secured courteous but evasive declaration in return. But Prince Adam did not feel strongly enough to disavow Pitt's and Novosiltsov's common work. In spite of his successes in concluding alliances with Austria and Sweden, Czartoryski's position was growing difficult, his isolation more pronounced, and the absence of Novosiltsov, the most active and influential of his friends and the only one who had a continuous, daily contact with the Emperor, deprived him of most valuable support. He was subjected to attacks from several sides: the elderly Catherine's and Paul's dignitaries, mostly pro-Prussian, and the young "brothers Gracchi," the Dol-

[18] Stroganov to Czartoryski, 19 (Mar. 31, 1806). Nicholas Mikhailovich, *Stroganov*, II, 227 f. Czartoryski's and Novosiltsov's connections with the Prince of Wales and the Whigs: Martens, XI, 89, 96, 124.

[19] Report of Jan. 20, 1805 (Martens, XI, 101).

gorukis as well, backed by the Dowager Empress, accused him of sacrificing Russia's interests to the British, or perhaps to his own mysterious Polish designs. The champions of the policy of appeasement with Bonaparte—like Count Rumiantsov and Prince Kurakin—denounced his adventurous warmongering; at the same time, Muscovite diehards, with their spokesman, Count Rostopchin, did not desist from hinting at the young stranger's concealed Jacobinism. The old chancellor, Alexander Vorontsov, dangerously ill and far away from the capital, could not provide any effective support, although he warmly approved Prince Adam's policy. The Emperor seemed to yield to the pressure of all the malcontents and critics; and a feminine intrigue contributed to poison for a while his relations with his Minister. Czartoryski was near to being overthrown, *de faire la culbute*.[20] So, instead of admitting the failure of the London mission, he only tried to redress the setback by restating the position in his own talks with the British Ambassador, Lord Granville Leveson Gower. And he expressed his appreciation of Novosiltsov's achievement.[21]

The Russian Ambassador in London, Count Simon Vorontsov, was informed in a friendly manner that he no longer enjoyed the full confidence of his sovereign and was invited to choose the appropriate moment for resigning.[22] He complained bitterly of being regarded as more devoted to Britain than to Russia, as "either fool or traitor." In actual fact, he had much more understanding for the policy of his Tory friends than for the policy of his government. England was to him his second fatherland and his choice because free, and he had already decided not to return to Russia—he preferred living in England as a private citizen to all the splendors of the imperial court. He had, how-

[20] For the crisis at the end of 1804 see D. P. Tatischev to Al. Vorontsov, Dec. 2, 1804 (*Arch. Vorontsova*, xviii, 386-388); P. V. Zawadowski to Al. Vorontsov, Feb. 12, 1805 (*op.cit.*, xii, 297); S. Vorontsov to Czartoryski, May 18-27, 1805 (*op.cit.*, xv, 303-322); Czartoryski to Novosiltsov, Feb. 16-17, 1805 (Martens, xi, 102-103).

[21] There is in Cz.M.(E), ii, 52-55 and Cz.M.(F), ii, 62-66 a "Note on the arrangement of the European affairs as result of a victorious war"; it was supposed by the editors to have been written in 1804 and was generally referred to the negotiations with Pitt (so A. Sorel, J. H. Rose, S. Askenazy); careful analysis shows that it could not have been drafted earlier than late 1806.

[22] See Czartoryski to Vorontsov, Mar. 24, 1805 (*Arch. Vorontsova*, xv, 285-290).

ever, an acute sense of reality as to the conditions and limitations of a real agreement between the two powers.

Czartoryski now realized the mistake he had made when drawing up his instructions for Novosiltsov: there had been no clear distinction between the conditions to be proposed to France as a means of avoiding war, and the final aims to be achieved by the coalition in a victorious war. St. Petersburg, London, and Vienna were agreed as to the necessity of a preliminary attempt at imposing on Napoleon such conditions as were compatible with general security. This move was proposed by the British Cabinet and although the purpose was rather "to tear off the mask" worn by the French government and "to convince all Europe of the justice of their intentions," there was in St. Petersburg and especially in Vienna the feeling that the conditions for that kind of ultimatum should not exclude the possibility of actual negotiations. So the formula of enforcing upon France her ancient limits was to be dropped. It was omitted even from the statements of the war aims, though it was there specified that the Low Countries should be given to Holland, Geneva and Savoy to Switzerland, the King of Sardinia should be reestablished in his dominions (although it was not stated whether these included his lost territories on the western slopes of the Alps) and Prussia should regain her former territories on the left bank of the Rhine with a generous *arrondissement* to form an "efficient barrier."

Napoleon was to be notified of the necessity of establishing barriers to protect Holland and Italy and of withdrawing the limits of France to the Moselle, the Rhine, the Alps, and the Pyrenees, which meant the "natural limits," though much modified in the Rhineland and in Belgium.[23] If he agreed to negotiate, measures of expediency were foreseen for the arrangement of Italy: namely, consent for giving the Kingdom of Italy to Joseph Bonaparte and even the exchange of Piedmont for other Italian territories as compensation for the dispossessed King of Sardinia. As a supreme concession and proof of good will, it was agreed

[23] See Gower to Mulgrave, Apr. 7, 1805 (*Despatches*, 127 f.). The intended concessions were overlooked by A. Sorel in his masterly indictment of Russo-British policy in *L'Europe et la Révolution Française*, VI, 410-419.

that Britain should give up all her conquests, especially Malta, which would henceforth be protected by a Russian garrison. The concession was meant as a measure for removing the principal obstacle to entering into negotiations with France. But England was expected to make a disinterested gesture in isolation, since "aggrandizements" were promised to Austria, Prussia, and Holland, and Russia had stated her right to equivalent acquisitions. There was a clause about establishing a congress after the war, "which may settle the public law in Europe"; the document itself, however, was a product of hard bargaining and the laborious adjustments of conflicting interests and claims, and it conformed more to the traditions of the *ancien régime* than to the noble ideas which had at first guided the policy of Alexander and Czartoryski. There was some irony in the fact that even the name of Poland was not mentioned and the only stipulation connected with her fate was the promise of "equivalent acquisitions" for Russia, which meant that some Polish territories were to be taken from Prussia and Austria and added to Russia's earlier share.

When Pitt read the treaty, he was exasperated. The clauses concerning Italy came as a shock, and he disapproved of the concessions made in the delicate matter of subsidies. But the clause on Malta was the worst, the more so because it was to be extorted as a *sine qua non* condition. Gower was disavowed and Russia warned of Britain's decision to renounce in such circumstances any collaboration with the Continental powers.

The attempt to enforce that concession from Great Britain was unexpected in London; there had been no mention of it either in the instructions to Novosiltsov or in the dispatches to Vorontsov, and neither of them had raised the question. In fact, as Czartoryski pointed out in his answer to Vorontsov's criticism, it had been Russia's view since the conflict on Malta had emerged, and "Russia could not contradict herself on that matter."

Prince Adam quoted his Emperor's words that he did not understand why Malta should not be safe under Russian guardianship, and he himself wondered why the British failed to realize the extreme advantage of giving themselves such an appearance of moderation and of devotion to Europe's tranquillity without really giving anything away, as there was no real chance of a peaceful arrangement on the proposed terms. He even suggested that Britain might give up Gibraltar as a very appropriate gesture. Apparently in spite of the prodigious amount of ink which has been used for a year or two in order to explain the necessity of Malta's being kept in British hands, the Russian diplomats did not grasp the importance for Britain of her positions in the Mediterranean, nor the suspicions which inevitably arose from their proposals.

No one in St. Petersburg expected Pitt's disavowal of the treaty. Both Alexander and Czartoryski had been sanguine about a common policy for Russia and Britain; they presumed that Britain would give way over Malta and that Gower's obstinate opposition to signing was to be attributed to his peculiar temper.[24] The negotiations with Austria for obtaining her accession to the treaty were pressed forward. For a year or more Czartoryski had established his private liaison with Vienna through the intermediary of the young and efficient General Wintzingerode, his personal and devoted friend. The Austrian Colonel Baron Stutterheim, on a mission to St. Petersburg, informed even his court that Wintzingerode was Czartoryski's only friend in that capital, and he added that it did credit to both of them: "They live in the greatest intimacy together and, may I add, with the Emperor himself." The Baron was told by the Emperor: "You have very good friends in Czartoryski and myself; and do not forget Wintzingerode."[25] That link was an important weapon of Czartoryski's diplomacy, as Wintzingerode was *persona grata* with the Austrians; he greatly contributed to the removal of obstacles in the way of Austria's accession to the coalition. He was sent to Berlin in order to discover Prussia's real intentions; the official Ambassador, old Alopeus, was rightly suspected of being more in Prussia's than in the Emperor's service. The evidence of Prussia's attempt to secure Hanover in connivance with Bonaparte and her threat to Swedish Pomerania prompted Alexander's decision to enforce Prussia's surrender to the common policy of

---

[24] Czartoryski to S. Vorontsov, April 16, 1805 (*Arch. Vorontsova*, xv, 290).

[25] Stutterheim's reports, June 23, Oct. 14, 1804 (Staats Archiv Vienna) quoted by Wertheimer, *Geschichte Oesterreichs . . .* 1889, I, 213-214.

the three powers by a display of force and even by military operation. He awaited the news on the English ratification of the treaty before sending to Paris Novosiltsov, who was chosen by both cabinets as the right man to speak to Bonaparte on their behalf.

On May 15 Czartoryski dispatched the projected plan of operations to London; he emphasized the Emperor's adamant attitude towards Prussia and recommended that the Ambassador stand firm on all that concerned the possibility of operations against that country.[26]

Less than a month later, the news of Pitt's refusal to ratify the treaty burst upon St. Petersburg. "I have never seen our Master more dissatisfied and more out of control," so Czartoryski summarized the effect on the Tsar. The Russian court decided, nevertheless, to carry on with Novosiltsov's mission to Paris, stating their pledge that England should not be involved in any commitment without her assent.[27]

Novosiltsov proceeded to Berlin to secure Napoleon's agreement to his trip to Paris. But shortly after he had left St. Petersburg a new *fait accompli* by Napoleon put the whole situation in a new light. The impending annexation of Genoa made, in Alexander's view, the entire negotiation of no avail, stultifying his plan for compensations in Italy, while Britain's refusal of Malta deprived him of his other trump card. Novosiltsov was accordingly warned that if Vienna did not insist upon the continuation of his mission, he should declare that his government had recalled him. The article on Malta no longer seemed of immediate importance, and the Tsar decided at last to ratify the treaty with the controversial article and annex omitted, while restating Russia's view in a special declaration. This solution was immediately endorsed by Lord Gower, and on July 28 the acts of ratification were exchanged. The differences between the two texts were explained away in the protocol. The three powers' declarations of August 9 stated Austria's accession to the treaty.

The significance of the treaty, however, had now greatly changed: it had become merely an instrument of a general war.

---

[26] Czartoryski to S. Vorontsov, May 15, 1805 (*Arch. Vorontsova*, xv, 298 f.).
[27] U.s., June 16 (*op.cit.*, xv, 323 f.).

Grand Design and Third Coalition

The date of the march of the Russian armies into Austrian and Prussian territories had already been fixed for August 16. It should have coincided with the delivery of Novosiltsov's ultimatum in Paris; instead, his declaration, printed in Hamburg papers, announced that his mission was cancelled by order of his sovereign. Thus, what was left of any diplomatic measures in the agreed plan vanished; there remained only Russian and Austrian armies; British, Swedish, and Hanoverian forces; British subsidies; the march of the Russians to the Danube, to the Vistula, and the Oder; landings in Italy and at Stralsund combined with operations of British and Swedish expeditionary forces; Austrian advances into Italy and Germany; a general onslaught against the Corsican usurper and against France. There also remained the unsettled problems of Prussia, the prospective ally, who had to be either induced at heavy cost or forced by military measures to join the coalition.

CHAPTER 5

"THE PLAN FOR MURDERING
PRUSSIA"

ONE OF THE MOST REMARKABLE FEATURES of the Third Coalition was the Prussian imbroglio at the start and the plan for a preliminary military occupation of Prussian territory at the opening of the campaign. The military operation was to be connected with a political one, namely, the restoration of Poland by joining the Prussian share of that country to the provinces annexed by Russia, in order to form a Polish kingdom under Alexander I. That plan, for which Prince Adam was undoubtedly largely responsible, was to be stigmatized by future German historians as Czartoryski's "Mordplan gegen Preussen." The execution of the plan was averted by Alexander's last-minute change of mind and his rather delusive Potsdam agreement with his Prussian royal friend.

Prussia was by no means an innocent victim of "the murderous attempt," and her recent extensions did not seem sacrosanct even to statesmen who disregarded the rights of nations and worshipped each successive *status quo*. It is obvious that Czartoryski was ready to seize the first opportunity of changing that *status quo* along the lines agreed upon between himself and the Tsar. But his plan of political and military action against Prussia had matured while he was in continuous contact with London and Vienna, as a consequence of Prussia's ambiguous and rapacious policy, which aimed by a secret compact with France at a seizure of Hanover and Swedish Pomerania. After having insisted in his note to Vorontsov upon the necessity of warning Prussia and concentrating a powerful army on her frontiers, Lord Mulgrave instructed his Ambassador in connection with the "crooked policy of the Court of Berlin" to suggest to the Tsar to "give immediate notice that a powerful Russian army was on its march to the frontiers of Prussia, with a peremptory declaration at the same time that the entrance of a single Prussian soldier into Swedish Pomerania will be considered as an act of hostility against Russia, which will be followed at once by war."[1] He approved of Czartoryski's idea of putting Prussia before the alternative of joining with Russia or with France.[2] On May 15 Czartoryski wrote to Vorontsov: "The Court of Berlin will not take a decision unless forced to do so; but if enforced, she will most probably decide in our favor. . . . I hope that this time we shall no more be her dupes. . . ."[3] And he added significantly: "I ask you to insist strongly upon all what regards the possible operations against Prussia."

At that time Wintzingerode was still sanguine that Prussia, when facing a coalition, would take sides with Russia. But several weeks later Novosiltsov's impression was less favorable: "This cabinet," he wrote from Berlin, "holds fast to the principle of isolation and is imbued with abject selfishness, which sooner or later must prove very pernicious for them." And he warned the Emperor that he could not rely upon the cooperation of his Prussian majesty in a struggle for the deliverance of Europe.[4]

According to the military plan expounded in Czartoryski's dispatch to Vorontsov of July 31, the movement of the first Russian army into Austrian territory at Brody in the second half of August was to be followed in a few days by the advance of another one from Brest towards Warsaw (then capital of "Southern Prussia"), and by the march of a third from Lithuania into Eastern Prussia. The Russian ambassadors in Vienna and Berlin should give ostensible declarations explaining Russia's action as a retort to Bonaparte's successive invasions threatening the independence of the European states; the Russian troops would be withdrawn if Bonaparte gave sufficient guarantees for the future security of the neutrals. Austria was asked to declare in Berlin her approval of Russia's action.

The political part of the plan was not fully explained in diplomatic dispatches. Immediately after the occupation of War-

---

[1] *Despatches*, pp. 88-92, 98-102.   [2] *Ibid.*, pp. 114-116.
[3] *Arch. Vorontsova*, xv, 298 ff.
[4] Novosiltsov to S. Vorontsov, May 15, July 10; to the Emperor, July 10, 1805 (*Arch. Vorontsova*, xv, 459-468).

saw by the second Russian army, the restoration of the Polish
Kingdom was to be proclaimed and the Polish nation invited to
welcome the Russians as liberators and to rise up as their allies.
Soundings were made in London and Vienna and, according to
Czartoryski's letter to the Tsar, the idea was favorably received
by Pitt and applauded by Fox. Even Austria did not oppose it;
in fact, it was the proposal for the disposal of Prussia which
allegedly induced the Archduke Charles to drop his opposition
to Austria's participation in the coming general war.[5] It seems
likely, from Stutterheim's reports, that there was a secret pact
between the courts of St. Petersburg and Vienna with a view
to overrun Prussia by an unexpected invasion.[6] The Archduke
Charles gave a warning that "Prussia seems not yet decaying to
such an extent as to yield to such a military pressure without
resistance."[7] Thus the Austrian consent to the action was probably given on the condition that Prussia should be taken by
surprise, thereby eliminating the risk of a serious contest and a
protracted campaign.

Poland was warned of and prepared for the coming events, and
for a while all the Polish leaders and political groups united in
support of Czartoryski's plan and accepted the union with Russia.
Prince Joseph Poniatowski, nephew of the last king, in 1792
commander-in-chief against the Russians and future commander-
in-chief of the army of the Duchy of Warsaw in the war of
1812 against the same enemy, was at that time ready to support
his cousin's design, and he gave to the latter's emissary an
unreserved assurance of the attitude of the Polish capital.[8]

In the second half of August, Prince Adam informed Simon
Vorontsov of the vigorous start of the war and assured him that
nothing would be neglected by Russia to ensure its success. He
was satisfied that the Emperor would show that "once he has
taken a great decision, he knows how to adhere to it with un-

---

[5] Czartoryski to the Emperor (April 5, 1806, Cz.M.(E), II, 125, and orig. text
Cz.M.(F), II, 104-131). The attitude of Archduke Charles as reflected in his
papers was rather cautious: see Wertheimer, *Geschichte Oesterreichs*, I, 221-226,
260-271. There also arise some doubts as to Fox's opinion; see his subsequent
letter to Czartoryski, Mar. 17, 1806 (CzM.(E), II, 132 f.).

[6] See Wertheimer, I, 274.   [7] *Ibid.*, pp. 260-261.

[8] See *Zamoyski*, I, 39; IV, 178-179.

shaken firmness."[9] But at that time, the military plan was already undergoing a dangerous modification: the march of the second and third Russian armies into Prussian territory was delayed for a month, until September 16, in order to await the outflanking of Silesia by Kutuzov's first army moving into Austria. It was a rather poor strategy and, as Czartoryski rightly pointed out, it gave Prussia time to prepare herself to check the Russian advance and denied to Russia all the advantage of surprising the Prussian forces, which were immobilized in their garrisons.

Another complication followed: contrary to Czartoryski's and Cobenzl's advice, Alexander decided to leave his capital and join his armies so as to be able to make decisions on the spot. On September 4 he sent a letter to Frederick William, demanding that he should agree to the passage of the Russian armies and announcing their movement for September 16. He proposed to meet the King. Thus having disclosed the secret of his intended operations, he modified the plan once more and ordered both armies approaching Prussia's border to stop upon reaching it and await his final orders. It was probably at that moment that Czartoryski, Wintzingerode, and Novosiltsov jointly intervened with the Emperor and implored him not to be deceived by Prussian promises and to stand firm by his original decision. They did so in vain.[10] On September 27 in Brest Alexander received the news from Berlin that the King would not refuse to meet the Tsar, though he was still opposed to the request for the passage of the troops. Alexander reacted by sending Peter Dolgoruki as a messenger of friendship to the King, bearing a letter in which he again urged him to grant the passage of his troops and an interview. A few days later he received Frederick William's pathetic letter dated September 21; the King persisted in his attitude of neutrality, announced his decision to resist aggression and reminded Alexander significantly of the late Emperor Paul's behavior on a similar occurrence: "He realized that by leaving nothing but the choice between disgrace and despair he would achieve the ruin of Europe." The Tsar was impressed; in his reply he insisted again on an early interview

[9] Czartoryski to S. Vorontsov, Aug. 21, 1805 (*Arch. Vorontsova*, xv, 408-409).
[10] Stutterheim's report, Oct. 4, 1805 (quoted by Wertheimer, I, 274).

and resorted to a sentimental tone: "I consider the moment when that desire would be accomplished as one of the happiest days of my life."[11] At Puławy, where he established his headquarters, he still appeared adamant; his attitude seemed unchanged, but the situation had altered with the passage of time. Stutterheim, who had before been a partisan of the plan, intervened now with the Tsar for an arrangement with Prussia, as she was already warned and preparing for defense. Alexander retorted: "I would bring disgrace upon myself if I withdraw; we must advance and make arrows of any available wood. We will make the Poles rise against Prussia."[12]

On October 3 a military conference was held at Puławy and orders were given for crossing the river Pilica (the frontier of "South Prussia"), but they were immediately canceled by the Tsar. Stutterheim intervened once more by orders of his government against embarking on a serious war with Prussia, who had decided to repel the invasion with arms. Even Prince Adam had to admit in dismay that the situation had changed and the momentum had been lost.[13] Nonetheless on October 10 he informed Razumovski, the Russian Ambassador in Vienna, "His Majesty is firmly decided to start war against Prussia," and directed him to inform Vienna of the forthcoming proclamation of a Kingdom of Poland and to sound that court about a partial exchange of Galicia.[14] But at that very moment the situation was completely reversed: on October 6 the King received the news of the violation of his territory of Ansbach by the passage of Bernadotte's army corps. He immediately announced his consent to the passage of the Russian armies and Dolgoruki hurried with the momentous news to Puławy. Thus the *casus belli* vanished and Alexander reacted by announcing his spontaneous visit to his royal friend: he was in a hurry to meet him, "he had never

[11] The letters exchanged by Alexander and Frederick William during the crisis were published by P. Bailleu, *Publikationen aus den Preussischen Staatsarchiven*, vol. 75, nr. 69-76.

[12] Stutterheim's report, *op.cit.*

[13] At the same moment the British Cabinet advised him to consent to Prussia's neutrality under the condition of the passage of the Russian armies; a few days later they even suggested dropping the plan of moving through Prussian territory. See Mulgrave to Gower, Oct. 15 and 20. (F.O.65/59).

[14] Vasilchikov, *Semeistvo Razumovskih*, 1887, IV, 74.

experienced a more unfortunate period in his life and he had never suffered more." Czartoryski tried in vain to persuade Alexander that Prussia's genuine adherence to the coalition could be secured only by vigorous and determined action. The Emperor hurried to his Prussian Canossa as a repentant sinner.

Alexander's grandnephew and biographer has regarded the sudden turn in Alexander's policy as a result of Peter Dolgoruki's efforts and the latter as having rendered an outstanding service to his country: "It can be reasonably admitted, that Prince Dolgoruki's exertions are largely responsible for averting at that time the possibility of a restoration of the Polish Kingdom in one form or another."[15] Certainly he had done much to prevent Poland's liberation and had been successful in that respect; but his increasing influence proved rather fatal to Russia, who had to pay a heavy price for it in a series of military and political catastrophes.

There was now a serious estrangement between the sovereign and the triumviri, since he himself had taken over the direction of his policy; he let Czartoryski feel the change in their mutual relations—even "dissatisfaction and regret." His scruples at having nurtured hostile intentions against Prussia became acute when facing his royal friends, and deprived him of countenance and determination; his vacillations were duly exploited by Prussian diplomats with the invaluable help of the Queen. Prince Adam was not given an opportunity to discuss the whole matter with the Emperor. As plenipotentiary for the conclusion of a treaty, he had to negotiate with Hardenberg and Haugwitz, and as dubious assistants their partisans Alopeus and Dolgoruki. The result was certainly not a masterpiece of Russian diplomacy and Czartoryski rightly told the Emperor some months later: "I will always reproach myself for having been compelled by circumstances to put my name to such a calamitous treaty."[16]

By the Treaty of Potsdam, Prussia pledged her armed mediation among Russia, Austria, and France on agreed terms. The terms

[15] Nicholas Mikhailovich, *Kniazia Dolgorukie*, 1901, pp. 12, 84 f.

[16] See Czartoryski's letters to the Emperor, Apr. 5, 1806 (Cz.M.(F), II, 104-131), and to S. Vorontsov, Feb. 18, 1806 (*Arch. Vorontsova*, xv, 359-362). For the Treaty of Potsdam of Nov. 3, see Hardenberg, *Denkwürdigkeiten*, II, 220 f., 324-333.

differed greatly from those which had been stipulated in the treaty of April 11, in the first instance as to the new French limits in Germany and Belgium, which were not called in question. If Napoleon rejected the mediation, Prussian armies should immediately join in operations against France. But the fulfillment of that pledge depended now entirely on Prussia's questionable good will; there was a separate and secret article providing for Russia's support for the acquisition of Hanover from the British King, and Prussia declared that acquisition to be the condition of which she would join the alliance.

Thus Alexander's trip to Potsdam was not only a betrayal of the promises given to the Poles; it resulted in a flagrant betrayal of his treaty with Britain. As a result, Oubril was to be sent to London to explain what had happened and to persuade the British Cabinet of "the necessity of pleasing Prussia" and of the expediency of exchanging Hanover for some other territory. In vain Vorontsov warned: "The weakness with which the Emperor has, in order to please Prussia, lent himself to a communication so offensive to the King of Great Britain and so contrary even to the true interests of Russia will be even more felt here, when his Ambassador presents a detailed memorandum on the subject."[17] After having thoroughly undermined his friendship with Britain, Alexander now hurried to the armies accompanied by his recalcitrant and gloomy Foreign Minister and stimulated by his buoyant aide-de-camp. The trip was bound to end on the battlefield of Austerlitz.

[17] See S. Vorontsov to Czartoryski, Nov. 29, 1805 (Cz.M.(E), II, 79-84, erroneously dated Sept. 17/29).

CHAPTER 6

AUSTERLITZ AND THE AFTERMATH
OF THE DEFEAT

A SILHOUETTE of Czartoryski appears at Alexander's headquarters at Olmütz in Tolstoy's *War and Peace*: haughty, surrounded by general dislike, taciturn and solitary, estranging people by the very fact of being a foreigner, but still regarded as the mainspring of the Emperor's actions. Actually all that happened at that time was done against his advice and despite his opposition: the Treaty of Potsdam with all its implications, the Emperor's stay at army headquarters and his taking over the real control of the operations, as well as his unfortunate decision to attack Napoleon instead of joining the armies of the Archduke Charles and John and waiting for Prussia's pledged armed intervention. All these decisions had been inspired by Dolgoruki's inconsiderate ardor and wishful thinking. The repudiation of Czartoryski's advice was avenged by Napoleon's crushing blow and the breakdown of Russia's policy as well as of the coalition.

On December 2 Prince Adam was on the battlefield with the Emperor and he repeatedly intervened to prevent outbreaks of panic and to restore the situation. The account of his experiences at Austerlitz given in his memoirs is a striking testimony to the inadequate generalship of the allied command, of the poor fighting spirit of the Austrians, and of the confusion which before long reigned everywhere, even in the Russian army. "While we were standing round the Emperor, General Miloradovich apostrophized me in a somewhat singular fashion, saying: 'How is it you are so calm?' . . ." It seems that even his countenance aroused suspicion. "Night came on, and we proceeded at a foot pace on the road that leads to Holitch. The Emperor was extremely depressed; the violent emotion he had experienced affected his health and I was the only one to bring him some relief. . . ." Alexander's behavior on the battlefield and after-

wards did not make things easier; it contributed rather to the breakdown of the fighting spirit of the army.

After a long talk with Czartoryski and Novosiltsov at Troppau on December 14, Lord Leveson Gower informed his government that "such was the disorder into which the Russian army had been thrown by that defeat that an armistice of a day or two was necessary to save it from total annihilation." Significantly enough, they did not conceal in their talk the seriousness of the moral and political crisis: "The disasters which had attended the Russian army have occasioned much murmuring among the officers against the war, and even those about the person of the Emperor talk loudly against its continuance . . . [as well as] against the Austrian government and people. No pains have been spared to impress the Emperor himself with the same feelings of disgust against the court of Vienna and to shake the influence of those who are the authors of the alliance with that power. The first of these objects has not altogether failed, for Prince Czartoryski acknowledged to me that the two Emperors had not separated upon terms quite so friendly as they had been during their residence at Olmütz. . . ."[1]

In fact, in those momentous days and hours of the retreat, Czartoryski had tried in vain to preserve the collaboration of the two emperors, to restore the alliance shaken to its foundations, and to prevent Russia's actual withdrawal from the war. Once more, fateful decisions had been taken by the Tsar against his Foreign Minister's advice: Austria was left alone, Prussia was absolved from her pledges and given a free hand to negotiate with France. Alexander's hasty return to his capital had the appearances of flight; his prestige had sunk heavily, and there was an increasing pressure for a wholesale change in Russian foreign policy and in the Tsar's advisers.

At Troppau, the British Ambassador tried in vain to induce both Russian ministers to go to Berlin before returning home; he had been instructed to suggest Novosiltsov's mission to Prussia and thought that they could contribute to Lord Harrowby's efforts to secure Prussia's actual cooperation with both allied powers. Czartoryski and Novosiltsov answered that by

[1] Gower to Mulgrave, Troppau, Dec. 15, 1805 (F.O.65/59).

doing so without the Emperor's knowledge they would incur his dissatisfaction. In fact—as Lord Gower noticed before long—Prince Dolgoruki, who was in Berlin as the Tsar's special envoy, was acting independently of the Foreign Department. And although Czartoryski still pledged Russia's military support for Prussia if she was willing to defend northern Germany, he realized the necessity of gaining time and of preparing negotiations. Therefore he suggested to Lord Gower the seizure and joint occupation of Egypt and of parts of European Turkey, especially of Greece, in order to have in their hands objects of exchange for Italy and Germany. The suggestion made some impression in the Foreign Office; Mulgrave wrote to Pitt: "You will observe that Czartoryski has already opened the subject of Greece and Egypt. . . ."[2] Pitt was now inclined to go far in order to meet Russia's plans of expansion in the east and Prussia's "land hunger" in the west, even by giving her Holland—in all probability a sufficiently high bribe. But Stroganov, who had been sent by Czartoryski from Holitch to London with the ungrateful mission of explaining the political and military failure of their common plan and discussing the basis of a new joint policy, called at Downing Street when Pitt was already fatally ill.

Czartoryski and Novosiltsov returned to St. Petersburg. Novosiltsov relates: "Fearing the daylight like owls we arranged to enter the city at dark; the entry was not a solemn one. . . . But can you imagine our surprise when we learned that the Emperor had been given an enthusiastic welcome . . . that the whole city of St. Petersburg was delighted with the distinguished conduct of our army in the last battle; that it consists of heroes only and that all three of us have also done very well; that finally the Austrians are but traitors sold to France. Victims and scapegoats were needed: so Count Razumowsky [the Ambassador in Vienna] was found guilty of not having sufficiently sounded out the public spirit when inciting the Court of Vienna to declare against the French. . . . Next came Wintzingerode, the real traitor . . . and as we arrived eight days after the Emperor, there was time to think things over, and a large part of the public

[2] Jan. 6, 1806; see *Cambridge Hist. of British Foreign Policy*, I, 581.

had already thought it convenient to give us a place next to the former. . . .

"But too many people who had witnessed the catastrophe soon arrived, and opinion changed. . . . Shortly after we came, we saw the Emperor's prestige sinking in an alarming way; they did not talk about treason, but they made him solely responsible for all the disasters. There had been plots against Prince Adam and both of us [Novosiltsov and Stroganov]; but shortly after we arrived, opinion became more just to us; they knew how the Emperor treated those people who did not share his opinion, that he listened only to a few young giddy-heads and that he had scolded me when I proposed to him just what the public thinks ought to have been done. At last they perceived that Prussia was fooling us all the time and that it would not have been bad if we had given her a good lesson when we were so close to her frontier. . . . The Dowager Empress (I do not speak about the young Empress, who is an angel) took our side most frankly; she made a gift to Prince Adam for not having left her son during the battle and after . . . and she treats both of us in a very distinguished manner. This enrages the plotters. . . ."[3]

But Prince Adam's situation was by no means easy. The Emperor no longer agreed to any of his proposals; he generally postponed any decisive steps and the long discussions of the state council produced only a divergence of views and thus an excuse for further delays. Kochubey warned Stroganov: "Czartoryski knows the situation pretty well. He rightly thinks that the ill is not incurable and that much energy ought to be displayed; but not all people think as he does and there are unfortunately a great many people who think that they are entitled to intervene in affairs and to do so by secret or crooked ways without understanding anything."[4] Prince Adam complained of the disorganization and inertia—even Novosiltsov admits having *perdu son latin.* "Several coalitions were formed in order to get rid of us; if such was the desire of many, it also is ours. After all

---

[3] Novosiltsov to Stroganov, Jan. 18, 1806 (Nicholas Mikhailovich, *Stroganov*, III, 106-108); on Alexander's enthusiastic welcome, see Countess Stroganov's letter, Dec. 24, 1805 (*op.cit.*, III, 123-124).

[4] Kochubey to S. Vorontsov, Feb. 12, 1806 (*Arch. Vorontsova*, XIV, 192).

that has happened, after so little confidence has been shown by the Emperor in us, when executing a plan which he had ordered us to conceive and to carry into execution, you will surely understand our strong desire to resign. The people who have contributed to establish the ministeries, who have contributed to entering the war, can hardly be useful any more."[5] Cruelly disappointed, he wrote to Stroganov confidentially: "The Emperor is always the same: fear and weakness in the highest degree. We are afraid of everything, we are no more able to take any vigorous step; it is even no more possible to advise him because he would not take any advice. The Emperor still prefers to keep us, in order to avoid embarrassment by making a change, but he would like to act only according to his own pleasure. The misfortune has not strengthened his logic, he has become more arbitrary than ever before. It is that agglomeration of weakness, uncertainty, fear, injustice, extravagance which inspires only desolation and despair." He gave Stroganov a warning: the Emperor had forbidden them to inform the British that Russia was having secret talks with Prussia: "Nous tripotons en grand secret avec la Prusse, which deludes us by the hope of her abandoning France."[6]

There has been much criticism of Czartoryski's policy during those three fateful years; some Polish historians have been inclined to present him as blinded by his sentiments for his imperial friend and deluded by Alexander's superior ability, astuteness, and cunning. The documents published long ago in Czartoryski's Memoirs, and especially his letters to Alexander written in the period following the disaster, seem to give a different picture of their mutual relations. The long letter of April 5, 1806, is conclusive. It is an account of their three years of common work from the time of Czartoryski's appointment to the Foreign Ministry. There is not any trace of weakness, compliance, or delusion. The language is that of tutor exposing his pupil's inconsistencies, weaknesses, and errors. He accused him

[5] Czartoryski to Vorontsov, Feb. 18 (*op.cit.*, xv, 359-360).
[6] Feb. 18, 1806 (Nicholas Mikhailovich, *Stroganov*, ii, 226). The same day Stroganov wrote to his wife: "I love our Emperor as much as is humanly possible, but I pity him for having a character such as his" (*ibid.*, iii, 127-129).

of having lost a year's time from the rupture with France until the start of the campaign by delaying military preparations; even the recruits were not called up in adequate numbers, and the concentration of the armies was postponed since the Emperor did not really regard the war as unavoidable and expected that some *deus ex machina* would give him victory without fighting. "There is but one sovereign in Europe who knows the value of time: it is Bonaparte and that provides him with continuous success. . . . Bonaparte has overwhelmed Austria, Prussia, and Russia because he knows how to exploit the present moment without being embarrassed by further prospective developments. That capacity doubles and trebles his armies. . . ." Czartoryski reminded the Emperor how the opportunity of surprising Prussia and enforcing his will on her was lost by his hesitations; how the interest of the Empire was sacrificed to his sentiment for Prussia, and his cabinet's policy stultified by his personal action undertaken without consulting the responsible minister. By joining his army and remaining with it, the Emperor had lost control of the general conduct of the war, had wiped out his generals' sense of responsibility, and had disorganized the command of his armies. "Your presence at Austerlitz was of no avail; just where you were present the rout was immediate and complete. Your Imperial Majesty participated in it and was forced to withdraw rapidly, a thing you should never risk. In Holitch Your Majesty's departure increased the spirit of dissolution and the general dejection. . . ."

There followed a lesson on what a sovereign's duties were when waging war: he ought to be the mainspring putting the whole mechanism in motion; he should concern himself only with general plans and with the general direction of their execution. "A man's capacities and mental powers are limited; the same person cannot be at the same time officer, colonel, general, secretary, minister, etc., and sovereign too." Czartoryski explained with a rare understanding of warfare what Kutuzov would have done if he had not been hampered by the Tsar's presence. He would have avoided battle until the Prussian armies had started operations. "It was in Bonaparte's interest not to waste time; it was in ours to win time. He had every reason for risking a decisive battle; we had every reason to avoid it. . . ." Prince Adam reminded the Emperor of what he had himself suggested: harassing the enemy by partial combats with limited forces, withdrawing the main army from contact with the enemy's and shifting it behind the Morava to Hungary in order to join the army of Archduke Charles. But even if a battle in Moravia had been unavoidable, Kutuzov—if left alone—would have acted more prudently, and the Emperor—if farther away from the impact of military events—would have taken decisions more calmly and less precipitately; he would not have acted, as at Holitch, under the pressure of panic-stricken people, who loudly denounced the Austrians as traitors and their own army as utterly disorganized and absolutely incapable of further fighting. Czartoryski denounced the baseness of the Emperor's advisers who had persuaded him that he had done enough for others and that he should think of himself—"as if his glory and safety had nothing in common with the fall of Austria and his other allies." It had been just what the Tsar had retorted to Czartoryski, when the latter ventured to speak in favor of the King of Naples; and he even told the Emperor Francis that he could no longer count upon the Russian army. He also told the Prussian minister, Haugwitz, that he would leave Prussia free to come to an arrangement with France—when Czartoryski insisted upon her fulfillment of the Potsdam stipulations. By doing so the Tsar had deprived himself of the opportunity of reacting to Prussia's flagrant complicity with Napoleon, by exploiting Prussia's isolation and her open breach and formal state of war with Great Britain over Hanover, in order to proclaim the Kingdom of Poland as it was expected again by the Poles at that moment.

Such a reckoning of one's sins by any fellow creature would in no case be easy to endure; written by a Minister to his sovereign, it hardly has a parallel in history—in Russian history at any rate. "I felt my duty," thus ended the letter, "to let my devotion speak even if taking the risk of displeasing you." It certainly was bound to displease.

Prince Adam's ministerial work became more and more complicated by the Emperor's personal interference and decisions, particularly with regard to the relations with Prussia. He insisted many times upon the necessity of restoring the normal way of handling foreign policy through the medium of the responsible minister; he suggested a meeting of the Secret Committee in order to draw up a plan which should be strictly followed. He suggested his own replacement. "My resignation," he wrote, "would make many people happy and most of Your Majesty's habitual and confidential society would be delighted."[7]

As usual, Alexander hesitated and postponed his decision. Probably he thought Czartoryski still useful if an understanding was to be reached with the new British Cabinet. As Czartoryski had long anticipated, his Whig friends and particularly Fox now had an important part to play; he attached an exaggerated importance to Fox's previous friendly attitude to Russia, to his hostility to Prussia, his ideological approach to the problems of peace, and hoped for the solidarity and unity of action of both cabinets. Neither Vorontsov, who had always shared Pitt's dislike of Fox, nor even Stroganov confirmed Prince Adam's expectations of the new Foreign Secretary; on the contrary, they were upset by the manner in which Fox entered into an exchange of views with Talleyrand without even consulting Russia, and Czartoryski himself thought it necessary to retort somewhat rudely. Later on, mutual relations improved. A long letter from Fox to Czartoryski a short time after the former's appointment was worded as an exhortation to a peaceful policy, while inviting Russia's pressure on Prussia in order to prevent her annexation of Hanover, and Czartoryski's long-delayed answer expressed mutual understanding and friendship. He was at that time approached by the Foreign Office with proposals regarding a common military operation against Prussia, but the Tsar "did not see fit to accept the English proposals."[8]

There thus remained a divergence of policy on a matter now most vital to Britain. The British negotiations in Paris were conducted in rather loose liaison with Russia, and it seemed neces-

---

[7] To the Emperor, Mar. 22, 1806 (Cz.M.(F), II, 95-103). The Emperor had told him by then that General Budberg was his prospective successor. See Novosiltsov's letter to Stroganov, Mar. 29, 1806 (Nicholas Mikhailovich, *Stroganov*, III, 108-109).

[8] Czartoryski to Vorontsov, Feb. 18 (*Arch. Vorontsova*, XV, 359-360); to Stroganov Feb. 18 (Nicholas Mikhailovich, *Stroganov*, II, 226).

sary to send a diplomatic agent there in order to join in the conversations. This was the purpose of Oubril's mission; he was instructed to act in closest understanding with the British plenipotentiary and to refer in all important matters to Stroganov in London. But Oubril knew that Czartoryski's ministry was drawing to its close; he did not feel bound by his instructions and was too much impressed by what he had been told by the Emperor about the necessity of making peace *coûte que coûte*. Thus his mission ended quite unexpectedly with his signing a separate peace treaty with France, three weeks after Prince Adam's dismissal.

The prospect of a general peace with Britain's participation had become at that time particularly undesirable to Prussia, and possibly the Dowager Empress acted under some inspiration from Prussian quarters when she suggested Czartoryski's successor. It was to be the General Baron Budberg, who had once been Alexander's tutor and who was a good German and a friend of Prussia.[9] Novosiltsov had known about it for a long time; he regarded the general as a most incapable, weak, and ridiculous man.[10]

Czartoryski was dismissed on July 1, 1806. Both his friends, Novosiltsov and Stroganov, resigned their governmental posts. His last weeks of office had been an agony. "I had," he wrote Vorontsov, "several sharp clashes with the Emperor; each report provoked a conflict. There were no principles involved; in each dispatch, simple phrases became the subject of unending discussions and of His Majesty's dissatisfaction. . . . That situation became unbearable to both of us; bitterness poisoned it. . . . Actually the Emperor was bored and tired with having a minister whose opinions did not correspond to his own and who showed it on each occasion."[11]

The sympathies of many prominent Russians were now for Czartoryski and his friends; something like a great though vague

[9] The political meaning of the change was clearly perceived by S. Vorontsov in his letters to Czartoryski, July 24, Aug. 5, Oct. 19 (Cz.M.(F), II, 162-164).

[10] Novosiltsov to Stroganov, Mar. 29 (Nicholas Mikhailovich, *Stroganov*, III, 109-112).

[11] Czartoryski to Vorontsov, Sept. 6, 1806 (*Arch. Vorontsova*, XV, 411-419).

expectation vanished with their departure.[12] Russia now entered a new phase of her policy, fully subordinated to Prussian interests and leadership. It was the path leading to Bartenstein and Friedland and to a new political collapse.

Czartoryski's part as Russian statesman was over and so was that amazing episode: a Pole as founder of a great program of the policy of the Russian Empire and responsible for its destinies.

[12] See Nicholas Mikhailovich (*Stroganov*, I, 78-81).

CHAPTER 7

AT THE CROSSROADS

THE defeat and collapse of Prussia in 1806 was a turning point in Polish history. The developments in November and December 1806 were precisely the opposite of those planned by Czartoryski a year before. Alexander was now Prussia's ally and Prussia had been overwhelmed by the French before the Russian armies could intervene. Poland rose in arms and Polish regiments and divisions were joining Napoleon's army. No political consideration could prevent or alter that spontaneous decision of the Polish people: no argument could prevail against the simple fact that the French Emperor had crushed two of the powers which had partitioned Poland and that he was struggling against the third. Though he carefully avoided formal commitments, Napoleon became *de facto* the liberator and restorer of Poland and, in the eyes of the Poles, their hero.

The solution of the Polish problem by the restoration of a Polish state in union with Russia, which a year before had been backed by the unanimous will of all the Polish political elements, was now for most Polish people only a delusion. Had not Alexander's trip to Puławy been followed by his trip to Potsdam and by the oath of eternal friendship with the Prussian King taken on the tomb of Frederick the Great, Poland's deadliest foe? The Poles were now ready to strive for a different solution, for an independent Polish state backed by a victorious France.

There remained but little chance for the success of Czartoryski's policy of Russo-Polish union. In spite of his bitter disappointment, however, he persisted in his policy and still tried to work for a restoration of Poland by Alexander. For several years two divergent trends existed in Polish political life, and the Polish cause found itself more than once at a crossroads—as did Prince Adam himself.

After having been released from his duties as acting Foreign

Minister, he still remained a civil servant: a member of the senate and of the state council, and curator of the educational province of Vilna. Like him, Novosiltsov remained a member of the senate and of the council. Stroganov, of the three the most embittered against the Tsar, relinquished his state functions entirely, but joined the army after the outbreak of the new war.

The triumviri, though refusing to share the responsibility for the Empire's policy, did not consider the breach definitive, nor did the "private committee" immediately cease to exist. In Czartoryski's correspondence with Alexander, sessions of the committee are still mentioned at the end of the year. Nor did Prince Adam think of his personal collaboration with Alexander as ending with his ministerial post. Their friendship seemed to survive that crisis, though it was certainly much altered by Czartoryski's feeling of frustration and the Tsar's resentment of the humiliating reprimands and of too much guidance and control generally. As to the difference of views, Czartoryski could still expect that the course of events would prove him right and that his policy would prevail. Some months later, the Tsar even gave him an amusing lesson on good parliamentary conduct, when with a hint at Prince Adam's excitement at a meeting of the committee, he reminded his friend of the example of English members of Parliament "who after saying the most bitter things to each other in the House in the heat of the debate, are excellent friends when the debate is over. . . ."[1]

Thus it was that after the catastrophe of Prussia in December 1806 Prince Adam drafted a paper "On the necessity of restoring Poland to forestall Bonaparte."[2] He rightly emphasized the military and political importance of Poland for Napoleon when facing war with Russia and the possible increase of his power if Poland's resources—both material and moral—were joined to those of the French. He still considered it as "desirable in the Russian interest to reverse that state of things" and suggested that there was "only one way: to proclaim Poland a kingdom, the Emperor declaring himself king. . . ." He still hoped that as a result of such a step "equally magnanimous and political," gratitude would

[1] Cz.M.(E), ii, 172.
[2] Cz.M.(E), ii, 165-170, dated Dec. 5, 1806 (Old Style?).

rally the Polish nation around the throne and repudiate "Bonaparte's seductions"; Poland would become for Russia a rampart protecting her in the west, and every cause of anxiety as to the conduct of Poles would be forever removed. He discussed the possible objections to the separation of some provinces from the Empire, and explained that the separation would be only external, as the crown of Poland would be irrevocably attached to the throne of Russia and the Empire would actually not lose those provinces but gain the remainder of Poland. Of course, in order to win over the Poles, they should be granted a government in conformity with their wishes and their ancient law; he quoted Hungary, which had for centuries been an example of fidelity to the Hapsburg kings. Czartoryski dealt further with the serious objection that, by reuniting Poland under her scepter, Russia would be despoiling her Prussian ally; "but the master of the Prussian monarchy is now Bonaparte," and the question at issue was the forestalling of that enemy (which would be the only means of saving Prussia) by forcing Napoleon to agree to an equitable peace. As to Austria, he thought that an arrangement could be obtained by frank and loyal negotiations. He insisted upon the need of making early decisions without waiting for Napoleon to make overtures to the Poles.

Probably at the same time, he wrote his "Article pour l'arrangement des Affaires de l'Europe à la suite d'une guerre heureuse."[3] That document has been erroneously classified by the editors of Czartoryski's papers as connected with Novosiltsov's mission of 1804; and very distinguished historians have raised no objection to that date, although the difference between the provisions of the instructions for Novosiltsov and the views expressed in that note is rather striking. What is even more noticeable, it seems to exaggerate the alleged negligence or distraction found in Czartoryski's writings, by admitting that he could promise to Prussia in 1804 the Grand Duchy of Berg, which was still to be created by Napoleon in 1806; to return to her Ansbach, which was then still her property; to promise to Austria the Tyrol, which was still an old Hapsburg "Erbland" and had not yet been taken away from her by the Treaty of Pressburg; and hint

[3] Cz.M.(F), ii, 62 sq.; Cz.M.(E), ii, 52 sq.

at Venetia as a suitable principality for an archduke, when it still belonged to Austria. In view of these considerations, that memorandum must definitely be rejected as part of the history of the Third Coalition, but it seems closely bound up with Prince Adam's political exertions in December 1806. When enumerating the war aims, he speaks of the Emperor of Russia's taking the title of King of Poland and of reuniting all the territories that belonged to Poland before the first partition.[4]

In 1804, when promoting the reunion of Poland, Czartoryski did not think it necessary to grant full compensation to Prussia; but now, when Prussia was fighting with the Russians, he realized the necessity of doing so, and he discussed the possible extension of Prussia in Germany, as it had been proposed by Pitt in 1805 and even, "if such a course should be absolutely necessary, and England consented to it," suggested that the offer of the Kingdom of Holland be made to her; that suggestion also conformed to Pitt's final ideas about bribes for Prussia in order to secure her actual alliance. Czartoryski recalled once more his conceptions of peace: he preached as before a close union of Russia and Britain, an alliance of all the five great powers (France included), and the establishment of "intermediary counterpoises" by regional federations. He hinted at a future solution of the Turkish problem along such lines: a federation of the former Turkish provinces in Europe with the Emperor of Russia as their protector and emperor.

In the redrafted program of Russian policy, Czartoryski insisted upon the necessity for ministerial changes, especially of the Foreign Minister and the Minister of War. A written memorandum of the Secret Committee was submitted to the Emperor and met with a rebuff. He also disagreed with Czartoryski's proposal that he should declare himself King of Poland at that moment.[5]

---

[4] Incidentally, the English translation of the name "Prusse Royale" as "Kingdom of Prussia" is misleading, "Royal Prussia" being identical with that territory (Polish Pomerania) which was restored to Poland by the Treaty of Versailles and which from 1466 to 1772 had been a province of the Polish Kingdom. So J. H. Rose's remarks about Czartoryski's idea of shifting Prussia to the west and of depriving her of the bulk of her former territory do not seem justified.

[5] Cz.M.(E), II, 170-172.

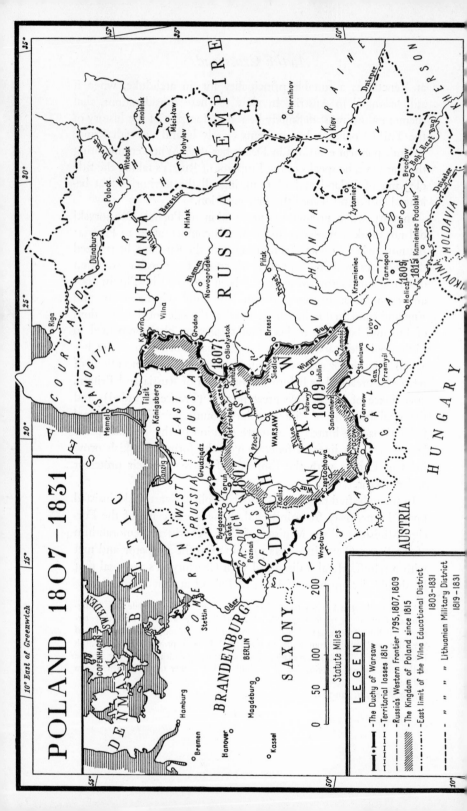

At the Crossroads

Two weeks later—on December 21—Czartoryski submitted another memorandum to the Emperor, insisting upon the necessity of treating for peace with Napoleon before the Russian armies were attacked. In fact they had already been so; the campaign of Poland was nearing its climax, and Czartoryski rightly hinted at the progress made by the French in winning Poland over.[6] The result was probably that Alexander encouraged Prince Adam to prepare detailed plans for the restoration of the Polish Kingdom. The British Chargé d'Affaires reported that Czartoryski's friends "just now exert every effort to effect his reestablishment in office," and two weeks later he still thought that the latter's policy might prevail; but he was aware of a strong Prussian counteraction and of Prussian insistence upon peace negotiations because of the increasing danger of a Polish rising.[7]

When leaving St. Petersburg to join his armies, the Tsar was accompanied by Czartoryski and Novosiltsov.

Prince Adam's efforts to gain the support of his countrymen for the Russo-Polish union coincided with a very serious crisis in Napoleon's position after the battle of Eylau. The conqueror was made to realize how numerically inadequate was his Grand Army (after the heavy losses inflicted by the recent operations) for defeating a tenacious and numerous adversary; the immense difficulties of campaigning in that theater of war; and, last but not least, the threat of an Austrian intervention, and the possibility of the Archduke Charles attacking in the rear and cutting the communications of the French armies.

He wanted peace and was prepared to sacrifice his new Polish allies. There were therefore some misgivings and hesitations among the Poles. Czartoryski invited to Alexander's headquarters at Taurogi two well-known figures from Lithuania and Volhynia: Thomas Wawrzecki, who succeeded Kościuszko as Chief of the National Forces in 1794, and General Charles Kniaziewicz, a distinguished commander of the Polish legions in the campaigns of 1798-1801 in Italy and on the Danube. It was proposed to them that they should take the lead in a national movement in favor of Alexander and against the French. But at that very

[6] Cz.M.(E), ii, 175-187.
[7] Stuart to F.O., St. Petersburg, Jan. 2, 1807 (F.O. 65/67).

time Poland already possessed a national army under the command of Prince Joseph Poniatowski, General Henry Dombrow-
ski, and other renowned military chiefs, and Warsaw had a provisional government composed of well-known patriotic leaders,
over which the old Marshal of the "Great Seym," Stanislas
Małachowski, presided.

Both Wawrzecki and Kniaziewicz declined Czartoryski's offer,
and the only result of his efforts towards uniting the Poles once
more around Alexander was to check to some extent the menacing pro-Napoleonic underground activities in Lithuania and
Volhynia.

Prince Adam's plans were partly ill-timed and partly inevitably
stultified by the Tsar as a result of the latter's new commitments
contracted at Bartenstein, in the shape of the restoration of Prussia and the defence of her special interests. At Tilsit the triumviri were no longer consulted, nor did they see much of the
Emperor; he was busy learning the art of war from General
Phull, former Chief of Staff of Frederick William during the
campaign of Jena, while most people around the Tsar were busy
deliberating on how to prevent him from once more taking the
command of the army. So Czartoryski duly informed Stroganov
that they were busy with Novosiltsov in reading German novels
and that it was having a salutary influence on the latter's morals;
he was even slowly becoming tenderhearted and sentimental.[8]
That outburst of "Galgenhumor" signaled the end of Czartoryski's career as a Russian statesman.

He was already aware of the rising of a new Poland, supported
by Napoleon, most probably as a small separate state, with the
Saxon Elector as sovereign.[9] He expressed to his friends his regrets that the Poles were getting into rather bad company, but
he could do nothing other than wish for his country's revival
and the restoration of the name of Poland.

A few days later, the battle of Friedland was fought. In the
momentous days which followed, Lord Gower addressed a mov-

[8] Czartoryski to Stroganov, Tilsit, May 23, 1807 (Nicholas Mikhailovich,
Stroganov, II, 257-259). Cf. H. Butterfield, *The Peace Tactics of Napoleon*, 1929,
p. 189.
[9] To Stroganov, June 4 (*op.cit.*, II, 255-259).

ing letter to Czartoryski, in which he expressed his hope that the Prince would still be able to prevent a separation of Russia from England, and thereby contribute to the salvation of Europe.[10]

Actually neither Prince Adam nor his friends had any influence with the Emperor at the time of his "disastrous transactions" at Tilsit.[11] The peace then concluded was exactly contrary to that for which Czartoryski had striven and for which he still hoped when the Russian armies stood menacingly on Prussian and Polish soil. Instead of restoring some kind of balance, it was a peace by division: Europe was now divided between the two Emperors and their spheres of interest. As seen by Czartoryski, the peace was a breach by Alexander of their common creed, their principles, and ideals; it was not just a change of policy but a turning point in Alexander's life.

Czartoryski did not know everything that actually happened at Tilsit. For instance, he heard only long after of Napoleon's offer to Alexander to restore Poland in personal union with Russia. Of course the restoration was to be made at the expense of Prussia, and Napoleon wanted on his side to have Silesia for his brother, Jérôme. Alexander declined the offer: "What was left of his regard for unfortunate Prussia prevented him from accepting it." So, instead of a Polish kingdom united under his royal crown, he agreed to the creation of a small separate state from the Polish provinces of Prussia—or rather of a mutilated trunk of them—called the Duchy of Warsaw. The Polish state was to be in personal union with Saxony and thus attached to the confederation of the Rhine and to Napoleon as protector. Thus it would be a French outpost on the Vistula, and nothing else could have been expected by the Tsar when he promoted that solution. He was supposed to have suggested a high governmental post in the new state for Czartoryski and Napoleon would allegedly have declined the proposal, suspecting an attempt to establish Russian influence in the Duchy.

Czartoryski looked with exasperation on a new partition of

---

10 Cz.M.(E), ɪɪ, 187-188.

11 Czartoryski to S. Vorontsov, Sept. 2, 1807 (*Arch. Vorontsova*, xv, 422-425); Novosiltsov to the same, Nov. 12. (*op.cit.*, xvɪɪɪ, 473-474). See also H. Butterfield, *Peace Tactics*, 287.

Polish lands: Polish Pomerania (Royal Prussia) cut off in order
to do less harm to the Hohenzollern; the district of Białystok
cut off and accepted by Alexander as a bribe to Russia. The Tsar
had asked for much more and Napoleon had to curb him by
warning him that he disliked the idea of having Russian troops
at the gates of Warsaw.

Russian policy as a whole suddenly returned to the old traditions of Catherine II and to those most hated by Czartoryski and
condemned by Alexander himself. The new Minister of Foreign
Affairs and later Chancellor, Count Alexander Rumiantsov, was
Prince Adam's old adversary, a defender of Catherine's conquests
in Poland, a promotor of a partition of Turkey in understanding
with France and against British opposition. Czartoryski fully
realized that the alliance between the two Emperors not only
meant Russia's leaving Britain alone, but also her joining with
Napoleon in his struggle against Britain; and he discerned the
impending danger of a rupture between England and Russia.
Just at that crucial time he became friendly with the young
Colonel, Sir Robert Wilson, "an excellent young man beloved
by all our army"; the latter had served with the Russians in the
recent war with outstanding merit, was much in favor at the
court and popular in the capital. His activities were later connected with an incident which provoked the final disgrace of
Alexander's Anglophile friends, and particularly that of Novosiltsov: the pamphlets on the Tilsit compact which Wilson had
brought from London were too eagerly circulated by them; the
Emperor was duly informed and his anger was menacing. Prince
Adam's position became more precarious than ever.

Rumiantsov succeeded in bringing about a declaration of war
against Britain.[12] "I expected the rupture," Prince Adam wrote
to Vorontsov, "but neither so early nor such a sudden one." And
he said farewell to that voluntary exile: "May the fortunate
island on which you are living be preserved intact during the
universal deluge, because with it only justice, freedom, and all
the sound and generous ideas can survive—in short all that is

---

[12] For Alexander's rupture with England, see K. Waliszewski, *Le règne
d'Alexandre I*, I, 238 sq.; A. Vandal, *Napoléon et Alexandre I*, I, 152-165.

most dear and precious for mankind. If England had to accept the yoke which had been laid on so many other states, Europe would be ultimately the prey of a new century of barbarism. . . ."[13]

Certainly Czartoryski exaggerated the "barbarism" of the Napoleonic conquest and its fatal consequences; he did not perceive its not unsalutary influence on the future of some of the nations which experienced Napoleon's "regime"—one of which was Poland. He had been too convinced a believer in Montesquieu and Rousseau, too ardent an *idolatre* of Fox to be able to recognize the greatness of the Corsican "usurper" and "tyrant." He did not—as did many of his compatriots from Eastern Poland—withdraw his allegiance from the Tsar in order to serve the new small Polish state, the Duchy of Warsaw. Although he no longer had a say in Russia's general policy, he continued to serve as a member of the senate and of the council of state as well as curator; he remained in fact Alexander's minister for his Polish provinces and their spokesman.

He was now more than ever isolated. Both his closest friends' were away: Novosiltsov traveling abroad for security reasons, Stroganov confining himself strictly to his military life. There was a marked coldness in Alexander's feelings for his friend and former mentor in that early period of alliance with France.

In July 1808 Prince Adam went for a long leave to his country. When parting he submitted to the Tsar a memorandum with a bitter criticism of the French alliance: "Napoleon has but one object, which he is pursuing exclusively and without respite since his taking over the government of France, and it is to abase, to subdue, or to destroy all the existing governments in order to make his own and his dynasty immovable. He must necessarily seek for Russia's abasement. As long as she will be obedient to his desires and concur in the execution of his plans, he will perhaps let her alone, but once he will perceive some opposition of hers, he will try to crush her by force. . . ." And he laid before his friend's eyes a gloomy prospect of coming developments: Napoleon invading Eastern Poland to the Dvina and Dnieper, lending assistance to the Turks, organizing a Polish kingdom,

---

[13] Czartoryski to Vorontsov, Nov. 12, 1807 (*Arch. Vorontsova*, xv, 425-430).

proclaiming the freedom of the Russian peasants, tearing the Empire to pieces and creating several separate kingdoms.[14]

At that time Alexander was already disappointed in his partnership with Napoleon and rather embittered by the obstacles the latter put in his way to Constantinople. He was also somewhat alarmed by the outburst of Polish patriotism focused in Warsaw—although he had himself been largely responsible for the Tilsit solution of the problem with its unavoidable implications. He went to Erfurt for a new interview with his great partner, with the firm intention of deceiving him and hindering his policy. At the price of Napoleon's important concessions to Prussia, he committed himself to joining in the war if Austria attacked France; but at the same time he reassured Austria and encouraged her to resist Napoleon. He had already found a secret adviser and ally in Talleyrand, who suggested that he should oppose Napoleon and back his adversaries in order to become the savior of Europe.

Strangely enough, the new private alliance of Alexander and Talleyrand affected Prince Adam's private life. At that very time he was wooing the young Princess Dorothy of Curland, a girl of fifteen, who adored Czartoryski even before she met him. Piattoli, who was then secretary to the Duchess of Curland and the preceptor of the Princess, was certainly responsible for having introduced his former pupil into her thoughts and dreams. Prince Adam decided to marry her—a *marriage de raison*—and he was undoubtedly impressed by the young Princess's affection. There were obstacles to be overcome: the mutual dislike of the two mothers. Princess Isabella's opposition was at last surmounted and Prince Adam was able to appear officially as a suitor, when an unexpected *deus ex machina* intervened. The Princess, the future Duchess of Dino, was heiress to a great fortune, and her dowry and prospective inheritance seemed to the Emperor to be a most suitable bribe for his new ally, Talleyrand; he decided to give her in marriage to Talleyrand's nephew, Maurice de Périgord, and undertook himself to secure the Duchess' consent. He paid her a visit accompanied by his protégé and explained to her that Prince Adam's courting was not serious: "I assure you that

[14] Memorandum of June 28 (July 10), 1808 (*Sbornik*, VI, 372 sq.).

he has no inclination for marriage; he always allows his mother, an old Polish intrigante and a dangerous one, to govern him. I guess that somebody had turned a young and sentimental head; because Adam is surely a perfect man, but he has become so wild and dejected that I cannot discern anything attractive for a person of fifteen. . . ."[15] It was rather peculiar service he thus rendered his old friend!

The following year Austria started her war of revenge; her armies crossed the Inn into Bavaria and invaded the Duchy of Warsaw. Czartoryski never knew—nor did historians for about a century—that the signal for starting the war came from St. Petersburg, from Austria's special envoy there, General Prince Schwarzenberg, after a private talk with the Tsar, and that the latter even concluded a formal secret convention eliminating any danger for Austria from the mock intervention of the Russian army, and reducing the latter's operations to a prearranged spectacle. A special provision was included ensuring secret cooperation in preserving the political *status quo* in the Polish provinces of both states.[16] Prince Adam was still unaware how pronounced was Alexander's hostility against the Duchy of Warsaw, and to what extent his imperial friend, who still used to call the restoration of Poland his *idée favorite*, had committed himself to the Austrians —as he had done before to the Prussians—to prevent Poland's rebirth.

Now the eyes of all the Poles were turned towards Warsaw. Their small national army, which Poniatowski successfully commanded against superior Austrian forces, succeeded in making a bold offensive into Galicia, a great part of which they liberated and called to arms. Polish patriots from over the Russian frontier, from Podolia and Volhynia, hurried to join their countrymen; they improvised several regiments of cavalry and a number of volunteers came from distant Lithuania.

In Galicia, Prince Adam's father, the old "Prince General," now titulary Austrian Field Marshal, was "taken in captivity" by

[15] See Duchesse de Dino, *Souvenirs* (4ᵉ éd.), pp. 162-164, 167-168, 185-189, 201-206, 226-237, 251-252.

[16] The secret of these negotiations was disclosed only in 1901 by A. Plutyński in the Polish Revue *Biblioteka Warszawska*, and later by the Austrian military historian G. Just, *Politik oder Strategie*, 1909.

Poniatowski by his own wish; and Princess Isabella was even more "captivated" at seeing the Polish army again. They provided funds for a new regiment with their younger son, Prince Constantine, as Colonel; and their son-in-law, Stanislas Zamoyski, equipped yet another and became President of a Polish provisional government of Galicia.

The unexpected invasion of the Duchy by the Austrians, and the even less expected Polish counterstroke and the Galician insurrection, as well as the peculiar kind of warfare displayed by Prince Galitzin's Russian army, did not fail to provoke a serious crisis in the Russo-French alliance. Napoleon was ignorant of the existence of the secret understanding between Alexander and Prince Schwarzenberg, but the lack of good will betrayed in Russia's military operations was obvious and the Poles could before long produce most convincing proofs of close contacts between Napoleon's Russian allies and his Austrian enemies. He failed to react otherwise than by complaints—"the Emperor's heart is hurt." Having however overcome a grave military crisis —the defeat of Aspern and its aftermath—by the victory of Wagram, he faced a dilemma: either he should appease his great though unreliable and somewhat unfaithful ally by sacrificing the Poles, who had done better and more than he could have expected; or he should do for Poland what he felt to be just and fair, by uniting at least a part of Galicia with the Duchy, a move which could not fail to provoke a hostile reaction from Russia. Czartoryski did not hear about Napoleon's words to Chernyshev, Alexander's aide-de-camp: "There may be some difficulties about Poland, but these can be settled, the world is so great!" He was never told of Alexander's answer: "When Poland is concerned the world is not great enough, because I do not want anything"— which meant he did not see any possible compensation for the restoration of a Poland not under his own control. Nor did he hear Alexander's exclamation that he could not tolerate Poland's specter haunting his frontiers. But he clearly perceived the attitude of both Emperors in regard to the Polish problem. He understood perfectly why Napoleon, while giving half Galicia to the Duchy of Warsaw, was trying to induce Russia to take part of that province (Tarnopol) as a bribe, why he consented to leave most of Old Galicia to Austria, and why he ostentatiously denied any intention of restoring Poland and declared himself ready to give any pledges to the Russian Emperor to that effect. Czartoryski knew that that was the price which Napoleon was ready to pay Russia for her consent to the extension of the Duchy, and that Alexander had eagerly seized this opportunity of securing a heavy political ransom in the form of an official declaration against Poland.[17]

Meanwhile Russian imperial decrees pronounced the confiscation of property of those Russian subjects who had joined the Polish insurrection; a policy of reprisals by arrests, interrogations, and deportations was started in the southwestern provinces.

Prince Adam first heard about the negotiation of the two Emperors concerning Poland from Novosiltsov, who brought the news from Vienna; most probably he did not conceal his own opinion of both partners, because the conversation had been reported to the Tsar. In a long talk with Alexander, Prince Adam tried to excuse their common friend; he even assured him that Novosiltsov was exultant when speaking about Napoleon's offer of a declaration, and that it was he as a Pole whose feelings had been hurt. The Tsar seized this opportunity to show his friend the dispatch of Champagny to Caulaincourt authorizing him to declare Napoleon ready to agree that the name of Poland should disappear "even from history." But Czartoryski reacted by a bold indictment of Alexander's handling of the problem: he had proved to be such an enemy of Poland that he was thought of as desiring her disappearance from history. Czartoryski exclaimed: "Could anything be more revolting than the conduct of the three powers towards Poland? And is it surprising that the idea of seeing their country restored should fill the Poles with enthusiasm and bring them together?" He asked the Emperor if in his numerous conversations with Napoleon he had ever touched on the matter of Poland's restoration. Alexander's answer was evasive, confirming Prince Adam in his belief that his friend's attitude towards Poland in all the negotiations with Napoleon

[17] The history of the anti-Polish guarantees has been detailed by both Albert Vandal and Albert Sorel; for some details from Polish and Russian material, see Waliszewski's more recent work on Alexander I.

had been hostile. When Alexander started sounding Prince Adam on the matter of a separate constitution for the Polish provinces, the latter replied with skeptical restraint that the only solution compatible with the security of Russia would be to unite the whole of Poland with her. Alexander mentioned that if the war with France broke out it would be advisable for him to declare himself King of Poland in order to win over the Poles. Czartoryski answered that it would then be too late.

Another talk, on November 26, started with Prince Adam's intervention for the participants in the recent events; the Emperor promised to stop the persecutions. Czartoryski strongly defended the conduct of his countrymen and explained why their hopes were bound up with Warsaw: "The Duchy is a specter of the old Poland and it inevitably greatly impressed all those who considered the annihilated state as their own fatherland. It is as if after the loss of a cherished person her ghost had appeared and assured us that she herself would join us before long." The moral and political significance of the Duchy of Warsaw has never been perceived as clearly and expressed as powerfully as by these few words spoken to the Tsar by Czartoryski.

Alexander now appeared to return suddenly to the old plan of 1805 in order to challenge Napoleon. He spoke of restoring Poland as a separate kingdom with its own national constitution, and of starting this restoration with his own Polish provinces. Instead of indulging in discussions about the realization of that idea, Czartoryski insisted once more upon the problem of an agreement with Napoleon on that subject, and asked again if there had been any exchange of views on that subject. Obviously embarrassed, Alexander spoke about the "levity" with which the Polish question had been approached by Napoleon at Tilsit, and said that at Erfurt they had not had time to discuss it.

Several months later, on April 5, 1810, Alexander once more raised the problem of giving a separate administration to the eight Polish provinces. Once more Czartoryski retorted by raising the matter of Alexander's negotiation with Napoleon concerning Poland; but he was already informed of the convention which had been concluded by the Tsar with Caulaincourt and which began: "Le Royaume de Pologne ne sera jamais rétabli." He knew all about Alexander's insistence upon this wording and about Napoleon's refusal to ratify it. Alexander then changed the subject of the talk; he spoke about his Polish plan of 1805, admitted that it had been a mistake to drop it, but refused to admit that the plan had been definitely frustrated: "The Poles would readily follow the devil himself if he led them to their restored country." He changed when speaking of the imminent crisis: "We are now in April—it will be nine months hence." Prince Adam noticed Alexander's severe and fixed look, which reminded him of his haggard gaze after Austerlitz.

Czartoryski did not put himself at his friend's disposition. He understood quite well that his object was to erect one altar against another, *autel contre autel*, of splitting the Polish nation in two. In a memorandum which he submitted to the Tsar, he protested against such a policy and refused to become an instrument of it.

He then drafted a note to his Russian friends and forwarded it to Stroganov on June 20. It was to explain why the Poles had followed Napoleon and why he himself was unable to raise anti-French feelings in Poland. "When people say Bonaparte should not be supported by the Poles because of his unjust and oppressive conduct towards other nations, they forget that there is not a single act of iniquity committed by Napoleon of which the powers who have partitioned Poland had not themselves set an example. It is not for them to become champions of principles which they have trodden under their feet. . . . Bonaparte has never done any harm to Poland; he alone has held out his hand to her and has done all he could for her. . . . The Poles find on one side interest, support, and help; on the other animosity, persecution, and discouragement. . . . Poland hopes through Napoleon's assistance to recover her name and her existence as a nation. If she is wise, circumstances may perhaps enable her to emerge successfully out of the general cataclysm which is approaching and by her efforts she may prove to the Russian government and nation that it would be useful to bring her over to their side and to unite both nations by bonds of mutual advantage and interest. . . ."

Thus he still allowed for the possibility of reconciling Poland's freedom and independence with Russia's true interest. As for himself, he plainly stated the conflicting obligations facing him at this juncture: his loyalty and friendship for the Emperor and his feelings for his own country. The latter must prevail. "To keep the esteem of my countrymen and to do good to my country is the only glory which could give me pleasure; and if her misfortunes continue and my reputation perishes with her existence, I shall at least have the consolation of knowing that I have never acted from any motive that was not just and honorable."[18]

By reiterated demands he succeeded in obtaining permission to leave for Poland. He left St. Petersburg in June 1810 never to return.

A few months later, in Sieniawa, he received from the Emperor the momentous letter of December 25, 1810, announcing his plan of surprising Napoleon by a sudden invasion of the Duchy of Warsaw and Prussia. The operations were to be preceded by a proclamation of the Kingdom of Poland. The preliminary condition was to be a unanimous resolution of the Polish nation and army to join the Russians; the resolution should be guaranteed in a declaration signed by Polish political and military leaders. He entrusted Czartoryski with the mission of sounding out his compatriots and of providing information about his country's attitude. He enclosed an estimate of the forces available for this great undertaking, proving their overwhelming superiority over the French in the first period of the war. It was as if he had learned the lesson of 1805 and was now showing his former mentor that it had not been lost.

Prince Adam's answer, dated January 6, 1811, was skeptical and showed that he was obviously reluctant to commit himself. He cited as necessary conditions if the evident interest of Poland was to prevail over the attachment of the Poles to Napoleon, the reestablishment of the Constitution of May 3, 1791, the reunion of all Polish provinces under one scepter, and the opening of a natural outlet to Polish overseas trade.

[18] The account of the conversations of 1809 and 1810 and Czartoryski's note of June 20, 1810, were published in Cz.M.(E), II, 191-212, with some omissions; the full original text of the former is in the French edition, II, 207-234; the latter in manuscript in the Czartoryski Museum.

Alexander's letter of February 12 announced his full acceptance of the above claims. All the former Polish provinces with the exception of White Russia (the provinces annexed in 1772 east of the Dnieper and the Dvina) were to be restored; the national character of the government and army ensured; a liberal constitution granted; and the restoration of Poland immediately proclaimed under the sole condition of a secular union with Russia and of a formal pledge to join, signed by leading Polish personalities. "Until I have been ensured of the cooperation of the Poles, I cannot start a war against France."[19]

Prince Adam felt it was his duty to inform the leading Polish figures in Warsaw, especially Poniatowski, of the Emperor's offer, and to discuss with him the path to be chosen by Poland in the forthcoming crisis. He went to Warsaw, and before having received Alexander's second letter he informed him of the failure of his mission.[20] Napoleon's ascendancy over the minds of the Poles was still overwhelming. They could not bring themselves to abandon him. Later, in a detailed report, Czartoryski explained their attitude.[21] "Loyalty, gratitude, confidence, and fear" as well as the undiminished prestige of Napoleon were preventing the Poles from accepting the offer. He suggested a long-term Russian policy of preparation for a Russo-Polish union and again, for the third time, asked the Emperor why he had failed to make any attempt to reach an agreement with Napoleon on the restoration of Poland. "Could not Your Majesty's generous intentions in the Polish cause become a matter of negotiations and help to reconcile the interests of the two Empires and to prevent a cruel European war?" He suggested a negotiation with Napoleon on the basis of a *iunctim* between the maintenance of the alliance and of the Continental system with Poland restored in union with Russia.

Czartoryski's suggestion was certainly submitted to Napoleon by Poniatowski or by Thaddeus Matuszewic, the Minister of Fi-

---

[19] Alexander's and Czartoryski's letters, Cz.M.(E), II, 213-228; for the full original text, see the French edition.

[20] Jan. 30, 1811 (Cz.M.(E), II, 218-222; for the full text, see the French edition).

[21] Mar. 12, 1811 (omitted in both editions; the full text has been published by Nicholas Mikhailovich, *Alexandre I*, I, 351; the original drafts of the whole correspondence are preserved in Czartoryski's papers).

nances of the Duchy and a friend of Czartoryski. Both of them made long sojourns in Paris in 1811 and had several private talks with the French Emperor. On July 24 Prince Adam wrote to Alexander: "I am informed from most competent sources that Napoleon has recently made the following statement: 'If one Cossack cross the frontier of the Duchy of Warsaw, I shall proclaim the independence of Poland. I am told that Emperor Alexander has the same intention, that he would like to become King of Poland. If it is to be done by agreement, I would not oppose; on the contrary, I would readily comply. I had once suggested that solution myself [at Tilsit], but then he was reluctant to accept. I also would agree to give the Polish crown to his brother.' —Those were his own words." Prince Adam recalled and insisted upon his suggestion of March 12.[22]

His idea is evident: to disarm the impending conflict by solving the Polish problem, and he hinted at the possibility of Polish mediation. Poland, Russia, and Napoleon himself would be spared many disasters.[23] But the animosity and mutual suspicion of the two emperors left Alexander no choice other than war; a revival of the French alliance would not be suffered by the Russians, and Napoleon, three weeks after Czartoryski's letter to the Tsar, closed the way to a friendly understanding with his "brother and ally" by his violent and provocative harangue to the Russian Ambassador, Prince Kurakin, at the official birthday reception of August 15.

Alexander was bitterly disappointed by his failure to win over the Poles. He tried the same proposals with the Prussian King, and received an equally negative answer. Both attempts resulted in alarming Napoleon and in provoking hasty actions on his side to avoid being taken by surprise and later preparations for war on an unprecedented scale.

After Czartoryski's refusal to cooperate, Alexander looked for a substitute for his Polish policy. He found some aristocrats

[22] Letter omitted in both publications of Czartoryski's papers; it has been published by Nicholas Mikhailovich, *Alexandre I*, 1, 361-362.

[23] Cf. Schiemann, *Geschichte Russlands unter Nikolaus I*, 1, 107-108: "Czartoryski hat in dieser ganzen Zeit ein doppeltes Spiel getrieben. Er verriet Alexander an Napoleon und Napoleon an Alexander." The letter of July 24, 1811 is quoted as evidence for that strange misjudgment.

from Lithuania: Prince Michael Ogiński, Prince Xavier Lubecki, Prince Casimir Lubomirski, and Count Louis Plater, who proved less reluctant to do so. There was a plan of proclaiming a grand duchy of Lithuania with similar rights as had been granted Finland, and thus establishing a union of Lithuania with Russia as a challenge to Napoleonic Warsaw. After consultation with leading people in Lithuania, the plan had to be dropped; they were prepared to rally around a Polish king, but not to disrupt the Lithuano-Polish union still alive in their minds. So the proclamation of a Polish kingdom once more came under consideration; the involved problems were discussed and drafts of decrees and constitutional acts were prepared.

After a prolonged silence Alexander wrote Prince Adam on April 1, 1812.[24] He informed him that his plan had to be postponed because of the publicity it had acquired: there were talks about it in Paris and Dresden—he hinted at the warning given by Poniatowski to Napoleon and suggested that Czartoryski should have dealt with the matter with more secrecy. Alexander now stated that a rupture was unavoidable, and very probably near at hand. He warned the Poles against trusting Napoleon too much: they were only being used as tools of his hatred for Russia. He dismissed as chimerical the idea of coming to terms with him on a restoration of Poland in union with Russia. The future war operations would be focused upon Polish territory; he therefore asked for advice: would it be better to proclaim the Kingdom of Poland at the very moment of the rupture, or rather later, after some military successes had been scored? Would not a proclamation of a grand duchy of Lithuania be a suitable preliminary move? He emphasized the important part which the Poles could play by joining him and hinted at the danger they would face if they were to provoke Russia's vengeance. "You cannot overlook all the calamities which would befall you if, by serving under French banners, you gave Russia a reason for avenging the wrong which might be done. . . ." And once more he asked for a list of Polish supporters, particularly of members of the Polish army.

Prince Adam refrained from replying hastily. He explained

24 Nicholas Mikhailovich, *Alexandre I*, 1, 362-365.

the reason for the delay by the fact that he expected to be able to entrust his message to the friendly hands of Novosiltsov, who had promised to see him when returning home from Vienna. The letter which he eventually wrote on June 4 was cautious and restrained: of the two sovereigns, the Poles would follow the one who would keep his promises to them; the project of a grand duchy of Lithuania was belated; he declined to name prospective followers or to make any suggestions; he referred again to the plan of winning over the Poles which he had already submitted seven years before. He mentioned his own difficult position and appealed to the Emperor in the name of their friendship to release him from Russian service at the critical moment. But the postscript added on June 13 was even more outspoken: in it Czartoryski announced that his father had already left for Warsaw in order to preside over an extraordinary meeting of the Seym, and he begged for his dismissal in order to obtain relief from his agony.[25]

Actually at that very moment the Czartoryskis had acceded to Napoleon's Polish policy. That momentous decision had been matured for more than a year. The French Resident in Warsaw, Baron Bignon, on April 8, 1811, expressed the view that they were ready to rally to any Poland if it were but independent. Prince Adam's younger brother Constantine, a colonel in the Polish army, as well as Matuszewic, a devoted friend of the Family and a supporter of Napoleon, were busy paving the way; the accession of the Czartoryskis was to be timed to coincide with Napoleon's proclamation of a restored Poland. While nothing was yet decided, they stayed at Sieniawa, in Galicia; both daughters, Princess Maria de Württemberg and Countess Sophie Zamoyska, were in Warsaw acting as the Family's liaisons, while Prince Constantine was its chivalrous representative in the Polish army. They raised no objections to the news that Jérôme, the King of Westphalia, whose military headquarters were in Warsaw, was the prospective candidate for the Polish throne. They humorously plotted how to persuade Jérôme to put on a Polish *kontusz* (traditional ceremonial coat), how to convert him to the principles of the May 3 Constitution, and how to make a

[25] *Ibid.*, pp. 365-370.

good Pole out of him. When the news came from Matuszewic that an extraordinary Seym was to be convoked in Warsaw and a confederation proclaimed there with the old Prince General as its marshal, there were no hesitations at Sieniawa. Princess Isabella wrote in her diary: "Mon mari is summoned to the confederation and he will proclaim Poland. . . . Since Racławice [Kościuszko's victory in 1794] I have not had such a moment. . . . My husband rewarded for so many virtues and so many services to his country. . . ."

But while his father hurried to Warsaw, Prince Adam still remained at the crossroads: his heart urged him to follow his father and his nation, while his affection and his sense of honor prevented him from betraying his allegiance to Alexander. In despair he implored Alexander with amazing frankness to absolve him by discharging him from his duties. "Poland has been solemnly proclaimed by a general confederation with my father at their head. The name of Poland pronounced by him is an order to me."[26] He also addressed a moving message to his Russian friends: "My dear friends," he wrote, "so we become enemies. . . ." He explained that his first obligation was to his country and that it had to prevail. He predicted with melancholy: "You will be bent on destroying us. The hatred on both sides will be exacerbated and it will not be appeased until the day when, after much bloodshed, it will be at last understood that the happiness and glory of one of our two nations are not necessarily to be founded on the oppression and misfortune of the other one."[27]

At the same time he wrote a long letter to Matuszewic explaining his attitude towards his nation—and towards Napoleon.

Napoleon attached much importance to Prince Adam's access and failed to understand his scruples. To him, over the heads of the Polish delegation, were addressed these words pronounced at Vilna on July 11, declaring that any other allegiances, obligations, and attachments had to give way to the love of one's own country. He was later induced by the Poles to replace this trans-

[26] Letter of July 4: Cz.M.(F), ii, 285-287.
[27] Letter to Stroganov, July 5, 1812 (Nicholas Mikhailovich, *Stroganov*, ii, 269-270).

parent allusion in print with the words: "The love of his country is the first virtue of a civilized man."

Prince Adam was well aware of it; he was also conscious—and so he wrote to the Tsar—that a people in the position of the Poles must regard their unity as their only hope. He hinted at Napoleon's utterance and repeated: "To be sure, one's first obligation must be that towards one's own country."[28]

Prince Adam's absence at Vilna at that crucial time hampered Napoleon's own commitment to the Polish cause as well as the extent and the intensity of the national movement in Lithuania and Volhynia. The importance of the national movement for the course of the war was by no means negligible.

In the talks of Napoleon's Foreign Minister, Duc de Bassano, with Polish representatives, allusions were made to the possibility of Napoleon himself taking the Polish crown and of Czartoryski holding the post of Great Chancellor. Czartoryski was then at Karlsbad and went later to Vienna; twice more he reiterated his appeal practically in the form of an ultimatum to Alexander. In October, impressed by rumors about peace negotiations, he made the suggestion that Alexander should agree to Poland's restoration as a fully independent state with the Grand Duke Michael as king. There was no reply to any of those appeals; Alexander chose the most sensible way—to ignore them.

The term put to the Tsar by Czartoryski was due to expire in November and his accession to the confederation was at last signed at the very time when the news of the disasters of the Grand Army and its impending catastrophic annihilation was received. The document remained in Prince Adam's portfolio.[29]

Czartoryski did not expect the war to take such a turn. Like Metternich and most of the Continental statesmen, even those who hated Napoleon, he had no doubts as to the latter's victory; he worried about Alexander's fate, and this feeling of sympathy increased his scruples. He had delayed his accession to the national cause but because he believed that Alexander would be

[28] Letter of Aug. 16, 1812 (Cz.M.(F), ii, 290-293).

[29] For Polish history in 1812 and the policy of Czartoryski, see J. Iwaszkiewicz, *Litwa w roku 1812* (Lithuania in 1812), 1912, and M. Kukiel, *Wojna 1812 roku* (The War of 1812), 1937. Cf. A. Mansuy, *Jérôme Napoléon et la Pologne en 1812*, 1931.

the victor. But now, when Alexander was winning—and the victory was to a great extent his own work—the fact that the relations between Alexander and Prince Adam had not been definitely ruptured seemed advantageous to the Polish cause. However, a few months later there was the following entry in Prince Adam's diary: "My duty was to have been in my country and to fight for it and to proceed along a straight path. The Russian allegiance fetters. . . ."[30]

Feeling somewhat guilty, he considered it more than ever his duty to redeem his *peccatum omissionis* by rescuing the Polish cause from shipwreck.

[30] See also Czartoryski's correspondence with his parents and sisters, and with Matuszewic, Kropiński, Linowski, Niemcewicz, etc., in his records.

CHAPTER 8

STRUGGLE AGAINST DESTINY

IN THE LAST DAYS of November 1812, members of the Warsaw government, Matuszewic, Mostowski and others, together with Count Zamoyski, the acting leader of the General Confederation, appealed to Prince Adam for his help and his mediation with the Russian Emperor. A few weeks after the final "ultimatum" which he had sent to his imperial friend, Czartoryski was expected to intercede with him to beg mercy for Poland. He was fully aware that it was his duty to undertake such an ungrateful mission in spite of his reluctance and aversion. In a letter dated December 18 he asked the Emperor now marching into Poland as conqueror whether he would return to his former intentions of becoming her liberator. If when conquering the territory, he also wished to conquer the hearts of its inhabitants? Was he eager to make the bonds uniting the two nations indissoluble, because voluntary? Writing with but little hope, he warned the Emperor in advance that Prussia and Austria would try to prevent him from realizing his intentions. He suggested a negotiation with the Council of the General Confederation.[1]

A few days later, on December 27, he sent another letter in which he stated his views on the Polish question.[2] He mentioned the possible "magical" effect of a magnanimous gesture towards the Polish people, who were expecting only revenge from the conqueror. He suggested that a Polish kingdom with a wholly separate existence, with the Grand Duke Michael, Alexander's youngest brother, as king should be created. He explained that the Grand Duke Constantine's violent temper gave rise to some misgivings among the Poles, who would prefer to have their own line of Romanovs on their throne. With a clear vision of the future, he emphasized that "a

[1] Cz.M.(F), II, 297-298.
[2] Cz.M.(F), II, 298-302.

Polish king who could command a Russian army of 300,000 to overthrow what his predecessor had built might be inclined to do so at any time." He insisted upon the necessity of constitutional guarantees. He declared himself satisfied as to the willingness of the Warsaw government and of the confederation to come to terms. In order to stress that he was acting as a representative of the Polish nation—and not as a Russian statesman—he asked once more for a *congé absolu.*

He had to wait a long time for a reply. Meanwhile, the situation in Warsaw had greatly changed. Napoleon's sudden appearance and the vigorous impulse he gave to the Polish leaders, Prince Poniatowski's return and his soldierly loyal bearing, prevented further drifting into capitulation; Poland remained Napoleon's ally. Alexander wrote to Czartoryski on January 25 from Leypuny.[3] He informed him of the proposals he had received directly from members of the Polish government (through the intermediary of Russian military commanders) and enclosed a copy of a memorandum by Mostowski containing an offer of a personal and genuine union with Russia. Thus Czartoryski's proposal of a *secundogeniture* was already disavowed by his own countrymen.

Alexander categorically declined to consider his suggestions: it could not be forgotten that Lithuania, Podolia, and Volhynia were already Russian provinces and that the Russian people would never tolerate their being transferred to any other sovereign. They must remain under the Russian Emperor even if called by a new name. He let his friend feel that their mutual relations had now greatly changed. He reminded him of the part the Poles had played in the last campaign, and he even charged them with the destruction of Smolensk and Moscow, an accusation quite without foundation, as the Polish corps, although it had taken part in the attack on Smolensk, had never entered the city, nor had it stayed in Moscow. He hinted at a revival of the old Russian hatred against Poles; as to himself, he declared that vindictiveness was a feeling unknown to him, and stated that to repay wrongs with good deeds was what he enjoyed above everything. Actually he could refer with pride to his noble and

[3] Cz.M.(F), II, 302-308.

conciliatory gesture made when visiting Vilna in December. He reassured Czartoryski that the military commanders had been ordered to treat Poles as friends and brothers. He was ready for an understanding with Warsaw, provided it should remain secret; any divulgation of his intentions regarding Poland would thrust Austria and Prussia into the arms of the French. A formal alliance with the Duchy's government should be concluded; he was ready to undertake to refrain from concluding peace "before the hopes of the Poles would be fulfilled" and stated with over-emphasis that "no one had ever relied on his loyalty in vain."

Prince Adam's messenger, Kluczewski, who carried the letter, was intercepted by the Austrians, who carefully copied it, to-gether with all the enclosed documents, and communicated it to Napoleon; it reached Czartoryski after several weeks' delay. So the negotiations with the Poles were actually interrupted.

Meanwhile, as a result of Prince Schwarzenberg's calculated retreat, Warsaw was occupied by the Russians; the Polish gov-ernment and army withdrew to Cracow. Alexander renewed his friendship with the King of Prussia. At Kalisz on February 26 he undertook to restore Prussia "to her previous power with re-gard to statistics, geography, and finances," and to return to her a part of her previous Polish provinces "in order to establish a frontier linking politically and militarily old [Eastern] Prussia with Silesia."

This meant the reannexation by Prussia of Chełmno [Kulm], Bydgoszcz [Bromberg], and Poznań. The Prussian interpretation went even further: the frontier, as suggested by their negotiator, Knesebeck, was to be pushed to the Narew, the Bzura, and the upper Pilica.[4]

A few weeks later Prince Adam appeared at Alexander's head-quarters at Kalisz. He was received with obvious embarrassment and displeasure. "Have you seen that specter?" the Tsar asked the Austrian agent, Lebzeltern, and he added that the kind of reception that Czartoryski had met with should reassure Vienna

[4] For the Polish overtures to Alexander and Czartoryski's action in 1813 see S. Askenazy, *Na rozdrożu* (At the Crossroads) in the review *Biblioteka Warszaw-ska*, 1911, and *Polska i Europa 1813-1815*, *ibid*, 1909, with long extracts from Czartoryski's diary and correspondence.

as to Poland. That utterance should not perhaps be taken at its
face value. The Tsar had many reasons to avoid discouraging
the renascent Austrian friendship and a possible alliance by the
evocation of the Polish specter. He had warned Czartoryski
about it, and now he forbade him further visits to his headquarters. But he had two long talks with him and he encouraged
him in his endeavor to prevent further bloodshed and asked him
to persuade the Polish government and Poniatowski to conclude
an armistice: "If all things ended well, Russia would have the
Duchy in the peace treaty and the Emperor would act after that
by himself without much ado as he had previously done with the
Finns."

Czartoryski fully realized how unfriendly was the atmosphere
at Kalisz to him, as well as to his country; how the Prussians
and many of the Russians displayed their hostility and how old
friends, former collaborators and protégés, now avoided him.
Of the two closest friends, Stroganov still had warm feelings
for him, but none for Poland;[5] as to Novosiltsov, after all the
years of disgrace, and semi-exile, he was only too anxious to
regain his position in the Emperor's counsels and he was certainly not inclined to risk anything for a lost cause. Alexander
was now almost alone among the Russians in holding his *idée
favorite*. Nevertheless, he dismissed his Polish friend without
giving him any definite pledge. Czartoryski knew about the
impending cession of the western parts of the Duchy to Prussia.
However, he advised Poniatowski to conclude an armistice with
Russia in order to preserve the nucleus of the national army
as a guarantee of political existence. The suggestion seemed
rather sensible. By changing sides and joining Alexander and
the Russians, the Polish government and its army would certainly influence the Tsar favorably and strengthen his position
with regard to the Polish problem. Politically they could hardly
be charged with disloyalty, as their legal sovereign, Frederick
Augustus, disengaged himself at that very time from the alliance
with France and tried to secure a neutral status for Saxony seeking Austrian protection. It was also evident that if peace negotia-

[5] See his letters to his wife, Dec. 29, 1812, and Jan. 11, 1813 (Nicholas
Mikhailovich, *Stroganov*, III, 155-157).

tions started, the first sacrifice Napoleon would be compelled to make would be that of abandoning Poland to the partitioning powers. But there were powerful emotional obstacles in Poniatowski's mind. His attitude was not so much determined by his feelings for Napoleon since he had many reasons for feeling embittered and frustrated; he was guided by his chivalrous sense of brotherhood in arms, the memory of the bloodshed in common and the common sacrifices, his abomination for anything resembling defection, and an intuitive feeling that nothing else was left but to "make the Polish name sound well" (*faire bien sonner le nom polonais*).

After having surmounted conflicting instigations, incertitude, and despair, he decided to march with his army through Austria (still neutral at that moment) to Saxony and there join the Grand Army. It is not easy to say what the Polish cause lost by that unpolitical decision. The fact that Poland continued to be represented by her soldiers on most of the battlefields and that the "specter" of Poland was not thus disposed of up to the very end of the war was not without consequence in the light of further developments.

Prince Adam went to Warsaw to stay there for a few months; it was to be his first long sojourn in the Polish capital since 1792. He wrote thence to Alexander, reassuring him about Prussia's possible reaction to the Emperor's Polish plan.[6] He managed to get in touch through the intermediary of Prince Anthony Radziwiłł, a cousin of the Hohenzollern, with the King, and Frederick William gave his blessing and suggested a public announcement, possibly even a joint Russo-Prussian declaration. It seems that, having by the treaty of Kalisz secured a guarantee that a large part of Western Poland would be returned to him, as well as the promise of Saxony in compensation, he was anxious to have his partner fully committed to that arrangement and to forestall Austria's efforts to prevent it; he was fully aware that Vienna would oppose to the last any extension of Prussia in Central Germany and particularly on the border of Bohemia.

So Czartoryski, in spite of his misgivings as to Prussia's part in the game, was bound to take her attitude into account and

[6] Warsaw, May 4, 1813 (Cz.M.(F), II, 309-315).

to try to exploit the King's personal political ideas, ideas not always consistent with Hardenberg's policy.

Once more he tried to explain to the Tsar the reluctance of the Poles to enter into negotiations. "The powerful does not degrade himself by offering his friendship; the weak abases himself by imploring mercy and so he procrastinates with distaste and reluctance." He strongly defended Poniatowski: "If it had been the case of a small Caucasian tribe or of a Persian Khan, the Russian commanders would have surely made more effort to win them over than they have done over coming to terms with Poniatowski and his Army."

But it was already too late to change the course of events; the roads of Prince Joseph and Prince Adam went in opposite directions for the last time: a few months later Poniatowski met his soldierly death at Leipzig.

In Warsaw Czartoryski became a competent, vigilant, and embarrassing observer of the Russian occupation and of the activities of the "Temporary Supreme Council"—a mixed Russo-Polish body presided over by the Russian senator Lanskoy and established as the civil administrative body of the country. He began to rally public opinion to his policy. He made contacts with the Senate of the Duchy—a body "comparable to the Roman"—at private meetings at its president's, Thomas Ostrowski's, home. An entry in his diary reads: "The Freemasons ready to elevate," which probably refers to his elevation to the seventh grade, the highest, but could also be interpreted as referring to their support for his policy. There was at that time a spectacular shift in policy among the Polish Freemasonry from the support of Napoleon to that of Alexander, and it seems that it was connected with wider changes in the political tendencies of Continental Freemasonry, particularly in France. Much remains to be explained about these important underground trends.

Czartoryski became more and more conscious of his responsibility for the fate of the Polish cause. The task was far from easy. He confided to his mother: "The *figure de bronze* is like the voice in the desert; nobody listens to it, either on one side, or on the other, and so it is difficult to make the thing go. . . . I try to do everything possible to help individuals and my country, but I do not always succeed."

He argued with the administration on the necessity of reducing the burden of the maintenance of the Russian armies. He begged Alexander to preserve his compatriots in Lithuania from renewed persecutions. Notwithstanding the amnesty, the Emperor's promises, his statement that the past should be forgotten—*passer l'éponge*—and his recommendations to treat the Poles as "brothers and friends," things went their usual way: there were more and more denunciations, arrests, beatings, and seizures of property.

On the other side, he tried to secure general support for the program of a constitutional kingdom under Alexander's scepter. He founded a secret league for giving leadership to public opinion. He became the unofficial leader of the central committee elected by departmental councils—a body, which, under the pretext of collaboration with the occupational authorities, was in fact a substitute for a parliament. He was invited by that body to inform the Emperor of the situation in Poland and the claims of its people.[7]

This invitation enabled Prince Adam to get to the headquarters at Reichenbach in June 1813—in spite of the previous interdiction. He appeared to Alexander as a personified remorse; it was just a few days before the conclusion of the three powers' compact stipulating the dissolution of the Duchy of Warsaw and its partition among the three eastern powers.[8] Alexander had submitted to Metternich's pressure and to British insistence in order to win over Austria for the coalition; he only later made the reservation that the liquidation of the Duchy did not necessarily mean a return to the boundaries of the Third Partition of Poland.

Austrian mediation followed, and among the four points presented to Napoleon as conditions *sine qua non* was the dissolution and partition of the Polish state—one of those "demands

[7] For the domestic history of the Duchy, 1813-1815, see J. Bojasiński, *Rządy Tymczasowe w Królestwie Polskiem*, 1901, and K. Bartoszewicz, *Utworzenie Królestwa Polskiego*, 1916. The memorandum of the committee and their letter to Czartoryski, Nov. 20, 1813, Bartoszewicz, pp. 50-54 and 286 sq.

[8] Czartoryski at Reichenbach, June 22; the treaty was signed on June 27.

so just and so moderate," as Castlereagh emphasized when calling upon the Allies not to hesitate to stand by it.[9] That first condition was accepted by Napoleon. He wrote to his plenipotentiary, Caulaincourt: "I am giving up a nation which has done so much for me."

Meanwhile, at Reichenbach and Peterswalde, Prince Adam tried in vain to get a glimpse into his imperial friend's mind; he was left in darkness as to the latter's intentions and undertakings. His diary contains entries full of exceptional bitterness: "Reflections on the Emperor's duplicity. He promised the Duchy to Prussia and gave it up for a new partition." And a few days later, before leaving, he wrote: "Impossible to discern whether he is frank or deceiving; there is ample reason for thinking the latter. Indifference and ill will surely." And he added: "But who knows the Emperor so well and from the worst side does not despise him, as even evil has not any system or character in his mind."

At Reichenbach, before leaving for Warsaw, Prince Adam decided to venture a diplomatic campaign of his own and to try himself to win Britain's support for his country and its union with Russia as the only way to preserve the existence of the Polish state against Austrian hostility and Prussian rapacity.[10] He wanted to achieve even more: a secret Anglo-Polish understanding and Britain's lasting interest in Poland's existence as a separate state if threatened by its powerful partner—Russia. What he strove for stood in flagrant contradiction to Castlereagh's policy of reestablishing a "just equilibrium" in Europe by reinforcing Austria and Prussia and by restoring to them—to Prussia especially—all or most of their previous share of Poland. Czartoryski was not yet fully aware of the extent to which the Foreign Office was committed in pursuing that policy and how it was resolved to prevent Russia's expansion in the basin of the Vistula and towards the Oder, even if it would go under the name of a personal union with a Polish kingdom.

[9] *Brit. Diplomacy*, pp. 16-18.

[10] For Czartoryski's relations with Britain at that period, see the monograph of E. Wawrzkowicz, *Anglia i Sprawa Polska 1813-1815* (England and the Polish Cause, 1813-1815), 1919. English, Prussian, Austrian, and Polish sources are fully exploited and much material given in original text in the Appendices.

Prince Adam's relations with Britain had been severed since 1807. In March 1813 at Kalisz he had tried in vain to establish some contact with Lord Cathcart, the British Ambassador; he spoke of this attempt harshly in his diary. He again met there Sir Robert Wilson, with whom he had recently exchanged information and views; a warm friendship revived between the Polish statesman and the brilliant, chivalrous, intelligent, and noble-minded young British general, who was always ready to champion a cause he considered just and fair.[11] Wilson was now very popular with the Allies, much more than with the Ambassador, Lord Cathcart, to whom he was attached, or with the Foreign Office, which disliked his exuberant political initiative and the independence of his views. Thus he was not the proper liaison with His Majesty's government, and his connections with the Whig opposition did little to improve the situation. However, after having been at first a convinced and somewhat too outspoken supporter of a Russo-Polish union, he changed some of his views under the influence of Metternich. He was rather impressed by the danger of an excessive expansion of Russia in Europe, and he became a partisan of peace with Napoleon; he was even denounced by Gneisenau as a danger to the unity of the Allies.

At Reichenbach his relations with Czartoryski were very close; he encouraged the latter's idea of sending his private secretary, Felix Biernacki, to London, and promised to provide him with letters of recommendation to his friends, Lord Grey and Sir Francis Burdett, the radical free-lance at Westminster. He was sanguine as to their influence and the probability of a governmental change. Czartoryski also obtained from Sir Charles Stuart a passport for his envoy and a letter of introduction to Lord Castlereagh. Some weeks later, Biernacki—an able, versatile, and highly educated man—left for London. By sending him, Prince Adam in a way disengaged his diplomacy from that of Alexander. He realized the risk involved and he undoubtedly bore in mind the catastrophe of his grandfather and great-uncle in 1766-1768, a warning that Poland if dependent on Russia's

[11] For Wilson's contacts and correspondence with Czartoryski, see Wawrzkowicz, *op.cit.*, pp. 14-38, 287-304, and Cz.M.(E), II, 240-246.

good will could not have connections of its own with the West without exposing itself to the danger of being forced into wholesale submission and of becoming Russia's impotent dominion.

Before Prince Adam had left the headquarters of the coalition, Wilson had been removed to Italy. "I went away," Wilson wrote in his private diary, "with low spirits, because I had to separate from Czartoryski, who from the misfortunes of his country has become quite melancholy and who inspires these feelings in his friends from love of him as well as of his cause. He is certainly one of the most gifted of the human race, and the more I see him, the more I attach myself."[12]

Prince Adam's memorandum to the British government[13] was conceived as an appeal to Britain's ideals of freedom and justice and her supposed mission as a protector of oppressed peoples and the leader of Europe in the building of a new international order. There was a striking contrast between such an idea of British policy and the realities of 1813-1815; ten years before, Czartoryski had had some difficulty in finding a common political language with Pitt, but the discrepancy became much more acute with Castlereagh because of the latter's "almost complete unconsciousness of the strength of national forces which had been called into new life by the French Revolution and the Napoleonic system. The aspirations of Poles, Italians, or Germans left him unmoved."[14] Justice meant to him an adequate balance of power, and while he stood for abolition of the slave trade elsewhere—after it had been banned by Great Britain—he felt no revulsion at the slavery of nations. When Prince Adam denounced the policy of self-interest called erroneously *raison d'état*, he addressed himself to a statesman who had never envisaged any other kind of policy but that of self-interest connected with a sense of moderation, "equilibrium," and stability. Of Prince Adam's lengthy treatise, little or nothing could capture Castlereagh's attention; nothing could influence his attitude.

No wonder that Biernacki's reception at Downing Street was rather cool, the more so as he submitted to the Foreign Secretary

---

12 R. T. Wilson, *Private Diary*, 1863, II, 81.
13 Puławy, Sept. 9, 1813 (Wawrzkowicz, *op.cit.*, pp. 307-324).
14 *Brit. Diplomacy*, XLI.

a plan for a Russo-Polish union. Castlereagh had been warned
long before by a memorandum of Baron von Stein against the
dangers of Russia's impact on Central Europe if, by her union
with Poland, her frontiers would be pushed as far as the Carpathian Mountains, Silesia, and Pomerania. He had also been
warned by Pozzo di Borgo, who advocated a new complete
partition of Poland as the best solution. Castlereagh gave Czartoryski's emissary a rather simple piece of advice: the Poles ought
to accept their fate; Great Britain could not intervene to alter it.

Czartoryski's letter to Canning recommending Biernacki did
not prove helpful. The letters promised by Wilson never arrived. The Polish emissary was stranded until he found a close
collaborator and supporter in the young and brilliant political
writer, the barrister Henry Brougham, at that time one of the
editors of the *Edinburgh Review*, and one of the future leaders
of the Whigs. With Biernacki's help and with the use of his
information, Brougham wrote an anonymous pamphlet, *An Appeal to the Allies and the English Nation on Behalf of Poland*.[15]
For the first time the British people were told about Polish
affairs with real understanding and knowledge of the facts and
of recent developments concerning Poland and her potential role
in Europe. Not only in Britain was public opinion impressed.
Frederic Gentz, whose opinion in the finality of Poland's partition was challenged by the pamphlet, immediately drew the conclusion that it must have been written by Brougham and that
it had been formally ordered by a distinguished Pole; he was
prepared to make a bet as to the latter's name.[16]

Brougham published a review of his pamphlet in the *Edinburgh Review* (January 1814), and a very outspoken one at
that; neither Alexander nor the Russian authorities in Lithuania
were spared. He exposed the "urgent reasons for a return of
public principles and honor, more peculiarly in the case of
Poland," and he warned his readers, "Let our ears be spared
the insulting titles—of restorer, liberator, avenger, lavished upon
or even claimed by those who, having got the upper hand by

[15] Published in London in 1814 and in French translation in Paris; Brougham's
manuscript in Cz. Mss.

[16] Mendelsohn-Bartholdy, *Briefe von Fr. V. Gentz an Pilat*, 1868, I, 121.

means of the peoples of Europe, use their power in perpetuating slavery and oppression and having driven out the French armies, think only of dividing the spoils among themselves, without ever wasting a thought upon the rightful owners, to whose assistance they have affected to come. But, most of all, let us be spared the ridiculous name of *pacificator*, given to those who are destroying every chance of lasting tranquillity and employing a moment of unexampled success, never likely to recur, in laying the foundations of new wars; when they might, by recurring to sound principles, only by keeping of faith which they have vowed, reestablish the system of European independence upon an immovable basis, and give to the world a real and lasting peace. . . ."

Here we are very near to the program expounded in 1804 in the instruction for Novosiltsov and very far from Castlereagh's policy of encouraging Austria's extension in Italy, Prussia's extension in Germany, especially on the Rhine, and advocating a new and complete partition of Poland. Alexander could easily discern his friend's inspiration even if he was not informed—which he certainly was before long.

The publication of the appeal proved a turning point in the attitude of British political circles, the press, and the Parliament on the Polish problem. Brougham proceeded to introduce the Polish emissary to many politicians; his most important contact was with the Chancellor of the Exchequer, Vansittart, who showed an interest in the problems of Poland and an understanding of the situation which had arisen; he was the only one among the British statesmen to perceive the difference, from the point of view of European security, between a simple annexation of a part of the Duchy by Russia and a Russo-Polish union with a liberal constitution for Poland as a separate state. His contact with Lord Grey was less useful; it resulted only in a vague allusion to Poland in the latter's speech after the fall of Paris.[17]

Early in 1814 Czartoryski, for the third time, left for Alexander's headquarters. With some difficulty he succeeded in obtaining an audience at Chaumont on March 8. He was better received than before. Alexander now felt strong enough to impose his

---

[17] For Biernacki's mission, see Wawrzkowicz, *op.cit.*, pp. 56-78, 325-328, and Cz.M.(E), ii, 246-282. See Brougham's letter to Vansittart, *op.cit.*, ii, 276-278.

policy on the Russians and to surmount external obstacles; he took the role of a victorious leader of the united nations and the liberator of Europe, eager to display his generous intentions and to appear a benefactor of Poland. "He announces that the larger part of Great [i.e., Western] Poland must be restored to the Prussian King, and Austria would like to have Cracow, but the Vistula is also a suitable frontier. And we must bear in mind that if he gives something up, he gives us seven millions Poles [i.e., the provinces annexed in 1793 and 1795 by Russia]."

At Chaumont, Czartoryski for the first time met Castlereagh, his most obstinate and formidable adversary in the forthcoming diplomatic campaign. The talk was courteous, but the Foreign Secretary had been well prepared for it by the Prussian Stein and the Austrian Stadion. The latter had reported to Metternich a month before that the Foreign Secretary seemed to be quite convinced that they must "not admit a distinct Kingdom of Poland either in fact or in name, either openly avowed or concealed under some subterfuge."[18]

Now Castlereagh expounded the same opinion on the Polish problem: "I have had communications with the Princes Czartoryski and Radziwiłł on the affairs of Poland and I hope I have succeeded in discrediting their views, considering them in truth a diversion in favor of France—the former [Czartoryski] who is a person both of principle and merit promised to absent himself from the headquarters if his presence was considered as calculated to create disunion, which I ventured with every possible sentiment of regard to assure him was the fact."[19] So Castlereagh managed to dispose of the specter of the Polish question, though not for as long as he expected.

The short and momentous campaign of 1814 was in its final phase. Alexander achieved what he had longed for: he entered Paris at the head of the Allies. The Polish troops, on Napoleon's own advice, surrendered to the Russian Emperor, invoking his protection. On Napoleon's insistence the Treaty of Fontainebleau stipulated their return to Poland with colors and arms, with their ranks, honors, and medals. The divergent ways of the Polish

[18] Stadion to Metternich, Feb. 9, 1814 (Webster, *Castlereagh*, 1931, p. 213).
[19] Castlereagh to Liverpool, Mar. 3, 1814 (*Brit. Diplomacy*, pp. 163-164).

statesman and the Polish soldiers met at last on the ruins of lost hopes. And then, Kościuszko reappeared.

The aged chief had lived in France in voluntary exile, in bitter opposition to Bonaparte, openly displaying his disdain for the Emperor, unshaken in his republican creed, and uncompromising in his opposition to Napoleon's absolutism. Now, like so many other republicans, he placed his only hope for Poland, for France, and for Europe in the noble ideas of a sovereign who had been a pupil of La Harpe and who was a friend of Czartoryski. He was enchanted with the *grand enchanteur*. He put at Prince Adam's disposal his great and honorable name in order to help him to save the Polish state and the name of Poland.

In a letter of May 3, Alexander promised to the old chief the freedom and independence of his country.[20] In their conversation the Tsar promised to return to the new Poland the land which had been annexed, as far as the river Dvina and Dnieper (namely the Russian share of the 1793 and 1795 partitions). The Tsar's soundings of his allies on the Polish question started even earlier, and Metternich boasted that he had refused proposals of exchanging Galicia for Alsace and Lorraine. This would be in striking contradiction to Alexander's approach to the problems of France, but the dispute over Cracow and the adjacent part of the Duchy of Warsaw came immediately to light in the Paris talks, and the plan of compensating Prussia's losses in Poland by annexation of Saxony complicated the situation.[21] Alexander faced more opposition than he had expected, and he was reluctant as usual to push the thing ahead when meeting resistance. He still hoped for a friendly response and appraisal from Western liberal quarters and he also thought it advisable to influence Russian notables at home, who were rather hostile to Poland's political existence. Even his next collaborator, the State Secretary Count Nesselrode, did not conceal his criticism of his sovereign's plans.[22] Thus Alexander consented to the pro-

20 Kościuszko to Alexander I, Apr. 9, and Alexander to Kościuszko, May 3, 1814 (Angeberg, pp. 599-601). See also Czartoryski's letter to Novosiltsov, Paris, June 1, 1814 (Schiemann, *Geschichte Russlands*, I, 530-531).

21 H. Nicolson, *The Congress of Vienna*, 1946, pp. 69-70, 104. C. Webster, *The Congress of Vienna*, 1937, pp. 42-45.

22 Martens, III, 212-216.

posal of postponing the solution of the problems not directly relating to France to a special congress to be held the next autumn in Vienna. Preparatory talks had to be continued during the intended visit of allied sovereigns and statesmen in London. Such a friendly invasion of Britain seemed an important step for securing support for Alexander's generous intentions.

To the great dismay of the Foreign Office, Czartoryski accompanied the Emperor. He was at that juncture once more indispensable to his friend as collaborator and adviser. The Tsar's aim was to seduce and conquer the proud and cold Albion. His success was not what he expected. Both Alexander and his beloved sister, Catherine, Duchess of Oldenburg, who had preceded him, had shown some disregard of British habits and diplomatic protocol; they irritated and offended the Prince Regent and proved rather shocking to their hosts.[23] Alexander's too obtrusive attempts to win over the Whig opposition for his policy were merely troublesome for its leaders and only strengthened the position of the Foreign Secretary.[24]

Czartoryski made contacts of his own. He struck up a warm friendship with the Duke of Sussex, the Grand Master of the Freemasonry, a liberally minded man who showed much interest in Poland. He used to tell a story of how for a moment he had had the Polish crown on his head (it had been shown to him in Berlin together with the Prussian jewels). To the very end of his life he remained a faithful friend of Prince Adam and his country.

Czartoryski renewed his friendly intercourse with Lord Gower and made contacts with many Whig leaders, most of whom he had known since his first stay in London: the Lords Lansdowne, Grey, Grenville and Holland. He met with some sympathy for Poland but with hardly readiness to support Alexander's plan. He approached Wilberforce, Romilly and their friends in the Commons; this move resulted, with Brougham's help, in the

---

[23] There were strange things in Alexander's and Catherine's mutual relations, and it could not be fully unknown. See Melgunov, *Dela i ludi Alexandrovskogo vremeni*, p. 105; and Webster, *The Congress of Vienna*, pp. 46-48.

[24] For Alexander's adventures in England, see H. Nicolson, *The Congress of Vienna*, Ch. 7, "London Interlude."

problem of Poland being raised by several members—Mackintosh, Ponsonby, and others. There were probably some exchanges of views with the Chancellor of the Exchequer, Lord Vansittart; the latter's intervention some month later against Castlereagh's handling of Polish problems reads like an echo of Czartoryski's own words.[25] There also took place a long political discussion with Castlereagh to whom a *pro memoria* had been handed containing suggestions as to the solution of the Polish problem.

Czartoryski discussed in the first instance the restoration to Poland of her old boundaries; most of Polish territory being in Russian hands, it could be achieved only under the Russian crown. If that solution proved impossible, partial restoration should be sought for: the minimal solution would be a Polish kingdom in union with Russia, leaving Poznań and Polish Pomerania with Prussia and Galicia with Austria. The condition should be to give to those provinces the name of Poland and national institutions. "If some parts of Poland remained in the hands of Austria and Prussia, the only and simplest way for ensuring the security of their possessions would be to grant the inhabitants such institutions as would attach them to their governments." He expounded a plan of national self-government for those provinces, with some common institutions for the whole of Poland.

In the main outlines, Czartoryski's suggestions surprisingly conformed with the agreement reached a year later in Vienna, although they were obviously more favorable to Poland in some important points.[26]

The Foreign Secretary showed a rather cautious restraint, and the Austrian Ambassador, Count Merveldt, fanatically hostile to the Polish cause, thought it his duty to intervene vehemently in a talk with Czartoryski. He said that Austria was ready to wage war in order to prevent a Russo-Polish union, and he warned Castlereagh once more against the peril which such an increase in Russia's power would constitute for Europe.

---

[25] He also contacted Jeremy Bentham, and invited him to collaborate on the Polish and Russian legislation; see Bentham's letters, 1815 (Cz.M.(E), II, 288-301). Cf. Nicholas Mikhailovich, *L'Empereur Alexandre I*, I, 150-151.

[26] Wawrzkowicz, *op.cit.*, pp. 349-351.

Struggle against Destiny

When leaving Britain, Prince Adam left behind more understanding for the cause of Poland than had existed there before. His endeavors had not been entirely in vain, but it was obvious now that the fourthcoming congress would become a sharp contest between the Allies, largely over the Polish problem, and that it would also be a contest between Czartoryski and Castlereagh.

CHAPTER 9

THE MAKING OF THE KINGDOM
OF POLAND

On his way from St. Petersburg to Vienna, Alexander paid a visit to Vilna and announced once more to the Lithuanians that he was pleased to forgive them their sins. Then he appeared at Puławy in high spirits, cordial, radiant, full of generous feelings and ideas, visibly delighted with the consciousness of accomplishing a good deed, and sanguine as to his success. Never afterwards did he perhaps feel so much a Polish king as at that time, when he had merely announced to the European powers his claim to the Polish throne. When greeting Prince Constantine, who wore his Military Cross won at the battle of Smolensk, he embraced him with the words: "I loved you always, but now I respect you more than ever since you have fought for your country."

If a certain chilliness appeared in his relations with Prince Adam—as the Tsar was certainly well informed of Czartoryski's highhanded action in London and had read Brougham's pamphlet and article—the ice quickly melted in the course of their talks, most of which were attended by Novosiltsov, who accompanied the Emperor. There was a long conference with the members of Prince Adam's Secret Committee: Count Stanislas Zamoyski, Thaddeus Matuszewic, and Alexander Linowski. Alexander restated his formal pledge of Poland's restoration and the reunion of the Polish provinces with the Duchy; he assured them that the future kingdom would have ten to eleven million inhabitants. He presided over the reading of the principles of the constitution as drafted by Czartoryski, and the only major amendment he moved was a clause, introduced with the object of "placating the Russians," stipulating that Poland was to be bound to Russia by the person of the present Emperor and his successors. When Zamoyski somewhat rashly suggested inserting a phrase that the Kingdom of Poland was to be incorporated in the Empire, Alexander briskly opposed him: it would not be incorporated but united with it forever under a common sovereign.[1]

Alexander went to Vienna with a program known in advance to the other powers: "The Duchy of Warsaw for Russia. If necessary I can give up Poznań and the district of Chelmno . . . but Toruń and its surroundings must be excepted. . . . Prussia will get Saxony. . . ." He was optimistic as to his partners' attitude, being assured of Frederick William's consent and underestimating Austria's opposition.

Unexpectedly Alexander's policy was challenged by Great Britain, and it was Castlereagh who became the inexorable protagonist of Poland's partition, more Prussian than the Prussians themselves and more adamant than Metternich in opposing the reappearance of a Polish state. The British Foreign Secretary adhered to what he believed to be Pitt's political testament: the main points of the memorable note for Vorontsov, dated January 19, 1805, the idea of preventing future French aggression by increasing Austria's power in Italy and Prussia's power in Germany, and establishing her as a guardian of the Low Countries on the left bank of the Rhine.[2] But Castlereagh went far beyond Pitt's legacy by committing the British policy to the defense of territorial arrangements in Poland as established by the treaties of her Third Partition, against Alexander's plans for a restoration of the Polish Kingdom. "He did indeed share [with his colleagues] an almost complete unconsciousness of the strength of the national forces which had been called into new life by the French Revolution and the Napoleonic system."[3]

What Castlereagh saw in the proposed Russo-Polish union was only "the introduction of Russia's influence into northern Europe" and he undertook to rally Hardenberg, Talleyrand, and even Nesselrode, Alexander's official plenipotentiary, to his opinion that

[1] For the meeting at Puławy, see Askenazy, *Szkice i Portrety*, 1937, pp. 126-131, 369-373, containing minutes from the conference. See also Talleyrand's letter to Louis XVIII, Oct. 4, 1814 (Talleyrand, *Mémoires*, II, 329).

[2] Webster, *Castlereagh*, pp. 386-387.

[3] *Brit. Diplomacy*, Introduction, p. xli.

nothing could be more fatal to Prussia "than to have the Russians on both flanks," and that they had to unite in order to oppose the "folly of Alexander's Polish policy."[4]

In his first talk with Alexander in Vienna on September 26 the latter told him "in considerable detail" the plan "to retain the whole of the Duchy of Warsaw with the exception of a small portion to the westward of Kalisz, which he meant to assign to Prussia, erecting the remainder, together with his Polish provinces, into a kingdom under the dominion of Russia, with a national administration congenial to the sentiments of the people." He declared himself "not prompted by any view of ambition" but by a "sense of moral duty," and he was ready "to give to the neighboring states every security as to their possessions." Castlereagh stated that his government "would view with great satisfaction the restoration of Poland to its independence" but that "they took a broad distinction between the erection of a part of Poland merged in the crown of Russia, and the restoration of the whole, or a greater part, into a distinct and independent state"— the Prince Regent did not suggest the latter solution, because he would not like to demand "unreasonable sacrifice" from his allies.

Alexander emphasized that his solution would be to the advantage of Poland. He hinted at the prospective constitutional evolution of Russia; a few days later he explained "that Russia, as at present constituted, was too large, but that when the Russian provinces [of Poland] were united under a free system and his Russian army withdrawn beyond the Niemen, Europe would have nothing to fear."

Castlereagh insisted upon the danger to the tranquillity of the Polish provinces of Prussia and Austria, and he even warned the Tsar of the hostile reaction of his Russian subjects.[5] They parted without any agreement having been reached, and Castlereagh did his utmost to stiffen the resistance of the two German

---

[4] *Ibid.*, pp. 190-195.

[5] *Ibid.*, pp. 197-199, 206-207; Wawrzkowicz, *op.cit.*, pp. 419-422; Nicholas Mikhailovich, *Alexandre I*, I, 140-141. For Russian reactions to Alexander's Polish policy, see the report of Hegardt (Sweden), Vienna, June 25, 1814 (Weil, *Les dessous du Congrès*, I, 8). Talleyrand terrified some aristocrats with the prospect of the abolition of serfdom in Lithuania if reunited with Poland (*op.cit.*, I, 574).

powers. He was obliged to report that they were "more likely to seek their own aggrandizement in other directions than to oppose themselves to the pretensions of their more powerful neighbor."[6]

In fact, according to Alexander's plan, without Castlereagh's and Talleyrand's intervention, both the problems of Poland and of Saxony would have been settled in a few weeks.

Castlereagh's first memorandum on the Polish question, dated October 4, invoked the treaties of Kalisz, Reichenbach, and Teplitz, stipulating the dissolution of the Duchy and its partition, and accused the Tsar of taking the opposite line. In his letter to Alexander he suggested that he should "ameliorate gradually" the situation of the Poles without ostensible measures.[7] But he was now aware of Alexander's firmness in pursuit of his Polish policy and he made a last-minute effort to bring the two German powers to a common stand against Russia. He tried to reconcile them by appealing to their common interest in the partition of Poland. He even secured Metternich's reluctant consent to the annexation of Saxony by Prussia on the condition that the latter would oppose the creation of a Polish kingdom and claim her former share of Poland. As a result, Prussia would swallow half of Poland, Saxony, and the Rhineland, and become not only the leading power in Germany, but also in Central Europe; and the political existence of all the north German states, of Hanover in the first instance, would be doomed to an early end half a century before Bismarck's conquests. No wonder that Frederick William thought that policy too ambitious and preferred to adhere to his compact with the Tsar, whose armies now occupied both Poland and Saxony. Metternich's consent to the annexation of Saxony was disavowed by his Emperor. Talleyrand, who had supported Castlereagh's action with regard to Poland in order to regain for his country a place in the European concert, was adamant with regard to Saxony. The British Cabinet felt uneasy about the Foreign Secretary's action.

Liverpool's instruction of October 14 recommended a settle-

[6] *Brit. Diplomacy*, pp. 201-202.

[7] Angeberg, *Le Congrès de Vienne*, I, 265; *Brit. Diplomacy*, pp. 208-210; Wawrzkowicz, *op.cit.*, pp. 424-426.

ment of the Polish problem *à l'amiable* by the three partitioning powers among themselves, and hinted at the serious embarrassment resulting from that problem. He clearly disagreed with Castlereagh's abiding by the principle of partition and suggested the idea that the Duchy of Warsaw be maintained as an independent state under an independent sovereign. A memorandum of the same date discussed the three possible solutions of the Polish problem: partition, maintaining an independent state, and handing over the Duchy to one of the three powers, i.e., to Russia.

The British government favored the second solution, on the condition that the Emperor of Russia would not be a prospective king of Poland. They were definitely against the third solution, but—emphasized the memorandum—even that would be less unpopular in England "than the measure of complete partition and consequently Poland's annihilation."[8]

When the memorandum is compared with the *pro memoria* written by Czartoryski for Castlereagh in August 1814, a certain link between the two documents is seen; Czartoryski's arguments had not been lost.

Meanwhile Castlereagh was faced with Alexander's uncompromising attitude on both questions—Poland and Saxony—and he suspected that Czartoryski's influence was behind it. In his new memorandum of October 23 establishing a common policy for the four powers with regard to Polish affairs, Castlereagh was paying lip service to the principle of Poland's independence.[9] Counterproposals were suggested: a complete reunion of Poland under an independent sovereign (as before 1772), or the reestablishment of the *status quo* of 1791, or a complete partition of the Duchy with the Vistula as the suggested frontier. If none of the above solutions should be acceptable to Russia—as was presumed —the powers would protest the Emperor's right to act with respect to his division of Poland in defiance of the stipulation of the Convention of 1797, concluded by the three powers to the effect of a final annihilation of Poland; they had then pledged themselves never to assume any title which would restore its name. Thus,

[8] *Brit. Diplomacy*, pp. 210-211.
[9] For its origin and date, see Wawrzkowicz, *op.cit.*, p. 431. Text see Angeberg, *Le Congrès*, I, 291-293.

against their will, Castlereagh committed his government to endorsing the act of the Third Partition; he seemed to be quite unaware of the major importance of such a move.

Alexander reacted by a sharp rebuff in a memorandum written by Anstett, his confidential collaborator and state secretary, and based on Czartoryski's notes.[10] *Inter alia* he denied the validity of the treaties and conventions concluded with Austria and Prussia with regard to Poland's partition, since both these powers had invaded Russia as Napoleon's allies; and he hinted at the conspicuous fact that the British Minister seemed to be more committed to upholding those obsolete agreements than were the interested powers themselves.

Oddly enough, Alexander's reply coincided with Liverpool's letter to Castlereagh enclosing an important memorandum by the Chancellor of the Exchequer Vansittart.[11] The latter expressed his apprehension that the British were making themselves "too much principals in the dispute respecting Poland," and that they were running the risk of being considered abroad "as actuated by jealousy of the greatness of Russia," and "at home as the advocates and instigators of a system of partition." "There is some weight," he admitted "in the Emperor's observation . . . that Russia would gain more power by acquiring half the Duchy of Warsaw as a province, than the whole as a kingdom." He pointed out that with a constitutional regime the Poles would be "less manageable"; in one or two generations "the nominal independence of Poland would become real." He insisted on the importance of good relations with Russia for the British trade, and he advised against irritating her by a "pertinacious opposition."

Vansittart's views slowly penetrated at Downing Street. Liverpool's instructions of November 25 to the Foreign Secretary emphasized the necessity of maintaining peace; he recalled Fox's frequent quotation of Cicero: "Iniquissimam pacem iustissimo bello antefero." He approved Castlereagh's "triumphant" reasoning and disapproved of Alexander's disregard for his engagements contracted with Prussia and Austria, but he insisted upon the moral significance of the Polish problem. "It would have been

[10] Oct. 30, 1814 (Angeberg, *Le Congrès*, I, 352-358).
[11] Of Oct. 28, 1814 (*Brit. Diplomacy*, pp. 219-221).

fully unnecessary and, I think, very imprudent for us ever to have started the idea of Poland or Polish independence; but it becomes very different to defend the partition of the Duchy of Warsaw, as one of the alternatives to Polish independence, when the question of Polish independence has been once brought forward. We must, however, do our best in this respect, fully satisfied that we have acted from no other motive than that which was likely to contribute most upon the whole to the peace and tranquillity of Europe. . . ."[12] And to Wellington next day: ". . . We are thus brought practically to struggle for a question of partition, which is always odious in itself, in which we might have acquiesced as the result of former engagements, but for which it is painful to be obliged to contend on any other ground. . . ."[13] An official instruction to Castlereagh conveyed a day later the Prince Regent's approval of the "firm and decided manner" in which he was handling the Polish case, but the emphasis was put on the impossibility of involving Britain in a new war.[14]

In the meantime—November 1814—Castlereagh was very much a "principal in the Polish question." He was even abandoned by Hardenberg and so had to defend Prussia's share in Poland not only without Prussia but even while bitterly quarrelling with her; and he strove for Austria's interests, halfheartedly supported by Metternich.[15] On November 4 he gave a rather malicious and sarcastic reply to the Tsar.[16] Alexander delayed his answer for two weeks; the second Russian memorandum of November 21 was not provocative in tone but it stated significantly: "A mediator is only useful in a discussion if he tries to conciliate; otherwise he had better leave the parties concerned alone."[17]

The deadlock seemed complete, and there was talk of war, particularly much sabre-rattling by Austrian officers and even ministers. Saxony was handed over by the Russian army to the

---

[12] *Brit. Diplomacy*, pp. 244-246. Similar scruples inspired Count de Blacas' dispatch to Talleyrand, Nov. 9, 1814 (Talleyrand, *Mémoires*, II, 435).

[13] *Brit. Diplomacy*, pp. 246-247.

[14] Nov. 27, *ibid.*, pp. 247-248. See also M. Nicolson, *op.cit.*, pp. 175-176.

[15] For Prussia's and Austria's political vacillations, see Wawrzkowicz, *op.cit.*, pp. 444-450; and *Brit. Diplomacy*, pp. 229-233, 240.

[16] *Brit. Diplomacy*, pp. 226-227; Angeberg, *Le Congrès*, I, 393-401.

[17] *Brit. Diplomacy*, pp. 242-244.

Prussians. In Poland the Grand Duke Constantine, who had been given the command of the remnants of the Polish army, issued on December 14 an order of the day calling for readiness to defend the country and the existence of the Polish state; the moving appeal was in fact addressed to the British Foreign Secretary and Metternich.

The negotiations with Alexander were resumed late in November; Hardenberg now came into the foreground as mediator. Castlereagh showed restraint and disappointment; he still believed that war was "the most likely case to occur," that Austria "would have to bear . . . the first shock," and that the part of the western powers should be that of an "armed mediation."[18] It is difficult to perceive what issue he expected from such a contest between the Austrians and the overwhelming combined military power of Russia and Prussia.

Hard bargaining over Polish districts and towns, on Cracow and Toruń, followed, complicated by the problem of Saxony. At that juncture a momentous decision was taken at Downing Street: Lord Liverpool's instruction of December 22 not only authorized the Foreign Secretary to agree to the acquisition of the Duchy of Warsaw by Russia, but even expressly recommended his so doing, "provided it is distinctly stipulated in the treaty that at least the Polish provinces incorporated to Russia since 1791 shall be reunited to the Duchy of Warsaw, so as to form a distinct Kingdom of Poland under a free constitution." He expressed the view that "it would afford some security to Europe, however inadequate, that the Empire should consist of two distinct kingdoms and that the crown and one of those kingdoms should be subject to the control of a government more or less popular." If the Emperor refused, Castlereagh should inform Czartoryski and the Poles what the British proposals had been.

The dispatch reads as if it had been inspired by Czartoryski himself, and it most probably was, in an indirect way. During the congress there was a private correspondence between Czartoryski and several British statesmen: Lord Grey and others. Joseph Sierakowski, one of the leading Lithuanian politicians, acted in

[18] Letter to Liverpool of Dec. 5 (*Brit. Diplomacy*, pp. 251-254).

London as liaison with Brougham's help, and the latter's contact with Vansittart proved, as was shown, most useful. The letters of that period from London to Prince Adam are not preserved; the portfolio disappeared from his papers some time later and served most probably to stir up the Emperor's suspicions. A British overture on those lines would be for Alexander *vis grata*, but Prince Adam's secret diplomatic action in order to provoke it could not please him.[19]

The confidential commentary given by the Prime Minister on his instructions some weeks later stated his purpose with genuine sincerity: the British government was "desirous of putting the sincerity of Alexander's professions to the test," but they did "not suppose that there was much chance of his acceding to any such proposal."[20]

In any case, Castlereagh was instructed to take a course exactly the opposite of that which he had taken heretofore. Before receiving his instructions, he was visited by Czartoryski, "who, although not in any official situation, appears now the actual Russian Minister at least on Polish and Saxon questions."[21] The talks, mostly concerning Saxony, started afresh. The Russian and Prussian representatives, Czartoryski, Stein, and Hardenberg, proposed once more the incorporation of the whole of Saxony into Prussia and the transfer of the Saxon King to the Rhineland. The suggestion was stubbornly opposed by Castlereagh and Talleyrand; Metternich was less adamant. The Foreign Secretary adhered to his policy of establishing the Prussian guardian on the left bank of the Rhine against a possible French threat to the Low Countries. How Talleyrand discovered that the interest of his country lay in promoting the same solution, and in opposing the creation in the Rhineland, as Alexander proposed, of a buffer state with a peaceful and Francophile sovereign, remains

[19] Alexander instructed Count Lieven on Dec. 15 to lecture the British government on the right of nations to have institutions of their own, based upon the harmony of their interests and those of their rulers. It was his principle with regard to Poland. See Martens, XI, 211-212, and Webster, *The Congress*, pp. 95-96. Czartoryski's hand in drafting this document is apparent.

[20] January 16 (*Brit. Diplomacy*, pp. 290-291).

[21] *Ibid.*, pp. 268-271.

an enigma.[22] Contemporaries were inclined to seek an explanation in Frederick Augustus's large contribution to the Prince of Benevento's secret financial benefits; posterity almost unanimously praised the splendid achievement of the "Prince of Diplomats."

On December 29 the dispute reached its climax; an "unheard-of menace" of Hardenberg provoked the hasty conclusion of the alliance of January 3, 1815, of Britain, Austria, and France against Russia and Prussia. But as soon as January 5 Castlereagh felt that the danger of war was over. Compromise on both problems was at hand. On January 8 he was still pressing Alexander to give up more Polish territory to the Prussians, and was told again that after the assurances the Emperor had given to the Poles the subject was both painful and embarrassing.[23]

Czartoryski made a new attempt to allay Castlereagh's misgivings that the restoration of a Polish kingdom would be a danger to the security of Austria and Prussia. He once more suggested the same solution which he had expounded in London a few months before. The Poles who would be left outside the new kingdom under the Austrian or the Prussian crowns should be granted national rights, their own institutions, and proper representative bodies. He laid down in a new memorandum for the Foreign Secretary an elaborate plan of some form of home rule for the Polish provinces of both powers.[24]

Castlereagh had already received Liverpool's instructions of December 22. He probably felt uneasy when reading them; after having stirred up Russian opposition to Alexander's plan of restoring the Polish provinces to a new Polish kingdom and having warned the Tsar of the risks involved, he was now instructed to insist upon this, as a *sine qua non* of any agreement.[25] He was aware that what the British government wanted was a generous gesture with regard to the Polish cause. Czartoryski's suggestions concerning the national rights for the Polish lands outside the kingdom provided him with an innocuous theme. In his "Circular

[22] A. Sorel's eloquent *plaidoyer* of Talleyrand's policy in *L'Europe et la Révolution*, VIII, 373-374, 409-411, does not give a satisfactory answer.

[23] *Brit. Diplomacy*, pp. 282-285.

[24] Wawrzkowicz, *op.cit.*, p. 491.

[25] Cf. C. Webster in *The Cambridge History of British Foreign Policy*, I, 483.

to the Plenipotentiaries on the Conference" on January 12, 1815, he emphasized his government's desire to see an independent Poland "under a distinct dynasty," explaining once more why he had not been directed to press such a measure. Now "the Emperor of Russia continuing . . . to adhere to his purpose of erecting the part of the Duchy of Warsaw, which is to fall under his dominion together with his other Polish provinces, either in whole or in part into a kingdom, under the Russian scepter, and their Austrian and Prussian majesties, the sovereigns most immediately interested having ceased to oppose themselves to such arrangement," the Foreign Secretary dropped his opposition, though he expressed misgivings as to the consequences of that solution for the tranquillity of that part of Europe. In order "to obviate such consequences" he strongly recommended that they "establish the public tranquillity throughout the territories which formerly constituted the Kingdom of Poland upon some solid and liberal basis of common interest, by applying to all, however various might be their political institutions, a congenial and conciliatory system of administration. . . ." "Experience has proved, that it was not by counteracting all their habits and usages as people, that either the happiness of the Poles or the peace of that important portion of Europe can be preserved." Thus he appealed to the three monarchs "to take an engagement with each other to treat as Poles, under whatever form of political institution they may think fit to govern them, the portions of that nation that may be placed under their respective sovereignties. . . ."[26]

It was not exactly what had been recommended from London; the emphasis was put, not on the extension of the new kingdom on Russia's Polish provinces, but on the special rights of the Polish people in all parts of the former Commonwealth. With the three powers adhering to this principle, Castlereagh's proposals became one of the main stipulations of the treaty concerning Poland, and the most contradictory in their meaning and spirit to the Convention of 1797 on Poland's annihilation, which he had obstinately invoked. [27] Both Liverpool and Castle-

[26] *Brit. Diplomacy*, pp. 287-288.
[27] Metternich scoffed at Castlereagh's "conseils philantropiques" (his *Mémoires*, II, 487).

reagh were anxious now to make the arrangements of the Polish affairs "more palatable" to the British Parliament and public. Further hard bargaining went on—the mutilated trunk of the Duchy of Warsaw was still to be hewn in order to preserve a trunk of the Kingdom of Saxony. On February 13 Castlereagh could report the settlement of both problems and his project of a "General Accord and Guarantee Declaration." He thought it necessary to adhere to Pitt's pledge connected with Alexander's suggestions of European unity and collective security. The specter of the "République Sully" reappeared in Vienna for a while, though little remained of the spirit of Czartoryski's "Grand Design" in the "phrases générales" of the treaty; as he himself sadly stated afterwards: "Vox, vox, praeterea nihil."

Castlereagh left Vienna as a successful "pacificator"; he was and still is regarded as largely responsible for having checked Russian impact on Central Europe. In fact his success was rather problematic. Alexander had secured for his kingdom of Poland the territory he had planned before, with the exception of two cities: Cracow, to be "free, independent and strictly neutral," and Toruń, to be given to Prussia as compensation for Leipzig. The loss was extremely painful for the new Poland, but devoid of any importance for Russia's position in Europe. But Castlereagh's exertions had another result: the disappointment of the Russian Emperor in Western Liberalism. He realized that the effort of restoring Poland's freedom not only failed to arouse a friendly response in Europe but provoked a hostile reaction, and, though he imposed his will as to the Polish crown on a reluctant Europe, he felt a sense of frustration and lost much of his interest in his *idée favorite*. Castlereagh and Metternich had not only mobilized the majority of European powers against Alexander's Polish plan, but their opposition had greatly influenced the attitude of the Russians and increased their aversion to giving up Russia's provinces to a Polish kingdom.[28] Instead of being encouraged by the Western powers to take that generous measure, Alexander had been warned and discouraged. As a result, the reunion of Poland's eastern provinces with the new kingdom

---

[28] See J. de Maistre's dispatch of Feb. 2, 1815 (*Corr. Diplom.*, II, 40-41).

was not even explicitly announced in the treaty; mention was made only of the Russian Emperor's right to give to the kingdom such "internal extension" as he would consider convenient.[29] The implementation of that vague proviso was indefinitely postponed as a result of Alexander's vacillations and of the growing pressure of Russian and European reaction upon the Emperor. What is more, his experiences in Vienna did little to encourage his intention to give liberal institutions to his own empire. It seems likely that British policy not only helped to frustrate the coming into being of a strong and liberal Poland reconciled with Russia, but also to impede Russia's own constitutional evolution along Western lines.[30]

During these five months of diplomatic contest about Poland, Prince Adam was once more Alexander's closest collaborator and at some periods his only confidential one. Not only had he to fight against such adversaries as Talleyrand, Metternich, Hardenberg, and Castlereagh, who were all backed by their governments and the states they represented, but he had to face Alexander's own advisers, the majority of whom were hostile or obstructive (the great German patriot Stein was their protagonist). Even Capo d'Istria and Anstett were not reliable, and Nesselrode, the official representative of the Emperor, ostentatiously abstained from defending his case. The solidarity of the three partitioning powers seemed to reappear in spite of Alexander's policy and against him. "In hostile waters where there is neither rescue nor shelter, and rocks everywhere, we must pilot our unfortunate boat."

In such circumstances Czartoryski succeeded in securing for his country the recognition of the kingdom of Poland as a separate state, though united by its constitution to the Russian Empire; the clause concerning the extension of its territory according to the Emperor's future decision; and the stipulation that the Polish subjects of Russia (i.e., living outside the king-

---

[29] "Extension intérieure," scil. inside Alexander's own states. In *The Cambridge History of Poland*, II, 270, the proviso is erroneously translated "interior improvement." The wording was clear to contemporaries, but not so to most modern historians, and the clause omitted in their writings. See the most recent study: H. A. Straus, *The Attitude of the Congress of Vienna towards Nationalism in Germany, Italy and Poland*, N.Y., 1949, pp. 131 ff.

[30] Cf. Webster, *Castlereagh*, p. 495.

dom), of Austria, and Prussia should be granted national representation and institutions in conformity with the kind of political existence which each government would think it "useful and just to bestow upon them."[31]

It was certainly vague, it could mean much or nothing, and Prince Adam's efforts to secure Castlereagh's and Wellington's support in order to obtain more precise concessions met with polite refusals.[32] But the specter of Poland was now to be seen over the whole territory of the former Commonwealth, and the three powers recognized in principle the existence of a Polish nation and its right to exist as such. It was indeed an important turn in Polish history.

Czartoryski felt that "it was Emperor Alexander who has saved the Polish cause by his firmness and the consistency of his action." He stated this in a letter to a British friend and repeated it on many occasions even after he became a rebel, an outlaw, and an exile.[33]

Prince Adam's own ordeal was not limited to his bitter struggle against overwhelming odds. There was again a new outburst of his love for the Empress, with accompanying qualms of conscience, dreams of a new life with her, requests for the Emperor's consent to a divorce, and the bitterness of his refusal.

He did not accompany Alexander in the forthcoming war against Napoleon. On May 25 the Emperor confirmed the principles of the Polish constitution (they had been elaborated according to the proposals approved by him at Puławy), and he delegated Czartoryski to Warsaw as his plenipotentiary, authorized to establish the new institutions.[34] Officially he was a deputy of the Russian senator Lanskoy, the president of the supreme council; in fact, however, he had, for some months, full control

[31] For the treaties concerning Poland, see Angeberg, *Le Congrès*, II, 1146 ff., and Martens, III, par. 80, 81.

[32] Wellington's *Suppl. Despatches*, IX, 569-572, 578-580. For Prussia's and Austria's *reservatio mentalis*, see Wawrzkowicz, *op.cit.*, p. 498; B. Gebhardt, *Wilhelm v. Humboldt*, 1896, II, 99, 113.

[33] Letter of May 29, 1815, to an unnamed Lord [Grey?]; see Wawrzkowicz, *op.cit.*, pp. 499-500.

[34] He left for Warsaw on May 27 after a conference with Kościuszko and Count Stanislas Potocki (the Prime Minister of the Duchy of Warsaw): see Weil, *Les dessous du Congrès*, II, 619, 625.

of the administration of the country. He made tremendous efforts: he organized anew the new state of which he was, with Alexander, the founder, and where it was generally expected that he would become the real ruler in the King's name.[35]

In fact the real ruler had already been in Warsaw for more than half a year: Grand Duke Constantine, Commander-in-Chief of the Polish army. Prince Adam had long realized the dangers of Constantine's ungovernable temper and his wild and brutal instincts. He tried in vain to persuade the Tsar to appoint old Kościuszko as commander-in-chief. But it was not possible for the veteran republican to take the command of a royal army reorganized on the Russian imperial pattern; nor was his appearance in Warsaw possible before the problem of Lithuania, Volhynia, and Podolia had been settled. The Grand Duke's arbitrary and violent actions provoked governmental confusion and administrative chaos, and caused dismay in the army and among the population. Czartoryski warned Alexander in several letters—outspoken as ever—and he even submitted to him the draft of a decree recalling the Grand Duke from his post.

That contest was not to be won. In November the Emperor came to Warsaw and took the control of all affairs into his own hands. He was assisted by Novosiltsov, who now became his closest confidant with regard to Poland (later he was appointed the imperial commissioner with the Polish government). Prince Adam was aware of a great change in Alexander's relations with him: the Emperor became cold and estranged. Perhaps it was the result of Novosiltsov's insinuations and the information he provided about Czartoryski's independent activities and his secret links with England. In any case, the Emperor's distrust was growing.[36] But most probably the chief factor was the impossibility of Prince Adam's collaboration with the Grand Duke and the Emperor's firm decision to maintain his brother in Warsaw as the Kingdom's future viceroy, because he considered that his

[35] For the founding of the kingdom of Poland, see *The Cambridge History of Poland*, II, 271-276; and *Cambridge Modern History*, x, 445-449.

[36] For F. Biernacki's betrayal of Prince Adam's confidential contact with Britain, see Wawrzkowicz, *op.cit.*, pp. 304-306; the fact was disclosed in 1819, but alarming symptoms appeared in 1816 and possibly Biernacki's partnership with Novosiltsov could be traced to 1815.

presence there would make the existence of the Polish state more palatable to the Russians.

Alexander's state of mind was reflected in his conversation on November 8, 1815, with Ogiński who came to Warsaw as delegate of the Lithuanian provinces: "Adam will tell you at what a cost the kingdom had been made and about all the obstacles I had to overcome in Vienna. . . . I have made it and I have built it on most firm foundations, because I have compelled the European powers to guarantee its existence in the treaties. I shall do what still remains to be done, according to my promise [to restore Lithuania to the kingdom] but all cannot be done at once. . . . You must be confident . . . and do not expose me [with regard to the Russians]. . . ."[37]

But he had already transferred his confidence from Czartoryski to other Poles, more compliant than he was, namely to Ignace Sobolewski, who was appointed State Secretary, and the aged, disabled veteran, General Zayonchek, who, blindly adhering to the new order, was to be appointed Lieutenant of the Kingdom.[38]

On December 2 a long nocturnal conversation took place between Czartoryski and the Emperor; Czartoryski, usually a *figure de bronze*, appeared to be profoundly shaken when leaving Alexander's room. Had he been told that his role as the sovereign's mentor was definitely ended? That the Emperor was not prepared to sacrifice his brother for his sake or to offend Russia? Did Czartoryski insist upon the implementation of the stipulation concerning Eastern Poland? Did they discuss Elisabeth and the divorce which had been refused by the Tsar? We can only guess that Alexander was already bored with his partnership with Czartoryski. By his efforts to liberate Poland he risked displeasing Russia and the rest of Europe, and now he was disgusted with his failure to please his Polish friend.[39]

[37] M. Ogiński, *Mémoires*, 1826-1827, III, 233. See also Alexander's explanations in a talk with Princess Maria of Württemberg: Bartoszewicz, *op.cit.*, p. 195.

[38] For Alexander's decisions in Warsaw, see Nicholas Mikhailovich, *Alexandre I*, I, 188-190; and K. Bartoszewicz, *op.cit.*, pp. 185-212.

[39] See Schilder, *Imperator Alexander I*, III, 356. Czartoryski wrote to Kropiński, Jan. 1, 1816 (Bartoszewicz, pp. 210-211): "There was more *finesse* than sensibility in the Emperor's actions."

Prince Adam's entry in his diary read: "My part seems finished. To put a poor Poland on its feet was my job. . . . Now I am at the end of a career. Let others work; my turn will perhaps come later. . . ."

Thus the small mutilated state, which was the product of his long efforts, was to be governed without his participation. His Grand Design of organizing Europe as a league of free nations was transformed now by Alexander and Metternich into the Holy Alliance of Sovereigns against nations.

CHAPTER 10

HOPES DYING AWAY

PRINCE ADAM was appointed Senator (*Voyvode*) of the new Kingdom and member of its Council of Administration. He never attended the council's meetings for he was unwilling to assume moral responsibility for governmental activities under the Tsesarevich's (Grand Duke Constantine's) arbitrary and unconstitutional rule, with Novosiltsov, now completely demoralized, corrupt, and *débauché* as Imperial Commissioner.[1] His intention was to keep away from politics and to devote himself to social activities, to the promoting of letters and sciences, and to his duties as curator of the University of Vilna.

His dreams of personal happiness were frustrated; he realized that he had now lost Elisabeth forever. No other sentiments could soothe his agony. In 1813 his love affair with the lively and witty Countess Anna Potocka brought but bitterness and frustration.[2] He repudiated the hand of the charming Sophie Matuszewic, who was his mother's beloved foster-child and her choice for a prospective daughter-in-law. But at last he decided to found his own home, and in 1817 he married the very young Princess Anna Sapieha, of great patriotic traditions and heiress to her mother's, Princess Anna's (nee Zamoyska), large fortune. Her father, Prince Alexander, a friend of Napoleon I, died in 1812; her mother, a friend of Kościuszko, was a brave, wise, and energetic lady who was to be an invaluable help to her son-in-law in his later difficult times.

There was no romanticism in that marriage; but a romantic imbroglio occurred and twice Prince Adam had to fight a duel

---

[1] "Tsesarevich" was the title bestowed upon Constantine by Paul I as reward for his service in Suvorov's campaign 1799.

[2] Her letters are preserved in Czartoryski's papers, and much is told about this in his private diary; some quotations from it are given by M. Handelsman, *op.cit.*, I, 44-45. Nothing about their relationship is mentioned by the Countess in her *Mémoires*.

with his less fortunate rival, Count Louis Pac, and was twice wounded.[3] Although at the start it was rather a *mariage de convenance*, in the course of time a very real affection grew up between the two which was to last to the end of Czartoryski's life.

Czartoryski was not, however, permitted to stay on the margin of political developments. Under the pressure of circumstances, he felt it his patriotic duty to intervene with the Emperor, either to implore his protection for the institutions which had been their common work, or to denounce the arbitrary acts and cruelties of the Grand Duke and the failures of the government, and to ask for the Emperor's intervention.[4]

As early as 1817 Prince Adam meditated an appeal to the liberal opinion of Europe. The next year, 1818, the Seym held its first session. Czartoryski had a strong influence on the proceedings in both houses and succeeded in inspiring them with moderation and dignity; his idea was to submit to the Emperor and King a fair and honest picture of the conditions prevailing and of the needs of the country. The remarks submitted by the Committee of the Senate (they were Czartoryski's work) were rejected by Alexander's personal annotation without even being taken into consideration. Prince Adam understood the meaning of the unfriendly gesture, and kept aloof from further sessions of the Seym for the rest of his imperial friend's reign.

He withdrew from politics to Puławy, his property and residence, where he laid the foundations of a large scientific library. To the existing collections of his family he added the invaluable ones of Thadeus Czacki, which he purchased after the great bibliophile's and collector's death. He inaugurated a systematic building up of that institution on the lines of the British Museum, of which he was an admirer. Thus he sent to Great Britain a young humanist, Charles Sienkiewicz, whom he had selected for the guardianship of his library, and provided him with letters of introduction to Wilberforce and Brougham. Sien-

[3] For Czartoryski's marriage, see his private diary, 1813-1817 (a copy was in Cracow in Cz's personal papers), and R. Rzewuska, *Mémoires*, 1939, I, 504-505, 518-520, 562.
[4] His letters to the Emperor, 1816-1821; see Cz.M.(E), II.

kiewicz had to learn the librarian's business, to trace the *Polonica* on the bookmarket, and to register those in public collections. Prince Adam followed with keen interest and with a rare competence his work abroad and the further increasing and completing of the library.[5]

He occupied himself the more thoroughly with his other and earlier work—the University of Vilna and the schools in its large educational district. He was fond of the youth, the students of Vilna, a high-spirited, broad-minded set of men. Little by little mutual understanding and affection brought the Prince Curator and the students closer together. One of their leaders wrote in 1822: "As far as I know him, he is a zealous and enlightened man and an unconventional mind. . . . He is neither proud nor uneasy to be approached, as he was reputed to be; he might be told everything, even from the bottom of one's heart."[6] Feeling had run high since the days of Vienna, and secret societies were established among them which aimed at national unity and freedom. The Society of the Philomates took the lead; Thomas Zan, a Freemason, was its chief, and the future great poet Mickiewicz one of his first associates. The semi-official Society of Radiants with a large membership was closed down as it became suspicious to the authorities; but soon a secret league of Philaretes took its place. The younger ones—the schoolboys of the secondary schools —founded societies and clubs of their own, much more romantic and sanguinary in words.

The secret police were unearthing several secret societies in the Kingdom and in Lithuania; in Warsaw the case of Major Valerian Lukasinski, Grand Master of National Freemasonry, was waiting to come before the courts. The police suspected ramifications of his activities in Vilna, and even Prince Adam himself. Czartoryski certainly knew much about what was going on in Vilna; he was doing his best to prevent any foolhardy action on the part of the young people and to protect them against unnecessary interventions by the police. But in 1823 the Grand Duke became alarmed by the alleged revolutionary manifestations in

[5] See the interesting diary of K. Sienkiewicz, *Dziennik podróży po Anglii 1820-1821* (Journal of the Voyage to England), 1953.

[6] *Archiwum Filomatów*, 1913, IV, 167-170.

the schools, an enquiry was ordered, and Novosiltsov went to Vilna to investigate the case with the firm purpose of putting an end to Polish educational self-government in the eight provinces and of eradicating "the spirit of the unwise Polish nationality." There followed mass arrests, interrogations, persecutions of professors and pupils, and purges among the educational bodies.[7]

Prince Adam pleaded for tolerance and moderation and appealed in vain to the Emperor, who—since 1820—had not only privately delegated Polish affairs to the Grand Duke, but had given him carte blanche and now trusted his commissioner in Poland, the actual grand inquisitor Novosiltsov. Czartoryski once more lost his case, and he could but ask to be released from his duties as curator. In vain he tried to see the Emperor; he finally succeeded in meeting him when he passed through Poland on October 31, 1823, and stayed for a night in a Polish country house at Wolosowce. He had a long talk with Alexander, another one with Elisabeth, and there was a painful revival of old memories, of extinct feelings and vanished hopes. He obtained from the Emperor nothing but his dismissal. He was promised that Novosiltsov should not be his successor as curator, but a few short months later he was installed. Elisabeth confided to Prince Adam her lasting agony, and they revived the bitter thoughts of her unhappy life, doomed to solitude and melancholy.[8] It was their last meeting. Two years later Alexander was dead and before long Elisabeth followed him. But their emotional link with Prince Adam had been severed at this last meeting.[9]

Thus ended the drama of the partnership of those two men—the Emperor of Russia and the Polish patriot, who tried to bring to an end the old contest between Russia and Poland by reconciling Poland's rights with Russia's greatness.

[7] For the history of the Polish Underground in the period 1816-1825, see S. Askenazy, *Łukasiński*, 1929, 2 vols. In connection with the tragedy of Vilna, esp. II, 219-249, 421.

[8] There is an entry about this in Czartoryski's notebook, written immediately after parting.

[9] There was in Alexander's and Elisabeth's last years (1824-1825) some kind of Indian summer of their marriage; see Nicholas Mikhailovich, *L'Impératrice Elisabeth Alexeevna*, III, 393-394. Alexander died Dec. 1, 1825; Elisabeth, May 16, 1826.

CHAPTER 11

NICHOLAS, CONSTANTINE, AND
CZARTORYSKI

"AN EVENT of immeasurable consequences for Europe occurred in 1796," thus read Czartoryski's Memoirs, "and a most disastrous one for Poland. It was announced that the Empress Maria was pregnant, and shortly after she gave birth to a son. The ceremony of the baptism took place in the chapel of Tsarskye Selo; the court attended gathered together in a large adjacent room. . . . The ambassadors were present; I do not remember which of them stood at the baptistery acting as godfathers for their monarchs: the child was called Nicholas. When looking at the baby in swaddling bands, crying because of the rather protracted ceremonies of the orthodox baptism, I did not guess that the small creature, so weak and so pleasant as babies usually are, should become a calamity for my country."

In reality the new occupant of the Russian throne in December 1825 signified a momentous change for Russia and Poland.

With Alexander there disappeared the Tsar who in spite of his yielding to powerful reactionary and autocratic impulses remained to the end under the spell of the idealism and humanitarianism of his early years, and of the principles of the "philanthropist infidels of our century," so abhorred by Nicholas. Some years before his death, he was still busy drafting a constitution for his empire on the Polish pattern. And although he was, after 1820, thoroughly disinclined to pursue his liberal policy in Poland, and sanctioned Constantine's arbitrary rule of violence; although he allowed Novosiltsov to strike at the university and Polish schools in Lithuania, and definitely parted company with Czartoryski, he nonetheless in the last months of his life revived the "favorite idea" of the early years of his reign, namely, the idea of restoring to Poland the eight Polish provinces of the

Empire. Constantine wrote to Nicholas the following year: "He [Alexander] twice plainly announced it to both of us [Constantine and the Duchess of Łowicz, his wife] . . . he repeated the same pledges to several military and civilian persons."[1] He had still tried to bring about his reconciliation with Poland and Poland's with Russia.

His presumptive heir had been the Tsesarevich Constantine Pavlovich. But under some pressure from the Tsar, in connection with his marriage to a Pole, Joan Grudzińska, the future Duchess of Łowicz, he had renounced the succession. The secret declaration, rather humiliating for the Grand Duke, was disclosed after the Emperor's death and Nicholas' accession to the throne automatically followed.

Having renounced his right to the imperial crown, Constantine felt even more bound to his post as viceroy *de facto* of Poland and Lithuania. His first brotherly recommendations to Nicholas after having handed over to him their brother's imperial inheritance read significantly: "Not any change of what our dear, excellent, adorable departed has done, either in the most important or in petty affairs," "undertake nothing rashly," "accept as a rule, that you are but a plenipotentiary of the will of the defunct benefactor." There was in those prospects some thought for the Tsesarevich's own position in Poland, but some also for Poland's position and rights.

The new Emperor, who was thirty years old—seventeen years younger than Constantine and nineteen younger than Alexander—differed greatly both physically and spiritually from his elder brothers. He had nothing in him of Paul's strange nature, of his inconsistencies, folly, and nervous instability, nothing of that peculiar mixture of good and evil, of humane reactions and outbursts of ferocious cruelty. Nicholas was a man on the Prussian pattern; he had the Prussian rigidity, ruthlessness, and fierceness, an acute sense of duty and adoration for a strict order based on military and police regulations. He was inaccessible to philanthropic ideas and ideologies, except perhaps to his religious creed in the divine mission of absolute monarchies. Poland was for

---

[1] Constantine to Nicholas, Feb. 27, 1826 (*Sbornik*, cxxxi, 52-54); see also L. Zamoyski's (Prince Adam's nephew's) important notes, *Zamoyski*, i, 204-205.

him merely a conquered country, and although he was not at first prepared to abolish the institutions which his late brother had granted, he felt these rights to be a generous and benevolent gift of the Russian Emperor and not a natural right of its people. The letters exchanged between the brothers reveal their contrasting approaches to Alexander's inheritance.[2]

Nicholas emphasized that he would be both a Russian and a Pole, but that "he would cease to be Russian in his own eyes if he believed that there was any possibility of separating Lithuania from Russia proper."

Constantine retorted in plain terms: "As regards Lithuania, the case is too long for a letter and the more so for one scrawled and conceived by me, but I take the liberty of saying that I am, I was, and I shall be Russian to the end of my life, by heart and soul, but not one of those blindfolded and blunt, who adhere to the principle, that they are to act at will, and other people not at all! 'Our dear mother Russia takes but by free consent, putting only her foot on the throat'! That proverb is much in use among our people and I am always horrified when hearing it. . . ." Although he reassured Nicholas in his other letters that he would always comply with the imperial will, he did not neglect any opportunity of recalling the deceased Emperor's generous intentions, or of reproaching him with their having been given up.

Some months later they argued about the system of reinforcements for the Lithuanian corps—an autonomous body under Constantine's command, recruited until then from the western provinces only. Nicholas, when insisting upon reinforcing the Russian element in that section of the army, stated his *sic volo, sic iubeo*: "I cannot allow all my lifetime any possibility of encouraging the idea of uniting Lithuania with Poland, because I regard the thing as impossible and the consequences for the Empire as disastrous. It does not prevent me from being as good a Pole as I am a good Russian; I shall prove it on any occasions by strictly and loyally adhering to the privileges which our Angel has bestowed upon the Kingdom, but I would not suffer as long as I

---

[2] Their correspondence appeared in 1910-1911 in *Sbornik*, cxxxi and cxxxii, with some unavoidable cuts and omissions (sometimes hinted at as being illegible).

am alive any attempt to push beyond to the detriment of the Empire."

Constantine's answer was chilly: "As to the political opinions of the late Emperor and yourself relating to the Polish problem, my part is not to be judge, but to comply with your orders." That was the moment, November 1827, when the decision concerning the western provinces was definitely taken and Alexander's policy regarding them plainly countermanded by his successor. Nicholas' profound dislike of Czartoryski was connected with the fact that he had been the Polish inspiration and confidant of the late Emperor's intentions with regard to a free and reunited Poland and a regenerated, liberal Russia.

Prince Adam spent the years 1824-1827 mostly abroad, at Geneva, in Italy, and in Southern France. One can only guess at his real preoccupation, and retrace the discreet links he built up with some liberal leaders of the west; his Freemason connections probably helped to extend his old friendships. He was deeply committed in Philhellenic activities and he renewed his old friendly contact with Capo d'Istrias, whom he had once introduced to Russia's diplomatic service.[3] Common political creed and philhellenic feelings gave origin to his close association and durable friendship with Sir Stratford Canning, whom he met in 1826 at Geneva.[4]

This period of his life was one of meditation and deep inward questioning. He was affected not only by his country's misfortunes and his own disappointments and regrets; the passing away of Alexander plunged him into melancholy. Elisabeth's death followed, and his heart was bleeding. He confided to his sister, Princess Maria: "Since the moment when I learned of her death I do not know more what I want or what I ought to do. I was always thinking of her. She constantly was the aim of all my actions, and, can you believe it?, even when embellishing Puławy, I still nourished a vague hope that she would come there and approve."[5] He suffered before long another heavy blow by the death of Leon, his beloved first-born child.

[3] See Czartoryski's letter to Capo d'Istrias, Florence, Feb. 7, 1827 (Handelsman, *Książe Adam Czartoryski*, 1938, pp. 39-41).

[4] Handelsman, III, 151.

[5] Quoted by Comtesse Rosalie Rzewuska, *Mémoires*, 1939, I, 562.

Suffering influenced the course of his thoughts. In his treatise "On Consolation" (never published) he took a long step towards Christian philosophy. Until then he had been somewhat indifferent to religion. The Polish Freemasonry, like the French, was radically anti-Catholic; almost all "enlightened" Poles—the Czartoryskis included—even if they formally preserved their allegiance to the church, were strongly anti-clerical and eager to promote the laicization of public education and the supremacy of the governmental authorities over the clergy. Prince Adam's feelings and ideas began to take a new turn.[6]

During his sojourn abroad he wrote his political opinions in a coherent and systematic treatise: *Essai sur la Diplomatie*. It was finished in 1826 and was to be published anonymously; M. Toulouzan, president of the local Philhellenic committee at Marseilles, was entrusted with it. It was 1830 before the book appeared in print.

When returning to Warsaw in June 1827, Czartoryski had to meet the crucial situation created by the case of the secret Patriotic Society, the leading Polish underground league. Its existence had been disclosed after the Russian revolutionary attempt of December 1825. The case was extremely serious, for not only was the whole organization revealed by the confessions of some of its members, but also its links with the Russian Decembrist conspiracy. The new Emperor, since he had been greeted on his accession to the throne by a military rebellion, concentrated every effort of mind and will on the disclosure and eradication of all the ramifications of the conspiracy; for several months it was his chief preoccupation. The Grand Duke Constantine, although he knew much about the Polish society, was reluctant to admit its having any connection with the Russian rebels, and he avoided any special investigations. It was his opinion that all Polish conspiracies had been liquidated in 1822, the matter having been brought to an end by Lukasiński's trial in 1824, when the late Emperor's orders had put an end to further prosecutions. He did not even believe the St. Petersburg confessions concerning

[6] See *Zamoyski*, 1, 26-27; Cz.M.(F), 1, 42-43; Małachowski-Łempicki, "Wykaz Lóż" (Register of Polish Freemasonry) in *Archiwum Komisji Historycznej Polskiej Akademii*, 1930.

the contacts with the Polish conspirators; he explained that Russian culprits would like to let the Poles share their responsibility, or that there were always people eager to arouse suspicions in order to display their zeal. But the evidence proved too strong. The Grand Duke was forced to order arrests and interrogations, and he appointed a committee for the investigation of the case. In Dresden the aged General Kniaziewicz was arrested at the request of the Russians and his papers seized; the only important document was a copy of Alexander's letter to Kościuszko of May 3, 1814. Constantine then invited Nicholas to read the document, saying he would find there the explanation of the whole case of the Patriotic Society; could the Poles, after they had received such solemn pledges, act otherwise than they did? In another letter, when already informed about the facts actually disclosed, he did not exculpate the Poles, but insisted upon the difference between what the Russian conspirators had planned, and partly carried into execution, and the activities of the Poles; in fact the latter had refused to cooperate in an attempt to liquidate the Russian dynasty. He agreed, however, that the Polish conspirators must be tried, and he strongly emphasized the fact that Polish public opinion was unanimous in condemnation of them and that the Poles would be their most severe judges. He was inclined to proceed as in Lukasiński's case when without regard for the constitutional guarantees of habeas corpus he had ordered the trial of the defendants—military and civilian alike—by a court martial; he had thereby secured a sentence in conformity with his wishes. Now a prompt and severe verdict of a Polish court martial seemed to be the best defense against dangerous repercussions of the Decembrists' and the Patriotic Society's affair on the destinies of Poland.

But Nicholas unexpectedly proved more legalistic: he announced that those accused of high treason were to be tried according to the constitution by the High Court composed of the senate *in corpore*. On June 15, the day of the inauguration of the High Court, Czartoryski had a long talk with the Grand Duke. The latter was aggressive. He felt well equipped for the attack. As "head of the Imperial family" he received from Nicholas the most secret papers found in the private apartments and cases of the deceased Emperor and Empress. There were Czartoryski's letters in which he denounced Constantine's brutal extravagances and demanded his recall from Warsaw. There also were "little ones"—Prince Adam's letters to Elisabeth. This the Tsesarevich disclosed with brutal bonhomie to the Prince. He bitterly reproached the Poles for their nonsensical conspiracies and sterile political demonstrations, which he considered responsible for endangering the very existence of the Kingdom. He demanded that Czartoryski should bring the senate to reason and convince them of the necessity of condemning and punishing the accused; the more severity they showed, the better would they serve Poland.

Czartoryski was somewhat stunned by this rude shock, and his reply was given only a few days later in another talk. He told the Grand Duke the whole truth about the system of violence reigning in the country under the latter's auspices and control, about the secret police and counter-police, the espionage and denunciations, the arbitrary arrests in complete disregard of constitutional rights. He stated that this regime of arbitrary measures was undermining confidence, provoking suspicion as to the intentions of the sovereign, and generating hostility. Injustice could not be beneficial to nations in the long run. And here injustice had been done; it ought to be made good, and the right way should be to restore the western provinces to Poland.

Now Constantine was shocked and confused. He did not tell the Prince that he was arguing with his brother on that very matter—the rights of Poland and her reunion with Lithuania. But his language became more conciliatory and friendly. They parted on rather friendly terms; there was something like a "reconciliation in the late Emperor's shadow."[7] But that reconciliation had not implied agreement as to Czartoryski's part in the opening trial. His influence was rightly thought to be decisive. The president of the court, Voyvode Peter Bieliński, an elderly statesman much venerated but old and sick, looked for his advice and guidance, as did almost all of his colleagues. The general feeling

[7] S. Askenazy, "Dwie rozmowy w Belwederze," *Nowe Wczasy*, 1910, p. 450 sq. Diary of Countess Sophie Zamoyska (Prince Adam's sister), June 20, 1827 (L. Dębicki, *Puławy*, IV, 315).

was that this was a test case for the dignity of the senate and its independence in acting as High Court. They refused to rely upon the findings of the committee of investigation which had been set up by the Grand Duke's order. The case was investigated with a most scrupulous impartiality, and they established beyond a doubt the absence of any responsibility on the part of the Polish Secret Society for the December outbreak. They appeared responsible only for having as a final aim the independence and unity of Poland; some of the leaders could also be accused of not having disclosed to the government the plans of the Russian conspiracy.

The indictment accused the society of "a remote attempt at high treason." The Emperor was angry when reading that formula; it obviously reduced the guilt of the defendants. The Grand Duke, on the contrary, fully agreed with the indictment and with the wording "remote attempt"; he refused to see anything more in the affair, and he wrote to his brother: "There is not a Pole regardless of his opinions who would not firmly believe that his country had been robbed and not conquered by the Empress Catherina in the three partitions, and that she had done it by employing the most abject means, which should be shocking to every honest mind. . . ."[8]

He did not, however, admit the possibility of finding the defendants not guilty of the charge formulated with so much restraint. Thus he himself did his best to enforce his opinion upon the senators, and they were under continuous pressure from Novosiltsov, while some Polish dignitaries were busy persuading them to pronounce accordingly.

The verdict was pronounced on May 22, 1828. By thirty votes to one, the High Court declared that the Secret Society "not having been a conspiracy in the meaning of the 67th Article of the Penal Code, the participation in that society does not make a remote attempt of high treason." For participation in an illicit society and for having failed to disclose the Russian conspiracy to the authorities, the chief defendant, Lieutenant-Colonel Severin Krzyżanowski was sentenced to three years imprisonment, some of his companions to minor penalties.

[8] Constantine to Nicholas, Dec. 12, 1827 (*Sbornik*, CXXXI, 204-206).

The Grand Duke reacted by a violent outburst of anger and indignation. In his letters to the Tsar he indulged in abuse of the "stupid and silly senate" and in denouncing the "wretchedness of the senate and its president," Bieliński, for his motivation of the sentence (Constantine knew perfectly that it was written by Czartoryski although he did not mention it). But when Nicholas answered—after some delay—that the president of the court should be tried for high treason, the Grand Duke quite sensibly explained that this *triste individu* could not be tried by the same court which had adhered to his opinion; if he was acquitted, who would try the judges? Thus he suggested that a "mercuriale" should be administered to the senate and especially to the president, to annul the sentence and to order the trial of the defendants by a special court.[9]

In the meantime he inflicted upon the senate a kind of garrison arrest, by forbidding them to leave the town. They remained quasi-interned for a year.

But Nicholas regarded the suggested solution as unsatisfactory; he now requested the condemnation of the High Court by the Council of Administration (i.e., the government). The council was ordered to establish whether the verdict of the senate had been prompted by a wrong idea as to the meaning of the term "high treason," or by a feeling of solidarity with the criminal activities, or—he still allowed an excuse—was it due to faulty legislation?

The council was ready to dissociate itself from the hazardous stand of the senate, but it was not inclined to condemn it, nor to suggest a far-reaching alteration of the existing law. After long discussions, in spite of Novosiltsov's efforts and Constantine's pressure, they agreed to make a scapegoat of Novosiltsov himself, who was responsible for the alleged faulty and misleading wording of the royal decree on the proceedings of the court.

There now followed a violent clash between Constantine and Novosiltsov on one side, and the council and the whole of public opinion on the other. The Emperor addressed stern rebukes to the president of the council, old Voyvode Sobolewski, and to

[9] Constantine to Nicholas, May 22, June 2 and 13, July 24, Sept. 5; Nicholas to Constantine, Aug. 23, 1828 (*Sbornik*, cxxxi, 227-258).

the Minister of Finance, Xavier Lubecki, who had been mainly responsible for the government's attitude and report, and had acted in close concert with Czartoryski. But the Tsar did not like to go too far, and he was rather inclined to let the crisis subside. He was now committed to his war against Turkey, which was neither easy nor costless; his army was dwindling from hardship, misery, and disease, and decisive results were still to be achieved by renewed efforts. He looked for Polish reinforcements and asked his brother to send him one division, but he met with a rebuff. He appeared to agree with the Tsesarevich's arguments, but was in fact offended and upset; the relations between them suffered badly.

The Tsar presented Warsaw with Turkish guns captured at Varna (where the Polish and Hungarian king, Vladislaus, had been defeated and killed in 1444) in order to commemorate the fact that "the Russian army with the Polish king at its head avenged the death of a Polish king." The compliment was not meant to please the Grand Duke since he had strongly opposed the war in general and in particular any participation of Polish or Lithuanian troops.[10] Now he was aware of impending changes in the status of the Lithuanian army corps and of the probability of his being deprived of its command. There are even some indications that Nicholas at that time considered removing his brother and Novosiltsov from Warsaw; there were people who suggested that if the Poles were granted such a favor, they would even put up with the absorption of the eastern provinces by Russia.[11]

The long-delayed decision of the sovereign was at last an-

[10] Nicholas to Constantine, June 21, Oct. 13, and Constantine to Nicholas, June 27, 1828, Jan. 7, 1829 (*Sbornik*, cxxxi, 239-242, 258-260).

[11] For the trial of the patriotic society by the High Court and its implications, see S. Askenazy in *The Cambridge Modern History*, and M. Handelsman in *The Cambridge History of Poland*. The most important documents, in addition to the correspondence of Lubecki, ed. S. Smolka, Cracow, 1909, iii, iv. The new monograph of that statesman, Jan Zdzitowiecki *Xiąże Minister Xawery Drucki-Lubecki*, Warsaw, 1948, gives an interpretation of the latter's policy somewhat influenced by recent developments. L. Sapieha, *Wspomnienia* (Memoirs), 1913, pp. 82 sq., recorded in 1828 an utterance of the Russian chief of political police, Count Benckendorff: "There is not any bear which could not be tamed; yours [i.e., the Tsesarevich] is an exception; you never will succeed."

nounced by a royal rescript of March 26, 1829. The verdict of the senate was confirmed. Two of the defendants (both Polish officers, but Russian subjects) were to be handed over to the Russian authorities, to be tried by Russian courts; Krzyżanowski was one of them. All the others were released. The senate was punished by a royal reprimand. The Emperor now decided to go to Warsaw and to accomplish at last the ceremony of his coronation as king of Poland—an action which he had thought unnecessary and even nonsensical before.

The senate listened to the royal message in deadly silence. The crisis was over and it ended with a moral victory for the senate and for the constitutional order in the Kingdom. It was as well a personal success for Czartoryski, and a disastrous defeat for the Grand Duke, who was repudiated at the same time by both the Poles and the Tsar.

The great historian of that period, Askenazy, had some doubts about Polish policy at that crucial moment. Would it not have been preferable for Czartoryski to have supported the Grand Duke and to have influenced him? Certainly, the former heir presumptive of both the Russian and Polish crowns, the designated though never nominated viceroy of Poland, infatuated by his love for his Polish wife, for his Polish and Lithuanian troops, and for Poland itself, now in disgrace and quarreling with the Tsar for the existence of the Kingdom and its union with Lithuania, could have been a strong trumpcard for the Poles to play. This trumpcard was lost not only because the Poles were unaware of the Tsesarevich's real feelings and intentions. His own conduct had made him definitely appear as a tyrant to all the Polish people. From the first days of his residence in Warsaw he had played the part of a lightning-conductor, attracting and accumulating all the hatred against Russian control in Poland. Obstinately adhering to Novosiltsov as his partner and adviser, he by that very fact estranged Czartoryski; moreover, as far as he was concerned, Prince Adam now became a state criminal. After a stormy conversation at the time of the trial, the Prince broke off his relations with the Grand Duke.[12] The case of Constantine and Poland was already tragically entangled and nearing the final catastrophe.

[12] *Zamoyski*, I, 220-221.

CHAPTER 12

CZARTORYSKI'S TREATISE
ON DIPLOMACY

BEFORE returning as statesman to the political scene, Prince
Adam—as mentioned above—had expounded his political creed
in a comprehensive and elaborated treatise entitled *Essay on
Diplomacy*. It was ready for print early in 1827, but appeared
late in 1830, well after the July revolution, as *Manuscript of a
Philhellene*, introduced by a rather strange and misleading fore-
word by the editor, M. Toulouzan.[1]

There were only a few of Prince Adam's contemporaries who
had heard about the Grand Design of the early years of his
political career, about his idea of reviving the old plan attributed
by Sully in his memoirs to Henry IV, and founding a "République de Sully" of united European nations under the common
auspices of England and Russia. That idea became, probably from
1803 at the latest, a favorite one of the young emperor and of
his few friends, and in 1804 it was systematically expounded as
a coherent political plan by Czartoryski as acting Foreign Minister
in Alexander's secret instructions for Novosiltsov's mission to
London. It has been explained above how their ideas of the
natural rights of nations, of natural equilibrium, supranational
organization, and collective security conflicted with the British
policy of security achieved in the first place by reestablishing the
balance of power. In spite of his failure in carrying through his
plan when it was sponsored and signed by Alexander as Russian
Emperor, Czartoryski adhered to his idea; his treatise was a broad
theoretical commentary on his old plan, connected by remarks on
the past, present, and future of European politics.

He quoted Montesquieu's sentence: "The laws of nature are
above all other laws," and he bitterly accused diplomacy of hav-

---

[1] *Essai sur la Diplomatie. Manuscrit d'un Philhellène, publié par M. Toulouzan.*
Paris-Marseille, 1830.

ing violated the former; he denounced the evil which diplomacy had done by uniting hypocrisy with violence. "The policy which is responsible for settling relations between nations was mostly an inexorable enemy of mankind and the main author of its misfortunes."

In his historical survey, Czartoryski displayed a great deal of that optimism peculiar to the 18th-century philosophers and historians when speaking of more remote times; he even praised the honesty and sense of justice of the monarchs of the ancient Orient, in contrast to the practice of more recent epochs. He extolled the alleged generosity and fairness of the policy of the early Romans; he accused Cato Maior of having despoiled Rome of honesty and pity—Rome had a heavy price to pay later for having forsaken the principles of humanity and righteousness. He emphasized the enormous influence of Christianity in history: "Equality before the Lord involved equality before the law. . . . Christianity leveled human vanities and elevated goodness and sacrifice only. . . . It even changed into positive law the natural law, uniting mankind. . . ." But there followed a sharp criticism of the Vatican's policy: it was not always inspired by the spirit of love and self-sacrifice; the secular power of the Popes affected the policy and made it dependent upon secular expediency. Czartoryski hinted at the necessity for the papacy to reconcile its policy with the future unity of Italy.

Prince Adam paid tribute to the Treaty of Westphalia, which became for a century a "political code for Europe"; we remember that in 1804 he emphasized the necessity of creating an even more stable work. There followed an indictment against the diplomacy of the following centuries for having pursued a policy of sanguinary conquest under the pretext of European equilibrium, for having adopted the principle: "You take, but let me take also." He attacked the idea of a division of Europe into two spheres of influence of two powers, as had been attempted at Tilsit. With much force he exposed the disastrous consequences for European policies of Poland's partitions: moral decay, solidarity of the participants which constantly revealed itself at the time of Napoleon and survived his fall, "so powerful and durable are the bonds of a common crime." That solidarity had been an obstacle to the generous intentions of some sovereigns, who were not themselves guilty of the crimes of their predecessors; they "constantly had before their eyes the specter of Poland arising from her tomb."

The few pages concerning the Congress of Vienna are written with much restraint in spite of Prince Adam's bitter feelings in connection with the attitude of the western powers towards Poland. He preferred to strike at Pradt's assertions concerning the issues which were at stake in Vienna and his view that "policy is a thing quite separate from religion and morality." He also attacked Kant's view that the recognition of the *status quo* should be the basis of eternal peace. The spoliations committed in Europe were also comprised in the *status quo*, which the Holy Alliance tried to stabilize forever. "A peace which sanctions lawlessness cannot be an eternal peace."

There followed a systematic exposition of Czartoryski's own theory. He assumed that nations had a deeply founded natural right to an independent existence. If a nation was not independent, it meant that it had been despoiled of its freedom by an unjust action, which had no value before the natural law. No nation should be master of another. All nations must submit to the common law of mankind, to the principles of justice and equity. This was the point of view from which the main international problems were to be surveyed. A striking example of Czartoryski's ideas is found in his remarks about India. With Warren Hasting's trial (to which he once listened) still in his memory, he denounced the monstrosity of the rule of a trading company over such an immense country; but he fully realized the enormous complexity of its problems and the responsibilities which the British government necessarily would have to assume before a new, united, and regenerated Indian nation could arise. That nation, he foretold, would be attached to Britain by bonds of grateful memory of the good works achieved and freedom restored; while an obstinate and unjust opposition to the emancipation of India, when already prompted by the "march of time" and by the progress of civilization, could break those bonds forever.[2]

[2] See *Essai*, 1830, pp. 198-200, 253-254.

The same applied to the problems of other colonies: once their people reached a certain degree of national consciousness and sense of unity, they should be granted a national existence. When reading the treatise we feel very near to the actual developments of 120 years later, and Prince Adam's book seems to defy the march of time. To the principle of monarchical legitimism, which had been cynically misused by Talleyrand in Vienna, the principle of the legitimism of nations should be opposed, "the oldest, most evident and most respectable one." The natural form of the "civil existence" of a nation was its own state, which was its property sanctioned by centuries of existence; no other nation had the right to destroy it. Czartoryski dismissed contemptuously the pretence of subordinating the rights of nations to geographical conveniences or to the interests of great powers. In a series of chapters he tried to explain why conscience must prevail in the counsels of European cabinets, why nations like individuals must submit to the natural law, why injustice to nations did not pay, and why a state built up by robbery must sooner or later drink from the cup from which it had made others drink. He hinted at Napoleon's fate in order to emphasize the vanity of all that is not virtue; to be invincible—in Prince Adam's view—Napoleon had needed only equity and goodness. He would have won the war of 1812 if he had aimed at the restoration of Poland instead of the destruction of Russia.

Particularly striking are Czartoryski's remarks about the consequences of the enslaving of nations by great powers. For Austria her domination of Italy was only a nuisance and a source of weakness; for Russia, the domination of Poland was a curse for herself, the cause of her corruption and internal decomposition. Political slavery poisoned the life of a nation; it produced mutual hatred, it corrupted the characters of both—the subjugators and the subjugated.

When monarchs appealed to the peoples against Napoleon, they promised them their liberation. In Vienna there remained but vague declarations about the prosperity and security of Europe and the world, mere phrases without any defined value— *vox, vox, preterea nihil*, and nothing had since been done for the

subjugated nations. Only the struggle of the Greeks for their independence managed to shake the conscience of Europe.

Czartoryski's ordeal in 1814-1815 left him highly critical of
Britain's foreign policy, and a special chapter about it reads like
an indictment: England's rights were imbued with the spirit of
liberty, humanity, and equity, but her foreign policy sometimes
displayed iniquity and ruthless ambitions. Her insular position
involved her opposition to the Continent's most aggressive power,
and her struggle against Napoleon had been "long and magnanimous"; she had "fought alone for the independence of
Europe against all subjugated Europe." But, after Napoleon's
fall, England no longer felt bound to ensure the freedom of the
Continent, and she did not realize the great benefits of her position. "She allowed a new arrangement of the Continent to be
made, without even pronouncing the word 'justice,' without
showing any interest for the rights of the weak and without
taking the trouble of forwarding the principle of the rights of
nations and of reconstructing Europe on stable foundations."
She proved that she had a Christian approach to the problem of
the slave trade, but an incredible indifference with regard to the
fate of Continental nations, and she still displayed indifference
when the freedom of nations was being violated by new encroachments.[3]

Czartoryski postulated for every nation the necessary conditions
of its separate existence: the guarantees of its independence, the
frontiers and outlets indispensable for its defense and its trade,
freedom to institute a government reflecting public opinion so as
to enable it to take part as a moral being in the great society of
peoples. Since the situation of that time was in sharp contrast
with that postulate, it was necessary to change it by a farseeing
policy imbued with tolerance, and a spirit of conciliation and
moderation. Wars were to be avoided, but intervention became
a duty if a nation was being subjugated by armed violence. Unions
and federations were recommended as measures of expediency
in many cases; but attention was drawn to the instability of such
solutions in the case of excessive disproportion of power between

[3] *Essai*, pp. 285-292: "De la Diplomatie de l'Angleterre."

the partners; in such a situation, the freedom of the smaller nation would depend upon the good or ill will of the stronger. The last remarks clearly hint at the actual situation of the Kingdom of Poland.

Czartoryski's program for a united Europe was expounded as a new version of Sully's Grand Design, which allegedly had been Henry IV's own and which had won Queen Elizabeth's approbation and King James I's support. It had been a plan for reshaping Europe by the concerted action of France and England along the lines of equity and solidarity of the peoples who were linked by their adherence to Western Christendom. The immediate purpose was to dispose of the Hapsburg supremacy and their world-wide domination by building up a powerful league and dismembering both the Austrian and the Spanish empires into independent national states or federations. There was the suggestion of a German federation (excluding Austria), of an Italian federation presided over by the Pope (an idea which was to become almost a reality in 1847-1848), of independent kingdoms of Hungary and Bohemia, of the inclusion of the Commonwealth of Poland as the eastern support of the whole structure (Muscovite Tsardom should either join or be left outside the European system); the Christian population subjugated by the Turks should be liberated by the common effort of the European league, and a Res Publica Christiana completed with a supreme council and a society of Amphictyons, and common armed forces. Czartoryski's suggestion in his treatise did not greatly differ: he strongly criticized the Hapsburg monarchy as an agglomeration of diverse lands and elements achieved by dynastic policy without any natural foundations; he pleaded for the independent existence of united Italy, a Bohemia and a Hungary, and for a reconstruction of a German federation without Austria; the map of Europe he thus drafted was surprisingly like the map of the Treaty of Versailles. His remarks with regard to Prussia were rather cautious; he admitted the possibility of the evolution of that rapacious and aggressive power on peaceful and liberal lines. It was one of the great illusions of the second quarter of the 19th century.

Following Sully's suggestions further, he advocated (as in his

Secret Instructions of 1804) the founding of a league of nations as a safeguard of equity and justice in international relations and of collective security.

He recalled the part which Poland had played in the 17th century's Grand Design, and the radical change in the European scene caused by the appearance of the Russian Empire with its pressure upon Poland, Sweden, and Turkey. He recalled also the great ideas of Alexander I (mostly his own) as being kindred to those of Sully and Henry IV; and he discreetly hinted at the necessity of a concerted policy of the two western powers and the possibility of winning Russia over to their plans—of changing, one could read, an entente cordiale into a triple entente. Thus, if compared with the plan of 1804, the point of gravity was shifted now to the West, the solidarity of the western powers recognized as a keystone; but Russia was not yet excluded as a powerful partner.

There were in Czartoryski's treatise a great many concepts which were to become embodied in world policy only two or three generations later.

As to the immediate future of the Kingdom of Poland, the treatise was rather reticent. There was a discreet warning of a possible crisis, and a still more discreet hint at the eventual necessity of revising the Vienna decisions concerning Poland's union with Russia. How far Prince Adam's ideas with regard to the future of his country were already influenced by his apprehensions and disappointments is to be seen when reading the allusion to a Prusso-Polish personal union as one of the possible solutions of the Polish problem—in connection with the alleged liberalism of Prussian policy and with the necessity for Poland of recovering her access to the Baltic. The treatise seems carefully to avoid any special emphasis on Polish problems, although it clearly hints at their crucial importance. It tries to appear genuinely as a work of a cosmopolite Philhellene.

It had been written before the *status quo* established in Vienna had been shaken by the Russo-Turkish war, and before Nicholas' approach to the Polish and European problems had revealed itself in his political moves. It had been written with some restraint, assuming a temporary stability of the political conditions in Europe rather than revolutionary changes in the next future. When it appeared in print, revolutions seemed to be shattering the whole European *status quo*, and much of what was told in the book about current political issues seemed outdated by recent developments. The outlines of a new European order, as drafted in the essay, were going much too far for that and for the coming generation of politicians; there prevailed in the treatise rather universal ideas, when it was immediate political solutions which were being sought. Czartoryski's name would have given much publicity to his book; but for good reasons it was carefully camouflaged, and even in the new situation, when Prince Adam was engaged in an open struggle against the Tsar, he was prevented for reasons of political expediency from revealing the identity of the author of the essay. There was too much plain talk about Austria and about Napoleon, whose legend became so powerful in France in the thirties.

So the book passed almost unnoticed and it still remains little known to the historians of 19th-century political ideas. It deserves to be recalled at a time when all the great issues involved in Czartoryski's Grand Design are at stake.

CHAPTER 13

LEADER OF THE OPPOSITION

BEING a thoroughly liberal statesman, Prince Adam was accustomed to act and to strive by argument and persuasion, winning over supporters, coming to terms with partners and making political friends, inspiring public opinion in his own country and appealing to that in foreign lands. He believed in the possibility of achieving real progress by evolutionary changes, yet he was far from being a revolutionary. At this time, in 1829-1830, he was actually the leader of his nation in the struggle for its rights, but he was still trying to win the battle by peaceful means. His popularity was greater than ever before. His nephew, the young lieutenant Ladislas Zamoyski, wrote to his mother: "My uncle faced the disgrace of public opinion for long years and he proved right, but he does not regard its present favors as an affair of major importance to him."[1] Important it certainly was for the cause of Poland's freedom.

When Nicholas I came to Warsaw in May 1829 for his coronation, the pupils of the Infantry Cadet School and some of the younger members of the Patriotic Society planned a military attempt against him, which would be the signal for a general insurrection. Little was known even to contemporaries about that "coronation plot," which some years later was to be the subject of one of the most outstanding works of Polish dramatic poetry.[2] But it had been more than a poetic fiction. Some of its participants were, even many years later, firmly convinced that they had needed only a word from Czartoryski or Bielinski to dispose of the Tsar and that then the whole country would have taken up arms. They still resented Prince Adam's intervention in directing the old poet Niemcewicz, whom they had approached, to dissuade them from their plan.

[1] *Zamoyski*, 1, 348.
[2] J. Słowacki, *Kordian*, 1883.

Leader of the Opposition

Czartoryski himself explained the history of the plot in his biography of Niemcewicz. The idea of "some young people" had been "to seize the whole imperial family and to start a general insurrection"; they thought that it would throw the Russian government into complete confusion and anarchy, the more so as the war against Turkey had not yet been brought to an end and was not progressing satisfactorily. "The moment was certainly much more favorable than the one chosen at the end of the following year. The young people approached Niemcewicz to ask his advice, as they relied upon his wisdom and patriotism. They asked him whether they ought to risk a deed which could not be achieved without violence, bloodshed, and the endangering of innocent people who had believed in the generosity of the Poles. Niemcewicz dissuaded them from an undertaking which would have been stigmatized in history as an act of treason and cruelty, and, I think, he was right and acted as a sensible and righteous man. The conditions were certainly favorable for starting an insurrection; but it would have been wrong to start by a ruthless, inconsiderate, and treacherous action, which would have provoked the indignation and horror of the Russians and of other peoples, and would have drawn upon Poland Russia's and her allies' forces eager to avenge the deed, as well as Poland's condemnation by the whole world. Our nation, if it had sought its salvation by means of perjury and cruelty, would have acted contrary to its own character, and that never succeeds; it would have spoiled the purity of its cause, the generosity and righteousness of which are the only elements of its superiority and power. By preventing it, Niemcewicz preserved Poland from greater and more severe calamities than those which she was to experience before long and which would have not been mitigated by the respect and sympathy of other peoples, but aggravated by their aversion."[3]

In fact, the attempt would most probably have provoked the destruction of Poland by the joint forces of the three powers of partition, with the embarrassed approval of the West. Besides, it seems that the conspiracy was at that time not very widespread

[3] A. Czartoryski, *Żywot J. U. Niemcewicza*, Paris, 1860, pp. 216-217.

nor the revolutionary tendencies—not to be identified with the spirit of opposition—really strong. Elderly statesmen were not to be expected to take the lead in such a risky and immature undertaking.[4]

During Nicholas' sojourn in Warsaw, Prince Adam remained in the background. It was his brother-in-law, Stanislas Zamoyski, the president of the senate, who had long conversations with the Emperor in Prince Lubecki's presence and who exposed the wrong done by the Tsesarevich and Novosiltsov; he even dared to intercede for Lukasinski's release from jail, and Lubecki's opinion was that the Emperor could not be told about the situation either more frankly or more convincingly. Nicholas made it clear that he would do nothing against his brother; but both Polish statesmen had the impression that there was a possibility of appeal to him with regard to the legal status of the country. On the other hand, they took notice of the emphasis he laid on the limitation imposed by his duty as Russian emperor; he even hinted at Alexander's having transgressed those limits. It became evident that the matter of reuniting the eight provinces with the Kingdom could not even be approached. But the constitutional order in the Kingdom seemed somewhat more secure now, and the Seym, which, contrary to the constitution, had not been convoked since 1825, was now to assemble the next year.[5]

Zamoyski now stood for caution and restraint until better times. He suggested that Prince Adam should take part in the council of administration (he had never attended its meetings).[6] It was not possible for Czartoryski to commit himself as participant of a government acting under the actual control of the Grand Duke and of Novosiltsov. But he agreed with Zamoyski's opinion that political manifestations and protestations were to be avoided and rights were to be vindicated with moderation, without provoking the autocrat, who ought to be gradually habituated to constitutional government and reconciled with the representational system.

[4] See S. Askenazy in *The Cambridge Modern History*, x, 464-466, and W. Tokarz in *Polska, jej dzieje i kultura* (ed. S. Lam), iii.

[5] For the political talks with Nicholas, see *Zamoyski*, i, 279-288.

[6] *Op.cit.*, i, 307-308, 328-329.

Leader of the Opposition

Czartoryski directed the proceedings of the Seym of 1830 along those lines. He was summoned by the Emperor immediately after the latter's arrival, received "with rare favor," and assured of the sovereign's best intentions. The Emperor allowed free discussion in the Seym and "even the submission of grievances."[7] "The Seym," thus reads an entry in young Zamoyski's memoirs, "displayed its independent spirit, but it also gave unquestionable proofs of prudence and moderation." The opposition of public opinion to the arbitrary regime was expressed by objective criticism. In some cases there was a danger of Nicholas' violent reactions, especially when the Seym rejected—not for the first time—the government's bill altering the articles of the Code Napoleon with regard to the marriage law. There had been since 1818 consecutive attempts at a partial restoration of the authority of the clergy in cases of divorce, attempts which had met a fierce and obstinate opposition of the "enlightened" opinion and of the successive Chambers of Deputies, while the Catholic hierarchy in initiating the proposal and the government in trying to enforce the new law were strongly supported by both successive Emperors, the Tsesarevich and Novosiltsov. The Tsar was furious; but the Polish statesmen succeeded in persuading him that such incidents were quite usual in constitutional regimes and that the rejection of a law did not mean rebellion against the sovereign.

Thus he also deigned to have some petitions of political importance submitted to him, i.e., one asking for Lukasiński's liberation. He behaved "as if he had guessed how to deal with Poles."[8]

He accepted with correct objectivity the report of the senate, a critical survey of the administration of the country since 1825, and in fact for the whole period since the creation of the Kingdom. The report, which was mostly Czartoryski's own work, drew attention to the extravagances of bureaucracy and the hypertrophy of centralism. It insisted upon the restitution of the Kalisz provincial council, which had had its functions illegally suspended since 1822. It demanded the implementation of the article of the constitution on the voting of the budget by the

[7] J. U. Niemcewicz, *Pamiętnik z 1830-31*, 1909, p. 20.
[8] J. U. Niemcewicz, *Pamiętnik*, p. 25; *Zamoyski*, I, 332-339.

Seym. It suggested giving to the council of state a proper part in the preparation of laws and recommended that in certain cases social organizations should be consulted in governmental and legal matters. Emphasis was laid upon the unsatisfactory situation of the schools and the decline of public education. The restitution of the freedom of the press was asked for; if the sovereign had decided to maintain the censorship, then most honorable and enlightened men should be entrusted with it. Problems of economy and social life were discussed in the same spirit of liberalism and freedom of private enterprise. Reform of the situation of the Jews was urged, but the greatest attention was given to the problem of the peasants.[9]

The extreme gravity of the peasant problem had been clearly seen by Prince Adam since he had worked toward a kingdom of Poland. He regarded its solution as his duty, and he had promised Kościuszko to achieve it. He recognized that the peasants were equal as men; he felt strongly that the system of field service must cease and that it should be superseded by a system of rents enabling the peasants to acquire the ownership of the land gradually. At the time when the Kingdom was being organized, the question was put before the departmental (provincial) councils. There was a hostile reaction against any reform on those lines, and there were even bitter attacks on the rather dubious personal freedom that the peasants had been granted by Napoleon in 1807. Since Czartoryski's part in the government came to an end a few months after, the solution of the problem of land reform was beyond his scope; however, he gave an example on his own estates of the regulation of the peasants' conditions and duties along liberal and humanitarian lines.

The liberal opinion of the Kingdom, though very sensitive to any governmental encroachments when constitutional liberties were at stake, and ready to risk a crisis most dangerous to the very existence of the state in defense of the liberal marriage law, was much less concerned about the day-to-day brutal violations of the rights and human dignity of the peasant masses. The peasants were abandoned to the arbitrary misrule of the landowners,

---

[9] The report of the senate of 1830 was analyzed and the identity of its author disclosed by Handelsman, I, 140-143.

who had the administrative authority over them, and to a most ruthless exploitation by the services imposed upon them.[10] With regard to this problem, the senate, though politically rather moderate, displayed much more understanding of the necessities of the time and of patriotic duty than the Chamber of Deputies, where only a few isolated voices demanding justice for the people were heard.

In the remarks of the senate, Czartoryski observed that no improvement had resulted from the government's good intentions toward the peasants. They were ruined as before by the "extraordinary tax" and the "general obligatory work for the state." For fifteen years the government had not made the slightest attempt to improve and stabilize the peasants' situation; nothing had been done even on the national estates that could prove a useful example and inspiration to the private estate owners. The senate recommended "that most salutary measure for the people's and country's welfare" to the special solicitude of the king.

King Nicholas departed from his Polish capital in a rather conciliatory mood. The constitutional order now seemed considerably stabilized, but there were indications of threatening dangers. When Stanislas Zamoyski tried to persuade the chancellor Nesselrode and the powerful chief of the political police, Count Benckendorf, that the rule of the Grand Duke and Novosiltsov must end before it would be too late, Nesselrode replied by asking him if he did not think that it was already too late. Some people from the Emperor's entourage did not conceal their opinion that a revolutionary outbreak in Poland would be regarded by many Russians as a desirable opportunity for putting an end to the separate existence of the Kingdom, that unnecessary and dangerous invention of Alexander.[11]

Therefore Czartoryski was not inclined to promote an armed uprising, and he did not even consider it a possibility until the French July Revolution had shaken the whole of Western Europe

[10] See Z. Kirkor-Kiedroniowa, *Włościanie i ich prawa w dobie konstytucyjnej i organizacyjnej Królestwa Polskiego* (The Peasants and Their Rights at the Period of the Constitutional Organization of the Kingdom of Poland), 1912, especially pp. 206 ff., 363, 393-394.

[11] *Zamoyski*, I, 351-352.

and occasioned Nicholas' plans for an armed intervention. The victory of the tricolor in France electrified many Poles, and the military conspiracy existing since 1828 in the Infantry Cadet School was now expanding and absorbing or contacting all the remaining elements of the former secret societies. It is not quite clear to what extent they were linked with the French conspiracies; a few years before, the Patriotic Society had had contacts with the French Underground through the channel of General Charles Kniaziewicz, living in Dresden. New links had certainly been established later, possibly through young Leonard Chodźko, who, while residing for several years in Paris, had made friends among leading Carbonari, and had emerged as Lafayette's aide-de-camp during the *trois glorieuses*. It was Szymon Askenazy's conjecture that Chodźko was the link between the Paris Underground authorities and the Warsaw conspiracy, and that the invitation to rise up in arms came in that way. The leader of the military conspiracy, Lieutenant Peter Wysocki, had some doubts whether the moment was the right one and whether there was in fact any chance of success. His influence was soon matched by that of the stronger and more ruthless personality of Lieutenant Joseph Zaliwski, who was undoubtedly a Carbonari and possibly a plenipotentiary of the Vente Suprême in Paris, of which he was to become a member immediately after the Polish revolution. The problem of the interdependence of the revolutionary activities in both countries was never elucidated, and it is doubtful if evidence about it is still available, especially after the catastrophe which befell the Polish collections in 1939 and 1944.

Nicholas was badly shaken by the Paris revolution, although he strongly condemned the illegal acts of Charles X. He immediately ordered all leaves to be cancelled and put the army on a war footing. Constantine was warned that if the war started he would be the first to march with the Polish army and the Lithuanian army corps; further army corps would join him. He was by no means delighted by that prospect; he strongly protested against starting a war, insisted upon the necessity of leave for soldiers who had already served their terms, and calculated the time necessary for the mobilization at three months. What mattered even more, the King of Prussia, who was invited to join in Russia's intended armed intervention, was not eager to do so. Furthermore, assurances had already come from Paris about the peaceful intentions of the Duke d'Orléans and both England and Austria had recognized the new state of things in France, and even Prussia followed.

There was some wavering in Nicholas' bellicose intentions. Appeasement seemed most probable when the outbreak of the Belgian insurrection and proclamation of independence came as a new shock, and provoked his decision to go to war; the allies should be forced to join. The Tsesarevich tried in vain to dissuade his brother from risking war; he emphasized the progress of liberal ideas in Europe, hinted at the general hostility which would be provoked by Russian intervention, and even quoted Alexander's words from the manifesto at the outbreak of the 1812 war: "God will be against the aggressor."

In October orders were given for the mobilization, and the most distant corps were ordered to move to the western provinces. The Emperor now informed his brother that there was almost no possibility of avoiding war; he expressed his peremptory will that Constantine himself should march at the head of his forces even if they were not entirely ready. At first Nicholas wanted to give him the supreme command of the whole army; when he proved reluctant (and loudly declared to the people around him that waging war was not his business), Fieldmarshal Count Diebitsch Zabalkansky was designated as commander in chief of the Russian army. He was expected to establish his army headquarters in Warsaw, and he went to Berlin to concert military operations with Prussia. The final term for the mobilization of the Polish and Lithuanian troops was to be determined by him; instead, he let the Grand Duke know that according to King Frederick William's opinion, he ought to mobilize the Lithuanian corps only, not the Polish army. This news annoyed the Emperor; it would be an insult to the Poles, a sign of his distrust. On November 6 he ordered the newspapers to publish an official communiqué of the military measures he had taken and enumerating the forces to be mobilized, the Polish army included. Now he enforced his definite decision to have the Polish army ready for operations by December 22.[12]

In the meantime, the news of an impending war, of an expedition of the Polish army and of the establishment of the Russian army base in the Kingdom, was widely spread among the Poles. Even those abiding by the union with Russia were now aware of the dangers of a protracted Russian occupation and a military government; there seemed to remain little hope of later recovering the political institutions of the Kingdom. In addition, the prospect of fighting against the French, who had been for many years brothers-in-arms with the Poles, or against the Belgians, fighting for their freedom, seemed intolerable to the Polish troops and to the Polish youth.

The conspirators were determined to prevent such developments by their own action. The date for the outbreak had been decided upon: October 18 or 20. The news about a relaxation of international tension induced the conspirators to postpone the date until the following spring. But in the second half of October rumors of the dispute between Nicholas and Constantine on the mobilization caused much agitation among the conspirators and renewed discussions as to the proper date for action.

Prince Adam was too experienced a diplomat to ignore the fact that the outbreak of a Polish insurrection would automatically remove any danger of a European war by preventing Russia from intervening in the west; France would feel secure and keep quiet, Prussia would be released from waging a war she disliked, and Poland would be left alone.[13] On October 23 he was invited to talk with the Grand Duke, who now longed for his help in maintaining tranquillity in the country. Most prob-

---

[12] For the successive decisions of Nicholas I, see T. Schiemann, *Geschichte Russlands*, 1913, III, 13-44; N. Schilder, *Imperator Nikolay I*, 1903, II, 307-320, 577-579. The State Secretary to Lubecki, Oct. 21, see Angeberg, pp. 769-770, and S. Smolka, *Korespondencja Lubeckiego*, III, 384-385. Nicholas' correspondence with Constantine in *Sbornik*, CXXXII, 35-93. *Zamoyski*, I, 279, 352. Also see M. Kukiel, "La Révolution de Novembre 1830 en Pologne et la Révolution de Juillet," *Revue internationale d'histoire politique et constitutionnelle*, 1953, No. 11.

[13] There is a letter of Ladislas Zamoyski to Mlle. d'Arnaud (his and Prince Adam's agent de liaison in Paris to French liberals), Dec. 16, showing such a view of the situation (*Zamoyski*, II, 24-26). See also L. Sapieha, *Wspomnienia*, 1913, pp. 111-112.

ably Prince Adam stiffened Constantine's opposition to mobilizing the Polish army—it might provoke a revolutionary outbreak. He recommended restraint in seeking out conspiracies; they should not be put, as in 1794, in a desperate situation out of which there would not be any issue other than to strike.

He was informed about the conspiracy by Ladislas Zamoyski.[14] His nearest collaborators, young intellectuals, his secretary, and his son's tutor, Hipolit Błotnicki and his librarian, the poet Charles Sienkiewicz, also had many friends among the most active group of the secret association, knew much about it, and kept the Prince informed. Some years later, when a prisoner in an Austrian jail, Zaliwski confessed that the conspirators' intention was to put Czartoryski at the head of the government and Chłopicki at the head of the army, and that both of them had been approached. But Prince Adam denied such rumors when he stated in a public speech: "I had not been asked from any side for counsel, nobody confided to me the undertaking, nor was the need of a general leadership discussed."[15] But it was quite possible that Błotnicki or Sienkiewicz had talks with Joachim Lelewel, who at that time was already the spiritual head of the revolutionaries and most probably (as later in Paris and Brussels) the chief of Polish Carbonarism. Prince Adam certainly suggested that they should wait and see how the European situation would develop. In the last days of October he left for Puławy.

Early in November two of the members of the conspiracy revealed to the Grand Duke and to the secret police a large part of its organization and undertakings and some of its leaders. Constantine reluctantly appointed a committee for investigation headed by General Count Stanislas Potocki, a noble-minded man and a patriot. The investigation proceeded without haste and in a most humane way, but much was disclosed. On November 15 Constantine reported the results and implored Nicholas for grace, or at least for indulgence towards the guilty. In spite of the pressure from many sides for action, he procrastinated over seizing the ringleaders. On November 17 Niemcewicz wrote to Prince Adam with visible anxiety; he feared that Nicholas' impetuous

[14] *Zamoyski*, I, 362-364.
[15] The speech of Nov. 29, 1841: A. Czartoryski, *Mowy*, 1847, p. 47.

reactions might precipitate the course of events, and added: "Our sovereign would like waging war, but his more prudent brother tries to stop him."[16] When writing, he had not yet seen the communiqué of November 6. Its publication in Warsaw had been delayed by the Grand Duke; it appeared in all newspapers on November 18 and 19; so it became generally known that the Poles were to march to fight against their French comrades-in-arms and against the cause of freedom.[17]

Czartoryski perceived the gravity of the situation and immediately returned to Warsaw. Once more he advised Constantine to avoid reprisals and to delay mobilization; once more he tried indirectly to influence the conspirators in order to prevent precipitate action. But a conspiracy usually behaves like a mine—once you strike it—it explodes. The Warsaw conspiracy was conscious then of being disclosed, and a feverish longing for action prevailed. In vain Wysocki tried to postpone the date and Lelewel opposed the outbreak; supported by young intellectuals, Zaliwski had gained full control. On November 26 it was decided to start the struggle on December 10. But the next day, warning was given from governmental offices of the Emperor's orders for the arrest of all suspected persons and their trial by a court martial. Hasty decisions were immediately taken to prevent this by starting the action on November 29 at night.[18]

Zaliwski carried the decision of attacking the Belvedere (the Grand Duke's residence) and killing Constantine. There was a tragic irony in such a decision, for the Tsesarevich—at the very moment when the bayonets of the conspirators were to turn against him—not only loudly proclaimed himself to be a Pole, but really felt himself a Pole and tried to plead for Poland and even for the men who meditated his death. After the attempt, he still appealed many times to his brother for clemency for the

[16] A. Czartoryski, *Żywot J. U. Niemcewicza*, p. 360.

[17] The announcement of the mobilization in a communiqué in Warsaw newspapers was overlooked by historical research until recently; it was disclosed by J. Dutkiewicz, *Francja i Polska 1831*, 1950, pp. 16, 31, 35-36.

[18] See S. Askenazy in *The Cambridge Modern History* and the more recent special study by W. Tokarz, *Sprzysiężenie Wysockiego i Noc Listopadowa* (Wysocki's Conspiracy, and the Outbreak of the November Revolution), 1925, esp. pp. 46-49, 75-76, 80-102.

Poles.[19] Zaliwski's idea most probably was that by killing him they would enforce upon Poland the necessity of a struggle for life or death without looking backwards, without any delusions of appeasing the Tsar or obtaining his mercy, with no possibility of retreat.

Constantine's narrow escape actually left some ground for an attempt at negotiations before the guns started to talk; it also left the possibility of appealing for help to the western powers.

Prince Adam was unable to prevent the outbreak of the revolution, and he was far from optimistic as to the chances of a war between the small Kingdom and Russia. But he met the events with a quiet determination not to separate himself from his nation and to serve its cause.[20]

[19] His letters to Nicholas, *Sbornik*, cxxxii, 62-63, 72-73, 76-77.

[20] That idea often finds expression in the correspondence of Czartoryski and his family during the weeks which followed; see also the letters of the Zamoyskis, *Zamoyski*, ii.

CHAPTER 14

LEADER IN THE WAR FOR
INDEPENDENCE

THE STRUGGLE started in Warsaw on the night of November 29, 1830. After a few hours, the fighting had spread over most districts of the town, and the arsenal was in the hands of the insurgents. At midnight the battle was still far from being won by the revolutionaries. The Tsesarevich, after having escaped the bayonets of his attackers, was joined by his Russian guards and by part of the Polish garrison; they held the southern suburbs. Only a part of the Polish troops joined the insurgents. Several Polish generals were killed by the rebels, among them some splendid soldiers and men with a fine record of previous struggles for independence. Several joined the Tsesarevich, or disappeared from the scene to avoid being committed to either side. No one espoused the cause of the insurrection.

Most of the town was in the hands of the revolt, but the chiefs, Wysocki and Zaliwski, when the failure of their plan became apparent, did not have sufficient moral courage or authority to retain the leadership in their hands. No revolutionary government was proclaimed, and no appeal issued to the people. At that moment Constantine probably could have crushed the revolt by one resolute attack. But he abhorred the idea of fighting against the Poles. He repeatedly declared: "No Russian will be involved in that affair. The Poles have started, they must finish it among themselves. It will be shown now, if they deserve so many favors. . . ." And he added: "As for me, I do not interfere; let the Poles settle it by themselves, it is their affair."[1]

After midnight on November 30, the Tsesarevich's young aide-de-camp, Ladislas Zamoyski, nephew of Czartoryski, knocked at

[1] W. Tokarz, *Wojna Polsko-Rosyjska 1830-1831* (Russo-Polish War), 1930, pp. 56-58. T. Morawski, *Dzieje narodu polskiego* (History of the Polish Nation), VI, 308-309. *Zamoyski*, I, 376-378.

the door of Prince Adam's house. After having reconnoitered the situation in both parts of the city, he had come to suggest an immediate meeting of the Council of Administration in Czartoryski's presence, and the reinforcement of the government by the addition of two or three influential patriots. Thus chaos and anarchy might be prevented and a national authority instituted. They both went to President Sobolewski's house; Lubecki and some other members joined the meeting. After a brief exchange of views, they decided to send Czartoryski and Lubecki to the Tsesarevich, to learn of his intentions. His reaction was the same as before: he wanted to be left alone.

The council then decided to issue a proclamation, still in the name of King Nicholas I, expressing concern over the previous night's "unfortunate and unexpected incidents," and inviting the citizens to remain calm and orderly. At the same time they announced the appointment of new members to the council, especially of General Joseph Chłopicki, the same man whom the conspiracy had intended to invite as generalissimo.

The next day, December 1, under growing pressure from the revolutionaries who had tried too late to take control of the government with the support of armed crowds, the council once more altered its composition. Some of the most unpopular members, servile reactionaries, were dismissed, and two representatives of the revolutionary left, Professor Joachim Lelewel and Ladislas Ostrowski, a member of the Seym, admitted. An executive committee was appointed, with Czartoryski as president.

On December 2 a delegation was sent to Wierzbno, the Tsesarevich's headquarters on the outskirts of Warsaw; Czartoryski and Lubecki were now accompanied by Lelewel and Ostrowski. Long discussions brought no immediate solution. It became evident that Constantine was not ready to be opposed to Nicholas as a challenge. He agreed only to a kind of armistice, to intervene with his brother in favor of some of the Polish claims and to beg him for an amnesty. Lelewel himself—the representative of the Underground—implored him to "obtain from the common father of the two nations his oblivion of all that had happened."

In the meantime the situation had grown more and more serious. The Polish regiments still remaining under Constantine's orders grew restive; regiments marching from other garrisons, instead of reinforcing him, joined the insurgents; and the revolutionaries succeeded in enforcing upon the government the decision to request an immediate release of the Polish troops still under the Tsesarevich's command. On December 3 armed crowds were marching against the Tsesarevich in order to "liberate their brethren." Zamoyski obtained from him an order permitting the Polish troops to join the new Polish authorities. Constantine was summoned to withdraw from the capital with his Russian troops; he decided to march to the south, to cross the Vistula at Puławy and to withdraw thence beyond the Bug. He entrusted his own person and the security of all Russians in Poland "to the generosity of the Polish people."

Thus a fratricidal struggle was avoided and the Polish army united under the authority of a national government headed by Czartoryski. It was achieved at the price of the undisturbed withdrawal of Constantine and his guards from the Kingdom.

The next day an imbroglio occurred. General Chłopicki, a veteran of the Napoleonic wars, whom the army and the people favored for his dignified attitude towards the Grand Duke in the early years of the Kingdom, was (as mentioned above) designated by the revolutionaries as their military chief. In actual fact, he had always been an implacable adversary of revolution and popular government; he refused to act as generalissimo under the collective authority of the national government and took over the power as dictator. Prince Adam found himself unexpectedly superseded by this ruthless and arbitrary soldier. Nevertheless he remained at the head of the government, accepted the presidency of the senate as well as of the dictator's supreme council, and tried to cooperate. He did not oppose the mission of Lubecki to the Emperor—a final attempt for a peaceful settlement—but he had little hope as to the success of the negotiations if not supported by formidable forces emerging in the country. He considered negotiations chiefly as a delaying action in order to win time for gathering forces and armaments.[2] He was early aware of the

[2] See Czartoryski's instruction for General Kniaziewicz's mission to Paris, Jan. 26, 1831 (B.P.Ms. 350, Nr. 1).

disastrous consequences of the dictator's policy of avoiding any "revolutionary measures" in building up the national army.

Nicholas, as was to be expected, was adamant in rejecting any negotiation with the rebels, but he offered oblivion if they immediately submitted to his will: the revolting regiments would be given an opportunity of rehabilitation in the vanguard of his armies. Most illuminating was the December 18 conversation of Colonel Wyleżyński, the dictator's delegate to the sovereign, with Benckendorff and Diebitsch; the Emperor was listening in the adjacent room. Benckendorff harangued the emissary of the rebels: "Eh bien, Messieurs les Polonais—your revolution has by no means the merit of right timing. You have risen up just at the moment when all the forces of the Empire were marching towards your frontiers. You certainly must feel that such an inequal contest cannot last long." Wyleżyński retorted that Poland was strong enough for stemming the flood so as to allow other powers to take the necessary measures and to avert the peril which threatened all of them. Here Diebitsch intervened: "Well, but what would you benefit from it? We have considered a campaign on the Rhine; we shall have one on the Elbe or even on the Oder, after having crushed your resistance. But, if you should desist, there is the Emperor's assurance that he would forgive all. You feel that the word of a sovereign has some value, particularly the word of a sovereign who will keep it even against all, as he is determined to keep the word given to King Charles X."[3]

Although Diebitsch for obvious reasons minimized the effect of the Polish revolution, it proved decisive for Russian foreign policy. On the very moment of the Warsaw outbreak the crisis was reaching its climax and war was in sight. The French Chargé d'Affaires, Baron de Bourgoing, who repeatedly demanded explanation of the warlike measures, was answered that Russia had not even the slightest intention of attacking France on her own boundaries; she was just arming against all the troublemakers elsewhere; and it was understood that order must be restored by a military intervention in Belgium and by a general onslaught

[3] Angeberg, pp. 769-770. The full reports of Wyleżyński and Count Jezierski (who had been delegated to the Emperor with Lubecki) are in the published diary of the Seym: M. Rostworowski, *Diariusz Sejmu 1830-31* (1907), I.

against France, if she was "foolish enough" to counteract.[4] France was "foolish enough" and announced a *levée* of 500,000 men; on December 1 her Foreign Minister, Count Sebastiani, instructed Bourgoing to give to Nesselrode, in addition to conciliatory assurances on the Belgian affairs, the stern warning that any move of Russia's forces beyond her frontiers into Prussia or any other German state would be regarded by France as a breach of peace. This statement followed by a few days the exclusion of the House of Nassau from the throne by the Belgian Congress. Thus two flagrant *casus belli* were on the way.[5] But before Sebastiani's instruction had reached its destination, the Tsar had learned about the Warsaw outbreak. The first news immediately provoked a change of his mood; as the situation in Poland proved more and more critical, he displayed a more and more conciliatory approach to the Belgian problem. In his private talks with Major General de Sainte-Aldegonde, a Frenchman in Russian service, he offered the King his friendship and Russia's gratitude if France refrained from interfering with the Polish affairs; and Nesselrode put the same idea in more diplomatic terms. Bourgoing did not wait for instructions; he spontaneously reassured Nesselrode and paved the way for the long-delayed Russian recognition of Louis Philippe as King of the French.[6]

The news of a Polish revolution caused immense relief in Paris; it was the *deus ex machina* they had dreamed of; some newspapers had even expressed annoyance and bitterness about the docility of the Poles before their Russian ruler. Even the King exulted; and with all his remarkable dexterity he immediately seized the

[4] Nicholas' expression in a letter to his wife, Oct. 29: "Assez folle pour vouloir s'y meler." Schiemann, III, 40.

[5] For the crisis of 1830, see the dispatches of Bourgoing and the instructions for him, Aug.-Dec. (Archives des Affaires Étrangeres, Russie, vol. 180 and 181), particularly Bourgoing's dispatches Oct. 13, Oct. 30, Nov. 9, Nov. 11, Dec. 7; and Sebastiani's instructions, Nov. 22 and Dec. 1. Cf. De Guichen, *La Révolution de Juillet et l'Europe*, 1917; J. Dutkiewicz, *Francja a Polska 1831* (1950); and Ch. Morley, "The European Significance of the November Uprising," *Journal of Central European Affairs*, Jan. 1952.

[6] See Bourgoing's dispatches, Dec. 9, 11, 20, 21, 22, 23; and Major Gen. Count de Sainte-Aldegonde to King Louis Philippe (copy annexed to the dispatch of Bourgoing of Dec. 23). The long-belated act of recognition of Louis Philippe by Russia took place on Jan. 8, 1831, when Pozzo di Borgo presented his new credentials to the King.

opportunity of reaching a *détente* with Russia. On December 11 a dispatch from Sebastiani promised what Nicholas was striving for: France would abstain from supporting the Polish insurrection.[7]

Not only popular leaders (like Lafayette), their exponents in the government (like the Prime Minister Laffitte), the still strong *parti du mouvement*, but also a very large sector of the public opinion and the working masses of Paris and elsewhere reacted to the news with an outburst of sympathy for the Poles. Even Sebastiani, who once had commanded a Polish division against the Russians, felt uneasy in selling them down the river. In a talk with Prince Adam's brother-in-law, Prince Leon Sapieha, he declared: "If what happened in Poland was merely a brawl, you must get out of it as you can; but if this is a national movement, you can count on our support."[8] And he allowed the Pole to report his words to Czartoryski.

The exact date of that momentous utterance is unknown. In any case, it was before the solemn declaration of the Polish Seym on December 20 proclaiming the insurrection as national.

French ministers had further contact with Sapieha, and he was directed by them to London, in order to present the Polish case to Lord Grey, who was once Czartoryski's and Kościuszko's friend and at this time the head of the British government, and to Palmerston; they also recommended him to Talleyrand.[9] That fact and other friendly utterances from leading French figures were reported to Czartoryski by an emissary on December 30 and seemed most encouraging; he was even worried by the dictator's skepticism.

Almost at the same time, Nicholas wrote to Constantine about France's recent friendly gestures; she was trying to exploit the circumstances by appeasing him.[10] He felt that the Poles were left alone; and after the declaration to the Seym he abandoned any hope of avoiding an armed contest. He wrote to his brother

[7] Instructions of Dec. 11 and 28, 1830.

[8] L. Sapieha, W*spomnienia*, 1913, pp. 112 sq.

[9] See the Diary of Alexander Krysiński, the Dictator's secretary (B.P.Ms. 382, f. 26-28) Dec. 30; and Sapieha, *loc.cit.* The emissary, Louis Szczaniecki, possibly exaggerated, when mentioning a French promise of military intervention.

[10] Dec. 28, *Sbornik*, CXXXII, 112.

on January 13: "Which of the two has to perish, because one of the two must, Russia or Poland, decide for yourself. I have exhausted all the possible means of preventing such a calamity. . . ."[11]

After the complete failure of negotiations, when the dictator was faced with an ultimatum from the Tsar which meant unconditional surrender, Prince Adam prevented a capitulation and enforced the convocation of the Seym. The ultimatum was rejected, and the dictator relinquished his power; military leadership was conferred upon a generalissimo elected by the Seym. In the meantime further reports from Paris contributed largely to the outburst of fighting spirit in the Seym and to further burning of bridges by the proclamation on January 25 of the vacancy on the Polish throne.[12] Czartoryski tried in vain to obtain from the Seym the organization of a new government enabling it to meet its enormous responsibilities, to ensure unity of leadership and efficiency in all governmental and military activities. The disastrous failure of Chłopicki's dictatorship left public opinion and the Seym suspicious of strong personalities and reluctant to allow much power to individuals. A national government of five members was elected and invested with the supreme authority short of the conduct of war; a generalissimo was to be appointed by the Seym and directly responsible to it. On January 29, 1831, Prince Adam was elected president of the national government—in actual fact merely its chairman—and he remained at this post until August 15, when the government was overthrown by a popular revolt chiefly because of the failures of commanders of military operations.[13]

Czartoryski was to be much criticized by his contemporaries

[11] *Ibid.*, pp. 97-99.

[12] See the letter of Count Gustave Małachowski, acting Foreign Minister to Gen. Kniaziewicz and L. Plater, Jan. 28, 1830 (B.P.Ms. 350, No. 7), accusing the French government of having induced the Poles to burn the bridges; and the account of E. Cabet, *La Révolution de 1830 et la situation présente*, 1834, pp. 313-317.

[13] For Czartoryski's part in the 1830-1831 revolution see L. Gadon, *Książę Adam Czartoryski podczas powstania listopadowego*, 1900, with large excerpts from the Prince's private correspondence, and a more recent and complete study by W. Nagórska-Rudzka in *Przegląd Historyczny* (Historical Review), 1930, Ser. 2, vol. 9, pp. 211-308.

and by later writers and historians for having failed to impose his leadership, for having permitted Chłopicki's coup d'état, and for having, after the latter's eclipse, assumed great responsibility without the necessary powers. Some of his biographers even discovered in his behavior at the time of the revolution a certain weakness of will and incapacity for action. Such an opinion does not seem justified in the face of the facts. During the whole period of the revolution and the war, Prince Adam was active and indefatigable; he tried to inspire others with fighting spirit, boldness, and defiance toward adversity. He was always ready to make decisions and to face perils and responsibilities. What was really lacking was the lust for power and the will to strive for it. It seems rather dubious whether he could in fact have challenged Chłopicki's immense military prestige and popularity in the first days of the revolution. After the latter's resignation he opposed, in vain, the new peril: the omnipotence of the Seym and its immediate control over the conduct of the war. He could certainly have declined the post of president when he had been refused the necessary powers. But he did not bother about his personal prestige or his record in history; his only aim was to serve his country in its desperate struggle and to try to prevent disaster instead of waiting until his warnings would be proved to have been right. When elected, he told the Seym: "I accept that honorable burden; I shall carry it with firmness and resolution, as I think that no one has the right to abstain from serving his country." His endeavor was "to seek the strength of the government by securing the confidence of the Seym and of the nation."

He was suspected by some of his Republican opponents of coveting the royal crown. That indeed was Tsar Nicholas' guess; he wrote to his brother about "Adam I" as his "successor" and the Tsesarevich indulged in rude insults.[14]

In fact Czartoryski did not approve the proclaiming of the vacancy of the throne; he regarded it as a vain and provocative gesture. But once it was proclaimed, he tried to make the most of it in his diplomatic action in order to secure foreign assistance and intervention. He used it as a trump card in Vienna, sug-

[14] *Sbornik*, CXXXII, 115-116, 167-168, 170-172.

gesting—not without the friendly reaction of some Austrian statesmen—Poland's dynastic union with Austria.[15]

There was yet another myth about Czartoryski's leadership: namely, that he relied too much on diplomatic negotiations and hampered military efforts and operations. Czartoryski's own words, pronounced when elected president, give the lie to such claims: "Our hope is now in armament and military effort. . . . If God granted a first victory, it would be easier to act. . . ." His letters to the three successive generalissimos, Prince Michael Radziwiłł, Jan Skrzynecki, and Henry Dembiński, emphasized repeatedly the very simple theory that there was no chance for negotiation with the enemy without previous victory, that foreign help could be secured only by military success. His diplomacy did not hamper strategy; on the contrary, strategy was required to pave the way for diplomacy. There was a great difference between his diplomacy and the amateurish diplomacy of generals like Chłopicki or Skrzynecki, who tried to substitute negotiations for military action in order to avoid or to postpone the contest with the adversary's overwhelming strength. Czartoryski did not like such military incursions in politics and he tried to counteract them. In his report for the Seym he wrote: "I bored them by repeating that diplomacy depends upon military success, that our political situation can be improved only by one more decisive victory."

By his diplomatic activities in Paris, London, Vienna, Berlin, Rome, and Brussels he tried "to gain, if possible, the confidence and understanding of governments, as well as the friendship of peoples" and to pave the way for a mediation of the powers in the Polish crisis.[16] His policy had at first good reason to count on

[15] In addition to the Hapsburg dynasty, other solutions were discussed. Sebastiani mentioned the Prince of Orange, Nicholas' brother-in-law who was *persona grata* with the British government; it could be helpful for the settlement of the dispute over Belgium. Later the Polish delegate in London, old Niemcewicz, suggested, when speaking to Palmerston, the candidature of an English prince (he certainly meant the Duke of Sussex) and he had the impression that it did not displease him. See A. Czartoryski, *Żywot Niemcewicza*, pp. 361-364.

[16] There is no complete history of the Polish diplomacy in 1830-1831. The study of the subject by S. Askenazy (first chapters published in *Biblioteka Warszawska* 1902 and 1903) remained a brilliant fragment. J. Dutkiewicz, *Francja a Polska 1831* (1950), recently gave an important contribution.

French support. His expectations were stultified when he received, three days after the vote of exclusion, ample evidence of the ambiguous policy of Louis Philippe. That disappointment did not deter him from further attempts to secure French diplomatic and material help; nor did his attempts seem hopeless. He directed to Paris General Kniaziewicz, whose name was associated with the glorious victories of the First Republic in 1798-1800, and Count Louis Plater, a distinguished politician devoted to the national cause.

Lafayette, the president of the Vente Suprême of the French Carbonari, the spiritual leader of the French Underground on the eve of the July revolution, the chief of the popular forces emerging from the revolt, and the inspiring spokesman of the "Parti du Mouvement" under the new July monarchy, was certainly largely responsible for the November insurrection in Warsaw. In any case, he was keenly aware of the part which that insurrection was playing by preventing Russian armed intervention in Western Europe. He championed the cause of the liberty of nations, and he regarded it as France's sacred duty to support that cause and to be prepared to wage wars for its sake. Now the cause of fighting Poland was in the foreground, and on January 15, 1831 he revealed to the National Assembly the tremendous importance of the fact that in the very moment when the Russian mobilization was nearly completed "the [Polish] vanguard turned against the [Russian] main army." He was fully informed by the Polish national government about Nicholas' decisions and measures, and he produced ample evidence.[17] He was supported in the National Assembly by Louis Bignon (once Napoleon's envoy in Poland), by General Lamarque, Mauguin, and others. The Polish delegates, Constantine Wolicki, Teodor Morawski, and later General Kniaziewicz and Count Louis Plater enjoyed his unreserved support.

But the control of French foreign policy was neither in his nor in Laffitte's hands. The King had the real lead, and the Foreign

[17] His parliamentary speeches in *Mémoires*, vi, and in A. Lewak's, *Le Général Lafayette et la cause polonaise* (Vars. 1934); see also the latter's introductory study on Lafayette and Poland. The documents he produced are to be found in his speech of Mar. 18, 1831.

Minister, Sebastiani, followed a tortuous middle course between Louis Philippe's policy of appeasement and Lafayette's policy of action, which had the backing of a growing popular movement.

Talleyrand, Prince Adam's old adversary, had been since the July revolution the French envoy in London. He worked on an Anglo-French understanding about Belgium and on the building up of a concert of powers in order to check Nicholas' pressure on Europe. His attitude to the Polish cause was now apparently more favorable, and his inseparable young friend, the Duchess of Dino, who had not forgotten Prince Adam, was there as Poland's friendly advocate. The aged statesman appealed to Sebastiani to give moral, diplomatic, and material support to the Poles; he even suggested military measures short of war.[18] So Sebastiani authorized him to sound out the British government on the possibility of a common mediation in St. Petersburg; but Anglo-French relations were still too much complicated by the Belgian problem to allow a common stand.[19]

Talleyrand had many talks with the Polish emissaries, especially with the very young Count Alexander Walewski, and the latter's numerous reports reveal how the old roué was amused by playing "diplomacy" with the boyish Polish agent and how he enjoyed the additional pleasure of having a son of Napoleon as an admiring pupil. He carefully avoided commitments and emphatically denied, in disregard of facts and documents, any real danger of Russian intervention in November 1830; but he advised the Poles to persevere, to fight, and to secure decisive military victories, which he regarded as a necessary precondition of the intervention of the Western powers.[20]

The response of the British government was even less encouraging. The Prime Minister, Lord Grey, explained to Sapieha quite frankly that there was some apprehension as to whether France's aim was not the annexation of Belgium. Therefore England wanted Russia to coerce France if necessary, and she desired

[18] Lacour-Gayet, *Talleyrand*, III (1931), 264-266; Pallain, *Correspondance dipl. de Talleyrand*, IV, 143-144, 153; *Ambassade de Talleyrand à Londres*, 142-145.

[19] Sebastiani's conversation with Kniaziewicz, Mar. 16, 1831 (B.P.Ms. 350, No. 60). Cf. Gleason, *Russophobia*, pp. 110-111.

[20] Walewski's letters to Małachowski, and to Kniaziewicz and Plater are in the papers of the Polish Legation in Paris (B.P.Mss. 352-353).

Russia to have a free hand and to liquidate the Polish rising as soon as possible. Palmerston's utterances were less harsh but not less peremptory. In Marquess Alexander Wielopolski's conversation with Palmerston on January 10, the only remark by the Polish emissary which seemed to impress the Foreign Secretary was that the Kingdom with its own army had proved a valuable obstacle against Russia's aggressive policy; what Poland wanted was to maintain and to reinforce that barrier. But when informed two weeks later of the breakdown of the negotiations with Nicholas, Palmerston interpreted the Tsar's ultimatum as rather conciliatory; the latter demanded capitulation only because he could not negotiate with rebels. In a later conversation in March, he told the Polish emissary that since France was the real danger for Europe, Britain was interested in Russia's strength; he denounced the French for having induced the Poles to rise, and hinted at Lafayette's secret contacts with Poland. He refused to consider any steps prejudicial to Russia's rights as stipulated in Vienna, and declined any discussion of a Hapsburg candidature to the Polish throne.[21]

The hopes of a foreign intervention and the efforts to secure a common intervention of the four-power signatories of the treaty of Vienna survived that first and bitter disappointment. The attitude of Austria seemed to reopen the way for Polish diplomacy. She was visibly not displeased to see the Tsar committed to a hard struggle against his Polish subjects and Russia's position greatly compromised. The Chancellor's wife, Princess Mélanie Metternich, noted in her diary on April 10 her husband's opinion that a military success for the Poles "could reduce to some degree the presumption of the Russians and ensure a brilliant situation for Austria."[22] Metternich's entourage considered the Polish insurrection as *ein wahres Glueck*.[23] Officially the most correct

---

[21] L. Sapieha, *Wspomnienia*, pp. 114-118. A. Wielopolski to A. Czartoryski, London, January 11, 1831 (A. Lisicki, *Margrabia Wielopolski*, 1878, IV, 340-349). Cf. Webster, *Palmerston*, pp. 181-183. Grey's letter to Kościuszko, July 1, 1814, was published on Apr. 5, 1831 in the *Morning Chronicle* without his consent; see *Correspondence of Princess Lieven and Earl Grey*, 1890, II, 204-205, and Angeberg, p. 601.

[22] Metternich, *Mémoires*, v, 94.

[23] F. Gentz, *Tagebücher*, 1920, p. 387.

relations with Russia were maintained, but unofficially the Poles were given discreet encouragement, even by friendly intercourse with Polish politicians and emissaries and an attitude of informal neutrality. The Poles were given numerous friendly assurances (*protestations d'intérêt et de bienveillance*).[24] The support of the insurrection by the Galician Poles was tolerated, and the viceroy, Prince Lobkovitz, a genuine Polonophile, did not conceal his preference for an Austro-Polish solution of the problem.

Soundings were undertaken at Lvov and in Vienna about offering the Polish throne to a Hapsburg prince. The Duke of Reichstadt was mentioned, who could please the Poles and the French. But the response in Vienna was not favorable to that candidature, and in February 1831 the Polish government tested Vienna's reaction to the candidature of Archduke Charles, and both Western powers were informed and asked for support. Later the Polish government was ready to accept as sovereign any other member of the imperial family chosen by the Austrian Emperor. He seemed to favor the idea, but before long it became apparent that Vienna was too cautious for any risky enterprise and would not act until pushed by the Western powers.[25] Constantine Czartoryski, Prince Adam's brother, reported in April from Vienna, where he remained during the whole period of the war in close touch with Metternich, Kolovrat, and the "Hofburg": "Victories, great victories are needed." Thus Vienna echoed Talleyrand's "diplomatic" advice.

The policy of a dynastic union with Austria was highly unpopular in Poland; the embittered hatred of the Hapsburgs by the Carbonari coincided with a general dislike of Austrian bureaucracy. This attitude was the main reason for a violent clash between Czartoryski and Lelewel on August 4, and it greatly contributed to the outburst of popular anger on August 15.

There was at first some uncertainty as to Prussia's intentions, largely due to the Prussian consul's strange utterances, and it was evident that Prussia was highly interested in the extension of the conflict between Poland and the Tsar. But before long it became certain that she would adhere to her policy of close col-

24 See Małachowski's letter to L. Sapieha, Feb. 25, 1831 (B.P.Mss. 350, No. 52).
25 Czartoryski to L. Sapieha, Mar. 21, 1831 (B.P.Mss. 350, No. 415).

laboration with Russia. What she wanted, in fact, was an abrupt end of the political existence of the Polish state.

The political situation deteriorated in March when Laffitte was superseded by Casimir Périer and Lafayette's party defeated. But it improved later in the spring, when a settlement of the Belgian problem seemed nearly achieved and the tiny Polish Kingdom not only survived the onslaught of the powerful Russian army but proved itself able to win battles. There were protracted talks about a common intervention of the Western powers and Austria in St. Petersburg. They vanished when new complications over Belgium suddenly revived the danger of war between Britain and France. Czartoryski's diplomacy, encouraged by Palmerston, successfully intervened in Brussels to induce the Belgian congress to accept the 18 Articles and thus to pave the way for a final settlement. In France exasperation was growing because Poland was left fighting alone, and in the month of July the government faced a revolt of the Chamber. They tried to disarm public opinion by claiming that the French diplomatic intercession in St. Petersburg was successful, and they once more tried to win over London and Vienna for a common mediation, but in vain.[26] Nesselrode before long expressed his gratitude to Britain for having declined the French proposals, and the Austrian reply was evasive. In August Talleyrand assured Niemcewicz of French diplomatic support with the proviso: "You must first succeed." At the same time, Palmerston, when explaining to Niemcewicz the reasons for Britain's inactivity in the Polish crisis, told him: "If you won important victories, the position could change."[27] But when they told it to the old Polish patriot, an Anglo-French war over Belgium was unexpectedly once more in sight as a result of the Belgian defeat and of the French army's march into Belgium. It was avoided, but the new crisis finally frustrated the efforts of Czartoryski's diplomacy.[28] He angrily reacted to Sebastiani's and

[26] De Guichen, *Revolution*, pp. 430-434.

[27] A. Czartoryski, *Żywot Niemcewicza*, pp. 228-230, 361-364. Grey felt that he could not refuse to receive Niemcewicz, whom he had known as Kościuszko's aide-de-camp in 1797. He tried in vain to disarm Princess Lieven's anger (*Correspondence*, II, 268-273). But she praised the "adorable" foreign Secretary. See Webster, p. 184.

[28] For the interdependence of the Belgian and Polish crisis in summer 1831,

The War for Independence

Talleyrand's demands of victories and perseverance: "Why did they not tell the truth from the beginning instead of deluding us, it was a vile and shameful policy. They still would like to destroy the common foe at the price of our blood and after having spent it to the last drop to leave us alone. . . ."[29] After Poland's defeat in September both Talleyrand and Palmerston expressed the opinion that the Poles should have continued their stand until—at least—the end of October; intervention would then have been possible. Austria showed a keen interest in the Poles just in the last critical phase of the war, and started something like a mediation on the eve of the fall of Warsaw.[30] The attitude of the three powers with regard to Poland was finally identical: they had allowed Poland to be overwhelmed; now they looked with regret on her disappearance from the political scene.

The disappointments of Polish diplomacy in 1830-1831 confirmed Czartoryski's opinion that the fate of the country would be decided on the battlefields. He did not omit the possibility of acting by means of diplomacy, but he did not subordinate to it military operations.

The military operations started early in February 1831 with an over-all offensive of Field Marshal Count Diebitsch's army against Warsaw. The disparity of strength was apparent. On a peacetime footing the Polish army had been more than ten times inferior in numbers to the Russian, and the ratio of the populations of the Kingdom and the Empire was approximately the same. The building up of the Polish army was hampered by the scarcity of arms and ammunition and the total lack of war industries. But great effort had been made by the little kingdom to meet the threat

---

see M. Handelsman in *Revue Belge de Philologie et de l'Histoire*, 1930, IX, No. 3, and F. Perelman-Liwer, *La Belgique et la Révolution Polonaise de 1830* (Bruxelles, 1948), with a detailed study of Count Roman Załuski's mission to Brussels. King Leopold of Belgium was an old acquaintance of Czartoryski. On their relations see *Zamoyski*, I, 290-292.

[29] Letter to Kniaziewicz Aug. 6, Dutkiewicz, p. 121. Sebastiani had recommended to Kniaziewicz, July 7, stirring up the spirit in Warsaw. *Op.cit.*, p. 115.

[30] J. Dutkiewicz, *Austria wobec powstania listopadowego* (Austria and the November Insurrection, 1933), a detailed study based on Polish and Austrian archives and collections, fails to elucidate that last episode; cf. A. Zamoyski, *Moje przeprawy* (My Adventures), 1906, II. Much of the Austrian policy of that year still remains an enigma.

of her giant adversary; at the start of the campaign the ratio of fighting men was one to two, and on some battlefields it was even more favorable for the Poles. In the first encounters a marked superiority of the Polish regular troops over the Russian became apparent, due to the qualities of the Polish rank and file, their fighting spirit, dash, and skill.

Operational leadership was the Poles' weakest point. The first generalissimo, Prince Michael Radziwiłł, was merely a nominal chief; the conduct of the operations was once more in Chłopicki's hands, who acted with vigor and skill, but without any definite position, as "military adviser to the generalissimo" or "commander of the first line forces." Much friction and confusion was involved, and Prince Adam discovered with anger and sorrow a lack of fighting spirit and energy on the part of some generals and senior officers, the chief of the general staff included. He insisted upon a purge, elimination of *longs visages et des mines renversées*, and promotion for officers "with ardor, faith, and a will to fight." In the series of battles on the eastern approaches to the capital, called the battle of Grochów, he watched developments closely; on the critical day of February 25 he was at Radziwiłł's battlepost, giving a good example of self-control and presence of mind. The battle was lost in spite of the outstanding gallantry of the Polish troops and their temporary successes; Chłopicki was severely injured; Radziwiłł lost his nerve. The army, nevertheless, managed to withdraw in good order on the left bank of the Vistula, keeping a foothold on the right bank—the bridgehead of Praga.[31]

There was some panic in the capital, which was now in the front line. Czartoryski prevented any collapse of the fighting spirit; the government, the Seym, and other authorities remained in Warsaw and he looked for a brave soldier as new generalissimo. General Skrzynecki, who commanded the Polish forces in

[31] Constantine, who was present at the battle of Grochow, wrote to the Tsar on Feb. 26, 1831: "The Poles, i.e., the regulars, fight marvellously well and if the numbers were equal, it would have been quite a different thing." Nicholas answered on Mar. 12, 1831: "It certainly does much credit to the Poles, speaking militarily, to have saved almost all their artillery and to have succeeded after such a defeat in crossing the Vistula during one night on one bridge only. . . ." (*Sbornik*, xxxii, 121-124.)

the last phase of the battle, became quite naturally the candidate for that post. He was unanimously elected, and perfect understanding seemed ensured between the president of the government and the generalissimo. Two young staff officers with outstanding talent and efficiency emerged as Skrzynecki's closest collaborators: General Chrzanowski as chief of staff, and General Prądzyński as general quartermaster. Both had been in touch with Czartoryski for some time and were selected by him. The more enterprising of the two, Prądzyński, a man of inexhaustible ingenuity, became before long one of the chief characters of the Polish drama. In the planning and execution of the Polish counteroffensive which started on March 30, two contrasting tendencies conflicted, greatly affecting the course of operations: the generalissimo's tendency to avoid the risks of a general battle against Diebitsch, and Prądzyński's daring and eagerness for a battle. Thus the counteroffensive was for Skrzynecki just a sortie. After having badly mauled Rosen's 6th Army Corps (the former Lithuanian corps) in a series of encounters between Praga and Minsk Mazowiecki (Wawer, Dembe Wielkie, Kałuszyn), he was anxious to avoid being cut off from Warsaw by Diebitsch's main forces which had been preparing to cross the Vistula at the mouth of the Wieprz, but would certainly hurry to Rosen's rescue. Prądzyński tried to enforce upon Skrzynecki the decision to advance as far as Siedlce, to destroy what was left of Rosen's forces, and even to strike at the flank of Diebitsch's army if withdrawing from the Vistula. After much arguing, operations against Rosen were resumed when the intervention of the field marshal was already quite possible and certainly not far off; Prądzyński, who himself commanded a force directed at Rosen's left flank, secured a new victory (Iganie, April 10) in spite of the lack of intervention of the main Polish forces, which appeared on the battlefield when the fighting was over. Diebitsch's army was near; Skrzynecki refused to imperil his own, and the victory remained unexploited. In fact the general quartermaster had already committed his chief to a position which the latter had been anxious to avoid.

The other great Polish counteroffensive, in May, was even more influenced by the contest of their conflicting wills. It was directed against the Grand Duke Michael's guard corps which occupied the area of Łomża, while Diebitsch's main army was to the west of Siedlce, menacing Warsaw. The Polish army, attacking the guards, was certainly exposed to the chance of being cut off from Warsaw and having to fight a major battle against Diebitsch on its retreat. Once more the Polish advance was stopped by Skrzynecki before the final blow was delivered; once more the advance was resumed too late, when the risks were out of proportion to the chances of success, but this time the general battle with Diebitsch's main army was no longer to be avoided. At Ostrołęka, on May 26, the Poles were out-generaled, out-numbered, and out-gunned, and in spite of Skrzynecki's personal bravery and the gallant stand of his army it was defeated. The military situation became critical.

Prince Adam intervened repeatedly in that conflict of two divergent tendencies at the Polish headquarters. He tried to reconcile Prądzyński's daring and Skrzynecki's caution. Many times he appeared on battlefields among the *tirailleurs*; at Iganie, where he accompanied Prądzyński's force, he galloped to meet the Polish cavalry, which was expected from another direction, and led them himself on the enemy's flank. He constantly tried to inspire the generalissimo with courage, fighting spirit, and initiative. He suggested and planned military operations as if he had been a regular soldier—and only a few people knew that he had once held the rank of Polish colonel and of Russian major-general, that he had seen campaigns and understood war. Even Skrzynecki, although greatly annoyed by his suggestions, admitted that the Prince discussed operations better than many generals and that he was *ad utramque paratus*.[32]

Because they demanded activity and offensive actions, Prince Adam's operational concepts were confused with those of Prądzyński. In actual fact they differed greatly. Prince Adam's idea was to avoid general battles, not to stake all on one card; he thought that the weaker side must not prompt decisions but delay

---

[32] For Czartoryski's military plans and opinions, see L. Gadon, *op.cit.* (most of his letters to the generalissimos are given in the full text or in long excerpts); W. Łopaciński, a special study in *Biblioteka Warszawska*, 1914; W. Nagórska Rudzka, *op.cit.*; Handelsman, I, 177-181.

the contest as long as possible by a system of active elastic defense. He suggested striking when possible with superior forces, surprising the enemy by launching unexpected attacks, and withdrawing before his main forces to the fortified capital, "like a beast to its burrow," to look for the right moment and to "exploit it with a celerity and energy equal to the patience with which it had been awaited." While Prądzyński, simplifying Napoleon's strategy, wanted always to attack the adversary's main forces and opposed secondary operations as prejudicial to the concentration of forces for the general battle, Czartoryski suggested "strong expeditions" against the enemy's weaker forces, offensive actions on the flanks and rear of the enemy's main army, making full use of partisan warfare. He attached the highest importance to the insurrection in the Lithuanian and Ruthenian provinces, which he encouraged and endeavored to support. He suggested winning the war by celerity of moves, beating the enemy with the feet of the Polish soldiers. For the time being, he suggested destroying Diebitsch's forces *en détail*, not all of it at once. But he would have liked to seize the opportunity of attacking and beating him if he were weakened and in an unfavorable position.

In his great work, the *History of the Art of War* Hans Delbrück showed that two different kinds of warfare are discernible in different periods of history and in the minds of different generals: the strategy of striking down (*Niederwerfungstrategie*), and the strategy of attrition (*Ermattungstrategie*). It was only the former which Prądzyński understood. As for Czartoryski, he very well understood the latter and would have known how to apply it if he had been commander-in-chief. There can be little doubt, for instance, that Rosen's army corps would have been destroyed and Siedlce reached not later than April 3, when Diebitsch was still far away and had not yet taken any decision as to how to meet the unexpected threat. Most probably the Russian army would have had to withdraw its dispersed units as far as Brześć before regaining its freedom of action. The expedition against the guards, if it had been undertaken at all, would have ended on May 19 at the latest in a final blow, and a speedy retreat would still have preserved the engaged forces from Diebitsch's vengeance. In June, the operation against Rüdiger's corps in the Lublin area, which failed on account of poor operational leadership, and Skrzynecki's halfhearted control, would certainly have been successful and could have greatly influenced the situation in the direction of Volhynia. It is difficult to say what would have been the result of such events on the general course of the war, but in any case it would have been greatly changed.

Some people realized too late that Czartoryski himself should have been generalissimo and that no one was more qualified for the position. But no one had suggested it at the proper time. There was a moment, after the battle of Ostrołęka, when Skrzynecki had lost control of himself and of his army. He wrote to the government: "Nous avons perdu la plus honteuse bataille. Finis Poloniae." There was no other sensible solution than to request the Seym to dismiss the generalissimo and to confer this function on the president of the national government. Instead, the reaction was to give comfort and consolation to the defeated general. Young Ladislas Zamoyski, who was already renowned for his exceptional gallantry and dash, and who was deeply moved by Skrzynecki's soldierly valor and misfortune, had the very bad idea of suggesting that he should intervene with the Seym in favor of establishing a strong government under Prince Adam's regency. So the rather feeble general, no longer very popular with the Polish people although still respected by the rank and file, thought it his duty to save his country from its internal weakness. The Seym, always inclined to adopt Roman gestures, met him, when returning after his defeat, with a vote of thanks. Prince Adam with his usual generosity protected him against criticism and accusations. But the project for governmental reform in spite of Skrzynecki's intervention was rejected in June by a majority of the Seym; and at the same time the shameful failure of the operation against Rüdiger provoked a crisis in the high command. It was aggravated by the subsequent generalissimo's inactivity at the time when the new Russian commander-in-chief, Field Marshal Count Paskievich, made his very risky encircling movement on the north of Modlin and Płock to the lower Vistula and beyond, in order to attack Warsaw from the west.

Czartoryski adhered much too long to Skrzynecki and opposed a change because he did not see any suitable successor to him.

The War for Independence

The circumstances of Skrzynecki's belated dismissal badly shook the spirit of the army, and his successor, Dembiński, an equally gallant soldier, was as a general unequal to his task. This was the main reason, although not the only one, for the crisis of confidence and the revolutionary unrest which ended with the revolt of August 15, and with the fall of the national government.[33]

Prince Adam left Warsaw, where his life was then endangered; he joined the army and was directed as a volunteer to General Ramorino's 2nd Army Corps.[34] Czartoryski's previous postulates with regard to the governmental powers were now, when he left, fully agreed upon. His successor, General Count Krukowiecki, a veteran demagogue, always fond of intrigue and seeking for popularity, was invested with full civil and military powers. He had neither the necessary talent nor the strength of character to make use of them otherwise than for starting negotiations and—after the first day of the bloody battle of Warsaw—for trying to enforce a wholesale capitulation (September 7). A revolt of the Seym prevented the final surrender of the government and of the army, but Warsaw was evacuated after a new and bitter struggle and the Polish army and government withdrew to Modlin, and later on towards Płock.

In the meantime, Prince Adam shared as a soldier the fate of Ramorino's army corps, which was directed to attack Rosen's observation corps in the direction of Siedlce and to clear the eastern approaches of the enemy. He took part in some encounters, looking as usual for danger and displaying his soldierly virtues in the belated pursuit of the adversary as far as the frontier at Brześć as well as in an equally belated march to the rescue of the capital. He clearly saw that the 2nd Corps' presence was necessary to prevent the defeat and the capitulation of Warsaw, and that time had been irremediably lost. When they were back at Siedlce, they received the news of the surrender of Warsaw. Now the Polish commander-in-chief ordered the 2nd Corps to join the main army at Modlin; but it could not be done

[33] For the origins of the revolt and the events of Aug. 15 see E. Oppman, *Warszawskie Towarzystwo Patriotyczne 1830-1831* (Warsaw Patriotic Society), 1937.

[34] Ramorino was an Italian who had served as a colonel in Napoleon's army; in 1831 he volunteered in Paris for the Polish army.

without a clash with the Russian main army of Field Marshal Count Paskievich, which already held Warsaw and the crossing of the Vistula. Prince Adam therefore did not oppose the decision which his nephew suggested and a council of senior officers approved, to march to the south, to cross the Vistula in the area of Lublin, and to continue the struggle in the provinces of Sandomierz and Cracow, the more so as there were misgivings as to whether a concentration at Modlin and Płock was not a step towards final capitulation.

On the other side, the absence of Ramorino's corps during the crucial days of the battle of Warsaw and its subsequent failure to comply with orders it received, became a source of suspicion and abuse against Zamoyski and Czartoryski himself. He witnessed Ramorino's katabasis under the growing pressure of the enemy and became aware of the increasing collapse of the fighting spirit of the rank and file; Zamoyski, who fought with his accustomed valor, was wounded twice more, and tried in vain to inspire his fellow-officers with perseverance and defiance in adversity. When they met difficulties in crossing the river, and the frontier of Galicia was near, it became apparent that the corps would seek for asylum and give up their arms to the Austrians. Prince Adam left them before they took that fatal step. He crossed the Vistula to join the small force of General Różycki, still operating in the province of Cracow. He organized at Kielce a provisional government for the three southwestern provinces which were now cut off from the national government by the Russian main army. But what remained of free Polish soil shrank rapidly and on September 26 Prince Adam took refuge in the "strictly neutral" republic of Cracow. The next day, surprised by the sudden invasion of the town by Russian troops, he made a last-minute escape. Piloted by the Austrian consul, he walked to the bridge over the Vistula and crossed it into exile.

CHAPTER 15

THE OUTLAW AND THE
AUTOCRAT

PRINCE ADAM became an outlaw. Before he had crossed the frontier, orders were given for the seizure of himself and his property.
All his estates in the Kingdom were immediately sequestrated,
especially Puławy, a focus of Polish national spirit and culture.
The precious collections (library, archives, and museum) were
secretly evacuated in two or three years' time, thanks to the daring and self-sacrifice of many people, members and friends of the
Family, officials, servants, and peasants. The Prince himself was
persecuted by imperial decrees depriving him of his title and
orders, calling him a traitor and unworthy of them. He retorted in a dignified statement that he had never been seen wearing the Russian ones; as to the Polish orders, he thought that he
had deserved them.

Czartoryski was to be tried for high treason with some hundred
participants in the revolution who were excluded from the amnesty. A special supreme criminal tribunal was instituted, composed of a few servile Poles and some Russian generals. The
proceedings lasted a long time; the verdict was dated November
29, 1833; it received the sovereign's final approval on February
4, 1834. Czartoryski was among the ten sentenced to be beheaded;
as he had been tried *in absentia*, it meant proscription. The court
emphasized that by his example he had induced others to usurp
royal authority, that he had incessantly stirred up the nation and
the army and encouraged them to fight against their sovereign;
that he tried by all means to extend the civil war and had even
induced provinces which were part of the Russian Empire to rise
up in arms against their sovereign and to share with the Kingdom the deplorable consequences of the revolt. The indictment
reads like a fine tribute paid to Czartoryski's patriotism and lead-

ership, and the tribunal in Warsaw was unwittingly more accurate in defining his role in the past revolution than were many of its authors, who after the catastrophe were looking for scapegoats.[1]

When Prince Adam heard of his material ruin, he had some feeling of relief. He refused to conform to the prudent suggestions of his mother-in-law and some old friends as to how the autocrat's vengeance should be disarmed. "I feel happy," he answered one of them, "to be released (although in a costly and rather violent manner) from bonds by which I had been fettered, and surely I shall not return to take them again, even at the cost of all my fortune."[2]

Not for a moment did he think of giving up the struggle for the freedom of his country. In September 1830, at Kielce, and later at Cracow, at the request of the Minister of Foreign Affairs his friend Theodore Morawski, he wrote a circular letter to all Polish agencies abroad, instructing them to demand diplomatic interventions by the signatories of the Vienna treaty for safeguarding its stipulations with regard to Poland. He decided to act as champion of his country's rights. He had no official position for representing his country, and he now regretted that he had declined the post of Foreign Minister which had been offered to him after the crisis of August 15. The only assets he had were his personal prestige and his long experience in statesmanship.

On October 23 he addressed from Leipzig a letter to the principal Polish representatives abroad: General Kniaziewicz and Count Louis Plater in Paris, and Niemcewicz in London. "It seems that the only thing which can be done is to exploit the good will of some courts for maintaining the stipulations of the Vienna Treaty intact." He instructed them to request a diplomatic *démarche* of both Western powers: "Let them not think that the Polish cause is finished. It is alive and will be." He foresaw a mass emigration of Polish officers and men of other ranks to France and hinted at the desirability of organizing a Polish legion there. The idea of rebuilding the Polish armed forces

---

[1] For Czartoryski's proscription and the fate of Puławy, see M. Kukiel, *Banicja Ks. Adama i katastrofa Puław* ("Kwartalnik Historyczny," 1930).

[2] L. Gadon, *Emigracja polska*, I, 208.

abroad was to be one of his main preoccupations for three decades to come.

Although Paris was to become the natural focus of the Polish emigration, Prince Adam decided to go straight to London, where he discerned the crucial point of the forthcoming political campaign for the defence of the treaty.[3] Talleyrand, his former adversary at the time of the Third Coalition and of the Vienna Congress, urged him to come. They were now led to cooperate for the first time in their lives. Not only were their characters different; they probably even repelled one another. The old master of diplomatic craft always displayed cynicism and a complete disregard for moral principles and scruples; he personified the type of diplomacy which Czartoryski had stigmatized in his *Essai*; in Talleyrand's policy there was no place for sentiment towards conquered or subjugated peoples, nor understanding of their cause. But he was brought closer to Czartoryski as he clearly discerned the danger of Russian pressure on Europe, the necessity for a common front on the part of England and France, for winning over the other Western powers and even Austria, if possible, to a common stand. Czartoryski appeared at this time an important associate, since in Vienna he had been the only intimate confidant of Alexander I, the best-informed witness, and the most competent interpreter of the intentions of the signatories, and especially of Russia with regard to the stipulations concerning Poland.

Czartoryski's interpretation was ready. The stipulations of the Congress of Vienna were more the concern of the European cabinets than of Poland: Poland had not been a participant; she had not broken any treaty by her revolution. The partitioning powers had for the first time obtained in Vienna the legal recognition of their possessions in Poland, but only under the specific conditions that the national rights of the Poles in all parts of the former Commonwealth of 1772 were respected, and that a Polish kingdom with its own constitution should have a separate existence. By the violation of those rights, the corresponding articles of the

[3] He met Plater at Strasbourg and they established permanent contact through the channel of Countess Tyszkiewicz in Paris and Talleyrand in London.

treaty would become null and void and the possession of Polish territories by the three sovereigns deprived of legal validity.

The first move for a diplomatic intervention on similar lines, although a very cautious one and limited to the constitutional status of the Kingdom, had already been made during the Polish war. Palmerston had instructed Heytesbury on March 22, 1831 to inform Russia of the British government's view that "the revolt of the Poles and their casting off the authority of the Emperor and King could afford to the Russian government no grounds for departing from the stipulations of the Treaty of Vienna. That revolt cannot release Russia from engagements of other powers, which had for their object not merely the welfare of the Poles, but the security of neighboring states." He also remarked that the article relating to national representation and institutions for the Polish provinces of the Empire has not been fulfilled by Russia. After Poland's fall on November 23, while recommending full and complete amnesty, he emphasized that, according to the stipulations of Vienna, "Poland should be attached to Russia by its constitution. A constitution the Emperor of Russia accordingly gave; and it is no forced construction of the meaning of that treaty to consider the constitution so given as existing under the sanction of the treaty."[4]

Talleyrand was now aware of the shifting of the balance of power by the fact of the annihilation of the Kingdom and of the danger of increasing Russian pressure on Central Europe. He was shocked by the declarations of the German powers: they hurried to state that order and security could no longer be maintained without desisting from the Vienna stipulations with regard to Poland. Thus the solidarity of three partitioning powers became evident, and a common stand by Britain and France was sought for by Talleyrand as an urgent necessity.

Prince Adam arrived in London on December 22, 1831. On the following day he had a long and friendly talk with Talleyrand, and they agreed upon the main lines and tactics of a diplomatic intervention. Talleyrand assured him that it could not even be supposed that France and Britain could refrain from demanding

[4] E. Ashley, *Life and Correspondence of Palmerston*, I, 273. Gleason, *Russophobia*, pp. 110-113. Webster, *Palmerston*, pp. 182, 185-186, 189-190.

a full execution of the treaty.[5] Talleyrand's ostentatious support was helpful to Czartoryski, but he had a standing of his own in London: he had old friends there, and the Duke of Sussex was the most constant and devoted of them; he was in friendly inter-course with Niemcewicz and welcomed Czartoryski at Kensing-ton. Lord Lansdowne had been his friend many years before at the time of his first sojourn in Great Britain, as had the Duke of Hamilton in St. Petersburg, and they both felt warmly towards the Polish exile. The Whigs, for whom he had always had a marked predilection, were now in power. The elderly Charles Grey, who in 1793 had raised his voice against Poland's Second Partition and in 1797 had organized the reception of Kościuszko in London and had supported Czartoryski's policy against that of Castlereagh in 1814, was prime minister. In spite of being en-chanted and influenced by Princess Lieven (the real and very influential Russian envoy), Grey could not decline conversations with Czartoryski and felt rather uneasy when trying to excuse his passivity during Poland's last struggle for independence.[6] He told Prince Adam about Metternich's memorandum to the Rus-sian government, and about the latter's view that the Treaty of Vienna did not exclude a change in the constitution of the King-dom. He did not object to Czartoryski's interpretation, but he helplessly repeated that nothing could be done now as Austria and Prussia were taking the opposite view.[7] But the next day he wrote the Lord Chancellor, Henry Brougham, their common friend, about his meeting with Czartoryski with some emotion, and confided some regrets at not having sent the British fleet to the Baltic Sea when Poland was still in arms.[8] Brougham himself, who had been once Prince Adam's confidential and most valuable

[5] For that period of Czartoryski's action, see his correspondence with the Polish legation in Paris, published in the *Album Muzeum Rapperswylskiego*, I, 1877, esp. pp. 130-142, 146.

[6] For the violent reaction of Princess Lieven, see her letter to Lady Cowper, Jan. 2, 1832 (*The Lieven-Palmerston Correspondence*, 1943, p. 31): "Indeed an action like that [entertaining of a state criminal to dinner by the prime minister] seems to indicate a desire to make war." Grey's sharp rebuke in a long letter of Jan. 4, 1832, and her reply (*Correspondence of Princess Lieven and Earl Grey*, II, 312-319). Webster, *Palmerston*, pp. 190-191.

[7] *Album*, I, 149-150.

[8] *The Life and Times of Henry Brougham*, 1871, III, 164.

collaborator, was not less embarrassed when meeting him, and he sadly remarked: "Unfortunately the cause of Poland is conflicting with the interests of all other powers." Prince Adam could hardly rely on any serious help from either of them.

For the first time he met Lord Palmerston, with whose policy his efforts were to be connected for three subsequent decades. He was introduced to him at a dinner given by Talleyrand and had conversations with him at Downing Street. The Foreign Secretary agreed with Czartoryski's interpretation of the treaty, but objected that the Poles had forfeited their rights by dethroning Nicholas. He mentioned the recommendations with regard to the Polish constitution which he had already sent (the previous November 23) to St. Petersburg. But later, when Russia answered by a sharp rebuff, he was reluctant to push the matter further. He wrote more than thirty years later with visible regret: "Mad. Lieven had great influence over Lord Grey and put much water into my wine."[9] And before long the news came of an important *fait accompli* in Poland, the abolition of the constitution and the promulgation of an "organic statute" with a kind of limited home rule. Actually it was never to be implemented; the country was to remain under Russian military law, the administration subordinated to military authorities, and political offences tried by military courts.[10]

That the Russian unilateral action was in contradiction to the stipulations of the Treaty of Vienna was evident. Palmerston hesitated as to how to react. Czartoryski, supported by Talleyrand, tried to prevent the recognition of the organic statute by Great Britain. He had already (as in 1813-1814) sought for the support of British public opinion and of the British Parliament.[11] The first champion of the Polish cause in the House of Commons, Colonel Sir George de Lacy Evans, had raised the matter three

---

[9] H. C. F. Bell, *Lord Palmerston*, 1936, I, 165. The "adorable" Foreign Secretary became "detestable" after November 1831, because of his intercession for the treaty rights of the Polish Kingdom. See Webster, *Palmerston*, pp. 183-185.

[10] In *The Cambridge History of Poland*, II, nothing is told about the fate of the kingdom and of Eastern Poland under Nicholas I in the years 1832-1855.

[11] For the attitude of the British press, almost unanimously pro-Polish and anti-Russian, see Gleason, *Russophobia*, pp. 114-118, 124, et passim. Count Louis Plater came to England to assist Czartoryski, and addressed several meetings.

times in 1831, and his remarkably farsighted warning of August 16 had met with no response. Now Czartoryski found a powerful spokesman in Robert Cutlar Fergusson, whose motion, announced in March 1832 and postponed until April 18, burst in the House as a challenge to the Tsar. His aim was "to bring the subject [of the abolition of the Polish Constitution] fairly before the Parliament." In a remarkable speech, he explained with irresistible reasoning and precision the meaning of the first article of the Treaty of Vienna relating to Poland; he related the history of the fifteen years of the constitutional existence of the Kingdom with a long list of flagrant violations of all the constitutional guarantees. He dealt with the argument that the Poles had forfeited their rights by their revolt and reminded the House (and Palmerston) that "the rights of the Irish nation were not forfeited by their rebellion of 1798, nor were the rights of Scotland affected by what was done in support of the Pretender in 1745." He insisted on the necessity for action, spoke of the interest shown by the French King and his government in the Polish cause, and emphasized that "nothing was so calculated to sacrifice the interests of England and of the Continent, as yielding to a fear of the power of Russia." In the Foreign Secretary's absence Lord Althorp stated that the government had no official information on the last act of the Russian Emperor; he expressed the "profound sympathy which the sufferings of the unhappy Poles must excite," but—significantly enough—he observed "that the government of this country had at no time held out any encouragement whatever, tending to excite the Polish nation to the late contest, which ended so fatally for their interests. He regretted that it was not in his power to say more upon the subject, that a sense of duty compelled him to be silent." It was a transparent allusion to the responsibility of France for the Polish revolution.

In the debate that followed, all the participants expressed their sympathy with the Poles and their concern about the fate of that country. Some denounced the "indignant and shameless conduct of Russia" (Labouchère), her "breach of faith" (Dr. Lushington), her cruel treatment of the Poles (Viscount Sandon). Doubts were expressed about "putting forward a threat" which one "was not prepared to carry into execution" (Courtenay); but there was expressed as well the view that "a strong opinion of the powers of Europe would preclude the necessity of going to war" (Hume), and criticism of the British government's attitude in 1831; it would have prevented France from affording assistance to the Poles (Hunt). Some of the members displayed a full knowledge of the problems involved and of diplomatic documents as well, and one of them, Sir George Warrender, involuntarily indicated the common source of their information when stating that "he had the happiness of knowing some of the illustrious men who were now exiles from their native country and he believed more enlightened patriots or more disinterested persons did not exist." The debate made a strong impression; Count Orlov, the Tsar's dreaded confidant, then on special mission in London, was infuriated and Princess Lieven even more so. Talleyrand was delighted and sanguine; he promised Czartoryski vigorous letters from Palmerston and himself to both embassies in St. Petersburg. Little or nothing came of it.[12]

Once more Fergusson raised the matter by a motion for papers relating to the organic statute, and on June 28 there was another Polish debate, even a stormy one. Lord Ebrington opened it by presenting a petition from Polish refugees; its reception being refused, he presented analogous petitions of his own Devonshire constituents. Fergusson's great speech expounded in a masterly manner the obligations with regard to the whole of Poland resulting from the Vienna Treaty; emphasis was laid on Russia's failure to fulfill the obligation to give to her Polish provinces national institutions and representations; ample information was given about their present ordeal. He informed the House of the cruel Russian persecutions, of Nicholas' own decision to send Prince Roman Sanguszko to Siberia "on foot," of children who had been carried away by thousands. Lord Sandon expressed the grief and sorrow of the House, and almost all the participants in the debate (O'Connell, Beaumont, Schonswar, Hume, Wyse,

---

[12] Czartoryski to the Polish Legation in Paris, London, Apr. 20, 1832 (*Album*, I, 169-170), *Hansard*, Apr. 18, 1832. Fergusson inspired Henry Rich's article "History, Present Wrongs and Claims of Poland" (*The Edinburgh Review*, Apr. 1832); it was submitted for approval to Czartoryski, Niemcewicz, and, at his own wish, to Palmerston. See Gleason, *Russophobia*, p. 124.

Sheil, even Sir Robert Peel) joined in the expression of concern at the Russian atrocities. Palmerston stated that he was ready to accede to the production of the papers; he agreed "that Great Britain possessed a full right to express a decided opinion upon the performance of the stipulations contained in that treaty"; but he denied any specific obligation "to adopt measures of direct interference by force." He alluded to certain communications which he had already made. Some members (Sir George Warrender, Lord Ebrington) expressed their satisfaction with the appointment of Sir Stratford Canning as ambassador to St. Petersburg (he was known as a friend of Czartoryski and *persona grata* to the Tsar and he was refused the *exequatur*). There were some outbursts of angry exasperation; O'Connell told of the "miscreant barbarian" who "had violated all compacts—had trampled on all rights," and when Sir Robert Inglis protested against "the improper use of freedom of debate," and the Foreign Secretary expressed his regret, two members (Thomas Wentworth Beaumont and Joseph Hume) rose to support O'Connell. Wyse insisted upon the liberty of speech and the necessity of a "moral barrier against the inroads of Russian despotism," and Sheil would not call the Tsar "miscreant" because the word was too poor. In connection with the impending case of Russia's Dutch loan and its promised payment by Britain, certain members (Pigott, Ruthven) protested against giving money to Russia "until the treaty of Vienna was fully carried into effect." Colonel Evans declared that "he should not shrink from a war, if a war became necessary, although he was glad that the peace of Europe had hitherto been preserved." Prince Adam's name was pronounced in Gally Knights' speech; after having alluded to the responsibility of the war party in Paris for having encouraged the Poles to rise in arms, he spoke with melancholy of the "weeping Fame" which "will blend in future eulogies the name of Czartoryski with that of Kościuszko. . . ." And Peel, in his final appeal for moderation and restraint, paid some tribute to the "dignified remonstrance" of the Poles themselves, when contrasted with the "violent speech" of some members.[13]

[13] *Hansard*, 3rd Ser., XIII, June 28, 1832. Princess Lieven to Grey and his answer, June 29, 1832 (*Correspondence*, II, 359-360). Webster, *Palmerston*, p. 191.

On August 7 in the debate on the Dutch loan, Evans raised the matter again and provided ample information about the Russian terror in Poland and the violation of the union of churches in Luthuania. In a powerful speech Sir Francis Burdett expressed his shame at the government's previous conduct with regard to the Polish cause.[14]

Palmerston had already instructed Lord Durham to raise the subject of the Polish constitution in St. Petersburg; but he stated in the House when answering Evans that "Russia had in neither of the cases [Persian, Turkish and Polish wars] been in the slightest degree the aggressor." With respect to Poland "in the late war the Poles, not the Russians, were aggressors," and he refused to discuss the question of "Russia having broken her faith to the Poles on the subject of the Constitution." So the burden of responsibility was shifted by the Foreign Secretary from the Russians to the Poles and the verbal *démarche* in St. Petersburg became automatically valueless.[15]

Ladislas Zamoyski wrote at that time to his uncle that the British ministers always expected to secure some concessions by appealing to the Tsar's equity and generosity. "They do not realize nor perceive that there is a war between them and Russia, a real and obvious one, and that nothing can help but strength and defiance."[16] He anticipated the developments which were to occur a few months later.

Prince Adam was more cautious in his considerations: "I do not yet see any war in the near future. The two constitutional governments are not yet aware of their situation, they will not start a war, their whole policy will be to avoid war."[17] They exaggerated the British government's unawareness of the real situation. The main obstacle for a more decisive action was—and

---

The "Iron Duke" showed his displeasure by ignoring Princess Czartoryski when seated at her side in Sir George Warrender's house.

[14] *Hansard*, 3rd. Ser., xiv, Aug. 7, 1832. *Zamoyski*, iii, 36-38.

[15] Grey rightly told Princess Lieven that she must be gratified with the Foreign Secretary's statement, "but if something could be done to mitigate the conditions of those poor Poles, what satisfaction it would give to this country and to Europe!" (Aug. 9, 1832, *Correspondence*, ii, 375-377). For Durham's handling of the Polish question see Webster, *Palmerston*, pp. 192-195.

[16] Letter of Aug. 8, 1832, *Zamoyski*, iii, 40-41.

[17] To Gen. Chrzanowski, Aug. 29, 1832 (Handelsman, ii, 52).

Czartoryski knew it perfectly well—their strong feeling that they could not risk war when facing a common front of the three partitioning powers, while being still in latent conflict with France. They were somewhat disturbed by the growing pro-Polish disposition of the Parliament. They asked Czartoryski: "What do you think to achieve with your motions and petitions?" He answered: "We want to have the rights of Poland engraved on the walls of the parliaments."[18] It was what he nearly achieved. When he left London in autumn 1832 for a few months' sojourn in Paris, he left behind many devoted and active British friends ready to raise their voice in defence of the freedom of his country even at the risk of displeasing the government. The Literary Association of Friends of Poland, founded by the exertions of Niemcewicz and presided over originally by the poet Thomas Campbell (then by Thomas Wentworth Beaumont, and later on for many years by Lord Dudley Coutts Stuart), became a valuable political instrument by organizing meetings, manifestations, and petitions and proved a real blessing for the Polish refugees in Britain.[19]

In Paris, *Vive la Pologne* was for two years the battlecry of the Party of Movement in their fight against Louis Philippe's policy of appeasing the absolutist powers. Prince Adam found in the government itself, at the post of Foreign Minister, an old acquaintance, the Duke of Broglie; he had known Poland as a member of the French Embassy in Napoleon's time, and still had some feeling for that country and even for Puławy, where he had once been a guest. He told Czartoryski that France would never recognize the present status in Poland and asked for legal arguments to be exploited in a diplomatic intervention.[20]

[18] *Zamoyski*, III, 26.

[19] See Czartoryski, *Żywot Niemcewicza*, pp. 234-235. Gleason, *Russophobia*, 120-125. For the origins of Lord Dudley Coutts Stuart's association with the Polish cause and of his friendship with Zamoyski, see the interesting account of M. Budzyński, *Wspomnienia*, 1880, I, 237 sq. The Lit. Association published in 1832 a periodical *Polonia*, and then annual reports and other pamphlets. Niemcewicz noted in his diary on Feb. 6, 1832: "Good Prince Adam purchased in spite of his present poverty all books on Polish history in order to leave them to the Museum Britannicum." *Dziennik podróży zagranicą*, 1876, I, 171, 355-356.

[20] *Zamoyski*, III, 58-60. Czartoryski's *pro memoria* for Palmerston of Oct. 1832 suggested a new intervention in intimate concert with France and hinted that it would help the final settlement of the Belgian affairs; see Handelsman, II, 58-59.

Czartoryski's efforts concentrated for several weeks on preparing a Polish manifestation in the French National Assembly; he seized the opportunity given by the forthcoming opening of the House and the debate on the address to the King. On December 3, 1832, Baron Louis de Bignon, once Napoleon's minister to Warsaw and Vilna, moved an amendment to the address warmly recommending to the government the Polish cause; it was voted by a great majority. It was now the Russian Ambassador in Paris, Pozzo di Borgo, once Czartoryski's protégé, who bitterly reproached De Broglie for his intimacy with Czartoryski. But the amendment to the address recalling the obligations towards Poland was not the last one. "It was because of Prince Adam's efforts that so many addresses to the throne were submitted by the Chambre des Députés during Louis Philippe's eighteen years of reign, so many times was Poland named and the violation of European law recalled." There was even an instance when Broglie, moved by a speech of Bignon, his former chief in the French Legation in Poland, gave in his answer an assurance of the government's will to intervene at the proper time for the liberation of Poland, a statement which he was later obliged to explain away.[21]

Prince Adam found followers among French intellectualists. The young Count Charles de Montalembert was the most devoted of all. Two years later he wrote in a note to be shown to the Prince that he asked to be relied upon on any occasion, to be employed according to the Prince's decision, and he affirmed that it was Poland and her future which occupied the first place in his heart after God.[22]

At the end of 1832 there was a deadlock on the Polish question; the cautious objections of the Western powers met with Nicholas' sharp rebuff, and there was left no further move short of an open conflict, which neither Britain nor France was ready to risk. Even Talleyrand told a British friend who mentioned Poland among the many problems absorbing the old statesman: "La

[21] *Zamoyski*, III, 208; Talleyrand, *Mémoires*, III, 308-312. Czartoryski himself wrote a pamphlet: *Le dernier mot sur le Statut Organique imposé à la Pologne*, Paris, 1833.

[22] Letter of July 12, 1834, see Handelsman, *Les idées françaises en Pologne*, 1927, p. 173.

Pologne n'est plus une affaire"; and, bored by old Niemcewicz's plaintive requests, he gave him the advice to drop delusions.[23] Zamoyski recorded a little later "the 'cripple's' indifferent, merciless talk." Even the Duchess of Dino made her separate peace with Russia and with Princess Lieven. In France, early in 1833, the Polish committee presided over by Lelewel was expelled from Paris. The committee members were Czartoryski's political opponents, and they had given to the Russian Embassy a good pretext for diplomatic intervention by paying a solemn tribute to the Russian Decembrists, but their expulsion affected the whole position of the Polish emigration. The War Minister, Marshal Soult, in a circular letter invited Polish officers and men of other ranks to apply for Russian amnesty.[24]

At the same time Prince Adam, who had returned by the end of January 1833 to London, informed the legation in Paris: "I have seen Palmerston; he was glacial and more taciturn than ever; I tried to discuss different matters in vain. In the course of the conversation he said that in spite of the present events in the east the powers do not see any possibility or need of Polish action, nor can they help our cause. . . ." But the Foreign Secretary seemed impressed by the pro-Polish disposition of the Chambre des Députés (and of the House of Commons, as well).[25] Prince Adam sadly remarked a few weeks later: "They do not care now about us. They look to their interests and they will do nothing for us."[26]

Some of his friends suggested that he should desist from further political action, which they now regarded as hopeless; they no longer believed that any help would come either from European cabinets or from the people. The overwhelming majority of the Polish emigration, if still believing in the solidarity of the peoples, was the more hostile to the governments. But Czartoryski persevered in his efforts. He was aware of the tremendous importance

[23] Niemcewicz's reports of Dec. 12, 1832, and Jan. 1, 1933; A. Czartoryski, *Żywot Niemcewicza*, pp. 394-395; A. Benis, *Une Mission polonaise en Égypte*, I, No. 10.

[24] *Zamoyski*, III, 101-103, 127.

[25] Letter of Feb. 1, 1833 (*Album*, pp. 189-191). Cf. Webster, *Palmerston*, pp. 226-235.

[26] Letter to Zamoyski, Mar. 9, 1833 (*Zamoyski*, III, 107-108).

of the events taking place in the Near East, of Russia's gaining control over Turkey and the Straits, of the inevitable serious political tension in Europe. He felt sure of a strong response on the part of public opinion in the West when he appealed for support for the Polish cause. On May 2, 10, and 27 he submitted to Palmerston several *pro memorias* giving him views on the situation of Poland and of Europe. He explained: "We do not demand war, or expenses or troubles for cabinets. We just demand words. Words can in course of time grow powerful and become reality. . . ."[27]

Before long such words were heard again in Parliament when on May 24 Thomas Attwood presented a petition from the Birmingham political associations. "The honorable member said, he thought, that Russia had by her tyrannic conduct laid herself open to the indignation and military attack of all the civilized powers of Europe, and that it was the bounden duty of all the European powers to see justice done to Poland."[28]

There followed on July 9 the presentation of new petitions (Glasgow, Birmingham) and a new Polish debate inaugurated by a motion of Cutlar Fergusson, concluding "that a humble address be presented to His Majesty praying that he will be graciously pleased not to recognize, or in any way give the sanction of his government, to the present political state and condition of Poland, the same having been brought about in violation of the Treaty of Vienna, to which Great Britain was a party."[29] Fergusson once more expounded the Polish case with ample and up-to-date information. He quoted the protest of the Hungarian Diet against the enslavement of Poland, and the declaration of the late Casimir Périer that Poland was under a provisional regime, but had not lost the rights which she held under treaties. He also quoted De Bignon's more recent words: "Facts change, but right and justice cannot change," and De Broglie's agreement with them. He once again shocked the House by quoting decrees and orders concerning the mass sequestration of Polish children if "orphan or poor" to be incorporated in cantonist battalions and

[27] Handelsman, II, 60-61.
[28] Hansard, 3rd. Ser., XVIII, *sub die*. Gleason, *Russophobia*, p. 127 sq.
[29] Hansard, 3rd. Ser., XIX, *sub die*.

mass deportations of Polish lesser gentry. Attwood's speech was once more warlike, and he hinted at the fact that Constantinople and the Straits were now in the possession of the Russians. Several members supported the motion. Palmerston stated that "he knew of no subject which deserved more to command the attention and engage the sympathy of an English association" and paid tribute to Fergusson's "generous feelings"; he restated his opinion that the revolt of the Poles did not absolve the Russian government from its obligations; he mentioned the fact that this opinion had not been concealed from the Russian government. But he emphasized that not only Russia, but also Austria and Prussia, took a different view, and that "it was not deemed prudent to support by force of arms the view taken by England," because of the risk of "involving Europe in a general war." He tried to mitigate the strong impression of the details of the Russian persecutions and remarked that many of the reported facts happened in Podolia and Volhynia "which were strictly part of the Russian territory." That remark was particularly painful to Prince Adam, who wrote to Zamoyski:[30] "We cannot forgive him that he has thrown Podolia and Volhynia to the wolves. . . ."

The conclusion of the Foreign Secretary was that the motion was unnecessary, "for no circumstances could arise under which the English government could give their sanction or acquiescence to the arrangements which the Emperor had made in Poland."

There followed a stormy debate; O'Connell, Buckingham, Hume, Sheil supporting the motion and denouncing the government's weakness, and Lord John Russell, Lord Althorp, Warburton, Stanley, and Sir Robert Peel preaching moderation and the preservation of peace. Fergusson, induced by Zamoyski's ardor, refused to withdraw the motion; there was a division, and 95 against 177 voted for the motion.[31]

The debate sounded like a salvo on the funerals of the 1st Article of the Vienna Treaty. Czartoryski himself was fully

[30] July 22, from Paris, where he had returned, leaving in London Gustave Małachowski (acting Foreign Minister in 1831) and Ladislas Zamoyski.

[31] Koźmian, *Anglia i Polska*, I, 83-92; *Zamoyski*, III, 143-158; Nesselrode, *Lettres et papiers*, VIII, 176 (sharp Russian reply to Palmerston's statement). Gleason, *Russophobia*, pp. 128-130 (size and composition of the minority was significant; the Tsar "incensed" by Palmerston's statement).

aware that the time for hopeful protests was over, that a long-term policy was necessary now, supported by a strong organization of Poles abroad and in underground Poland, exploiting conflicts among European powers, building up barriers against despotism and slavery, and preparing for a final struggle.

CHAPTER 16

PRINCE ADAM AND THE GREAT
EMIGRATION

IN THE SUMMER of 1833 Prince Adam decided to settle in the center
of the Polish emigration, the main part of which had found sanctuary in France. Princess Anna had followed him into exile with
their two boys Vitold and Ladislas, and the little Isabelle.[1] They
had lived since 1832 in Paris. Niemcewicz, already too old for
any political activity, also left London for France. Gustav Małachowski, former Foreign Minister in 1831, and Ladislas Zamoyski
were entrusted with the representation of the Polish cause in
Great Britain. Zamoyski performed that delicate mission with
some interruptions—special missions to Rome, Germany, Italy,
Hungary or Turkey—for three decades.[2]

The so-called Great Emigration was certainly larger than any
Polish emigration before, although it was far below the figures
of the political emigrations of our times. Less than ten thousand
Poles, mostly officers and men of other ranks, went to France
after crossing the Prussian or Austrian frontiers and refused to
return. For most of them it was a triumphant journey. Those
vanquished soldiers were enthusiastically greeted in Germany,
and the "Polen-Lieder" written mostly at that time, are a lasting
memorial of that unique phenomenon of Germano-Polish brotherly relations.[3] The exiles were welcomed by the French, especially
by the Party of Movement and by the radical elements of the

---

[1] Vitold was born Aug. 6, 1822, Ladislas on July 3, 1828, Isabelle on Dec. 14,
1830, two weeks after the November outbreak in Warsaw, and nicknamed
"Princess of Revolution."

[2] His papers, *Zamoyski*, III-VI, are important for the history of Czartoryski's life
and policy, 1832-1861.

[3] Julius Mosen's "Die Letzten Zehn vom vierten Regiment," when translated,
became a Polish national song, even more popular for some decades than Casimir
Delavigne's "La Varsovienne" in Charles Sienkiewicz's powerful translation. Only
the latter has survived the events of the last fifty years.

intelligentsia and working classes. Lafayette's Committee for Poland provided sums for their relief; later, when their number increased, the ex-servicemen were granted allowances from the French treasury equivalent to the military half-pay. The emigrants were concentrated in several dépôts, away from the capital. Political refugees continued to come over, and there were still several hundred Polish soldiers interned by the Prussians; Prince Adam made continual efforts to obtain their release. After long delays, the Prussians decided upon their deportation to America, treatment which at that time was regarded as very harsh. The British friends of Poland, on Prince Adam's request, organized their landing at British ports and prepared a provisional sanctuary for that handful of soldiers. Thus the problem of Polish refugees, their relief and resettlement, became from 1834 the concern of the British government and Parliament as well.

In Paris, the Polish Legation became a nucleus of a strong group of generals, senior officers, civil servants, and politicians who looked to Czartoryski for guidance and were ready to back his efforts. But a new political body emerged when members of the last Polish government, of the Seym, and of the radical Patriotic Society gathered in Paris. A Polish Provisional Committee was elected with the last president of the Polish national government, Bonaventura Niemojowski, as chairman. In the course of a few weeks it was superseded by a Permanent National Committee proclaimed at a meeting of refugees, dominated by the Carbonari and other radicals, and sponsored by Lafayette. Lelewel was president, and their first manifesto of December 1831 read like an indictment of the political and military leadership of the recent war. Prince Adam's diplomacy was accused of having deluded itself and the nation by promises of foreign mediation. The manifesto even mentioned the inactivity allegedly imposed upon the army by diplomats—a very unjust reproach and particularly surprising when endorsed by Lelewel, who himself had been a member of the government and should have known better. The rank and file were inclined to blame for the defeat those who were formally responsible for the government and the conduct of war;

there was bitter ill-feeling against the aristocrats, diplomats, and generals.

But it was something more than a crisis of confidence that estranged the majority of the exiles from Czartoryski. There was a deep divergence in their feelings and ideological creeds. Prince Adam persevered in seeking support from the constitutional monarchies of Western Europe—the July monarchy included; he looked for allies among the liberal sovereigns and statesmen, among influential members of parliaments and other leading politicians; he tried to win over the public opinion of the ruling élites. He considered the Polish soldierly emigration as the nucleus of a future Polish army, and he wished to see them organized as soon as possible in Polish legions in national uniforms, commanded by their old military chiefs. In 1832 he wrote to General Bem: "When a nucleus of a Polish army is formed, a great, decisive step forward will be made."

He tried therefore first to induce the French government to create a Polish legion, and Marshal Soult seemed inclined to do so. But concern for Russian susceptibility prevailed, and the admission of Poles to the Foreign Legion in Algeria was all that the French government was prepared to risk. In 1832 there were hopes of the formation of a Polish force in the Belgian army; King Leopold was eager to have as many Polish officers and men of other ranks as possible in order to use them as a skeleton for the young Belgian army. Ladislas Zamoyski joined him in the siege of Antwerp as aide-de-camp,[4] but all that the King of Belgium could achieve, when faced with the political implications of such an alliance with the Poles, was the help of a handful of Polish officers who served Belgium for years and earned good records in the military history of that country.[5] At the same time, Czartoryski made an agreement with Count Palmella, the representative of Don Pedro, providing for the formation of a Polish legion in Portugal in the service of the little Queen Dona Maria.

[4] He had known King Leopold as Prince of Sachsen-Coburg in 1829. At Antwerp he also became a friend of the Duke of Orléans, and that friendship lasted up to the latter's premature death.

[5] General Kruszewski was one of the most outstanding. For details, see J. R. Leconte, *La formation de l'armée Belge*, 1940, and Ladislas Zamoyski's notes and letters, *Zamoyski*, III.

The Great Emigration

The brave General Bem undertook the task in 1832-1833; his efforts ended rather sadly after bitter experiences and quarrels.[6] Soon after, in 1833-1834, there was the Polish military mission of General Dembiński to Mehemet Aly with a view to employing Polish officers in the organization and training of the Egyptian forces, as the Russian military intervention against Ibrahim's army in Anatolia seemed imminent. But the Polish general and his companions were sacrificed before long for the sake of appeasing the Tsar, and their mission came to an abrupt end.[7]

The civil war in Spain provided another opportunity for trying to raise the Polish banner against absolutist Europe; a large formation was to be organized and equipped in France to serve with the constitutionalist Spanish army. That plan, although originally agreed upon, met with serious political difficulties on the French side and all that proved possible was the transfer of the Polish units of the French Foreign Legion from Africa to Spain and the admission of a few Polish officers to the service of that country.[8]

Difficulties were due mostly to the reluctance of the constitutional and liberal governments to provoke Tsar Nicholas' anger —little Belgium had taken the risk and for long years no diplomatic relations existed between her and Russia. General Skrzynecki's admission to the Belgian army in 1838 caused a new and violent diplomatic conflict with all the three participants of the partition of Poland. But there were other causes for the failure of Czartoryski's endeavors. The majority of the Polish emigration was hostile to all monarchic governments; the exiles hated the French government because it had left Poland alone in 1831, and that feeling also prevailed in their attitude towards kings in general. They sought allies among the peoples of Europe identified with revolutionary elements, with the Carbonari and later, after 1833, with Mazzini's Young Europe, where Young Poland fraternized with Young Italy, Young Germany, Young Switzer-

[6] J. Freilich, *Legion gen. Bema w walce o sukcesję portugalska*, 1912.
[7] See the large publication of documents: A. Benis, *Une mission militaire polonaise en Égypte* (Le Caire, 1938), 2 vols.
[8] *Zamoyski*, III and IV.

land, etc. They hoped to achieve Poland's liberation as a result of a general uprising of the people in a world revolution; many of them marched in 1832 from their French dépôts to Switzerland to support the revolutionary outbreak in southern Germany. They arrived too late, when the revolt had already been crushed, and they stayed marooned in friendly Switzerland; but, incited by their Italian comrades, they made under Ramorino's command an irruption into Savoy to help the revolution in Piedmont. Most of them believed that Poland's peculiar mission was to take the lead—was she not, as Słowacki called her, "The Winkelried of Nations," ready to throw herself on the common enemy's spears to pave the way for Freedom for others.[9]

Thus Zaliwski decided to start a guerrilla movement in Poland against the powerful Russian army and in 1833 organized an expedition of several small groups of heroic desperados. They were wiped out without any serious fighting. Although the people did not join the struggle, cruel repressions followed, and the country was once more tormented by terror and overwhelmed with sorrow.

But even less adventurous Polish officers and soldiers were no more inclined to serve Portuguese or Spanish queens, and waging war in the Foreign Legion against Arabs, who were fighting for their country, seemed quite a different thing from fighting for Poland and for the cause of freedom. Thus, when in 1832 at a meeting at Bourges, delegates of all military dépôts elected a committee as a common representative body, the president was General Dwernicki, a favorite of the former Patriotic Society; and his first manifesto strongly opposed any plans for employing Poles in foreign armies. "Our blood," it read, "entirely and exclusively belongs to our own country. Europe is already indebted enough to the Poles, and there is no need for further sacrifices to acquire brotherhood and friendship with other peoples. We are ready to fight against any despotism oppressing Europe, since such a struggle might lead to the future liberation of Poland, but we shall not hire ourselves to foreign service or participate in any struggle if

[9] J. Słowacki: *Kordian*, 1833; cf. Freiligrath's later poem "Der Freiheit eine Gasse."

not undertaken for European freedom and the interests of our own country."[10]

Bem's recruiting for the Legion Dona Maria provoked not only violent protests but even an attempt on his life from which he had a narrow escape. The same sharp opposition occurred in other cases, and protests were often poisoned with abuse and slander.

At the same time as the death sentence was promulgated on Czartoryski in Warsaw, another sentence of civil death was pronounced by a large part of the Polish emigration. A declaration of the Community of the Dépôt at Poitiers of July 29, 1834, signed by nearly three thousand people, stated that "Adam Czartoryski not only does not enjoy their confidence but is regarded as an enemy of the Polish Emigration." The dépôt at Nevers went even further, declaring him "unworthy of the name of a Pole, traitor to his country" and "exposing him to the public contempt and the curse of posterity."[11]

An unusual amount of patience and perseverance was needed to continue the service not only for the cause of Poland but for the welfare of the same people who had joined in that campaign of ostracism and abuse. Prince Adam reacted by pitying his adversaries: "Poor people, they more deserve commiseration than condemnation" and he did not desist from doing everything possible to help Polish communities and individuals in exile. After some years, in one of his great speeches (November 29, 1839), he alluded to those sad incidents, saying that in the past years he had experienced slanderous attacks as well as manifestations of attachment and confidence. "Against the first I used to have as defence inadvertence, often even ignorance and always oblivion; for the others I have sincere feelings of friendship and gratitude. But neither abusive attacks of any kind or degree nor friendly encouragement could deflect me from the way, on which I had been put long since by the force of circumstances—the way of serving my country with all my means, and by doing so I do

[10] Manifesto of Oct. 3, 1832; see Gadon, *Emigracja Polska*, III, 302-304.

[11] *Ibid.*, pp. 19-25. The coincidence of those pronouncements with the Warsaw verdict was perhaps not fully accidental, as their chief promoter, Adam Gurowski, a would-be-champion of radical democracy, was in secret contact with the Russian Embassy in Paris and shortly after openly changed sides.

not ever implore or expect Providence to help me, without being strongly convinced that what I am doing is for the good, for the salvation, and, God willing, for the glory and happiness of our beloved country."

That dignified statement was a development of the simple idea, expressed by Czartoryski's device: *Bądź co bądź* (*Quand même*). It exactly recorded Prince Adam's actual conduct. In 1833, after the adventurous expeditions to Switzerland and Savoy, he did, together with his nephew, all that could be done to get assistance for the unfortunate legion of political opponents—Lord Dudley Stuart collected and sent an important contribution—and for obtaining for them from the French government once more the hospitality of the French dépôts and their former allowances. When, as result of his exertions, the soldiers who came from Prussia in 1834 were permitted to land in England and were granted provisional sanctuary until the French vessels could transport them to Algiers, to join the legion, they refused to go there and claimed the permanent hospitality of Britain. Prince Adam not only excused their conduct, but appealed to his British friends to assist them, to help in their employment, and to obtain from the Parliament allowances for Polish refugees on the French pattern.[12] Thanks to the devoted friendship of Lord Dudley Stuart for Zamoyski, Czartoryski, and Poland and his inspiring activity, these goals were achieved.[13] Thus the first Polish Socialist communities, founded by some noble idealists among those wandering soldiers, had their cradle on English soil, under Prince Adam's forbearing and discreet protection.

He stimulated the charitable activity of the British friends of Poland and he sponsored Princess Anna's activity in Paris, as the "grand almoner" of the emigration: her concerts, balls, *ventes* for the relief of the poorest.[14] Chopin was her last and infallible reserve, and George Sand wrote to her with a melancholic smile: "Chère Majesté, Regina Coeli." The full meaning of that title will be explained later. The French aristocracy and intellectuals

---

[12] A. Czartoryski to Lord Dudley Coutts Stuart, Paris, Mar. 9, 1834 (H.Mss., xxv, 166-167). The first fund for their relief had been provided by the Prince; see L. Niedźwiecki to Dudley Stuart, Jan. 20, 1834 (*ibid.*, xxvi, 194).

[13] A. Czartoryski to Dudley Stuart, n.d., June 1834 (H.Mss., xxv, 168-169).

[14] She was President of the "Charitable Society of Polish Ladies," founded 1834.

often yielded to Princess Anna's requests, reading for instance: "I have behind me a whole people of outlaws." But the material needs of the Polish outlaws were not the only matter to be cared for. In 1832, under the auspices of the Legation in Paris, a Polish Literary Society was founded (later the Historical and Literary Society), as well as a Society for Education; in 1835 under Prince Adam's auspices and assistance, General Bem organized a Polytechnical Society; later, in 1843, there was the Polish School at Batignolles (which survived the 19th century), and in 1844 the Institution for Polish Girls under Princess Anna's personal care, which existed up until the end of the century.

In 1838 he was one of the founders of the Polish Library in Paris, which was to be the most durable memorial of the Great Emigration; it survived the momentous political changes of our times and the perils of three wars, and remains for a hundred years in the building where Czartoryski used to address the public meetings of the Historical and Literary Society.

In 1849 a Polish Higher School at Montparnasse was founded. And one should not forget the military courses organized several times for some periods, General Chrzanowski's great map of Poland drawn and printed at Prince Adam's expense, periodicals, innumerable books and pamphlets either financed or subsidized by him.

His ever-growing diplomatic activities will be recounted in another chapter; they must however be taken into account when speaking of Prince Adam's position in the Great Emigration.

The material means for all those institutions, agencies, and publications were either supplied by himself, or by his family and friends in Poland and abroad, and Zamoyski took the lead by taxing heavily his own estate and his brothers' much larger fortunes as well. But important support came from Britain, where Lord Dudley Stuart collected certain sums for Czartoryski's political undertakings and sometimes in critical moments became himself the grand treasurer of the Polish state in exile.[15]

That state *in partibus*, some components of which seemed to emerge abroad, suffered badly from lack of a generally recognized

[15] See Czartoryski's letters to Lord Dudley (H.Mss., xxv), 1846-1848; esp. the letter from Berlin, Apr. 10, 1848, pp. 210-212.

supreme authority. The last Polish government of 1831 made no serious attempt to take the control and the lead abroad. There was the possibility of resurrecting the Seym of 1831. During the revolution it had been the supreme national power; it had never abdicated and a law voted at the time of the battle of Grochów (February 1831) allowed for its functioning even abroad and with a much reduced quorum (of 33 members including senators). It was easy to gather as many as that in Paris, if the members themselves were willing to resume their parliamentary duties. Some of them were ready to do so, and there were many private meetings to discuss the opening of the proceedings, but neither Prince Adam's friends and followers nor the revolutionaries were inclined to confide the destinies of the Polish cause to such a rump parliament, and neither side regarded it as really representative of the national will.[16]

No possibility was left untouched, therefore, for uniting the emigration under the lead of one national authority. The gulf between the right link of the emigration and the revolutionaries grew wider and deeper than ever before when the Democratic Society founded in 1832 became in the late thirties predominant at the left wing, and gradually extended its control over most of the underground societies and conspiracies in all parts of Poland. The society was egalitarian and preached social revolution. This meant radical land reform, full political rights for peasants, and a popular government according to the device: "All for the people, by the people" (thus read their manifesto of 1836). They were uncompromising in their decision to crush the political and social power of the landed gentry; they declared: "Who is against us is against the Fatherland." Czartoryski was for them a symbol of a monarchic and aristocratic regime, the leader of the landed gentry—an adversary and even a foe.

Czartoryski had no other way than to seek for the support of a political party of his own. A secret organization, the League of National Unity, was founded on January 21, 1833, by Czartoryski, Barzykowski, Bem, Dembiński, Plater, Małachowski, Swirski, all of whom had played an important part in the last insurrection.[17]

---

[16] For the problem of the Seym abroad, see Handelsman, I, 257-259.
[17] S. Barzykowski, G. Małachowski, and J. Swirski had been ministers.

The Great Emigration

The program they agreed upon was far from being reactionary; it was progressive and liberal. The main points were: Equality for all before the law; liberty of individuals; freedom of religion and opinion; security of property; peasant ownership of lands; unity and efficiency of government.

There was a distinct tendency to establish monarchical and constitutional government, sensibly liberal. The social changes which had been achieved in the French revolution were accepted. Emphasis was laid on an early solution of the problem of the peasants by granting them property in land, where they already were freed from serfdom, and freedom and property if they were still serfs.

It meant a full recognition of the overwhelming importance of that problem and of the fatal consequences of the neglect which it had suffered in 1831. Czartoryski and the national government had tried at that time to start the land reform by abolishing the statute labor on the national estates; but the liberals in the Seym had not shown any understanding of the project, and a handful of reactionary extremists, led by Marquess Wielopolski, succeeded in delaying any reform until the very end. After the catastrophe the conviction was growing that the full liberation of the peasants had been the only way of winning the struggle for independence. That was rather an overstatement. The land reform if proclaimed would certainly have sharpened the valor of the rank and file and the willingness of the common man to make sacrifices for his country's sake. But it was not lack of valor and devotion that had caused the final defeat. In any case a great opportunity had been lost for winning forever the masses of people to the cause of independence. Now the Polish revolutionaries thought they had invented a panacea for a victorious insurrection: the release of the immense potential energy of the millions of peasants by proclaiming their social freedom.

Czartoryski's League of National Unity did not oppose the tendency of enfranchisement; only the approach was different. The great measure was to be accomplished by acts of good will on the part of the landed gentry and was regarded as a necessary precondition of a future insurrection. They decided to act in full secrecy, to adopt the organization of a religious order, or rather one on a masonic pattern, to establish links with the homeland, to maintain there a strong patriotic spirit; the part of the emigration was "to appeal to the opinion of the peoples and to influence the policy of the governments."[18]

Prince Adam, when sending Charles Marcinkowski as emissary to Poland in October 1834, pointed out the respective tasks of the emigration and of the homeland. "Poland cannot regain her existence, except by an uprising, which must be strong, general, and undertaken at the proper moment." Until such a moment would come, "the homeland must refrain from action; premature and partial undertakings and unauthorized military moves can only bring new disasters. The emigration must unite, work, and organize a Polish armed corps."[19]

L. Gadon, a historical writer who often expressed the views of Prince Adam's son and political successor, rightly emphasized the utmost importance of the attitude of the league with regard to the enfranchisement of the peasants. "Those measures ought to have been put before any other matters and promoted by all available means." The granting of land to the peasants should have been accomplished by the landowners themselves; if the governments prevented such action, the people would have known at least that it was Poland which tried to liberate them from slavery. It would have dispelled any menace of social revolution and disarmed the radical propaganda of the Carbonari, of the Young Poland, and of the Democratic Society. But Prince Adam's great and salutary idea met with some passive resistance in the ranks of his own party and in the class of landowners, on whom he mostly, although not exclusively, based his political action. The opinion of his followers was too slow in following him; years elapsed before any serious action was undertaken, and in the meantime tendencies to start an insurrection by a social revolution were growing up in the underground conspiracies in Poland and among the emigration.

Czartoryski's position abroad was unmatched by any other Polish politician or political group. The leaders of the league

[18] On the League of National Unity, see Handelsman, I, 264-271; Gadon, *Emigracja*, IV, 300-317; *Zamoyski*, III, 102-103.
[19] Quoted by Handelsman, *Francja-Polska*, 1926, p. 240.

and many other prominent Poles became aware of the asset he was for the Polish cause and considered how to elevate him above the party feuds and petty affairs of the emigration. The great poet Mickiewicz suggested in 1834 that the Prince must not become too involved as leader of the emigration, but reserve himself as future king. At the same time Prince Adam's former violent opponent, Maurice Mochnacki, the leader of the Patriotic Society in 1831, suggested to Ladislas Zamoyski the conception of an insurrectional monarchy. He would unite the whole emigration under one leading personality, in order to pave the way for unity of leadership and action in the future national rising. Czartoryski's supreme authority was to be imposed as a measure of salvation in the future struggle for independence.

The suggestion of that young and inspiring politician probably aimed at Prince Adam's provisional monarchical power, as a regent of the realm, not at proclaiming him king. Charles Hoffman, a distinguished political writer and historian, one of Czartoryski's ablest collaborators, considered his part in Poland's struggle for independence similar to the part of William of Orange in the Netherlands, and while stating emphatically that Prince Adam was the only Pole who in certain circumstances should be proclaimed king, he did not propose taking such a step before the proper time.[20] But there were among Czartoryski's young followers tendencies to make of him a living symbol of their monarchic idea, by proclaiming him king *de facto* and his family a dynasty *de facto*. Those tendencies, fostered by Ladislas Zamoyski and championed by Janusz Woronicz, one of the Prince's secretaries, ripened in the years 1837-1839 and prevailed in Czartoryski's party in spite of his own reluctance and the almost general opposition of his old friends and of his family as well. The program of rebuilding a Polish kingdom under the Czartoryski dynasty was loudly promulgated, and although Prince Adam refused to proclaim himself king and reacted with anger when some of his followers spoke or wrote about it, he never publicly disavowed the program. He tolerated his nephew's and Woronicz's "dynastic

[20] K. Hoffman, *Cztery powstania* (Four Insurrections) 1837, and "Odpowiedź Lelewelowi na La Couronne de Pologne et la Royauté," in *Kronika Emigracji Polskiej*, vi (1837).

propaganda" and thus exposed himself to a great deal of criticism, slander, and ridicule. He was under the strong influence of Zamoyski, who tried to force upon him a final decision by persuading him that it was one more sacrifice he must make for Poland's salvation. The Prince knew very well that it would be a crown of thorns, and that very fact prevented him from simply rejecting the offer. Without taking the title, he accepted the charges and responsibilities of a king.[21] But the throne erected in exile did not prove helpful for uniting the Poles. On the contrary, it repelled many people who were ready to follow Prince Adam as a national leader but refused to admit the right of the emigration, or of a part of it, to dispose of the Polish crown. Moreover, the Prince was seventy years old and his health seemed to have been affected by several serious illnesses. His sons—the heirs presumptive—were too young to be looked upon as continuators of his work.

But the spectacular challenge in meeting a difficult situation by no means remained without response. The Monarchical and Insurrectional Party of May 3 founded by Zamoyski reached the important total of 1,500 members in exile, and had many devoted and influential adherents in Poland. It was a real achievement of the old Prince that in spite of the delicacy of his situation he imposed respect even for his kingdom of exiles.

Czartoryski used to speak to his fellow exiles publicly twice a year, at solemn meetings of the Historical and Literary Association, on May 3 and November 29, and those speeches were styled as announcements of the chief of the Polish nation.[22] In the November 1841 speech he explained how his leadership in 1830-1831 had been hampered by the memories of his former friendship and collaboration with Alexander I, a relationship which

---

[21] For Czartoryski's kingship *de facto* see Handelsman, I, 270-290, and in *Przegląd Współczesny*, 1838, esp. Czartoryski's letter to L. Sapieha, June 7, 1841, with an explanation of the whole affair. Most illuminating is Zamoyski's correspondence, *Zamoyski*, IV, 53-54, 86-87, 91-93, 103, 153-155, 181, 334, 368-381, 403, and V, 414-416. Also see Czartoryski's letters to Col. Łagowski, May 9, 1836, and to Col. Bystrzonowski, May 12, 1840 (B.P.Ms. 54, Nr. 22); and M. Budzyński, *Wspomnienia*, I, 299-305; F. Breański, "Autobiografia," *Przewodnik naukovy i literacki*, 1913, pp. 1068-1071.

[22] Those from the years 1838-1847 were published in 1847; some were published separately in French.

deprived him of the full confidence of his countrymen. But now, when he had given such evident proofs of his devotion to his country, he felt his right to demand the establishment of one authority, of a common center of action; the lack of centrality had been the cause of the disaster in the last struggle and Poland would never rise again without it. The nation deprived of material power must the more concentrate her moral strength for action. He declared that by assuming leadership he rendered possibly his last service to his country and that by doing so his sacrifice was the greater, the more painful and difficult, than if he had simply covered himself with a cloak of disinterestedness and, protected by it, quietly lived what was still left of his life. At that time he added to his armorial device *Bądź co bądź* (*Quand même*) another one so familiar to British ears, the Black Prince's *Ich diene*.

He expounded in his speeches his ideas with regard to the Polish cause, always considered in close connection with the general developments in European policy. His general ideas were expounded with particular lucidity in his speech of 1840. He admitted as axiomatic that the defeat of 1831 "was due not to the superiority of the enemy's forces, but to the lack of sufficient moral strength for making the proper use of all the forces of Poland, to the lack of order, of unity, of efficient government, and of self-confidence." General war, which had seemed inevitable in the early thirties, was not to be expected in the near future. The divergence of policy in England and France greatly favored Russia's impact on Europe, and the West was inclined to withdraw before the possibility of a conflict. Poland's situation was different: "We are the only ones who do not fear war; first, because nothing short of war can return to Poland her independence, and, secondly, because our oppressors maintain a state of war against our nation." The sufferings of the so-called peace even made the Polish people expect their salvation from a war. But, "in order to become a factor in European policy, Poland must rise in arms by a general and unanimous effort," and when fighting for independence "she must be just a military camp." Two things were deemed necessary for that purpose: her own strength and propitious circumstances. Czartoryski did not expect Poland's liberation from foreign support only; he emphasized, as he had in 1831, the fact that no one would liberate Poland without the efforts of the Polish nation itself. He was aware that her own forces could not expect to break the forces of the three partitioning powers. Thus in another November speech, in 1842, he restated his idea: "I shall not deviate from the way I have chosen and in the face of all odds I shall remain loyal to my vocation and my creed. I shall gather together separate grains; I shall seize separate fibers and link them in common threads, bind them at one focus to create if possible a strength for Poland, to prepare spirits for internal order and hearts for daring action at a moment when a favorable situation and foreign support can be secured."

No vital problem concerning either any part of Poland or the emigration was neglected in those speeches. At the end of that period—1845—Czartoryski dealt twice with the problem of the peasants, the most crucial of all. He spoke of Father Ściegienny's recent case and trial. Father Ściegienny, an outstanding leader of the underground Polish People's Association, had organized the peasants in several districts of the Kingdom of Poland in order to start a revolution aimed at the liberation of the country and their own social enfranchisement. The movement was radical, the ideas egalitarian, and there was a marked hostility against landowners. Father Ściegienny was arrested by the Russians, his activities disclosed, and cruel punishments followed.[23] Czartoryski did not indulge in denouncing the "communists"; he warmly defended the Polish peasants against such an accusation and had for them only sympathy and commiseration. But when hinting at the importance of the fact that the peasants took part in a political conspiracy for liberating Poland, he insisted upon the duty of the nobility to prove themselves worthy of leading the Polish people in their struggle, and he gave a grave warning against further neglect of that duty. He had expressed this sentiment plainly a year before in a secret instruction for his friends in Poland: "It is a principle for the future insurrection, that it must be so arranged that the landowners ought to be leaders of the popular movement." In the November speech he emphasized the necessity of the immediate enfranchisement and granting of land to the peasants. "Moments come in the progress of human

23 See M. Tyrowicz, *Sprawa ks. Ściegiennego*, Warszawa, 1948.

affairs when words become devoid of value and acts become necessary to restore it." The enfranchisement was "the principal and most efficacious measure, if we want to have at the decisive moment the whole nation—millions of people—burning with the same uniform and common ardor." He pointed out that it was the only way of avoiding social calamities. He recalled old secular wrongs which were done to the Polish people and demanded that they should "be repaired by a sacrifice which is a common command of patriotism, of Christian charity, of necessity, of justice, and even, it may be added, of the nobility's own interest as well."

Other problems of the utmost importance were treated in the same speech, especially the problems of the Lithuanians and Ruthenians, "who are our brothers and parts of the same nation." For many centuries of common history they had been mixed with the Poles and were now united by common sufferings. The only hope of freedom for the Poles and for themselves lay "in unity and brotherhood." Czartoryski demanded that their peculiarities, rites, customs, and tongues should be respected and protected. As to their emerging tendencies towards a separate existence, he considered far-reaching solutions in the spirit of equity and Christian charity.

There was in Czartoryski's speeches a slow but transparent evolution from the language of a liberal statesman of his time, opposing any influence of the Church and paying mere lip service to the sanctity of the Christian religion, to the more humble language of a believer. As mentioned before, Czartoryski had been an active Freemason from his early years; he had the highest Polish degree in the Society, and when in exile he was greeted as a brother in 1839 by the English Freemasons presided over by their Grand Master, the Duke of Sussex. He was, in the same year, a guest of honor of a Masonic lodge in Edinburgh; and in 1848 the Polish National Lodge, when conferring its highest degree upon Lord Dudley Stuart, informed him that Prince Czartoryski was an active member of the lodge.[24] Czartoryski had undergone

---

[24] A. Głogowski to Ld. Dudley Stuart, London, Feb. 5, 1848 (H.Mss., xxv, 286-287). Cf. H. C. Iverson, *The Polish National Lodge*, 1937, p. 40. Lord Dudley Stuart had a leading part in the founding of the lodge (1846-1847). Incidentally,

long before some ideological evolution; and his young French friend and admirer, Count Charles de Montalembert, one of those who undertook to reconcile liberalism and the Catholic Church, did much not only to promote that evolution, but also to reconcile the Polish liberal statesman with Rome.

Prince Adam denounced with vigor and powerful evidence the persecution of the Catholic Church in Poland and especially of the Greek Catholics (the Uniates) in the Lithuanian and Ruthenian provinces. The defence of the Church became a part of the struggle for Poland's national existence; and he appealed several times to Rome for support for Catholic Poland and the persecuted Catholic Church in Poland. In 1831 he had sent to Rome an emissary, Count Stanislas Badeni, whose mission met with little success; the only result was a suggestion from the Vatican made to the Austrians to try to mitigate Nicholas' vengeance. But the next year, on June 9, 1832, Pope Gregory XVI, yielding to the Russian envoy Prince Gagarin's pressure, and to Metternich's persuasion, pronounced in his breve, "Cum Primum," a harsh condemnation of the participation of the clergy in the insurrection and a strong warning against any subversive activities directed against the government. It was a terrible blow to Polish national feelings; a serious crisis emerged in Polish Catholicism, and for many years to come there was a growing spirit of revolt against the Pope.[25] Prince Adam tried to appeal "a Papa male informato ad melius informandum" and to reconcile him to Polish patriotism and to the cause of Polish independence. Soundings were made in 1834 with disappointing results.[26] The Pope, as in 1831, regarded all of the national movements with the same enmity, as the actions of the Italian Carbonari, which were a direct threat to his own state; and Tsar Nicholas, although he persecuted the Catholics in his Empire, seemed at the same time to be a defender of the security of Europe against any menace of revolution.

---

no *Masonica* were preserved in Czartoryski's papers and relics. They probably had been disposed of in the last period of his life.

[25] For the policy of Gregory XVI and his attitude towards Poland, see M. Zywczyński, *Geneza i następstwa Encykliki Cum Primum* (The Origin and Consequences of the Encyclic Cum Primum), Warsaw, 1935.

[26] Mission of Adam Soltan, 1834-1837.

The Great Emigration

In 1837 Montalembert at last succeeded in paving the way for Ladislas Zamoyski at the Vatican, and there were several dramatic conversations between the Pope and the Polish patriot. The Pope was well aware that in spite of Austrian interventions the Tsar did not repay his friendly gesture and that the situation of the Church in Poland was growing intolerable. He warmly assured Zamoyski that his only idea was to spare the Church in Poland persecutions and not to offend the Polish nation. Zamoyski was impressed by the Pope's tears; he even thought that the Vatican policy would change.[27] This proved to be a delusion. The main points of the encyclical "Cum Primum" were repeated in the encyclicals and allocution of 1839 and 1842. But contact continued.[28] In 1842 Prince Adam warmly greeted the Pope's allocution as denouncing to the Christian world the cruel and ignominious conduct of the Tsar's government with regard to the Catholics in Poland. He tried to placate Polish opinion as to the policy of the Holy See, and his own position in Rome grew slowly stronger. From 1844 there was in Rome a Polish chief agency—an informal legation of Czartoryski's. Its chief, Louis Orpiszewski, was to be for many years an *agent tacitement reconnu*. His and Zamoyski's friendship with the young Count Luigi Mastai Ferretti and their acquaintance with his uncle, the Cardinal and future Pope, paved the way to more intimate relations in the future between Rome and fighting Poland.

Prince Adam was at that moment not only a defender of the Church against Russian persecutions and of the religious Union in Poland; he also tried to extend the Union of Churches to the Balkan countries, especially to Bulgaria, and thus to emancipate them from the Russian religious protectorate and to bring them nearer Western Christendom. That great undertaking was near success; it was crushed in 1845 by Russian pressure, and the Bulgarian Unionists had their first martyrs.

Czartoryski's work for the Balkan Union of Churches contributed to the *rapprochement* with the Vatican. It will be remembered in connection with the development of his foreign policy, especially with his continuous efforts to build up a barrier

[27] *Zamoyski*, III, 431-441.
[28] Mission of Cezary Plater, 1837-1840.

of freedom-loving nations to check the expansionist policy of Nicholas I.

From 1843 Czartoryski's activity as the chief of the Polish state in exile was focused in a miniature capital. The improvement of his material situation allowed him to acquire the old Hôtel Lambert on the Ile-St.-Louis, and the name of the house meant to a generation of Poles in their country and abroad almost the same as did La Cour des Tuileries or the Court of St. James to the French and British. The house became not only the home of the Prince's family, but also the seat of his political offices, of his wife's charitable activities, of educational institutions. The court was somewhat austere in displaying the spirit of self-denial more than any royal splendor.[29] The cabinet was never officially appointed. Stanislas Barzykowski, Prince Adam's colleague in the national government in 1831, was for many years his official deputy, Teodor Morawski his chief collaborator for foreign affairs, and General Chrzanowski his chief military adviser. But other younger collaborators, such as Colonel Louis Bystrzonowski and Major Feliks Breański, played an important part, especially in the work of the Monarchist party, as did the Prince's secretaries, Charles Sienkiewicz at first, then Woronicz, Niedźwiedzki, and others. The role of Ladislas Zamoyski is not easy to define; it was more a father-and-son relationship than a formal one of chief and subordinate. Zamoyski acted as his uncle's deputy in Britain; he undertook important trips to Italy, Germany, Austria, and to Prussian Poland. He was an ardent man full of exuberant energy, sometimes too prompt in taking decisions, but always ready to submit to the Prince's authority, and serving him with devotion and self-sacrifice.[30] The impression of some contemporaries that he was the real chief and Prince Adam's brain was misleading; their correspondence does not permit any doubts as to who was the actual chief. Zamoyski was in fact the *spiritus movens* of the Monarchist party, and by enforcing upon his uncle and his family the dynastic principle, he automatically ab-

---

[29] See Charles C. F. Greville, *The Greville Memoirs*, 2nd Part, III, 44-45, on his visit of Jan. 26, 1847, at Hôtel Lambert. Also see A. Jełowicki, *Moje Wspomnienia*, 1891, pp. 414-417; M. Budzyński, *Wspomnienia*, I, 299 sq., 314 sq.

[30] See J. U. Niemcewicz's letter to Lord Dudley Stuart, Feb. 13, 1834 (H.Mss., xxvi, 199-200). Also see M. Budzyński, *op.cit.*, I, 298-299.

dicated his presumptive role as Czartoryski's political successor.

Once the principle was admitted, the political succession was to pass to the older of the young Czartoryskis. The situation was complicated by Prince Vitold's growing reluctance to assume the burden of such a succession and his revolt against the continuous and increasing exigencies of effort and self-sacrifice. His younger brother, Ladislas, devoted himself early without reservations to the service of his father and of the Polish cause.

The atmosphere of this "court" grew more and more monastic. Prince Adam said in one of his speeches: "Blessed is the man and the people, who in prosperity as well as in cruel misery feel themselves standing before their Lord." Thus he was living himself, and he demanded of his family the same courage, constancy, and self-sacrifice. There were moments when he felt almost alone, when even the Princess abandoned hope and asked him to resign his self-imposed duties.[31] But the monastic spirit of obedience and self-denial gradually prevailed as expressed in his motto, "Ich diene."

---

[31] For the serious crisis in 1845, see the extracts from letters of the family, Handelsman, I, Appendix.

CHAPTER 17

CZARTORYSKI'S FOREIGN POLICY

IN EXILE

ALTHOUGH the term "cold war" had not been invented in the 1830's, there was at that time a protracted state of continuous disagreement, tension, increasing hostility, and alarming incidents arising from deep-rooted distrust and enmity between Nicholas I and the constitutional Western powers. War seemed at several times very imminent, especially so when the Russian fleet anchored in 1833 in the Bosphorus, and the Russian army as Turkey's ally appeared on its Asiatic shore, opposite Constantinople. The treaty of Unkiar Skelessy (July 8, 1833) surrendered Turkey to Russian protection and control. Czartoryski wrote: "Turkey is now just a Russian province—what more is wanted?"[1] He had handed Palmerston his considerations on Russia's policy, with a long list of Russian encroachments and threats. He mentioned Poland, the Belgian question, Turkey, German affairs, Spain and Portugal, where Russia encouraged and supported the pretenders and fostered civil war, and Russian preparations for future interventions in India. He suggested a strong common stand of the Western powers to check the Russian impact with as much energy and determination as Russia herself was wont to display.[2]

Palmerston's own considerations of December 6, 1833 did not greatly differ. The list of Russian encroachments had increased; the border region of Persia, Turkestan, Khiva, Afghanistan, and Trans-Caucasia were mentioned as recent inflammatory matters. He was aware of the threat menacing the West European liberal states and firmly decided to check Russia's expansion and to build up a western league to be opposed to the block of the three

---

[1] To Zamoyski, July 19, 1833 (*Zamoyski*, III, 162).
[2] Memorandum of May 10, 1833 (Handelsman, II, 4).

absolutist powers, whose solidarity had been renewed and re-stated in Muenchengraetz in September 1833. He gave Prince Lieven a grave warning: "In the long run peace and war are in the Emperor's hands." He built up the Entente Cordiale into a quadruple alliance of four Western powers for the defence of Spain and Portugal against absolutist interference. He was never-theless anxious to achieve his aim of checking Russian expansion and pressure without actual war. He tried to break up the eastern block by winning over Prussia and even Austria. Although the latter was in Palmerston's view but a "slave of Russia owing to her fear of revolution" and Metternich more than ever bound with Nicholas I by their common absolutist creed, Vienna was not always ready to support Russia's expansionist policy in the Near East. Thus Palmerston considered the possibility of impos-ing upon Russia a lasting peace based on some kind of partition of Europe between the liberal West and a sphere of Russian in-fluence, but without sacrificing any country or peoples still free of Tsarist control.[3] So he was not inclined to embark upon a crusade of a united liberal Europe against the eastern tyranny—Czartoryski's final aim. Nevertheless, there was a parallelism in their views and actions, and the permanent contact of the British statesman and the Polish exile, directly or through intermediaries, led to a close though discreet collaboration.

The Foreign Office not only exploited the information supplied by Czartoryski and carefully considered his suggestions, but also aided his action by forwarding his correspondence, granting pass-ports, and employing his friends and collaborators in the British diplomatic service. For some years he had a strong foothold in-side the Foreign Office since the Under-Secretary (1835-1840), William Fox Strangways, was his and his country's devoted friend and convinced supporter.[4] Prince Adam and Zamoyski

---

[3] Webster, *Palmerston*, pp. 303-319 et passim; Gleason, *Russophobia*, pp. 148 sq. See also H. Temperley, *England and the Near East. The Crimea*, 1936; C. K. Webster, *Palmerston, Metternich and the European System*, 1934; H. C. F. Bell, *Palmerston*, i, esp. Ch. 8 and 12; Handelsman, ii, Ch. 9.

[4] W. Fox Strangways, the future Lord Ilchester, had visited Poland and had been in 1826 a guest at Puławy. His correspondence when British minister pleni-potentiary at Frankfurt in the Forties with Lord Dudley Stuart (H.Mss., xxvi) demonstrates his perfect knowledge of Polish, German, and Austrian problems

had friendly contacts with most of the leading British diplomats. In some cases—as with Sir Stratford Canning, the future Lord Stratford de Redcliffe—the relationship developed into intimate friendship.

The situation in Paris was similar, although Czartoryski's relations with Louis Philippe remained rather cool to the end, and Zamoyski's friendship with the Duc d'Orléans failed to bring the expected political opportunities.

There was a friendly contact with the Duc de Broglie, and when he was superseded in 1836 by Thiers, and then by Molé, neither of whom were Anglophile or friendly to the Poles, the collaboration with the Affaires Etrangères continued, the consecutive Chefs du Cabinet, Désages and Cintrat maintaining the contact from the French side; and Thiers' own relations with the Prince became gradually warmer, the more so, when returning as Prime Minister in 1840, he realized the value of such a friendly link with the then estranged Downing Street and with British political opinion. The same pattern occurred later with Guizot.

If Palmerston was the founder of the Entente Cordiale, Czartoryski was certainly its most convinced champion. He considered it a cornerstone of the whole political system, and England and France the two powers who stood for justice and freedom in Europe; their disunity, he felt, would be disastrous for the future of the European peoples and of his own country. Thus his political exertions both in Paris and in London were always inspired by the idea of strengthening the solidarity of the West and preparing an effective alliance on a wider basis than the Quadruple Alliance, which was limited to peninsular problems.

Certainly he was aware of the importance of those battlefields in the contest between liberalism and absolutism, the more so that the cold war had there given rise to real civil wars; he was far from being neutral, and he even tried to raise the Polish colors

---

and a remarkable perspicacity and independence of mind. After his departure from Downing Street, his successor, Lord Leveson Gower (the future Lord Granville) immediately offered Zamoyski his support. Charles Greville, the Clerk of the Privy Council, was also Zamoyski's permanent link with the British government and with *The Times*. See *Zamoyski*, III, 13-15; IV, 188; S. Koźmian, *Anglia i Polska*, I, 43 ff.; Webster, *Palmerston*, p. 65.

on the battlefields of Portugal and later of Spain on the side of constitutional queens.

Of the two Western powers, England was regarded by Czartoryski as the stronger, more active, and resolute in action, "more sincere, less dissimulated, not concealing her faults under a cover of vanity." She was also more interested in the problems of the east, which now came to the fore. "Nothing is to be done without England; all depends upon her. She must satisfy herself of our reliability and usefulness for the common cause."[5] Czartoryski's good wishes for Lord Dudley Stuart in 1835 read: "May we see England making use of a part of her prodigious power for the happiness of Europe and of Poland, of the nations of the world, and acquire by doing so greatness, prosperity, and glory greater than ever before, and well deserved."[6] Lord Dudley echoed his appeal when he addressed the House with these remarkable words: "If we allowed Russia to proceed in her present policy, we should someday be forced to enter under disadvantageous circumstances into that war which now we might prevent by only a slight demonstration. The moral power of this country is immense; she has only to express her will decidedly and she will see Russia—that power which is so much talked of, but which is so intrinsically weak—quail at her firm attitude."[7]

Prince Adam's political activity shifted more and more to eastern problems, which demanded of him a new approach. During the first three decades of the century and of his political career, he regarded the decay of the Ottoman Empire as leading inevitably to its collapse, its liquidation, and to the consequent liberation of the Balkan people. He thought this to be the great mission to be achieved by a liberal Russia in cooperation with a liberated Poland. As a Russian statesman he had done his utmost to stir up the spirit of freedom as well as the hopes of those people. Later in the twenties, when a semi-exile himself, he had espoused wholeheartedly the "sacred" cause of fighting Greece; he had renewed his former friendly cooperation with Capo d'Istrias and he signed his book on diplomacy as *un Philhellène*.

[5] Czartoryski to General Dembiński, Apr. 5, 1836 (Handelsman, II, 54) and n.d. (1836?, *ibid.*).

[6] Letter of Feb. 22, 1835 (H.Mss., xxv, 170).

[7] *Hansard*, 3rd. Ser., xxvi, 987: Mar. 13, 1835.

The events of 1831 threw a new light on that part of the political scene: the common danger of annihilation by the same ruthless adversary—absolutist Russia. Czartoryski's emissaries found in Constantinople a most friendly reception. His diplomatic representative was received by the Seraskier, who warmly approved the idea of a Turko-Polish alliance, but made its negotiation dependent on the recognition of the Polish national government by France, since after the recent disastrous war Turkey did not feel strong enough to face a new contest alone.[8] In February 1833 in London Prince Adam had his first friendly conversation with a Turkish diplomat, Namyk Pasha, and was surprised by an unexpected offer that he establish himself, with all his fellow exiles, in Turkey, to take a place in the Divan, with Polish generals and officers joining the Turkish army. A district or an island was to be allotted for the resettlement of Polish refugees, provided, of course, that they chose to become Mohammedans. The offer was of course not acceptable, and Turkey's surrender to Russia immediately put an end to any further exchange of views.

Czartoryski then considered the possibility of an armed conflict between Mehemet Aly and Russia, of an intervention of the Western powers against Russia's expansion in Turkey, and of the creation on the ruins of the Ottoman Empire of a new, more dynamic, and modernized power under the ruler of Egypt. His plan for a Polish military mission in Egypt was frustrated and the contest between Turkey and Egypt was in suspense. There was no general war, but the tension continued as did also the efforts of the Western powers for stiffening Turkey's attitude towards Russia and rescuing if possible her independence. In Prince Adam's opinion "if Turkey recovered something of her independence she should be approached as a prospective ally and real friend. . . . But the spirit of the Turks can be animated only by the hope of England's help."[9] He early discerned the possibility of a war in the east, starting by a Russian armed intervention in Turkey and developing into a general war. He wrote to General Dembiński early in 1835: "You are right in calling

[8] See A. Lewak, *Dzieje Emigracji Polskiej w Turcji*, 1935, pp. 9-19.
[9] Handelsman, II, 70.

the governments sluggish, but there is no remedy and there are no better ones to choose. The true spirit has only now entered some very able and efficient second-ranking persons, but has not yet reached the great leaders upon whom the direction of the government's policy depends. The fire is still feeble; and, being kindled, if we puffed too strongly we would not stir it up but put it out. The logs are wet and frozen. It is not possible to dictate conditions to them in advance; they [the principals] do not care about us, nor do they think that we could be of any use to them."[10] Those gloomy remarks were written at the time of the Tory interlude at Downing Street, with Robert Peel as Prime Minister and Wellington at the Foreign Office, when the King's speech praised the benefits of lasting peace, assured by the increased confidence of the great powers towards the British government. Lord Dudley Stuart retorted with bitterness that the confidence of the three despotic rulers could not be considered a matter for congratulations, and he once more denounced the acts of the three despotic governments in Poland and elsewhere and the weakness of British policy as well.[11] In March there was an outburst of indignation in the House against the sending of Lord Londonderry as ambassador to Russia, since he had shown in a recent debate marked partisanship for Russia and had spoken against the Emperor's "rebellious subjects of Poland" and against Turkey as well. He felt compelled to resign, and the criticism of Wellington's previous political achievements was overwhelming.[12]

Before the end of the year, Palmerston was back at the Foreign Office and in fighting mood. Czartoryski was more confident about the future, when he wrote in 1836 to General Chrzanowski: "The irresistible trend in the East European situation must sooner or later produce a new outbreak, and it is not possible either to foresee or to calculate its moment, but it should be the right

---

[10] Letter of Feb. 8, 1835 (Handelsman, ii, 52-53).

[11] See *Hansard*, 3rd. Ser., xxvi, 350-355, Ld. D. C. Stuart's speech of Feb. 26, 1835. Cf. Czartoryski's letter to him, Paris, Feb. 22, 1835 (H.Mss. xxv, 170-171).

[12] See *Hansard*, 3rd Ser., xxvi, 938-990. For the Polish questions in the British policy in 1835, see *Zamoyski*, iii, 295-306. Lord Melbourne, whose administration was not spared in the debates, was reported to have complained: "Stuart is quite mad about the Poles."

moment for our new rising in arms. Neither France nor England
will start a war, but they would be compelled to enter into war
once it had started—and we hope that they will and in a direction
most favorable for us. Our future must be considered from that
viewpoint, and we should have plans for combining the outbreak
of a Turkish war with our insurrection, so that it can be supported and maintained."[13] Prince Adam foresaw the situation
which was to arise in 1853, seventeen years later.

Since 1834 Czartoryski had observed with keen interest the
struggle of the Caucasian highlanders against Russian invasion.
Early in 1835 he made close contact with David Urquhart, the
free-lance diplomat and political writer, who had just visited the
Caucasus and made friends with Circassian rebels. Urquhart, who
had once been an ardent champion of the Greeks, was now a
fanatical supporter of the Turks and a real expert on Near Eastern
problems. He was admired and backed by Sir Herbert Taylor,
the King's private secretary, and his writings were greatly appreciated by King William IV, who showed great interest in
his plan of making a rejuvenated Turkey a bulwark against
Russia's advance in the Near East. He now advocated the cause
of the Circassians. The revolt in Circassia and Georgia, if supported and supplied with arms and equipment, seemed to provide
an opportunity for wearing down Russia's military power and
checking Russian pressure in the Middle East. It was for the Poles
the more interesting since many thousands of former Polish
soldiers had been deported to the Caucasus to serve with Russian
troops and many political prisoners were also deported there for
penal military service in Russian ranks. There was therefore
some possibility of organizing mass desertions and of raising the
Polish colors on the side of the insurgents against the Tsar. In
1835 a Polish mission was sent to the Caucasus, and links were
established between the Prince and the rebels.[14] That quasi-
alliance lasted up to Czartoryski's death and even survived him;
he was to the end a protector, a spokesman, and even an author-

[13] Letter from June 17, 1836 (Handelsman, II, 53).

[14] For Polish contacts with Circassians, see the detailed study by L. Widerszal,
Sprawy Kaukazkie w polityce europejskiej 1831-1864 (Affairs of the Caucasus
in European policy, 1831-1864), Warsaw, 1934.

ized representative of the fighting Circassian in the Western world.

His collaboration with Urquhart was connected with two important diplomatic incidents: the publication of the *Portfolio* and the case of the *Vixen*.

The *Portfolio,* Urquhart's periodical, started in November 1835 by printing Russian diplomatic documents which had been left by the Tsesarevich in his Belvedere in Warsaw in 1830, and evacuated to safety by Prince Adam. He had put the material at Palmerston's disposal and left it for a year in his hands. Since Palmerston, though highly interested and attracted by the prospective publication, seemed unwilling to commit himself, Ladislas Zamoyski confided the documents in 1835 to Urquhart, who had just once more attracted the attention of the Foreign Office by his new pamphlets and his remarkable articles in T. W. Beaumont's *British and Foreign Review*. Zamoyski arranged the matter with Fox Strangways, under whose and Sir Herbert Taylor's benevolent supervision the publication was planned, and who discreetly informed his Minister about its progress.[15] It resounded like a bombshell. At that time, when the world was accustomed to secret and discreet diplomacy and to apparent correctness in international relations, the publication seemed an international scandal and the documents terribly compromising for Russian diplomacy, especially for her policy in the Near and Middle East. In December 1835, Lord Grey entertained Prince Adam, Zamoyski, and Lord Dudley Stuart at Howick, and duly informed Princess Lieven once more of the deep feeling with which Czartoryski inspired him. He put to her with some malicious delight indiscreet questions relating to the documents published in the *Portfolio*. The Austrian chargé d'affaires, Hummelauer, suspected that Palmerston was behind the *Portfolio* and so did the Russians.[16]

Urquhart's, Henry Reeve's, and Sir John McNeill's contribu-

---

[15] For Urquhart's activities, Gleason, *Russophobia*, pp. 153-156, 177-181; Webster, *Urquhart, Ponsonby and Palmerston* (English Historical Review), t. 67, 1947, pp. 332-337; W. Weintraub, *Marx, Palmerston i sprawa polska*, Kultura, 1950; S. Koźmian, *Anglia i Polska*, I, 42-45; *Zamoyski*, III, 328-333; Ch. de Greville, *Memoirs*, Part 2, I, 117-120.

[16] *Correspondence of Princess Lieven and Earl Grey*, III, 175-176. Webster, p. 567.

tions to *The British and Foreign Review* and the *Portfolio* largely
concurred with the growth of the anti-Russian trend in British
public opinion. And the Tsar did his best to help. His Warsaw
speech of October 1835 included the statement (not printed, but
reported to London), that he was now for the Poles just a Russian
Emperor, to whom they belonged, and the warning that in the
case of a mutiny he would not hesitate to destroy Warsaw and
he certainly would not take the trouble of rebuilding it. Even
Metternich felt uneasy as the *Portfolio* duly exploited the theme,
and the whole of British press and the House of Commons echoed
it.[17] Before long the affair of the *Vixen* came as a shock to British
national pride, and poisoned still more the Russo-British relations.

The plan was conceived by Urquhart, now a member of the
British Embassy at Constantinople. A ship was to be sent under
the British flag with supplies to the Circassians. As the Russian
annexation of the part of the coast near Sudjuk Kale was not
recognized by His Majesty's government, Britain's right of trading freely with the inhabitants should be attested by a *fait accompli*, as a challenge to Russian *faits accomplis*. Prince Adam,
Zamoyski, and their British friends contributed to the expedition.
A schooner was made available; it was owned by two brothers,
George and Stanley Bell, who were already engaged in the affairs
of the Caucasus. The cargo was officially listed as salt; in fact,
mostly ammunition and some arms. Both Palmerston and Ponsonby, the Ambassador in Constantinople, had been informed by
George Bell about it and asked for advice; they avoided commitment but did not insist upon cancelling the expedition.

In December 1836 the *Vixen* sailed towards the Caucasian
coast. She managed to unload a part of her cargo at three points,
in complete disregard of Russian police, customs, and sanitary
regulations. The challenge was met by a prompt action on the
part of Russian light naval units; the *Vixen* was intercepted off
Sudjuk Kale and seized. George Bell, the captain, and the crew
were released by an act of imperial mercy and sent to Constanti-

[17] Webster, *op.cit.*, pp. 567-568; Gleason, *Russophobia*, pp. 186-187: Vail to
Forsyth (U.S. Dept. of State), Nov. 28, 1835, on Nicholas' speech and the
influence of Czartoryski and other Polish exiles, "who receive from the people
new and spontaneous remarks of interest and admiration."

{ 237 }

nople; the ship was confiscated. A sharp diplomatic conflict ensued, and peace and war seemed at stake in 1837. Palmerston's first reaction was a serious warning. The Tsar declined to discuss the restitution of the ship. The Foreign Secretary realized that he could not force the issue without inviting war. Thus after some arguments he admitted that the Russian occupation of the coast entitled Russia to establish quarantines there. So the guilt of the *Vixen* was admitted and the incident turned into a Russian diplomatic success, but British public opinion was shaken for some years by waves of anti-Russian hostility.[18]

Urquhart was shortly after released from his diplomatic post, as his wilfulness became unbearable to Ponsonby. He once more became a free-lance journalist, writing with as much competence as venom about Russian encroachments and aims in the East; but the first enemy now was Palmerston. Urquhart's acute Russophobia degenerated into an anti-Palmerston monomania, with the *idée fixe* that Palmerston was selling Britain's prestige and interests to the Tsar.

For Prince Adam and Zamoyski he became an uncomfortable partner, although they still highly appreciated his outstanding talent and his indomitable energy. In 1839 Prince Adam wrote from Paris: "Urquhart is here. Always the same. He thinks that he will make all single-handed and that he must succeed where all the others fail, as they are in darkness. He came to promote the Ottoman business. . . . He is more Turk than the Turks (from the Embassy) whom we have met this morning. . . . I fear sometimes for his head, but he is still reasoning perfectly. Much must be forgiven to him for his heartfelt hatred of Moscow. . . ."[19] But he came slowly to the same conclusion as Beaumont, who wrote a few months later: "Urquhart is a clever man, wonderfully so, and a fool, wonderfully so."[20]

[18] See Gleason, *Russophobia*, pp. 191-196; Webster, *Urquhart, Ponsonby and Palmerston (loc.cit.)*; H. Temperley, *England and the Near East*, pp. 407-409; Bell, *Palmerston*, I, 280-283; the Russian documents relating to the seizure of the "Vixen" in *Krasnyi Archiv*, 1940, vol. 5; G. Bell's letters to Lord Dudley Stuart, 1837, 1838, 1840 (H.Mss., xxv, 66-71).

[19] Prince A. C. to Zamoyski, Paris, June 27, 1839 (*Zamoyski*, IV, 87).

[20] T. W. Beaumont to Lord Dudley Stuart, Dec. 7, 1839 (H.Mss., xxv, 53-54). About Karl Marx's later partnership with Urquhart, see W. Weintraub, *Marx, Palmerston . . . Kultura*, 1950.

Palmerston's policy was very far from selling anything to Russia, especially anything in the Near East.[21] When he returned in 1835 to the Foreign Office after the short interlude of Tory administration, he decided to check the Russian impact on Turkey by a bold diplomatic move: he proposed to De Broglie a joint treaty of guarantee of Turkey's independence. That initiative was frustrated by Louis Philippe's reluctance, and shortly after the cabinet of the Duc de Broglie was superseded by the cabinet of Adolphe Thiers, unwilling to continue the policy of an Entente Cordiale, reluctant to provoke Russia, and looking for a *rapprochement* with Metternich.[22] British diplomacy however did not desist from reasserting its position to Turkey and restoring close cooperation with the Porte. Early in 1836 Czartoryski succeeded in persuading Palmerston to send there General Chrzanowski, who had some knowledge of the country and the people, and to make him a military adviser to the Turkish Army. Prince Adam himself introduced the General to the Foreign Secretary. Chrzanowski was admitted to the British diplomatic service, and spent several years in Turkey. He enjoyed Lord Ponsonby's "unlimited confidence," proved useful to the Turks, and paved the way for a large-scale Polish action on the Bosphorus.[23]

Prince Adam's emissaries were active at Teheran, and their contacts reached Kabul, Bukhara, and Khiva. Links were established with Rumanian patriots, whose leader, Colonel Campineano, sought his political guidance and support. Stourdsa, the Prince of Moldavia, had confidential talks with his emissary, J. Woronicz, and plans for Rumania's unity, independence, and emancipation from Russian control, and for securing British and French support were matured.[24]

[21] See his letter to Melbourne, Oct. 30 and 31, 1835, Webster, *Palmerston*, pp. 562-563.

[22] See C. K. Webster, *Palmerston, Metternich and the European System*, pp. 18-22; C. F. Bell, *op.cit.*, I, 209-211.

[23] For Chrzanowski's service in Turkey, see Webster, *Palmerston*, pp. 544-546 (with a wrong spelling of the general's surname); H. Temperley, *England and the Near East* (*sub voce*); *Zamoyski*, III, 375-376; the Polish Biographical Dictionary (*sub voce*).

[24] *Zamoyski*, IV, 75-76. P. Panaitescu, *Planurile lui Campineano* (Annuarul Institutui de Istoria National), Cluj, 1924. For the enigmatic role of Jan Witkiewicz, the Russian diplomatic agent at Kabul, see Handelsman, II, 24-25, 79.

Foreign Policy in Exile

The crisis of the Entente Cordiale had a paralyzing effect upon both Western powers when the Republic of Cracow was occupied in February 1836 by the troops of the three powerful neighbors of that miniature state. The occupation was accomplished without previous knowledge of the other signatories of the Vienna Treaty, and its violation was evident. In both Paris and London public opinion demanded action from the governments. In the House of Commons, Palmerston indignantly denounced the action of the three powers, sent strong notes of protest, and announced his intention of appointing a consul at Cracow. Thiers refused to join, and went so far as to defend the three governments in the parliament. Thus after some argument the British protest proved fruitless, Palmerston was isolated. The sending of a consul to Cracow —Henry Reeve had been proposed for that post—was postponed, and in spite of Prince Adam's, Zamoyski's, Lord Dudley's, and Fox Strangways' continual exertions, finally dropped.[25]

Prince Adam was accustomed to setbacks and disappointments, and to persevering nonetheless. Thus he wrote to Chrzanowski: "Such has been my own life for several years: incessantly bitterness, refusals, frustrated exertions; all that is nothing new for me and all of you must endure the same."[26]

In February 1839 he went to England to discuss with Palmerston the situation, which seemed once more a critical one. There were new crises over Belgium, Egypt, and Persia. There was no serious divergence of views between them as to the dangers and the necessity for action; but there was a great difference of opinion as to the tactics. When the Polish statesman demanded support for the Circassians and hinted at the danger to India from further Russian expansion in the Middle East, Palmerston retorted: "True, but John Bull will not go to war to save the Circassians."[27] He alleged the solidarity of the absolutist powers

[25] For Fox Strangways' opinion and his efforts see his letters to D. C. Stuart (H.Mss., xxvi). Henry Reeve was in 1835 at Cracow; after 1835 he was for several years the editor of T. W. Beaumont's *British and Polish Review*.

[26] N.d. (1836) Handelsman, II, 54.

[27] Conversations of Feb. 12 and Mar. 10, 1839 (Cz.M.(E), II, 339-342; Zamoyski, IV, 49-71). The crisis over Belgium was complicated by General Skrzynecki's admission to the Belgian army, followed by the breach of diplomatic relations of Austria and Prussia with Belgium. The Tsar was furious, but could not react in a diplomatic way, having no official relations with King Leopold.

and the French cabinet's unreliability in spite of Prince Adam's assurance of the favorable disposition of the new French cabinet (Marshal Soult's). He did not conceal his eagerness for coming to terms with at least one of the adversaries and his preference for Austria; such terms might have a good effect on Poland's fate. Czartoryski probably mentioned Metternich's utterances in 1836 of his readiness to accept Poland's independence; before long the Austrian Chancellor once more told the same thing to a British politician and there were rumors that he intended to raise the Polish problem at the new congress of Vienna, which he tried to bring together unsuccessfully.[28]

Prince Adam was received in England and Scotland with more regard than ever. The Freemasons under the auspices of the Duke of Sussex came to the fore in celebrating the visit of the old champion of continental liberalism. On June 15 a meeting organized and presided over by the Duke of Sussex with Palmerston's blessing was a great manifestation for Polish and European freedom and the solidarity of the West. A great many British politicians rose to speak for Poland—Lord Breadalbane, Joseph Hume, Lord Rosebery, Lord Sandon, O'Connell, Lord Dudley Stuart, Thomas Attwood, Sir George Sinclair, Lord Loftus. Many of them paid tribute to Czartoryski. Montalembert was the spokesman of Prince Adam's French friends. There followed an exchange of letters between Czartoryski and the Duke of Sussex which were meant as a public declaration of principles—a program for a new liberal Europe.[29] Britain seemed to be informing the Continental powers that in spite of diplomatic isolation, she had on the Continent allies in the forces of liberalism.

At that very moment the crisis in the Near East became acute because of the Turkish catastrophe, when the war against Mehemet Aly was started again in spite of the peaceful propositions of the powers. On June 24 Ibrahim's victory at Nisib seemed to

---

[28] Metternich's words were reported by British diplomats Henry Fox (1836) and McGregor (1839); see *Zamoyski*, III, 395; IV, 99. Earlier similar utterances had been reported by Fox Strangways, then Chargé d'affaires in Vienna (see his dispatch of Aug. 25, 1835, quot. Webster, p. 583).

[29] For the behind-the-scenes report of the meeting, see *Zamoyski*, IV, 80-90; the letter of the Duke of Sussex of July 16, 1839, see Cz.M.(E), II, 345.

seal the destiny of the Ottoman Empire. Sultan Mahmud's death followed and the defection of the Turkish fleet.

Palmerston had to choose between abandoning Turkey to its fate and to Russian protection as it had been stipulated at Unkiar Skelessi, or taking the lead in a joint intervention of the five powers to save Turkey and coerce the Egyptian aggressor. By doing so, he hoped to achieve what he had planned since 1833, which was also Metternich's aim: supersession of the bilateral Russo-Turkish compact by a multilateral guarantee of the powers, and the consequent nullification of Russia's special rights with regard to Turkey. His decision had been made in advance, and he acted accordingly and was surprised by Tsar Nicholas' readiness to cooperate, and also by the opposition of France in taking sides with Mehemet Aly and leaving him Syria, and by the outburst of French patriotism and expansionism. The Entente Cordiale was dead, France isolated but adamant, and England cooperating with the three Eastern powers. A four powers' treaty on imposing the terms of settlement between Egypt and Turkey was signed on July 15, 1840. Britain became an ally of the absolutist powers; and there seemed to be a renewal of the Great Coalition against France.

Such a dramatic turn in the general situation was the worst that Czartoryski could apprehend. He did all he could to prevent it, by trying to persuade British statesmen and British public opinion of the necessity of coming to terms with France and to convince those in France of the necessity of compromise. There was a last-minute attempt on the part of Thiers—now back at the head of the government—to appease Palmerston, and Zamoyski rushed from Paris to London as a messenger of friendship. The move came too late; no concrete proposals were made, and Palmerston's decision to sign the treaty had already been taken.[30]

The fate of Cracow became once more a subject of debates in the parliaments in connection with a petition of its authorities to both the Western powers. In the French Chambre de Pairs, Marshal Soult made a strong declaration on January 7, 1840, which produced a diplomatic conflict with Russia and contributed

---

[30] *Zamoyski*, IV, 128-132. His conversation with Thiers on June 25, with Palmerston on July 4, 1840.

to the change of the government.[31] A debate in the House of Commons followed some months later, on July 13, when Sir Stratford Canning presented the facts about Cracow to the House, and Sir Robert Peel sharply crticized the failure of the government to maintain the Treaty of Vienna.[32] Zamoyski was preparing an intervention of several members to raise the cause of the fighting Circassians, when the news about the four-power treaty shocked Britain and Europe. Zamoyski and his British friends did not see in the treaty anything else but Palmerston's surrender to Russia. Efforts to stir up liberal opposition against the new alliance were immediately made. Zamoyski reported Lord Holland's and Lord Clarendon's deep concern, Lord John Russell's reservations, the interventions of Henry Reeve and George Bell with *The Times*, Lord Dudley's exertions, and Urquhart's increased fury and his "wonderful power" in attacking Palmerston.[33]

The majority of the government was for compromising on the issue of Syria, reconciling France, and inducing her to join the treaty; but Palmerston defied the storm.

Prince Adam's situation became the more difficult as war seemed imminent. France was once more challenging the three powers who had partitioned Poland, and it was obvious that if war broke out, the Poles would spontaneously take sides with the French. Zamoyski reported from London on August 4: "Nobody admits the possibility of war against France, and people leave for the country as if nothing had happened. French armament and the tune of French papers irritate the Duke of Wellington."[34] The dangers seemed more real when observed from Paris or other Continental capitals, and the part of the Poles in a European war was discussed in September by Zamoyski with the Duc d'Orléans and Thiers, and by Prince Adam with the latter.[35]

There was a tremendous revival of French bellicose nationalism. The Napoleonic legend was at its height in spite of the

31 *Zamoyski*, IV, 122-126; Barante, *Souvenirs*, VI, 428-430.
32 *Zamoyski*, IV, 132-136.
33 *Ibid.*, pp. 133-145. Cf. King Leopold's opinion in his letters to Queen Victoria, Sept. 22 and Oct. 2, 1840 (*Letters of Queen Victoria*, 1907, I, 288, 294).
34 *Zamoyski*, IV, 140.
35 *Ibid.*, pp. 145-149. Cf. Bell, *Palmerston*, I, 311-312.

pitiful failure of Louis Napoleon's attempt at Boulogne. On the other hand there was a momentous awakening of the German national spirit expressing itself succinctly in *Die Wacht am Rhein*.

A crisis in the friendly relations between the Polish emigration and Britain seemed imminent. General Chrzanowski ostentatiously resigned his post at Constantinople; Prince Adam consoled himself with the hope that the British would always distinguish the Polish cause from French policy.[36]

Palmerston's prompt decisions, the daring operations of Admiral Stopford's squadron and Sir Charles Napier's spectacular victories rapidly cleared the way for peaceful solutions by crushing Mehemet Aly's resistance and enforcing his submission without any cooperation from Russian forces. Britain's political triumph was unquestionable and the French faced a *fait accompli*. Though estranged and embittered, they had no choice but to join the concert of powers and to sign on July 3, 1841 the Treaty of the Straits—a pledge of Turkey's integrity. Thiers was forced to resign and Guizot, who was regarded as more pacific, to take over; but Palmerston's diplomatic triumph coincided with the electoral setback of the Whigs and the return of a Tory administration.

Czartoryski went to London and made contacts with some of the Tory leaders. Those links were exploited and widened by Zamoyski, who was only too eager to make friends with Palmerston's victorious adversaries. A Polish debate in the House of Commons on June 30, 1842, in connection with new encroachments of the legal status in Poland by imperial decrees, was well prepared by Dudley Stuart and preceded by Zamoyski's memorandum and his conversations with Lord Aberdeen and Sir Robert Peel. The debate was a political event of major importance, as Peel not only agreed with Gally Knight's motion and restated the international character of the cause of the Polish Kingdom, but he emphasized that imperial "Oukases" could not change the laws of a country which was not a province of Russia and he called the Russian policy "unwise and unsafe." It was more than Palmerston had ever said, and Prince Adam wrote to Zamoyski:

[36] See Handelsman, ii, 54.

"When I consider the present dispositions of England, the government's inclination for Russia, and their reluctance to offend her, I must admit that the debate was a sort of miracle." The Russian envoy could only suggest to his Chancellor that he adhere to their statement of 1833 "as nobody can invent anything new in that damned Polish question."[37]

Collaboration with the British and French diplomats in Constantinople became closer than ever before, when Czartoryski's chief diplomatic agent with the Porte, Michael Czaykowski, was sent there by an understanding with Guizot and Reshid Pasha, to fill the gap caused by Chrzanowski's departure. He was soldier, novelist, and politician; versatile, enterprising, and inspiring. From Ukrainian descent, with Cossack tradition, he had a Cossack temperament, being impetuous and audacious.[38] In a surprisingly short time he won popularity and influence with the Turks; this was due not only to his personality, but even more to Prince Adam's policy, of which he was spokesman and agent. _1842

Czartoryski's policy was a far-reaching and long-term political program concerning the Slav peoples and other Christian nationalities of the Ottoman Empire, and it was connected with the problems of the subject nationalities of the Hapsburg monarchy and the Tsar. Czartoryski had always been a Slavophile and had a keen interest in the revival of the Slav peoples: Czechs, Slovaks, Slovenians, Croats, Serbs, and Bulgarians. He fostered their cultural life, made contacts with their political and cultural representatives, and obtained from the French government the creation of a chair of Slavic literature in the Collège de France for Adam Mickiewicz.[39] The idea of a Slav federation which he had promoted as a Russian statesman revived when his efforts were directed against Russia's domination and expansion. He planned

[37] *Zamoyski*, iv, 242-257.

[38] For Czaykowski, see *Polski Słownik Biogr.*; A. Lewak, *Dzieje emigracji polskiej w Turcji 1831-1878* (1935); Handelsman, ii. Czaykowski's correspondence with Czartoryski and others was published by F. Rawita-Gawroński: *Materiały do historii polskiej XIX w.*, 1911. His memoirs in Russian transl. in *Russkaia Starina*, esp. vols. 94, 95. Also see M. Czapska, *Ludwika Śniadecka*, 1938.

[39] See Czartoryski's "Notes à l'appui du projet d'établissement d'une Chaire de Littérature Slave au Collège de France à Paris, Mars 1840" (Mickiewicz Museum, Paris, Ms. 726).

the building of an eastern barrier of free peoples under Poland's lead and closely linked with the Western powers. The Turkish domination was undermined by separatist tendencies of subjugated Christian peoples, and their rights of national existence could not be denied. Russia stirred up their hatred of their Mohammedan masters and fostered revolts which provoked cruel massacres in Bulgaria. Czartoryski's policy tried to discharge the mines and aimed at removing the charges of explosives by continuous friendly mediation between the Porte and her Christian subjects and vassals, preaching patience and mutual good will, and protecting them against persecution and oppression. It tried to obtain for them political home rule or at least local self-government, and thus to pave the way towards their peaceful emancipation, without breaking for the time being their links of allegiance with Turkey, but under the protection and with the support of the Western powers and with Poland's brotherly help.

The Prince implored the Turks to respect their nationality and religion and promised in return their loyalty; and he persuaded the Slavs that Turkish sovereignty was milder in fact than Russian tyranny. That policy found in Czaykowski and his colleagues —Louis Zwierkowski (Lenoir), Francis Zach, and others—devoted and clever exponents, and it met with surprising success; their work was welcomed by the Balkan peoples and appreciated by the Porte. Polish diplomacy in exile managed for several years to check Russian influence and pressure, and in 1844 Tsar Nicholas complained, when paying a visit in Berlin to his brother-in-law, that all the difficulties he was meeting in Serbia were due to Prince Czartoryski.

In 1849 when Paskievich's victorious Russian army was on the Danube, the Porte, yielding to Russian pressure, considered the deportation of Czaykowski; the French Ambassador, General Aupick, while interceding in his favor, pointed out that it was Czaykowski's help which allowed Turkey to keep the Slav peoples in allegiance to her and that his departure would be a disastrous blow.[40]

[40] See Handelsman, *Czartoryski, Nicholas I et la question du Proche Orient,* 1934; L. Widerszal, *Sprawy Kaukaskie,* 1934; *idem, Bułgarski Ruch Narodowy,* 1937. *Zamoyski,* IV, 268-276, 282-283 et passim. M. Budzyński, *Wspomnienia,* I, 401 sq.

Foreign Policy in Exile

The diplomatic duel between Nicholas and Czartoryski became a European affair in 1842, when Prince Michael Obrenovich was expelled from Belgrade and Alexander Karageorgevich elected Prince of Serbia under the influence of the progressive and liberal politicians Vuchich and Petronevich, Czaykowski's friends, and with the friendly acquiescence of the Porte. Russia requested the annulment of the election. Guizot, persuaded by Czartoryski, backed the new Prince and stiffened the attitude of the Porte; but she gave way to Russian and Austrian pressure, the more so when Lord Aberdeen recognized Russia's special right to demand a fair election in Serbia, as liberator of that country. Sir Stratford Canning, now Ambassador in Constantinople, was instructed accordingly.[41] Lord Dudley Stuart wrote to Czartoryski when the crisis was over: "Lord Beaumont thinks that he [Lord Aberdeen] had not read the papers you sent him and that he would not read them for fear of being too well informed."[42] Palmerston, now ready to attack the Foreign Office for appeasing Russia by giving her a free hand in the Balkans, "pursued" Zamoyski to secure material for a motion.[43]

The Porte annulled Prince Alexander's election. A new one was ordered. Russia and Austria did everything to prevent his reelection and to extort from the Turkish government the temporary banishment of both leaders of his party, the more so as they perceived Czartoryski's hand behind the scenes.[44] But the Serbs offered a long resistance. Deprived of their Prince and their leaders, they adhered to their resolution and to their friends. Garashanin, who acted as deputy for Vuchich as head of the government, secured the full support of the Serbian people. Prince Adam's instruction of January 1843 for Serbia became an outline for Serbian policy for decades to come. His goal was liberating and reuniting all Serbs who were under Turkish or Austrian domination in one national state; but it was to be achieved gradually by a cautious and long-term policy, without giving pretexts for intervention in the current unfavorable circumstances. His suggestions were even more eagerly followed in Belgrade than

41 *Zamoyski*, IV, 271-275.
42 Letter of Aug. 7, 1884 (Handelsman, II, 64).
43 *Zamoyski*, IV, 284.   44 Handelsman, II, 101-103.

they had been in his own country. Prince Alexander was unanimously reelected. Both the Ministers were once more victimized and banished by the Turkish government in order to appease Russia. Their return to Belgrade now became a test case. Prince Adam obtained this from the Turks with some French support, and the returning Serbian leaders formally accepted the principles of a common policy. It was an outstanding diplomatic success.[45]

Prince Adam pointed out to his British friends the importance of the new Slavonic friendship, of making the Slavonic national movement independent of Russia, and of delaying the fall of the Ottoman Empire by so doing. He emphasized the service rendered by Poland to Europe not only in hampering Russia's advance, but by revealing to the Slav peoples the truth about Russian domination.[46]

His agents were busy in Bosnia, in Montenegro, in Bulgaria as disinterested friends, advisers, and mediators. Emissaries were sent to the Caucasus and to the Cossacks on the Black Sea. A living memorial of the Polish political activities in the Near East has survived until our times. There was, as Czartoryski had expected, a steady flow of Polish soldiers escaping from the Russian ranks to join the Circassian rebels. Many of the fugitives were treated by the Circassians simply as their slaves and some of them sold to the Turks. The Polish agents tried to redeem them from slavery and to care for their livelihood. The problem of their resettlement was solved by founding on the Asiatic side of the Bosphorus a Polish village called Adampol. The land was acquired by the Prince with the help of the Order of Lazarists. The settlement was autonomous and enjoyed French consular protection. The settlers were hereditary leaseholders of their shares.[47] The settlements of Cossack refugees in Dobrudja became for Czartoryski a starting point for infiltration towards the Dnieper

---

[45] Handelsman, II, 103-115, 181-183; Idem, *La Question d'Orient et la politique Yougoslave du Prince Czartoryski* (Séances et Travaux de l'Académie de Sciences Morales et Polit., 1929). Garashanin's "Nachertanye" (Outline of Serbian Policy) followed strictly Czartoryski's instructions.

[46] To Ld. D. C. Stuart, Feb. 15, 1844 (H.Mss., xxv, 182-183).

[47] A. Lewak, *Dzieje emigracji polskiej w Turcji*, pp. 50-51; P. Ziółkowski, *Adampol*, 1929; M. Budzyński, *Wspomnienia*, I, 373-377, and 398 sq.; *Zamoyski*, v, 3-7.

and the Don. A mass revolt of the Ukrainian people was taken into account and Poland's brotherly union with a free Ukraine. Prince Adam warmly greeted the first signs of the awakening of the Ukrainian national spirit. He considered the Ukrainians (or Ruthenians) a branch of the Polish nation. Was he not himself a Lithuanian by descent and a Ruthenian, as his family had lived for centuries in Ruthenian provinces? He did not see any possibility of liberation for that people, except through union with Poland, and he was aware of the crucial importance of the enfranchisement of the peasants in those territories. He demanded that the problem should be solved "with warm hearts and minds not blindfolded by selfishness."[48]

The possibility of a European war had seemed remote after the Treaty of the Straits, especially when the unhappy affairs of the Spanish marriages finally poisoned the Entente Cordiale and the Western powers became once more seriously disunited and estranged. Czartoryski's contacts with Spain had become even closer in the forties: his elder son Vitold was ordered to serve with the Spanish army (because he could not be admitted to the French army without becoming a French subject); and after a decade there was even a Polish "Spanish marriage" in Paris, when Prince Adam's younger son was married to a daughter of a Spanish queen.[49] Fortunately this alliance had little political importance and could not alarm Czartoryski's British friends. In the forties he tried in vain many times to disarm the growing suspicions and hostility on both sides of the channel, which was bound to be fatal to the Polish cause.

For the time being, he expected evolutionary changes. His hopes, which were connected with the recent change on the throne of Prussia, were shared by Fox Strangways, the Duke of Sussex, and other British friends. The new King, Frederick William IV, was known for his dislike of his brother-in-law, Nicholas; for his German patriotism, liberal views, and Anglophile feelings. He displayed more tolerance than his father for Polish

[48] For his Ukrainian policy see Handelsman, *Ukraińska polityka Czartoryskiego*, 1937, esp. pp. 98-128.

[49] Maria Amparo, Countess of Vista Allegre, was a daughter of Queen Christina from her morganatic marriage with Fernando Muñoz, Duke of Rianzares. She married Ladislas Czartoryski in 1855.

national life in the Grand Duchy of Posen; and shortly after he took over, his confidential aide-de-camp, Colonel Radowitz, told Zamoyski in 1841 that "the King does not intend to close his frontiers to Polish émigrés; they all might at some time settle there"; and he made bellicose allusions to Russia. In two of his November speeches, 1841 and 1842, Czartoryski alluded to the brighter prospects of the Prussian part of Poland under the new reign; and in fact, he hoped that the small Grand Duchy might become a substitute for the Kingdom of Poland as an embryo national state under the Prussian crown. It was the cherished idea of Fox Strangways and he discreetly worked at Frankfurt for its realization.

In 1842 the King visited London, and the Duke of Sussex handed him a petition of the Literary Association of friends of Poland, asking him to grant sanctuary for the exiles, whose extradition could be requested by Russia. There was an exchange of friendly views on Poland between the both. Both Czartoryski and Zamoyski were mentioned by the Duke; and when Nicholas went in 1844 to Berlin he failed to get a renewal of the cartel on the extradition of refugees from his brother-in-law. It was the last service rendered to Poland by the Duke; that old and devoted friend died a few months later.[50]

The following few years seemed hopeful for Prussia's evolution on liberal lines and for the prospects of a home rule in Posnania. But at the same time the underground revolutionary trends increased in power and the first eruptions of a new volcano occurred in Poland and shattered much of what had been built up by Czartoryski's diplomacy.

[50] For Prussian overtures to Zamoyski and Charles Marcinkowski in 1841, see *Zamoyski*, IV, 188-191, 194-195. The Duke of Sussex as intermediary, *op.cit.*, IV, 217-219, 226-227. Cf. W. Fox Strangways to Ld. D. C. Stuart, Mar. 14, 1846 (H.Mss., XXVI, 313-314).

CHAPTER 18

THE YEARS OF REVOLUTIONS

THE UNDERGROUND MOVEMENT in Poland, which had grown strong in the later Thirties when it was inspired and partly directed by the Young Poland organization, grew stronger in the Forties under the overwhelming influence of the Democratic Society with its slogan of social revolution as inseparable from a future insurrection.

The intelligentsia, students, small gentry, and townsfolk followed its lead with enthusiastic devotion. Strong propaganda measures were made among the peasants, who were urged to be ready to free themselves from social oppression and foreign tyranny by rising in arms. Especially in Galicia, where social unrest was at its height, did the revolutionary propaganda contribute to the excitement among the peasants. The landowners in that part of Poland were generally convinced of the necessity for enfranchisement, and a committee of the provincial Diet was busy preparing long-belated solutions. But the revolutionary leaders were not ready to wait for or accept evolutionary social changes without shaking off the foreign yoke. In Poznania the situation seemed ripe for a popular uprising although the social problem was less acute in that province, the peasants having been enfranchised more than a quarter of a century before.

In the Kingdom of Poland, under the terrible regime of Field Marshal Paskievich, now adorned with the title "Prince of Warsaw," the situation was nebulous: social unrest was great, but the extent of the influence of the conspiracies remained an enigma.

The Centralization—the governing body of the Democratic Society, sitting at Poitiers and then at Versailles—stood for the Jacobinic conception of revolutionary leadership: a strong central government with dictatorial powers, man power, and property at its unrestricted disposition, *levée en masse* militarily organized, improvised mass armies, the supreme command invested with all authority needed to secure unity of action. The young and inspiring military and political writer and orator, Louis Mierosławski (a second-lieutenant of 1831), was the principal champion of those ideas, as opposed to the rather anarchical concepts of a war of revolution, held by the able and influential economist-writer and underground leader, Henry Kamieński, and to the theory of guerrilla warfare, which Major Charles Stolzman recommended as a panacea. Mierosławski's ideas prevailed and he was the Generalissimo designated. But the conspiracies in the homeland were imbued with the idea that a spontaneous revolutionary movement of the peasant masses, even without any help from abroad, without adequate armament and organization, could submerge the occupation forces of the three partitioning powers, and "young enthusiasts" preached immediate action without further delay.[1]

In the Underground the sense of reality was even more obscured by emotional factors than it was in Paris or Versailles, and the revolutionary creed was more exalted. Their appeals induced the Democratic Society to take the fateful decision of starting a general insurrection in all parts of Poland in February 1846.

The decision was taken in the autumn of 1845, and it was announced by Mierosławski in a speech on November 29. Prince Adam knew that that kind of insurrection was something very different from what he had himself considered. It was evident that it would be a desperate struggle for the soul of the Polish peasant between the three powers and Poland. There was only one way out of it: to postpone the outbreak, to start on a large scale the enfranchisement by the landowners themselves, to relieve social tension, to win the peasants over to the Polish cause and to prepare them by long years of education for a future struggle. That path was clearly indicated in the rules of the League for National Unity in 1833 and in Prince Adam's several statements and instructions. His last strong warning of November 29, 1845, came too late; and he was already aware that there was no longer any possibility left of his party's preventing their dynamic opponents from starting the insurrection. It could be

[1] See M. Kukiel, "Koncepcje powstania narodowego" (The Polish Conceptions of National Revolution before 1848), *Teki Historyczne*, 1948, II, No. 3.

done only by means of civil war, in which the counter-revolution would appear as the ally of foreign powers against the Polish people. He could not admit such a solution and in his speech he prepared the minds of his party and of the Polish gentry in general for the necessity of an over-all sacrifice. He meant by this not only in accepting a radical land reform, but also in joining the insurrection—if one were to come—and doing the utmost for the victory of the national cause.

It was a kind of political surrender to the radicals, with the afterthought that only by so doing could the Polish nobility still secure—at the cost of material sacrifices—great moral prestige and maintain an important place in Poland's future life.

The decision was a momentous one, and Prince Adam's instructions were widely followed by the gentry in the homeland. It resulted in the unique phenomenon of the revolutionary attempt of 1846 in Poland. Although Jacobinic in its aims and tactics, egalitarian and republican, it was not resisted by the landowners, whose social privileges were at stake, and was even supported by most of them, especially in the Grand Duchy of Posen, in the Republic of Cracow and the adjacent districts of the Kingdom of Poland, and in Galicia. That attitude preserved Poland from the deadly danger of a civil war between insurgents and landowners, but at the same time it exposed the latter, particularly in Galicia, to the dreadful vengeance of the Austrian bureaucracy. The Austrian provincial and district authorities were already prepared to meet the impending national revolution by themselves stirring up a peasant revolt against their landlords.

The Polish leaders were not completely unaware of such a danger. Kamieński himself emphasized in his renowned book that slaves had no fatherland.[2] Czartoryski many times invited the gentry to forestall such a possibility by coming forward themselves as popular leaders. Rumors of secret contacts between Austrian officials and peasants were already widespread in the spring of 1845. But the optimistic view prevailed: the radicals hoped to win the battle for the soul of the Polish people, and many peasants and townsfolk joined the insurrection. But the Austrian

---

[2] Filaret Prawdoski (ps.) *O prawdach żywotnych Narodu Polskiego* (Axioms Vital for the Polish Nation), Brussels, 1844.

officials proved stronger: they succeeded in controlling the masses in the districts of Bochnia, Tarnów, and Rzeszów, and in mobilizing them for the defense of the good Emperor against his and their enemies, the landowners.

The ill-fated insurrection was to be started at the same moment in all parts of Poland; Poznania and Galicia were to be liberated from their Prussian and Austrian garrisons and to become bases for an overall onslaught on Warsaw.[3] That ambitious plan was frustrated as Mierosławski himself, who had established his headquarters near Poznań, was arrested before the outbreak and most of the active members of the conspiracy in that province fell into Prussian hands.

An insurrection in Cracow broke out, a national government was proclaimed, and a small army emerged; but in Galicia the action of the insurgents met with a counter-action of peasant bands led by Austrian officials. There was a massacre of groups of insurgents and landed gentry as they did not fight against the peasants and words proved in vain. The insurrection of Cracow was finally crushed by Austrian troops supported by peasants from Galicia.

In the Kingdom the outbreak was called off and there was only one isolated attempt against a Russian garrison. In all parts of Poland several hundred men of the Polish underground were detained and executions followed in the Kingdom, in Lithuania and Galicia.

When Prince Adam received the news of the insurrection in Cracow and the proclamation of a national government, he hurried to recognize the new national authority and to declare his allegiance to it by a public statement.[4] Naturally enough the sequestration of his Galician estate, Sieniawa, resulted. The political consequence was the surrender of his position as chief of the Polish nation; thus the Monarchist Association of May 3 ostentatiously cancelled its activities. He later explained his decision: "We behaved like honest soldiers: when hearing the roar of guns they hurry to support their fighting brethren without

---

[3] There were widespread conspiracies in Austrian regiments and the Hungarian regiments were considered as unwilling to fight against the Poles.

[4] Of March 7, 1846, published by the *Journal des Débats*, March 8.

worrying too much whether there is any hope of success or as to who is in command."[5]

What actually happened was a disastrous failure of the radicals, and their poor leadership in Poland was discredited for many years to come. The Monarchist and Insurrectionist Party could not show a much better record, as it neither managed to prevent the outbreak nor to take over its control. There was a new crisis of confidence in the homeland and abroad. For the first time Czartoryski's policy was publicly attacked by right-wing critics and opponents, and the most outspoken and ruthless of them, Marquess Wielopolski, in a "Letter of a Polish gentleman to Prince Metternich" denounced the Hôtel Lambert for begging the Western powers for help, and he suggested the allegiance of the Polish nobility to the Russian Emperor, who was a gentleman and who would surely wish to avenge the massacre of the Polish nobility by the Austrians.

That rather unwise address to the Tsar's noble feelings met with no response in St. Petersburg, and Tsar Nicholas I, instead of avenging Poland's treatment by Austria, sent his army before long to her support against the Hungarians and Poles. But Wielopolski's suggestion was not isolated and it was followed by a declaration of Count Tytus Działyński, a friend of Czartoryski, at the Russian Embassy in Berlin, that the Polish nobility would throw itself at the Emperor's feet. Czartoryski suggested a dignified reply to General Francis Morawski about Wielopolski's pamphlet, exposing its suicidal idea. But even Prince Adam's closest entourage were stunned by the terrific blow. He himself wrote to Zamoyski: "Among all the bitter experiences, the most painful is that there is no one person at home who would look upon me with encouragement. The nearest ones look upon our works and efforts sadly and with commiseration. My sister only [the old Princess Maria of Württemberg] persevered in supporting us, not by firm conviction, but as she is used to approve everything I do."[6]

There were attempts to enforce Prince Adam to withdraw completely from political life. His brother, Constantine, who had

---

[5] Speech of November 29, 1846.
[6] Letter of May 18, 1846, *Zamoyski*, IV, 457.

lived for three decades in Vienna on good terms with the Hof-burg, obtained the promise of releasing Sieniawa from sequestra-tion in exchange for Prince Adam's declaration condemning conspiracies and insurrections. He disavowed that bargain; and he also declined the offer of his one-time friend, Lord Brougham, of a British intercession on similar lines. He wrote to Lord Dud-ley Stuart: "As to my estates: *j'en avais fait mon deuil*. Lord Palmerston must be satisfied, that I never shall give any pledge to Austria, the more so after the recent massacres she had or-dered. . . ."[7]

He received a letter from his mother-in-law, Princess Anna Sapieha, once a friend of Kościuszko, an ardent patriot, who had given at the time of the emigration invaluable help to Prince Adam in financial matters and in the activities of Hôtel Lambert. It was a most disagreeable communication, containing bitter re-proaches and a request that he cancel his activities, whose con-tinuation would prove madness. Much worried, he sent the letter to his nephew, and Zamoyski answered: "Loyalty to our own past is not madness. Who has lived, like you, is a slave of his past; he cannot relinquish his post at will, as long as he is still surrounded by a lot of loyal men, as he is the only one with power of leadership, and nobody can stand for him. . . ."[8]

Prince Adam knew perfectly well that he could not cancel his action. There were steps to be taken without delay to arouse the indignant protests of the free world against the recent Austrian crime and the cruelties perpetrated by the Russians. Poland had to be defended against Metternich's indictment (he tried to lay the blame of the massacres on the victims). Parliamentary debates were to be suggested and inspired, the Pope kept informed and Metternich's influence at the Vatican checked. Nor could the cause of the Bulgarian Uniates or of the Circassians be dropped. A moral breakdown of the emigration had to be prevented, and new efforts made for its reconciliation and for national unity. A new wave of political emigration reached Paris—young, ardent people, ready to organize a military school and to provide funds—

[7] Letter of Nov. 30, 1846 (H.Mss., xxv, 194-195).
[8] Letter of May 22, 1846, *Zamoyski*, IV, 458.

and Czartoryski looked with more confidence to the future.[9] The salvation of the Republic of Cracow was now in the foreground. Czartoryski tried to persuade the Western powers to oppose in advance its impending annexation by Austria. The attitude of Lord Aberdeen's government was rather evasive and events in Poland were confused enough to give a pretext for restraint. Fox Strangways wrote from Frankfurt: "From what I can learn of the opinions of our government I foresee they will profess to believe everything Austria and the others choose to say on the subject, concluding with 'it is not our business.' The Foreign Office has never had much of the faculty of discriminating, at least in Polish affairs."[10] When Palmerston once more returned to the Foreign Office, and in high spirits, he showed more concern for the "shabbily dishonest" French intrigues in the affair of the Spanish marriages, than for more distant events in Poland. He admitted that what the three powers were doing was an "abominable shame," but he was anxious not to challenge Russia. On August 17 he spoke in the House of the concern of the British government with regard to events in Galicia and to the occupation of Cracow, and gave a strong warning to both German powers: "if the Treaty of Vienna be not good on the Vistula, it may be equally bad on the Rhine and on the Po." But both Nesselrode and Metternich realized that he was not ready to act.[11] Nor were Czartoryski's efforts and Montalembert's inspiring indictment of Austria's crime successful in provoking a reaction on the part of the French government. Guizot, like Palmerston, only restated his government's adherence to the respective clauses of the treaty. But the Austro-Prussian declaration on Cracow, announcing its incorporation into Austria, was a shock to French public opinion and was resented as an injury. Prince Adam wrote to Lord Dudley Stuart about the necessity for joint action on the part of both governments, and he pointed out the effect of their disunion on the affairs of Poland, of Germany, and of Italy. "I think," he added sadly, "that Palmerston and M.

[9] *Zamoyski*, IV, 460.

[10] To Ld. D. C. Stuart, Apr. 18, 1846 (H.Mss., XXVI, 317-318).

[11] Bell, *Palmerston*, I, 389; *Zamoyski*, IV, 466-469; Nesselrode, *Lettres et Papiers*, VIII, 339. Hansard, 3rd Ser., LXXXVIII, 815-832.

Guizot will *se renvoyer la balle* and expect what the other will do and excuse themselves by the reluctance of the colleague and the lack of entente cordiale. . . ."[12] But the next day he was satisfied with Guizot's readiness to act, provided that Palmerston would also do so. "If Palmerston withdrew he could not excuse himself with the French weakness."[13] He repeatedly insisted upon the necessity of England's cooperation. "It should be most unfortunate if your government repeated Lord Grey's deplorable error in declining French proposals of intervention in favor of our revolution in 1831."[14] Palmerston's reaction was disappointing.[15] Czartoryski once more insisted in a memorandum to Palmerston on the necessity of acting; he explained that there would be no war if there was no fear of war. But he had little hope of influencing the Foreign Secretary: "I think sometimes, that my *démarche* is but *un acquit de conscience*." He once more assured him that France would join England if England were willing to take common action.[16] But the wording of Palmerston's protestation was "as civil and moderate as it could be made," and Nesselrode himself was charmed and surprised—the result surpassed his expectations.[17] Cracow was safely swallowed by Austria without any serious diplomatic complications.

The final destruction of that small but valuable sanctuary of free Polish life was a heavy blow. There was the hope of securing a new one in the Grand Duchy of Posen. Prince Adam's long-term policy with regard to that part of Poland which he hoped would become an embryo Polish state had been submerged by the revolutionary movement, and the situation in 1846 and 1847 was a peculiar one: hundreds of Polish patriots tried for high treason by the Supreme Court in Berlin at a time when Prussian policy still aimed at liberal reforms and at compromise solutions of the Polish problem. Fox Strangways deplored the revolutionary

---

[12] Letter of Nov. 20, 1846 (H.Mss., xxv, 188-189).

[13] Letter n.d. (Nov. 21, 1846), (*ibid.*, 228-229).

[14] Nov. 23, Nov. 26 (*ibid.*, 190, 192).

[15] Czartoryski to Ld. D. C. Stuart, Nov. 30 (*ibid.*, 194-195).

[16] Letter of Dec. 6, 1846 (*ibid.*, 196-197). There is a striking parallelism between Czartoryski's remarks and Nesselrode's considerations in his letters to Meyendorff; see Nesselrode, viii, 337-339, 342-343, 359-361.

[17] Bell, *Palmerston*, i, 389-390; *Nesselrode*, viii, 359.

attempt in Poznania. He wrote to Lord Dudley Stuart: "I very much regret the Prussian part of the business, because it entirely destroys the hope of making use of this King of Prussia at some future period as a support of the Poles against Russia, and because it sets a number of Prussian liberals in the army as out of it, against the Poles. . . ." But he already discerned symptoms of decay in both the German monarchies, and as early as May 1846 he gave the first warning of an impending danger of revolution in Germany.[18] He became more and more skeptical as to the future of Prussia: "The King has lost ground." "How can you trust a king who gives a constitution with his right hand and buffets his Polish subjects with his left? I give him up."[19]

Prince Adam was conscious of the great changes impending in Germany. He had friends and contacts there; the *Deutsche Allgemeine Zeitung* edited by Gervinus at Heidelberg was considerably under his influence. His emissaries attended the Prussian Landtag in 1847 as observers, and in spite of the tension in Prusso-Polish relations, discreet contacts with the King through the Radziwills were continued and the matter of provincial self-government for Poznania was under friendly consideration. Czartoryski's postulate for it was home rule in personal and economical union with Prussia, but a government, Seym, and army of its own.[20]

The matter was discussed on the eve of the outbreak of the Revolution. First, however, great events took place in Italy in 1847. The national movement grew powerful and general, and the liberal reforms and pronounced national feelings of the new Pope, Pius IX, made of Rome the focus and the temporary capital of the Risorgimento. Palmerston promoted the idea of a federated Italy to be presided over by the Pope; and Czartoryski was also its protagonist. Palmerston's special envoy in Rome, Lord Minto, an old acquaintance of Zamoyski, had intimate contacts with him and with Orpiszewski, and found common friends in Conte

[18] Letters of Frankfurt, Mar. 14, May 11, 1846 (H.Mss., xxvi, 313-314, 319-320).

[19] Letter of July 17, 1847 (H.Mss., xxvi, 336-337).

[20] Handelsman, ii, 192-194, and S. Kieniewicz, *Społeczeństwo polskie w powstaniu poznańskim* (The Polish People in the Insurrection of Poznania), 1935, pp. 83 ff. et passim.

Luigi Mastai Ferretti and the Piedmontese liberal, Massimo d'Azeglio.[21] Fox Strangways, when paying a visit to Rome, was impressed by the large and influential Polish colony in Rome, and he wanted to establish a link between them and the British Catholics.[22]

The Polish action in Rome aimed not only at winning the Holy See's support for the Polish cause. Prince Adam and Zamoyski were thinking of Poland's active part in the liberation of Italy, and especially of the help of a Polish military mission in organizing the Italian army against Austrian armed intervention. The outbreak of the Sicilian revolution in January 1848, and the developments in central and northern Italy accelerated the solution; the Roman Consulta unanimously decided to invite a foreign general as expert and adviser: Chrzanowski was selected, and many Polish officers were admitted to the papal army.

In April 1848, a military convention with the papal government was concluded by Orpiszewski in Czartoryski's name. There had been a romantic imbroglio with Mickiewicz, who had taken separate action on his own; the poet appeared in Rome as a new Pierre d'Amiens of a crusade for the freedom of nations, and organized the nucleus of a Polish Legion, apostles of national revolutions in arms. A stormy audience of the poet at the Vatican took place and a clash with the diplomats and military experts of the Hôtel Lambert. The handful of Mickiewicz's followers left Rome to join the Lombardians in their fight against Austria.

Zamoyski stuck to his plan of military cooperation with the papal government, and he wrote: "A legion in Italy under the Pope's banner will be a good thing. I have never dreamed of becoming *un soldat du Pape*, but I now feel happy that the chance has come for me. I like the idea."[23]

But the Pope, although an Italian patriot and a liberal, disliked war and preferred to rely upon "canons, not cannons."[24] Before long Zamoyski realized that Piedmont was to become

[21] See *Zamoyski*, v, 40-41, 44-45.

[22] Fox Strangways to Ld. D. C. Stuart, July 17, 1847 (H.Mss., xxvi, 336-337).

[23] To Ld. D. C. Stuart, Rome, Apr. 13, 1848 (H.Mss., xxvii, 308-311). Cf. M. Budzyński, *Wspomnienia*, ii, 94-123 et passim.

[24] He spoke thus to Zamoyski in Jan. 1848: see *Zamoyski*, v, 63.

the only possible nucleus of a free and united Italy. He went to Turin to prepare the ground for Polish collaboration with the emerging Italian Kingdom.[25]

The February revolution in Paris turned Louis Philippe and Guizot into exiles, and the French monarchy into a republic, inspired by memories of 1793. In spite of his "kingship de facto" Prince Adam was neither terrified nor mortified by such an unexpected change in the French and European situation. He even shocked his nephew by confiding to him bluntly: "You know perfectly that I adhered to monarchical principles at the time of the Commonwealth [at the time of the Great Seym] by reasoning only, not by feelings. I had cherished Republican dreams, and I could share them once more without too much difficulty if there was but a chance for their fulfillment."[26]

The Second Republic seemed ready to follow in the steps of the First, and conflict with absolutist powers seemed imminent. Lamartine received Czartoryski as a potential ally, and the formation of a Polish force was once more under friendly consideration; common political action was discussed. Prince Adam wrote on March 7: "The sky is clearing up over us. Maybe the Lord will allow my mortal remains to rest in native soil."[27]

But news came even more directly affecting the situation in Poland: the revolution in Vienna and the Hapsburg Monarchy in complete dissolution, Metternich an exile; the revolution in Berlin and the King, at the request of the Berlin people, greeting the Polish conspirators released from the Moabit gaol with the words: "Long live Poland!" No wonder that the old man excused himself to his young British friend: "Events past belief are developing with such miraculous speed that time is lacking to think it over and to write what one thinks; a phrase hardly written and it becomes already out of date." He realized that the affairs of Italy were receding into the background, and those of Germany had taken on a decisive importance. The Prussian and Austrian government seemed no longer hostile to the cause of freedom, and even in the case of a Russian intervention they

25 For the events in Rome, see *Zamoyski*, v, Ch. 2 and 3.
26 Letter to Zamoyski of Feb. 27, 1848 (Handelsman, II, 202-203).
27 Handelsman, *loc. cit.*

could be discounted as potential allies. He secretly informed Lord Dudley Stuart: "I am leaving myself in two days' time for Berlin, where Polish colors were flown together with the German ones, and Polish prisoners of state were liberated and led in procession to the King, who ought to appear on the balcony to salute them. I feel compelled to go there and to put myself in the foreground, since I was criticized on previous occasions that I had not told what I suggested and wanted to be done, and that it was the cause of many misfortunes, as the people had followed wrong counsels, because they had not known mine."[28] On the same day, March 22, he wrote to his nephew, that "Berlin and Vienna are changing from enemies into allies and are no longer menacing powers," but two days later, when leaving, he considered the situation in a different light. He had been warned by Bystrzonowski, who was on the spot in Berlin, that war with Russia was regarded as inevitable by the new Prussian government. Decisions were now taken in a hurry. A Polish legion, mostly officers and non-commissioned officers, rapidly organized, was to be dispatched to Prussia. The Prince went to Berlin with his military adviser, General Chrzanowski, and his diplomatic assistant, Theodore Morawski. Barzykowski remained in Paris as his deputy and was joined by Zamoyski, who had been called up from Italy. Plans for a coalition war were hurriedly discussed. Turkey and Sweden were to be won over for common action, an emissary to be sent to Stockholm, and diversions on the coasts of the Black Sea and of the Baltic Lithuanian coast considered. It was Zamoyski who inspired Lamartine with the idea of sending a general as ambassador to Constantinople; he reminded him of the part which had been played in 1807 by Sebastiani. General Aupick was selected—a friend of Zamoyski—and sent to him for advice.[29] Franco-Polish collaboration in the Near East became closer than ever. A French diplomat reported later from Belgrade: "Prince Czartoryski's diplomacy is perfectly organized and efficient and it works here for us as we do not have our own."[30]

Prince Adam was welcomed with much enthusiasm in Ger-

[28] N.d., Mar. 22-24, 1848 (H.Mss., xxv, 226-227).
[29] See *Zamoyski*, v, 99-105.
[30] Consul Fabre, Jan. 19, 1849 (Handelsman, ii, 295).

many, especially at Cologne. He addressed the Germans in terms which provoked some dismay among his British friends, for he went so far as to mention democratic institutions, and he explained to Lord Dudley Stuart that the atmosphere on the Continent was quite different, and besides—had Britain herself no democratic institutions? He was anxious to solve the peasants' problem without delay, and informed Lord Dudley Stuart that he was insisting upon granting them lands without any indemnity, and that he had already given proper instructions for his estates in Galicia, which he hoped would be restored, and for all others, which he should eventually recover.[31]

In Berlin his arrival was a nuisance for the King, the government, and the British and French embassies, as it provoked an immediate menace of Russian intervention. But negotiations with the Foreign Minister Baron Arnim were begun, and problems of a reorganization of the Grand Duchy of Posen, of the formation of the Polish army, and of possible war with Russia and its implications on Poland's future were discussed; in Arnim's view there was a great probability of war.[32] "The course of events has miraculously brought us nearer to Poland's restoration"— such was Czartoryski's mood after several days in Berlin.[33] He was already aware of obstacles in the Prussian government, public opinion, and the Western embassies, and of the impending danger of collision between the Poles and Germans in the Grand Duchy. His instructions for both Poznania and Galicia aimed at securing *via facti* a separate existence of both provinces, with Polish administration and a national armed force. He wrote to Prince Sapieha, his brother-in-law, whose influence was growing in Galicia:[34] "The statute labor must be abolished immediately and completely. . . . Petitions are to be presented and concessions requested on the same lines as in other provinces. . . . Insurrections and riots are to be avoided. You must state your purpose as being not separate yourselves from other provinces and re-

[31] Letter of Apr. 10, 1848 (H.Mss., xxv, 210-212). Zamoyski to Czartoryski, Paris, Apr. 4 (*Zamoyski*, v, 99), with warm approval.

[32] See J. Feldman, *Sprawa polska w roku 1848* (1933), pp. 123, 171, 337-340. Cf. L. B. Namier, *1848: The Revolution of Intellectuals*, 1944, p. 61.

[33] Letter to Ld. D. C. Stuart, Berlin, Apr. 4, 1848 (H.Mss., xxv, 208-209).

[34] Mar. 24, 1848 (Handelsman, ii, 245-246).

quest from them and from the central government support against the external enemy [Russia]. . . . Not insurrection or a national flag is needed now, but claiming concessions as a separate province, like the other ones, and taking them *de facto* by your own action. . . ."

He was firmly convinced of Nicholas' impending intervention. He asked Lamartine, in understanding with Arnim, to send arms for the Polish force in Poznania.[35] Lord Dudley Stuart was instructed to explore the possibility of a British loan for the Polish armaments in both provinces. Czartoryski's hopes vanished rapidly during his five weeks' sojourn in Berlin. They were based on the probability of Russia's armed intervention against Prussia or Austria. But Nicholas proved more cautious and reasonable than expected, and in spite of the outburst of German patriotism, neither Berlin nor Vienna was ready to start a war against Russia. Baron v. Arnim, the new Prussian Foreign Minister, strongly anti-Russian, sounded out France about her attitude in the case of a Russian invasion of Poznania; he suggested "a solemn declaration of alliance and political solidarity in matters pertaining to the restoration of Poland," and the sending of a French squadron to the Baltic. But he met with no response; both he and General Willisen, like him a protagonist of the Polish cause, were gradually isolated at home and submerged by a wave of militant nationalism, rising against the Polish separatism in Poznania. The German minority in that province violently resisted the taking over of the local government by the Poles and the formation of a Polish army. They were backed by most Prussian bureaucrats and officers and found strong support in Prussia. The negotiations on the "national reorganization" of the Grand Duchy were brought to a close by the Prussian cabinet order on the partition of the Grand Duchy, which left a large part outside the autonomous territory. The small Polish forces, already reduced in number by a convention imposed upon the Polish National Committee in Poznań, instead of being regarded as a spearhead in a war against Russia, were now considered as the first enemy to be disposed of, and before the end of April a "war" against

[35] Mar. 30, 1848. See Handelsman, II, 251-252.

the handful of Poles was started with surprise attacks on the Polish camps by overwhelming Prussian forces.[36] Even before, on April 26, the Austrian General Castiglione submitted Cracow to heavy bombardment, putting an abrupt end to the short "springtime of nations" in Galicia.

Not only Czartoryski's hopes for a liberal Prussia and even for a liberal and federalized Austria as Poland's prospective allies had been deceived; his confidence in French and British support had also proved misplaced. He became aware that Lamartine's denunciation of the Treaty of Vienna and his pro-Polish declarations were aimed at appeasing the Paris radicals, but his real endeavor was to placate the European sovereigns and to avoid any conflict with Russia. The French envoy in Berlin, M. de Circourt, was not friendly to Czartoryski and a convinced adversary of Prussia's anti-Russian policy; but Lamartine's own attitude differed more in words and gestures than in deeds. In spite of his "energetic declarations to European nations" he was anxious to let the sovereigns and the governments know about his peaceful intentions and he did not reply to Arnim's request for a "solemn declaration of alliance and political solidarity in matters pertaining to the restoration of Poland."[37]

The British government stood for the territorial *status quo* and peace; both John Russell and Palmerston were anxious to discourage and prevent any action which could produce a *casus belli*. At the same time, as Czartoryski discussed with Arnim the problems of Poland's restoration, the former friend of Poland, Sir Stratford Canning, who was on a diplomatic visit in Berlin, agreed with King Frederick William about the danger of granting a national army to Poznania, stiffened the opposition of the King on that matter and tried to confirm him "in every pacific sentiment." Palmerston directed him to recommend that the Prussian government abstain from any proceedings which could justly be considered by Russia as aggressive; and the Russian Ambassador Meyendorff was informed what kind of good advice Sir Stratford was giving in Berlin.[38] Palmerston told Lord Dudley

[36] See L. B. Namier, *Revolution*, Chs. 13-15.
[37] L. B. Namier, *op. cit.*, pp. 35-37, 61.
[38] *Ibid.*, pp. 63-64.

Stuart that he would do nothing that would encourage a Polish insurrection, and that the British government wished matters to be settled. He once more felt uneasy when sacrificing the cause of Poland to the cause of European peace and, while appeasing the Tsar, he tried to make a gesture to placate his own conscience: he instructed the British Ambassador to suggest confidentially to the Russian Emperor "to be before hand with events and to place the crown of Poland upon the head of some member of his family [he meant the Duke of Leuchtenberg]"—with a good constitution, a free press, independent judges and open courts.[39] Czartoryski seemed not to have been told about Palmerston's *ballon d'essai*. But he received ample information from London and was aware of the unexpected collision of British policy with Polish aspirations and activities.[40]

Czartoryski's political setbacks in April and May 1848 coincided with another bitter disappointment: his failure to secure control of Polish political activities. In Berlin he had to face a strong and energetic group of Polish radicals under the leadership of Louis Mierosławski and Charles Libelt, the two chief defendants in the recent mass trial of the Polish conspiracy who had been freed from the Moabit gaol by the revolution. Mierosławski was called "the resurrected chief" by his younger followers and was more popular than ever; he was even much appreciated by the Prussian General Willisen, a liberal and Polonophile, who had been impressed by his military writings and backed him as the prospective chief of the Polish national army in Poznania. Libelt, an ideologist, a thinker, and an ardent champion of democracy, was representative of the left-wing intellectuals and very influential in Poznania.

Nothing could be done to prevent a duality of action. Nor did

[39] Bell, *Palmerston*, I, 438-439; *Feldman, Sprawa polska*, pp. 201-202; Handelsman, II, 208-209 and 242-245. See Ld. D. C. Stuart's letters to Czartoryski of Mar. 27, Mar. 30, Apr. 5, Apr. 11 (Cz.Mss. 5518, pp. 503, 513, 535, 551).

[40] Ld. D. C. Stuart to Zamoyski, Apr. 6, 1848 (*Zamoyski*, v, 107), gives interesting details on anti-Russian and pro-Polish moods at the Prussian Embassy. He had been introduced to Prince William of Prussia, then self-styled exile from his rebellious Fatherland, at the Prince's special request; and Count Pourtalès, the latter's companion, told him that they were conscious then what a crime had been committed by the partition of Poland and that the time to redeem it was at hand, even if by self-sacrifice.

the conservative elements in Berlin, Poznania, and Galicia subordinate themselves to the Hôtel Lambert. Prince Adam found
several devoted adherents and made converts; but he also met
much cautious restraint and even opposition against any political
leadership from abroad. He was regarded by many as too much
advanced in his opinions, too much committed in the struggle
for independence against Russia, and rather unequal to the task
of securing provincial self-government and organizing Polish life
inside Prussia or Austria. His program of home rule for both
provinces was scuttled by less ambitious claims for local self-
government put forward by leaders on the spot, and for the first
time he became aware that he had to reckon with dangerous
obstacles on the right.

In Poznań the Polish National Committee was dominated by
the revolutionary left and so was the secret National Provisional
Government which they appointed on April 5, without any
understanding either with the emigration or with other provinces
of the homeland. The secrecy of its existence was so complete
that hardly anyone knew about it, and it was regarded as a myth
until the instrument of its nomination was discovered.[41] The
"government" did not reveal its existence even after the outbreak of hostilities, but was strong enough in April to check any
interference from outside Poznania.

The influence of Marquess Wielopolski, hostile to the Hôtel
Lambert, was strong at Cracow and among the reactionary elements in the Kingdom of Poland, and although he could not
muster anything like a political party, he did succeed in inducing
the participants of an assembly of notables from Galicia, Cracow,
and Poznania, when they met at Wroclaw, to vote a resolution
denying to the emigration any say in the political affairs of the
homeland. The meeting, which was intended to establish a
common central authority for Poland, failed to achieve its goal;
but the fact of its repudiation of Czartoryski's leadership remained and affected his political position abroad.[42]

[41] See M. Tyrowicz, *Polski Kongres Polityczny w Wrocławiu 1848 r.* (1946),
esp. the facsimile, p. 80.
[42] For the conferences at Wroclaw, see Tyrowicz, *op.cit.*, and Handelsman, II,
258-259.

Meanwhile, the short campaign in Poznania came to an end. Mierosławski, the "resurrected chief," who imposed himself as dictator and even won two battles before being surrounded by overwhelming Prussian forces, vanished from the scene when capitulation seemed inevitable, to reappear later in Sicily and in Baden at the head of Italian and German republican forces respectively. Prince Adam's further sojourn in Berlin became of no avail; he returned to Paris and planned to go to Frankfurt to address the German National Assembly in the name of Poland. His emissaries were already on the spot. One of them, Dr. Szokalski, made important contacts at the time of the Vor-Parlament, and the resolution of April 24 condemning Poland's partition was partly his personal success.[43]

But the wave of German militant nationalism before long submerged most of the Germano-Polish friendship, in spite of the courageous opposition of Robert Blum, Arnold Ruge, and a few other idealists against voting a new partition of Poland, that of Poznania, the major part of which together with the city of Poznań was to be incorporated into the Germanic federation.[44]

Thus Czartoryski remained at his post at the Hôtel Lambert. He had to deal with the problem of a Polish national representation. In his absence, preliminary measures had been taken in order to resuscitate the Seym of 1831 by inviting members from abroad and from the homeland, and by inducing Galicia and the Polish provinces of Prussia to send their representatives. He realized that Polish politics in Poznania and Galicia, and the solving of the autonomous life of those provinces under Prussian and Austrian sovereigns, must be left to the local leaders, and his own interference was only advisory and discreet; but he felt the paramount importance of a body representative of the whole nation, which would speak in Poland's name, and he was greatly upset by the lack of response.[45] Nevertheless, in spite of all adversities and setbacks, Czartoryski continued his work acting as if he was the Minister of Foreign Affairs of a Polish state.

After the catastrophe of the Polish national movement in Poz-

---

[43] See E. Kipa, *Misja Szokalskiego* ("Biblioteka Warszawska," 1913).
[44] See Namier, *op.cit.*, pp. 78-91.
[45] Handelsman, II, 264-266.

nania and the breakdown of the policy of cooperation with a new and regenerated Prussia, there still remained grave problems arising from the apparent dissolution of the Hapsburg monarchy. Czartoryski expected to see Hungary and Bohemia emerging before long from the chaos as independent states; Galicia was for him now as precious for the future as the Kingdom had been before the November revolution. No European statesman was more aware of the complexity of the problems involved, especially of the problems of the Slavonic peoples in Austria and Hungary. Before leaving Berlin, Czartoryski directed Colonel Bystrzonowski to Hungary as emissary to both the Magyars and the Slavs and to act as mediator in their feuds.[46]

He did not attend the Slav Congress in Prague, but his friends, emissaries, and collaborators were there and his ideas were set forth in a comprehensive instruction.[47] Poland faced the difficult problem of how to preserve friendly relations with the Germans, Hungarians, and Slavs. Hungarian friendship—which proved sincere and helpful—was a condition of the liberation and security of Galicia, and Czartoryski considered the possibility of an alliance; but he clearly discerned the crucial problem of Hungary— her relations with the Slavs. "Our part," he wrote, "is to try to prevent a sanguinary struggle between them and the Magyars, to suggest concessions, to secure an armistice, at least. . . . May they postpone their quarrels to the moment when Poland rises again; she is necessary for both sides as a disinterested and impartial friend." He did not dismiss the Czech idea of turning Austria into a Slav federation under the Hapsburg imperial crown, although he considered this solution as only a temporary one, as he expected a complete dissolution of the monarchy in the near future, with Galicia returning to an independent Poland.[48] He realized the necessity of a peaceful solution of the emerging problem of the Ruthenians, whose representatives pretended to act as a separate nationality and claimed the partition of that province; he insisted upon a compromise. Men closely

[46] *Ibid.*, p. 262.
[47] For Anthony Walewski, June 9, 1848.
[48] For Czartoryski's influence at the Slav Congress, see Handelsman, II, 272-278.

connected with him, like Prince George Lubomirski and Prince Leon Sapieha, worked in Prague for an understanding with the Ruthenians. The Czech patriot Francis Zach, who had been Czartoryski's diplomatic agent in Belgrade and who was now one of the most active Czech leaders in Moravia and Slovakia, helped as intermediary. "The idea," as Bystrzonowski pointed out a few weeks later, "was to let the Ruthenians in Galicia develop their nationality if they so wished, and even to help them to do so, and to inculcate their national feelings to their brethren beyond the Dnieper and to the Cossacks. . . ." An agreement was signed on June 7, postponing the problem of Ruthenian self-government but pledging the rights of the Ruthenian language and culture.

Even Bakunin contributed to the Polono-Ruthenian agreement; a Russian "old believer" monk, Olymp Miloradov, who had collaborated with the Hôtel Lambert, almost won over the inexorable revolutionary for Czartoryski's policy in Eastern Europe. The main lines of the address to the Emperor, which was prepared but not yet voted when the Congress dispersed, conformed with Czartoryski's views. But Windischgraetz's bombardment of rebellious Prague put an abrupt end to the expectations of a peaceful solution of national problems under the Hapsburg crown. The war in Italy neared its climax and a new one in Hungary was in sight.

Zamoyski returned to Italy; he was most warmly received by King Charles Albert and by the Duke of Savoy. The King was eager to have Polish officers; Zamoyski himself joined his army and many Polish officers, who had formerly volunteered for the papal army, followed him to Piedmont. Prince Adam's older son, Vitold, had already served and fought in the Sardinian ranks, and the small Polish Legion, which had been founded by Mickiewicz, had fought with the forces of insurgent Lombardy. There was the problem of the future of the Polish legion in the Italian army; Prince Adam had explained to the King in a substantial memorandum its political importance and its possible influence upon the Slavs in the Austrian army of which they formed the bulk. Zamoyski tried to secure the decision of the King. Charles Albert was rather reluctant at first, as he was careful not to provoke the Tsar; but he was greatly impressed by Prince Adam's arguments, by his idea of a common stand for freedom on the part of Italy and Poland, Western civilization, and liberalism, of the emancipation of the Slav peoples and of Poland's part as a link between them and the Western powers.[49]

The decision was delayed by the campaign in Lombardy; Zamoyski, Breański, and others took part with the King, who himself commanded his army, and Kamieński's legion served with distinction. After the defeat of Custozza, the disastrous retreat and the conclusion of an armistice, the King was even more ready to accept the support of Polish exiles. On Zamoyski's suggestion, General Chrzanowski was invited and appointed Chief of the General Staff and later deputy C.-in-C. [Major General]. The formation of the legion was accepted; but obstacles arose from unexpected quarters, as the British and French envoys intervened to prevent the formation of a force with a Polish name, emblems, or colors.[50] Prince Adam complained with bitterness: "I have considered since my boyhood England and her government as promoting all good and noble tendencies in the world. I still cannot become accustomed to seeing that creed of my early years stultified, especially when it concerns things which are not very important in themselves, but which are of extreme importance to those who are the victims of such decisions."[51] The result was the failure to build up a real Polish force; even the small existing detachment was discouraged when it was denied its national colors, and a part of them left the Sardinian army.

Chrzanowski's mission was doomed to failure; his prudent warnings against breaking the armistice were in vain; and the General, though gifted, intelligent, and efficient, was neither an inspiring leader for an improvised army nor a powerful personality able to impose his will on foreign and unruly commanders. He could therefore not prevent the new disaster of Novara in March 1849.

Polish diplomacy had made efforts to help Italy by mediating

[49] Letters of L. Niedźwiedzki to Ld. D. C. Stuart, Paris, July 20 and 24, 1848 (H.Mss., xxvi, 190-193; *Zamoyski*, v, Ch. 5, esp. pp. 140-144).

[50] *Zamoyski*, v, Ch. 6, esp. pp. 171-173, 181-182.

[51] To Ld. D. C. Stuart, Nov. 6, 1848 (H.Mss., xxv, 213-216).

an agreement with Hungary and trying to arrange a secret understanding with the Croats. All this was of no avail after the defeat of Novara, and Zamoyski wrote on April 19, 1849: "It is as if the earth had vanished from beneath our feet." Old absolutist Austria had succeeded in crushing the revolution in Vienna and in regaining her Italian provinces. There still remained the Hungarians and their gallant struggle against Austria, against their Croat vassals, and against their Serbian, Rumanian, and Slovak populations as well. Zamoyski saw clearly the further course of events: Hungarian victories must provoke Russia's armed intervention, and the fact that the Polish generals Bem and Dembiński commanded Hungarian armies with success, that a strong Polish legion under General Joseph Wysocki bravely fought on the Hungarian side, could only foster Nicholas' enmity and prompt his intervention.

Prince Adam in vain suggested a French and British mediation between Austria and Hungary, and his agents did their utmost to win over the Turks to her support. But his efforts aimed in the first instance at an understanding between the Magyars, Slavs, and Rumanians; he tried to persuade Kossuth and his government of the necessity of reorganizing Hungary as a federation, and to prepare the Slavs and the Rumanians for a compromise. He even achieved an outstanding success when on May 19, 1849, the Magyar representatives, Ladislas Teleky and Francis Pulszky, met the plenipotentiary of the Slavs, the Czech statesman Francis Rieger at the Hôtel Lambert, and after a long conference, at which Prince Adam acted as chairman and mediator, they signed an agreement providing for the restoration of peace and the unity of St. Stephen's Kingdom on the lines which he had proposed.[52] But the Hungarian representatives were sharply disavowed by Kossuth, who violently opposed the terms; a suicidal attitude, which he regretted too late in exile.

Nevertheless, Prince Adam's and his emissaries' continuous efforts to disarm the hostility of the Croats and Italians, of the Croats, Serbs, Rumanians, and Magyars, were not entirely in vain,

[52] See L. Russjan, *Polacy i sprawa polska na Węgrzech 1848-1849* (1934), esp. pp. 152-176; J. Feldman, *Sprawa polska*, pp. 304-322; F. Pulszky, *Meine Zeit, mein Leben*, 1881, II, 330-331.

partly because both the Polish army commanders in Hungary, Bem, and Dembiński were properly instructed, had with them Czartoryski's diplomatic agents, and tried to put an end to the civil war by appeasing the national minorities and inducing the Magyars to compromise. Bem was especially successful with the Rumanians; and although Bystrzonowski's protracted exertions with the Croats and Serbs to turn their bellicose feelings against Austria were in vain, he paved the way for the appeasement imposed upon the Hungarian Serbs by their Polish conqueror, General Bem; Bem's *faits accomplis* in turn, as well as Prince Adam's mediation, largely contributed to the belated decision of the Hungarian government to make formal concessions to the Rumanians, as well as to the final decision of the Hungarian Parliament reached *in articulo mortis* on July 28, granting all nationalities and confessions full equality of rights.[53]

The Russian army of Field Marshal Paskievich entered Hungary to annihilate that last rampart of revolution and the resurgent specter of Poland at one blow. Zamoyski came just in time to take part in Bem's last desperate counter-attack and to prevent the Poles and the Italians from being involved in Görgei's capitulation; he obtained the order for the Polish legion to march to Orsova on the Danube, he protected the retreat and the passage of the river, and Bystrzonowski obtained from the Serbs hospitality and permission to cross their territory into Turkey; Czaykowski was working there, with General Aupick's support, to induce the government to grant them sanctuary. Kossuth accompanied them in Zamoyski's carriage.

But they had to face another and unexpected ordeal. The Porte, when summoned by the Russian and Austrian governments to hand over the Hungarian and Polish rebels, and threatened by the imperial armies on the Danube, found only one solution and considered it to be a generous offer. The refugees were invited to accept the Mohammedan faith and to become the Sultan's subjects. Even Czaykowski did not think of any better issue, and there was some hesitation, since the alternative of being handed over to the Austrians or Russians was a terrible one. The most distinguished of the Polish commanders, "Father Bem," was

[53] See Handelsman, II, 318-335.

among the few who decided to accept the offer. Zamoyski succeeded in preventing the moral breakdown of the rank and file, and the proposal met with an almost general refusal. He wrote to Lord Dudley Stuart: "We are here in a fine mess. . . . The Turkish Minister had sent me word that I might be excepted [from extradition] *if all* the others only comply [with becoming Mohammedans] and that *in such a case* the Pasha would have orders to facilitate my escape, notwithstanding the threat of Russia that a single refugee escaping from Viddin would be a *casus belli*. . . ."[54] And he familiarized himself with the prospect of long years of hard labor in Siberia. But the Porte stiffened by Sir Stratford Canning, Czaykowski, and Aupick, wisely applied delaying tactics and evasive replies to the summons of both Emperors, and did not capitulate when diplomatic relations were severed.

Public opinion in the West became indignant and demanded intervention. At Canning's request, Palmerston sent the fleet to the Straits, and Louis Bonaparte dispatched the French fleet to Smyrna. This had a salutary effect. Instead of extradition, the deportation of refugees was negotiated. The refugees had to be removed from Turkey, and there was hard bargaining over the list of deportees; Czartoryski's friends and agents were largely taken into account. Czaykowski's deportation was a test case for Russia and Austria. The French protection proved lukewarm, and Sir Stratford Canning was even less eager to intervene, as he disliked the man.

This crisis in the East coincided with another in Czartoryski's own position. He was personally attacked by a Prussian diplomatic intervention in Paris; they produced his letters to Kossuth and Dembiński and demanded his deportation from France, and he had to justify his conduct before the French Ministers. Even at the moment of the demonstration of the British and French fleets, when war seemed in sight, he had no more delusions about the cause of his country. He stated bitterly: "Even if a war broke out, France and England would try to keep us aloof, in order not to complicate the problems and to make a peace of compromise

[54] Letter of Viddin, Sept. 20, 1849 (H.Mss., xxvii, 312-317).

easier." There was a moment when he considered retiring from politics. Nevertheless, he continued to work as before, inspiring politicians and journalists, informing governments and parliaments, dictating memoranda and even articles for the *Revue des Deux Mondes* which for years to come echoed the views of the Hôtel Lambert. But his primary aim was now to prevent the expulsion of the Poles from Turkey, to organize the care of the refugees, whose number again increased, and to secure the welfare of Polish life abroad. It was the subject of his long talk with the Prince-President on November 22, 1849.[55] It marked the end of the period of revolution and opened one of a *modus vivendi* of the Hôtel Lambert with the new regime in France.

No sentimental links existed at first. For Louis Bonaparte, Czartoryski was a liberal *idéologue* and thus connected with his political opponents; in addition, he had been an enemy of the Great Napoleon. In actual fact, Prince Adam disliked Napoleonic methods and traditions; he had never been an admirer of Napoleon the Great and had little confidence in his nephew, who seemed as much committed in Italian affairs as he was indifferent to the fate of Poland.

Three years elapsed before a more intimate association was established between the Hôtel Lambert and the Tuileries. But close contact was imposed by imperious necessity. Early in 1850 Czartoryski suggested to the British, French, and Turkish governments the steps to be taken in order to appease the Christian populations of the Balkans: a hereditary throne for the Karageorgevich family in Serbia, and an outlet to the Adriatic Sea; in Bulgaria, concessions for the national tongue, liberation of the Church from Russian control, and local self-government; in Bosnia, concessions to the Christian Churches. He emphasized the importance of the Polish emigration in Turkey, as being a natural link between the Porte and her Christian subjects. With Palmerston's approval he discussed the plan on April 23, 1850 with Louis Napoléon and insisted upon the necessity of his *rapprochement* with England. The Prince-President promised his full protection for the Poles in Turkey.[56]

[55] Handelsman, II, 342-353.
[56] Handelsman, III, 23-29.

In spite of it, Czaykowski was sacrificed by his Turkish friends. The French Ambassador, General Aupick, reported sadly on May 25, 1850: "Henceforth Turkey will be given up to the secret activities of Russian agents, who thus far had been countered only by the action of Polish émigrés."

To escape expulsion, Czaykowski chose to become a Moslem and the Sultan's subject, Sadyk Effendi (later Sadyk Pasha), in spite of Zamoyski's and Prince Adam's warnings and imprecations.[57]

That heavy blow affected Czartoryski's position in Constantinople, his diplomatic agencies in the Near East, and his influence with the Christian peoples of the Balkans, on the eve of the events he had foreseen, foretold, and prepared for.

[57] Czaykowski's love affair with Louise Śniadecka (once adored by young Słowacki), an ambitious and clever lady, was largely responsible for his decision. His wife and children were in Paris and his return there would have put an end to the romance. Now he married her as his Moslem consort, and there was much embittered argument between him and Zamoyski with regard to his sons, whom he would have liked to make Moslems too. For that imbroglio and its implications, see Handelsman, III, 29-33, 39-43 et passim. Cf. M. Czapska, *Ludwika Śniadecka* (1938).

CHAPTER 19

THE WAR IN THE EAST

SOME YEARS LATER the war broke out in the East, as Czartoryski had expected for two decades and under the conditions he had foreseen.[1] Possibly he was the least surprised by the course the events took. He had warned Napoleon III in time. On January 24, 1853 he discussed with him the European situation and handed him a treatise on French foreign policy, pleading the cause of oppressed nations and summoning the new Emperor to become its champion. Although the leading ideas of his memorandum were the same as those he had advocated for half a century, they strangely harmonized with some of the *Idées Napoléoniennes*, and a link of mutual understanding was established between the two men. Prince Adam persuaded the Emperor that a rapprochement with Great Britain must be the cornerstone of his policy.

In a memorandum of February 10 for Drouyn de Lhuys (drafted in his own handwriting), he advocated once more an Anglo-French alliance as the only means to prevent Russia from encroaching in the East. He pointed out the existing difficulties, rivalries, and frictions and insisted upon the necessity of overcoming them. He strongly advised a concerted action, a common stand in order to deny to Russia and Austria any protectorate over the Sultan's Christian subjects, and a common effort as well to persuade him of the urgency of reforms. "There is no salvation for Turkey and her peoples but in a joint and simultaneous action on the part of France and England."[2]

In May 1853 the ultimatum of Prince Menshikov, Nicholas' special envoy—a request to recognize the Russian protectorate

[1] For the diplomatic prelude of the war, see H. Temperley, *England and the Near East. The Crimea*, 1936. Cf. E. Tarle, *Krimskaya Voyna*, 1944, a vindication of the Russian cause. Handelsman, III (1950), gives a complete diplomatic history of the war, with emphasis on the Polish question. The present chapter has little to add to the material which he has expounded, but differs in some cases in its interpretation.

[2] Handelsman, III, 89-92, 234 sq.; Cz.M.(E), II, 349-351.

over all Orthodox subjects of the Porte—was rejected and the rupture followed. In June, Russian troops crossed the frontier into Moldavia and the British and French fleets sailed towards the Straits.

The Hôtel Lambert and its Eastern agencies, which barely survived the crisis of 1849-1851, were now more active than ever, and the aged Prince (already 83) displayed almost juvenile energy. Early in June he wrote to Reshid Pasha, the Great Vizir, his acquaintance, with an earnest request to postpone no longer the emancipation of the Christians. He supervised the drafting of a general political plan; it proposed a simultaneous solution of the Eastern and Polish questions. He admitted the importance of winning over Austria for the common cause, and he suggested that this might be achieved by an offer of the Danubian principalities in order to build up a united Rumania under the Hapsburg crown; Transsylvania should be included. By such a sacrifice Turkey would obtain the safety of her Balkan possessions and a natural alliance, the Moldo-Wallachs national unity, and Austria could be induced to restore Galicia to an independent Poland and to concur on her liberation. Some compensation could be found for Prussia's part. The new Poland should be a neutral state, under a joint guarantee of the European powers, as was Belgium. The memorandum underlined the fact that Russia's impact on Europe ought to be eliminated by pushing her back to the East; she was a formidable power as an empire, but if revolutionized she would produce even more destructive power and provoke more disintegration elsewhere than any other revolution. He considered the Balkan Christian peoples as future separate states and natural heirs to the Ottoman Empire, but since they still were politically immature, this could be achieved only by the friendly and disinterested care of the West under Turkish sovereignty; thus the prolonged existence of the Ottoman Empire was thought desirable for the future of those peoples. A special memorandum suggested the formation of special Christian troops, under Christian officers: the Poles would be the most reliable and suitable for that task.[3]

[3] Handelsman, III, 239-242. *Zamoyski*, VI, 4-6. The memorandum was drafted by Lenoir (Louis Zwierkowski), the Prince's secretary.

The French Emperor was sounded by the Prince; he agreed with the main lines of the plan on condition of securing British consent and support. Prince Adam hurried to London, to discuss with British statesmen the problems of the coming war and the solutions he proposed.

He was received at 10 Downing Street by Lord Aberdeen, and he wrote later to Zamoyski, who was deputizing for him in Paris: "I found him much morally and intellectually declining and debilitated; his opinions are timid and wavering. In the Cabinet he must be a great nuisance and hindrance for any decisive act beyond usual routine. He explained that he is for maintaining the peace *quand même* and that this was the principal aim and principle of British policy. I told him that peace must be a real one, that Russia, if aware of the general and insurmountable aversion to war, would feel able to do anything at her will, etc., that this was the right moment for strengthening the Ottoman Empire temporarily at least, etc.—but it was in vain. . . . Such an aged person, slumbering, always gloomy, whose blood is cold and sluggishly circulating, cannot inspire confidence for the administration of which he is the head. He received us very kindly and in friendly manner, but it seems rather desirable that he should enjoy rest and repose." Incidentally, Aberdeen was fourteen years younger than his Polish guest. But the Prime Minister's attitude was by no means just a by-product of senility. Czartoryski could not know Aberdeen's earlier commitments with regard to Nicholas' intended solution of the Turkish question, nor his genuine readiness to allow the submergence of the Ottoman Empire by the Russian deluge. His colleagues, Lord Clarendon, Lord John Russell, and Sir James Graham, seemed more impressed by the peril and more concerned with checking it; but "they dreamed that trade, railways, continuous progress on every field should promote freedom, stop Russia, and prevent her from imposing her yoke upon other peoples." Prince Adam found Palmerston, now Home Secretary, buoyant, outspoken, with a clear vision of realities; he was gratified also by his talk with Disraeli. Palmerston showed much interest in the plan of settling the Polish question and was not inclined to appease Russia by abandoning Turkey to her mercy. But the House of Commons was definitely for preserving peace at any price; Lord Dudley Stuart, who said that peace could not be paid for by agreeing to the violation of treaties, the abandoning of weaker allies, and the forfeiting of moral credit, found no response.[4] At the same time Zamoyski noticed, when speaking to Drouyn de Lhuys and other French statesmen, a general reluctance to raise the Polish problem. "They know that it would be a powerful weapon, but too powerful, as they estimate, for their present convenience. Besides, they do not know how to make use of it. They are satisfied that it could be available if wanted at any time, and so they prefer to avoid premature commitments. We have no reason to complain, as it is evident that they do not regard us as dead, but as too much alive for their needs."[5] Actually, both the Western governments, especially the British, were anxious to find a peaceful solution and inclined to let the Turks accept the Russian claims, if made more palatable and less injurious to the sovereignty of the Sultan. When the Anglo-French naval demonstration did not prevent the Russians from occupying the whole of Moldavia and Wallachia unopposed, a four-power mediation followed and protracted negotiations took place in Vienna, with Austria, the real mediator, in the foreground.

Both Russia and Turkey were drifting into war and the general crisis promptly became acute. The so-called Turkish "ultimatum" of July 20, a sensible and conciliatory one, a quasi-spontaneous promise to Russia with regard to the privileges of the Sultan's Orthodox subjects, was dismissed by the four-power diplomats in Vienna as unpalatable for Russia, and they substituted the "Vienna Note" for it, which was not only unpalatable, but even insulting to Turkey. Lord Stratford, the friend of the Turks and champion of their independence, was directed to enforce the note upon the Porte. He tried to fulfill his painful task, but in vain. As Burke once had said, "an Englishman is the unfittest person on earth to argue another into slavery."[6] The Turks made amendments which Russia was to reject; and Nessel-

---

[4] Czartoryski's letters of July 2, 4, 10, 1853 (*Zamoyski*, VI, 7-10). Cf. Cz.M.(E), II, 349 ff., and Handelsman, III, 127-131, 242-247.

[5] *Zamoyski*, VI, 3-6.

[6] Quoted by Temperley, *The Crimea*, p. 343.

rode's interpretation of the Vienna Note, as revealed in a German newspaper, made of it something like another version of Menshikov's ultimatum. France and England abandoned the note; the Turks boiled with rage, demanding the evacuation of the Principalities within fifteen days; and on October 23 hostilities started on the Danube. Count Buol's last-minute new proposals could not prevent the outbreak of war.

Neither Czartoryski nor Zamoyski was unaware of the key position of Austria and of the apparent necessity for the Western powers of avoiding any complications which could restore her close association with Nicholas I. While sounding the Turks on the possibility of a Polish legion, they were inclined to disguise Polish military action, at first under the cover of Turkish Christian formations, as suggested in Bystrzonowski's plan. It coincided with a *fait accompli*: a crypto-Polish formation actually arose in the East, although with no Christian pattern. The renegade Czaykowski, now Sadyk Pasha, who still claimed to be Prince Adam's devoted and faithful servant, was organizing a regiment of "Ottoman Cossacks." The regiment was manned by Cossacks from Dobrudja, deserters from the Russian army, fugitive Ukrainian serfs, and volunteers from Balkan Slav countries, and commanded by a number of Polish officers. Before long, Sadyk's name became legendary in Poland. At the Hôtel Lambert he was supposed to be a useful link with the Turks and willing to act as Prince Adam's confidential liaison. He was directed to approach the Porte with proposals of the military collaboration of the Polish emigration under Czartoryski's lead, and the Seraskier accordingly invited Zamoyski, Chrzanowski, Bystrzonowski, and Charles Różycki to serve as generals in the Turkish army. The Prince was invested with the power to select and dispatch Polish officers to the East and was semi-officially recognized as the head of the Polish Emigration and treated thus as the Sultan's ally.[7]

In December 1853 an extraordinary envoy appeared in Constantinople with Prince Adam's letters of introduction. It was Lord Dudley Stuart who undertook to sound the Turks and his old friend Lord Stratford de Redcliffe as well, on the raising of the

[7] Handelsman, III, 252-260, 268-270.

Polish colors and of the Polish cause. He had long talks with the Ambassador and with Turkish ministers, and an audience with the Sultan. His visit greatly impressed the Porte and enhanced the position of the Prince, but the main object—the creating of a Polish legion—could not be obtained. Lord Stratford told him that it would be practicable only if England entered the war. And this was said just two or three weeks after the "massacre of Sinope," at the very time of the fateful decision of dispatching of the allied fleet into the Black Sea.[8]

Czartoryski decided to send Zamoyski to Constantinople as his permanent representative and introduced him to Reshid and to the Seraskier as "his most trusted collaborator for 24 years, whose every word could be considered by the Porte as the Prince's own." He brought a letter of the Prince to Abdul Medjid with the solemn words: "May we live to see the day when Your Imperial Majesty will raise the Polish colors and summon me with my sons to carry it in the vanguard of his victorious armies."[9]

Zamoyski reached Constantinople on January 24. He was well received, even by Sadyk Pasha, and the matter of the Polish legion was discussed with the Turks and the Ambassadors. He was recommended half-heartedly by the French Ministry, backed by the Embassy, and on excellent terms with Lord Stratford. In March 1854 he was invited by Reshid Pasha (at Lord Stratford's suggestion) to organize a Polish legion. But he was not the only Polish emissary on the Bosporus. The Poles in exile were divided, and the Hôtel Lambert had its democratic counterpart, now focused in the Polish circle in Paris, a strong political group led by Mierosławski. The ideas about the war and Poland's part were almost identical on both sides; nor was there any divergence between the Prince and his opponents as to the necessity of the enfranchisement of the peasants. But the old party feud and inveterate hostility prevented collaboration. And there was now in Constantinople a delegate of the circle, General Wysocki, as Zamoyski's opposite number, with exactly the same purpose and

---

[8] For Dudley Stuart's visit to Constantinople, see Handelsman, III, 263-265, 276. He left Constantinople on Jan. 25, 1854. His dispatches to Czartoryski were destroyed in Warsaw in 1939.

[9] Handelsman, III, 264-265, 275-277.

similar plan. He was backed by Prince Napoleon, who favored
the Polish radicals and was their candidate for the Polish throne,
as the former sturdy republicans now promptly evolved towards
Bonapartism. What was even more serious, Lord Stratford also
showed some preference for Wysocki, as he often quarrelled with
Zamoyski. Even Reshid Pasha, while seeking for a solution
which could be satisfying for all concerned, invented a curious
one: two separate Polish legions, the "aristocrats" with Zamoyski
in Asia and the "democrats" with Wysocki in Europe. And instead of a Polish legion, as proposed at first, the Ambassadors,
duly instructed by their governments, suggested a foreign legion
or a foreign corps only, which would be less alarming for both
German powers. The war had already started, and Lord Stratford
suggested that the matter be postponed until the arrival of Lord
Raglan and Maréchal St. Arnaud. In the meantime, the decisions
taken in Paris and London put an end to the imbroglio, as the
Prince was recognized as the unique representative of the Polish
emigration, and Zamoyski as his deputy.[10] Wysocki had no more
chance of achieving anything, but to hinder Zamoyski's work.
The old Prince, in his speech on May 3, 1854, mentioned with
sorrow the idea of "two opposed legions" and he warned his
countrymen: "How could we expect to bring our ship safely into
harbor if there were two or more captains, and two helms steer-
ing in two opposite directions?"[11]

At that time he was more conscious than ever that if anything
could be done for his country, he was the only Pole in a position
to try. So, as the outbreak of the general war was imminent, he
tried to gain over the Allies for the Polish conception of its conduct.

General Chrzanowski had been invited early in March by a
British minister to draft a plan for the war in the East.[12] They
discussed the main lines with Czartoryski, and the note of March
28, 1854 (the day of the declaration of war) quoted in the English

---

[10] Handelsman, III, 272-282.

[11] Printed in Polish in 1854.

[12] Czartoryski to Zamoyski Mar. 6 and 8, 1854 (*Zamoyski*, VI, 33-34). The
invitation came through the usual intermediary, Lord Dudley Stuart, who did
not name the destinatary; it was Palmerston, who knew Chrzanowski well
and appreciated his services.

edition of his papers expressed most probably their common views.[13] The Prince suggested offensive warfare; as long as the neutrality of the German powers protected Russia's western frontiers, she could be attacked at other points: "The first of these is the Crimea and the adjacent territories. The second is the Lower Danube and the Polish Ukraine on the borders of the Black Sea. The third is the coast of Lithuania on the Baltic. These three points if attacked simultaneously would all have the advantage of being in territories inhabited by populations which wish to throw off the Russian yoke. It would first be necessary to conquer the Crimea and Sebastopol, which would entail the destruction of the enemy's fleet. . . ." He also advocated an expedition to occupy the border of the Caucasus and to give support to the people of that country, who would rise en masse if supplied with arms. He suggested displaying the Polish flag, since the Russian army in the Caucasus consisted largely of Poles. On the Lower Danube a strong Cossack legion with infantry and artillery under Polish colors would attract the Ukrainian people. An expeditionary corps landing in Lithuania or Courland would find support from the Catholic people of Samogitia, "who are thoroughly Polish in sentiment, and would at once join the national colors."[14] He considered a combined operation upon Riga, or an attack on Vilna, with the final aim of cutting off the Russian forces in the north from those in the west and the south.

The declaration of war sounded in Prince Adam's ears like a voice of the Angel of the Apocalypse. He stated in an open letter to Dudley Stuart: "The *status quo* in Europe, in which Poland had been condemned to a complete annihilation, is already shaken in its foundation, and a new era seems to come for all peoples, in which nobler and more elevated principles should prevail in politics over the views of an egoism, often as blind to own interests as deaf to the claims of truth and justice. . . . The salvation of the whole of humanity seems to repose now almost entirely upon the new alliance of the two great and generous nations, England and France."[15] Early in March he was informed by

[13] See Cz.M.(E), II, 351-354.
[14] So did the Lithuanians in 1831 and later in 1863.
[15] Lettre à Lord Dudley Stuart, Mar. 24, 1854 (printed in French).

Cintrat that both the Foreign Minister and Marshal St. Arnaud recognized him as "the center and the intermediary in all matters pertaining to the creation of a Polish legion" and Zamoyski and Dudley Stuart as his plenipotentiaries in both allied capitals. On March 16 Drouyn de Lhuys announced it himself to the Prince, and on April 3—six days after war was declared—an instruction to Baraguey d'Hilliers in Constantinople settled the matter. The Prince was received by the Emperor on April 13 and assured of the latter's "warmest and sincere desire to restore Poland," with the restriction that Austria must be first induced to cooperate. The Emperor mentioned his idea of first creating a Duchy of Warsaw; he thought it the proper way for introducing the Polish problem. He also authorized the Prince to announce to his countrymen that he was recognized as their spokesman.[16]

Prince Adam was by no means enchanted with the idea of a Duchy of Warsaw, a *pars pro toto* of the Polish question. But even the proposal of such a partial solution was by no means agreed upon by the Western powers, nor even thought opportune by the French Foreign Ministry. He was told early in March by Persigny, then its *éminence grise*, that the Polish question was like a pot, where the key of the situation was hidden, and nobody dared to grasp it. They were negotiating with Austria and Prussia, and they could not raise the problem without a previous understanding with them; but he was satisfied that Austria was sincerely for a concert with France; later he mentioned that there were even talks about compensations for Galicia. His only advice for the Poles was that they must wait. Drouyn warned even more strongly against any Polish action, against the raising of Polish colors, and against a new insurrection. France could undertake nothing, except in concert with Austria; so the Poles must wait and keep their strength for the proper moment, which would come later. The Duc de Morny expressed it still more emphatically: "The Poles must behave as if they were dead, as *we* are taking care of them."[17] And Walewski, whose diplomatic career had started (in 1831) under Prince Adam's orders, was

[16] Handelsman, III, 211-212, 278-280, 309.
[17] *Ibid.*, pp. 107-108, 115-118, 310.

now more cautious with regard to Polish affairs than most of his French-born colleagues; he even exasperated Lord Dudley by his reluctance to commit his name by taking a ticket for a Polish ball. He was later regarded by Lord Clarendon as "more Austrian than the Austrians themselves," and suspected by the Austrian Minister of Foreign Affairs, Count Buol, to be too subservient to Russia.[18] His suggestions to his Polish countrymen sounded like Morny's: "Keep quiet. Poland will be restored without any Polish initiative by a concerted action of the Western powers and Austria." The attitude of the French diplomacy conformed with the views of the British government. Clarendon was against Polish formations and moves, for he thought that they could deter the German powers from taking part with the allies and expose the Poles themselves to new disasters.[19] Thus all was subordinated to the main issue: an alliance with Austria.

The results of that policy were to be felt before long at the Hôtel Lambert and even in Constantinople and the Danube. Prince Adam's letters to Dudley Stuart from July 1854 on stated with an increasing certitude and precision that the Allies were withdrawing in the matters of collaboration with the Poles, because they were anxious not to alarm Austria, that they still hoped to make a peace settlement promptly, if Austria joined them as an ally, and since she showed some inclination to do so, all action connected with Poland was paralyzed.[20]

There was in fact an alarm both in Berlin and Vienna about the Polish question. The Duke of Cambridge, who was in Vienna in April, warned the Queen of the susceptibility of the Austrian court. In May, the Austrian envoy in Paris, Count Hübner, mentioned the Polish question and Czartoryski's activities; he was told by the Emperor on May 21 that if Russia would push things to the extreme, then a Duchy of Warsaw should be restored, leaving the Austrian and Prussian possessions intact. He also mentioned plans for attacking Russia by crossing Germany; he mentioned Italy and Hungary and the reshaping of the map of

---

[18] See Dudley Stuart to Czartoryski, Dec. 1, 1851, pr. by Handelsman, III, 28; and *op.cit.*, III, 111-115.

[19] Handelsman, III, 143-145, 308-309.

[20] Letters of June 25, July 12, 21, 24, 29, 30, 1854, quoted by Handelsman, III, 320-322, destroyed in Warsaw, 1939.

Europe. No wonder that Hübner was much impressed, Vienna and Berlin alarmed, and Drouyn de Lhuys hurried to placate the Austrians (May 31) by assurances in all those delicate matters, if only they were willing to cooperate. All diplomatic action was now focused on enforcing the evacuation of the Danubian principalities upon Russia by Austrian intervention, and the Polish question was dropped.[21] Prince Adam clearly discerned the consequences of that policy: if Nicholas yielded to Austrian intervention, the Austrian army would separate the belligerents and prevent any decisive operations; and if a general peace followed, it would be a peace of compromise, safeguarding the *status quo* in Poland and Russia's dominating position in that part of Europe. He was aware, that not only a Polish legion but even the Cossack formation was becoming "inopportune."[22]

The Polish conception of bold offensive warfare met with little response. The idea of a war on a limited scale and with limited objectives prevailed, and the expedition to the Crimea, not combined with landings at Nikolayev or Odessa as the Poles suggested, inaugurated a long and costly campaign of attrition without any possibility of a decisive result. That kind of limited war seemed to conform most with British policy, and Gladstone congratulated Palmerston upon having suggested the Crimea as the main objective.[23]

Sigismund Krasiński, the poet and thinker, wrote to General Zamoyski:[24] "The Western people have always nourished the wishful idea that it would be possible to restore the peace they cherish at a minimum of expense. So they do not mention us and they fear pronouncing our name more than anything else. But a commercial approach cannot suffice when struggling against the incensed passions of the barbarian colossus. Either they must yield, or change their feelings and tactics. . . ."

On July 6, 1854, the Prince had a conversation with Napoleon III at St. Cloud and was impressed by his reiterated promises of

---

[21] Handelsman, III, 292-293, 312-316.

[22] Letters to Dudley Stuart, June 2 and 25, July 5; to Zamoyski, June 13, 23, 28, July 3 (quoted by Handelsman, III, 316-320).

[23] Bell, II, 104-105.

[24] June 17, 1854 (*Zamoyski*, VI, 169-170). Krasiński was a friend of Zamoyski. He had his own links with the Tuileries and easy access to Napoleon III.

raising the Polish cause in favorable circumstances. "Why should the Emperor delude us?" that question repeated itself several times in Czartoryski's letters. But later in July, when they met again at Prince Jerome's Palais Royal, the Emperor approached him to give him secretly the grave warning: "Do not delude yourselves. We just demonstrate against Russia from the South. Prevent the Poles from making any inconsiderate move."[25] The Prince reacted on July 26-27 by a memorandum to the Emperor as "the only man" who understood the position of Poland and her possible contribution to the future of Europe. Russia could be vanquished only if she lost both Poland and Finland, and Poland's restoration was necessary for the future security of Austria. In a bold vision of the future, he anticipated the events of the years 1914-1918, a Russo-German war, armies struggling from the Black Sea to the Baltic, and many hundred thousand Poles fighting on both sides. How then could the Polish question be left unsolved? He hinted at the possibility of winning Austria over for a bold solution of the Polish question, but such a solution must be proposed and she must be summoned to become a partner. The Poles were ready to accept any government which would be proposed by France and England, as advice coming from a good and generous friend.[26] He alluded clearly to the possibility of an Austro-Polish solution.

Prince Adam was aware that pledges of maintaining the *status quo* in Poland were not necessarily the best way for inducing Austria to wage war against Russia. The Austrians were not anxious to get into war only for the sake of Turkish independence and for preserving the *status quo*, and then to be left alone, to face a still powerful and embittered Russia, and be exposed to her revenge. It is not necessary to suppose that there was too much astuteness in their diplomacy of 1854. They were simply at the cross-roads between their Russian partner and ally of 1849 and the Western powers, who could not be considered as natural friends of the old Hapsburg monarchy. They tried to secure a settlement of the Turkish dispute which would prevent Russia's control of the Ottoman Empire without offending her.

[25] Handelsman, III, 320, 354-355.
[26] *Ibid.*, pp. 347-353.

They declined Nicholas' overtures at Olmütz and after; but they were reluctant to commit themselves without real guarantees for the future settlement in that part of Europe. So they procrastinated and sounded the Western powers about their final aims. By doing so, they were obviously careful and eager to display their moderation, restraint, and preference for the territorial *status quo* and for a peace of compromise. They became aware that it was exactly what the Western statesmen (with the possible exception of Napoleon III and Palmerston) had in mind and that there was not any clear conception of an offensive war against Russia and of the pushing back of her European borders. On the other hand, they were blackmailed by the Emperor's and Drouyn's threats of putting into action the revolutionary forces of the Poles, Italians, and Hungarians. So their first thought was to demand guarantees for their own *status quo* and to prevent such Polish activities which could endanger their possession of Galicia. But in their talks in Vienna, in Paris, and in London they used to suggest the proviso: if Russia would push the conflict to extremes, it would be necessary to wage war on the largest scale with the most powerful means. Count Buol stated it with some emphasis, and Francis Joseph restated it later in his letter of February 2, 1855 to Napoleon III. The texts could be safely interpreted as an indirect and conditional consent to Napoleon's Polish conceptions. Austria's Polish policy could be interpreted as one of avoiding and even opposing any Polish *fait accompli* or Polish activities as long as the conflict was limited to the Turkish problem; should it be extended to become a really offensive war of the coalition, they reckoned with the necessity of raising the Polish question.[27]

The young Austrian Emperor was indignant about being treated by Nicholas like a vassal. He was inclined to see the future of his Empire in the East; he regarded a future contest with Russia as unavoidable and the present situation as a favorable

[27] See Hübner's conversations with Napoleon III and Drouyn de Lhuys, his reports and discussions with Buol, and Francis Joseph's letter, quoted from Vienna Staats-Archiv by H. Wereszycki, in *Kwartalnik Historyczny*, vol. 41, 1927, pp. 51-77. Cf. Pope Henessy's interpretation of Austrian policy, July 2, 1861 (*Hansard*, 3rd Ser., CLXIV, 217-218).

opportunity. Thus he did not discard the necessity of waging an offensive war with far-reaching aims.[28] The concentrations of his forces in Galicia, Bukovina, and Transylvania in July 1854 were so powerful that the Russian Guards were sent to the Kingdom, and its evacuation was considered and prepared; the threat of an attack from Bukovina in the rear of the Russian army in Moldavia was even more strategically decisive.[29]

When inviting the Tsar to hand over the Principalities under such a threat, the Austrian ministers were conscious that they were shocking the world by a display of ingratitude. The more so, that they even tried to conspire with the Poles. Two Polish patriots known for their popularity, Count Peter Moszyński in Cracow and Count Alexander Dzieduszycki in Lvov, were approached by the local heads of the Austrian government, Graf Mercandin and Graf Gołuchowski and told of "possible changes in Austria's Polish policy"; she was conscious that Poland's partitions had been "a curse which had encumbered her ever since" and fettered her with the Russian policy; now she was willing to repair her fault and even ready to give up Galicia to an independent Poland; and she was anxious to know the reaction of the Poles to that overture. Both Poles independently gave the same answer: the policy of Austria since the First Partition has been one of destroying the Polish nationality, and it would hardly be possible for Austria to win the confidence of the Poles in Galicia; the events of 1846 were fresh in their memory (inquisitions and executions took place as late as 1851). But they suggested an approach to Czartoryski, who was in a better position to negotiate and who enjoyed the full confidence of the homeland. Prince Adam informed Lord Dudley about it; he expected to be approached from the Austrian side and asked the British government for advice.[30] Drouyn de Lhuys had already been sounded by Hübner about Poland; he gave a rather vague answer: if the most interested powers, Austria and Prussia, put forward a proposal,

---

[28] See Francis Joseph's letter to his mother, Oct. 8, 1854 (*Briefe an seine Mutter*, 1930, p. 232); and his letter to Napoleon III of Feb. 2, 1855, *loc.cit.*

[29] The extreme seriousness of the situation is shown in H. Friedjung's *Der Krimkrieg u. die oesterreichische Politik*, 1907, Ch. 6 and 7.

[30] Letter to Dudley Stuart, Aug. 15, 1854 (H.Mss., xxv, 223-225). See also for that and other similar overtures, Handelsman, iii, 330-338.

France would support it. It seemed rather discouraging, and Count Buol disavowed Hübner's approach in that matter.[31]

The course the events took in the month of August seemed to foretell an early settlement. The Austrian intervention proved successful: on August 7 Russia informed Count Buol of her intention to evacuate the Principalities, and on August 20 the Austrian army entered Wallachia. A limitation of the land operations of the Allied armies was the inevitable result, and the French Emperor's warning seemed confirmed by the facts.

Czartoryski felt it his duty to give a guiding advice to his countrymen in the homeland. On May 5 he had sent them a message of hope, warning against hasty and inconsiderate action, but recommending preparations and readiness. Caution was even more advisable in the new situation. So his public appeal of August 26 recommended that they persevere in the "conspiracy of restraint and prudence." He advised them: "Receive advances and offers from whatever side they will come, but before undertaking action insist upon substantial guarantees for your future." Such guarantees would be offered by "the creation of a Polish force under Polish leaders to serve as a nucleus for an army to be formed out of those, whose ranks are filled by our countrymen; by the recognition of independent Polish authorities; and by a declaration on the part of the powers, or of one of them with the consent of her Allies, that Poland had a right to an independent existence. . . . We have been too often deceived by promises and been made victims of our too adventurous and trusting spirit. . . ."[32]

The statement was published in London, and it provoked a storm of indignation among the Polish radicals; but the response in the homeland was strong and Prince Adam's conditions were before long sponsored by Polish public opinion in the homeland and abroad. The political leaders in Poznania, after careful investigation of the activity of both centers of the emigration, accepted Prince Adam's leadership, and so did a few months later the leading patriots in the southeastern provinces of the former Commonwealth. There was some wavering in the Kingdom,

[31] See Handelsman, III, 332-335.
[32] See Cz.M.(E), II, 354-355; and Handelsman, III, 354-357.

largely because of Czartoryski's progressive social policy, and even in Galicia, where provincial problems had already come to the foreground. But the response was a very strong one, and Prince Adam could safely assume the role and the title of "Supreme Chief" as he did following Kościuszko's style. Among the many declarations of allegiance, the most moving for the old man was certainly the one of Mattias Palacz, a peasant deputy to the Prussian Landtag, made in the name of Polish peasants. Old friends gathered closer around him, and new ones joined. Among the former, Mickiewicz was the dearest one. The great poet always had a kind of filial attachment to the Prince, in spite of frequent divergence of views which arose in the forties because of his mysticism and social radicalism. He was at this time connected with the democratic circle, but before long he felt compelled to change sides in order to become what he wanted to be, a servant of the Polish cause.[33]

The policy of the Western powers was clearly one of limited war aims and limited warfare, but they tried to extend the alliance to Austria and to the secondary powers, to Sweden in the first instance, because of her key position on the Baltic Sea. Their efforts coincided with Czartoryski's endeavor to win that country over for the Polish cause; his emissary, Alexander Wołodkowicz, was already on the spot and had made contact with the Royal Prince Oscar. There were most friendly talks, and he even alluded to the possibility of a Swedish candidature to the Polish throne. The report seemed promising and a more influential personality necessary for further talks. Lord Dudley Stuart undertook to go to Stockholm as Czartoryski's envoy. On his arrival he fell ill with typhoid cholera. Hardly recovered, he went to the inauguration of the memorial of Charles-Jean and was invited to a state dinner and developed thereafter a feverish activity.[34] "He had a long audience of the King, which was followed by a second at His Majesty's desire; Lord Dudley had also an audience of the Crown Prince . . . and on the very day of his last attack he had an audience of the King's second son Prince Oscar." He had to be carried downstairs and returned fatally ill; he succumbed on

---

[33] Handelsman, III, 385-400 et passim; also see his *Mickiewicz, 1853-55* (1933).
[34] For his mission, see Handelsman, III, 358-364.

November 17 to an attack of dropsy in the chest.[35] When feeling that he was to die, he said that his greatest sorrow was that he would pass away when events seemed to run to Poland's rescue.[36] Palmerston paid tribute to the defunct: "It is true that a nobler nature never lived and his death will be extensively lamented."[37] For Prince Adam it was a "terrific blow." He wrote to Lady Harrowby, Lord Dudley's sister: "I have lost one of the very few men whom I really loved and venerated" and "Poland has lost her best defender."[38] His speech of November 29 extolled Lord Dudley's virtues and services, and he proclaimed two months of national mourning.

The Prince asked Lord Harrowby to assume part of the task of the defunct and to serve as intermediary between him and the British government and Parliament. He accepted and became the semi-official liaison and the spokesman of the Polish cause for the whole period of the war and its aftermath. On March 12 of the next year he was appointed a member of the government, Chancellor of the Duchy of Lancaster, and later Lord Privy Seal, with the task of taking care of Polish affairs.[39]

In October 1944, Napoleon III once more sounded the Austrian envoy on Polish affairs. He spoke of enforcing a solution of the problem either against Austria, if she was on the Russian side, or in understanding with her, if she should join the Allies in the war. Hübner was impressed by this utterance, but Drouyn de Lhuys immediately disapproved of his master, and he even quoted the lesson he was alleged to have read to him. Thus the effort of the sounding was nil, the more so as Drouyn mentioned the

---

[35] Charles Szulczewski, *An Address of Condolence on the Death of Lord Dudley Stuart*, 1854. See also the article in *The Examiner*, Nov. 22, 1854. Ld. D. C. Stuart to Rev. E. Mortlock, Stockholm 8 Nov.; A. Magenis (The Brit. Minister) to Ld. Harrowby, Stockholm Nov. 13, Nov. 20; Mjr. Pringe (The Brit. Consul) to Lady Harrowby, Stockholm Dec. 6 (H.Mss. XLIII, 185-190, 193-196, 225-232).

[36] Letter from Lobstein, the French Minister in Stockholm, Nov. 18, quoted by Cintrat in a letter to Czartoryski Nov. 27 (Handelsman, *loc.cit.*).

[37] Letter to J. A. Smith, Nov. 21 (H.Mss.).

[38] Letter of Nov. 23 (H.Mss.).

[39] Czartoryski to Harrowby, Dec. 9, 1854 (H.Mss., XXVIII, 140-141). Handelsman, III, 406-407, 433-439. Dudley Stuart's wartime political correspondence was sent to the Hôtel Lambert and remained in the Prince's papers. In 1939 it was destroyed in the siege of Warsaw.

special rights of both Austria and Prussia as the powers immediately concerned; he wanted the initiative to be taken by their common accord—an accord which was possible only if directed against the restoration of Poland, but not for promoting it.[40] It is probable that Drouyn's diplomatic exploit contributed to his removal from his post and to his final disgrace. But Austria once more had convincing proof of the unwillingness of the Allies to push things beyond the limits of a dispute on Turkish affairs. She certainly resented the blackmail in the French Emperor's statement and retaliated by a violent campaign against Polish military formations, Zamoyski's and Sadyk's activities and his Cossacks, and demanded their removal from Bucharest, and even from European Turkey.[41] Czartoryski had to wait a long time for an audience with the Emperor, and when received on November 12 he was encouraged to hope for the best, but was told that the proper time for raising the Polish cause had not yet come. He retorted by a sharp criticism of French policy and suggested a discussion of the problem with Palmerston, who was expected in Paris.[42]

When the four-power conference in Vienna agreed upon the Four Articles for settlement of the eastern question, Poland was not mentioned; the Allies were too anxious not to complicate their new partnership with Austria and their even less promising relations with Prussia. Aberdeen discarded any idea of pushing beyond, even if the war was to be waged for another year, and he informed the Queen that there was no intention of promoting such extravagant claims as a cession of the Crimea, of Finland, or a restoration of Poland.[43] On December 2—the fiftieth anniversary of the coronation of Napoleon I and the forty-ninth of Austerlitz —the treaty of the Triple Alliance was signed, and Austria was now to be both ally and mediator, but more mediator than ally.

Prince Adam looked back at the passing year with a feeling of frustration. In his speech of November 29 he did not indulge in

---

[40] See Hübner, *Neuf ans de souvenirs*, 1904, p. 270. For Prussia's desperate efforts to prevent reappearance of the Polish problem, see Handelsman, III, 416-422.

[41] Handelsman, III, 379-383.

[42] *Ibid.*, pp. 369-373.

[43] F. Balfour, *Life of Aberdeen*, 1922, II, 264.

fostering hopes; he stated that "the name of Poland was nowhere pronounced, by no government." There still was a stalemate in the important matter of a Polish military formation, and Zamoyski was busy raising a new Polish regiment under the cover of the Ottoman Cossacks, and even that was regarded as dangerous for cooperation with Austria. The Prince wrote to Zamoyski: "I feel depressed and in darkness, as probably many others do. Things are going badly not for us only—as is our usual lot—but for all, because nobody knows where."[44] And he admitted in a letter to Lord Harrowby that the Western governments were careful not to give to the Poles vain hopes and not to provoke moves, which could expose that country to great calamities. But he also mentioned the suspicion arising among Poles that there was in the British government some kind of prejudice against the restoration of Poland.[45] The only light in that "darkness" was Reshid's proposal to Czartoryski of a Turco-Polish alliance after the war; it was proof that the Turks still did not despair of Poland's liberation.[46]

Thus he felt it his duty to restate his policy in a message sent to the homeland by the emissary of the southern provinces: "According to my own opinion and to the will of the homeland of which I had been recently informed, I declared and I undertake the obligation of continuing to state that the Polish nation should not rise in arms and start any struggle against her oppressors, until she had seen allied forces within her borders and with them a Polish force with national colors, and until the Allied governments had recognized a united and independent Poland, as she had been before the partitions. These conditions are indispensable and *sine qua non.* . . ."[47] In an almost desperate position he returned to the attitude of intransigeance and his defiant *Quand même.*

The situation in the early months of 1885 became more favorable for Czartoryski's action, not only because of Palmerston's succession to the Prime Minister's office and his vigorous leadership

[44] Dec. 4, 1854.
[45] Dec. 9, 1854 (H.Mss., XXVIII, 40-41).
[46] Handelsman, III, 400-402.
[47] *Ibid.,* pp. 382-383; and his *Mickiewicz,* p. 71.

of Britain's war policy, but also because the prospects of an early peace vanished in January and the prospects of Austria's taking part in the forthcoming campaign diminished. The Crimean war proved costly and troops were needed for its continuation; so the building up of a Polish formation was now considered with more interest, and a prospective insurrection in the Ukraine, of which plans had been sent to the Prince by the Polish leaders in that province, was now discussed with keen interest by French and British ministers, as was the suggestion of reviving and fostering the struggle of the Circassians.

British public opinion evidently took sides for Poland: numerous meetings demanded a statement of the British policy for her liberation, and petitions to the Parliament came from twenty towns. When questioned in the Commons on March 23, Palmerston answered with caution, trying to appease Austrian suspicions but "leaving the doors open for Polish hopes."[48]

Drouyn de Lhuys thought it advisable to instruct Bourqueney in Vienna (January 19) to sound Austria about her prospective approach to the Polish problem in the case of operations in Poland, and Hübner once more sounded Drouyn after Francis Joseph's letter of February 2 about some action for creating embarrassment to Russia from the Polish side. In his talk with Czartoryski on February 12 Napoleon III accused Austria of evasive answers and deluding tactics, but the language of his own diplomacy was neither firm nor precise.[49]

Early in March the unexpected news of the death of Nicholas I complicated the political situation. Prince Adam considered its effect as unfavorable for the Polish cause; with the new reign, changes would be expected and waited for and all combinations postponed.[50] In his conversation with the Emperor on April 10 he found him more helpless and undecided than ever before.[51] But the war was continuing and so were the affairs of the Polish formations, and the British government was willing now to have a Polish force under British command.

[48] Handelsman, III, 385-392, 402-408, 433-439. *Hansard*, 3rd Ser. LXXXVII, 882.
[49] Handelsman, III, 403-404, 423-424.
[50] Letter to Harrowby, Mar. 4, 1855 (Handelsman, III, 451-452).
[51] Handelsman, III, 455.

The marriage of Prince Ladislas Czartoryski with Maria Amparo, Countess of Vista Allegre, a daughter of the Spanish Dowager Queen Christina, was concluded in March 1855 and it created a new link between the Hôtel Lambert and the Tuileries, because of the affection of the Empress for the old Queen and her friendly feelings for the young Princess. In May the young Czartoryskis went to England for their belated honeymoon; it was rather a busy time as the Prince had to make personal contacts with the new British government and leading politicians, and to obtain a decision in the matter of a Polish corps. He was introduced to the Queen on her own wish by the French chargé d'affaires, who later was severely blamed by Walewski for having taken such a dangerous step. He had several talks with Clarendon, who informed him that Great Britain was ready to have a third regiment of Cossacks in Asia on her pay, but as a Polish national force, with Polish name and colors.[52] It seemed promising enough for starting negotiations, and for drafting a general plan of organization of the Polish forces in three corps, each of them armed and maintained by one of the three Allies; the corps in Asia under Polish and those on the Danube under Cossack name. If a force of 15,000-20,000 men was organized, a pledge was to be given in return to raise the question of the Polish national rights as stipulated in the Treaty of Vienna; if there was a Polish force of 25,000-30,000, the Allies were expected not to make peace without a guarantee for the independence of Poland. He was ready to limit the Polish uprising to the part of Poland under Russian domination.[53] The answer was rather disappointing. Lord Harrowby informed the Prince that Prince Ladislas had misunderstood Clarendon as to the Polish colors, that the raising of them was inadmissible even in Asia, as it could be interpreted only as a recognition of the existence of Poland as a separate state. The offer of organizing a third regiment of Cossacks was confirmed, and the Prince was asked for

[52] Letter of Lenoir (L. Zwierkowski) to Prince Adam, May 7, 1855, Handelsman, III, 468. In March Palmerston had given orders for transporting every Pole willing to go to the east to join the Polish formation, and war prisoners could volunteer. See Clarendon's letters to Harrowby, Mar. 13, April 11, 22, 24 (H.Mss., XXVIII, 125-131).

[53] Letters to Harrowby, May 27, June 8, 1855, quot. Handelsman, III, 485-487.

conditions.[54] He still insisted upon the national character of the
formation and the name of Polish Legion or at least Legion of
the Alliance. He did not succeed, and it was agreed that a Cossack
force, nominally in the Sultan's service, should be taken over by
Great Britain, with Zamoyski as commanding general.[55]

Early in May, Count Buol's proposals for compromise were
accepted by Drouyn and Gorchakov, but rejected by Napoleon
III, who had been stiffened by Palmerston; Drouyn was disavowed and dismissed, Walewski took over the Foreign Ministry,
as he was considered more compliant to the Emperor's wishes.
There was much irritation against Austria, and protracted war
seemed inevitable. Prince Adam was received by the Emperor
on May 9 more warmly than ever, and on the next day there was
an official audience of a Polish delegation headed by him; he was
accompanied by his old collaborators and friends, Barzykowski,
Morawski, Chrzanowski, Mickiewicz, and General Skarżyński.
His declaration was published in the *Moniteur*. Bismarck interpreted that gesture of the French Emperor as intended to blackmail Vienna; possibly it was, and a warning to the new Russian
Emperor as well. But Napoleon III's confidential talk with Czartoryski the day before had been rather a new display of incertitude
and helplessness. A month later, on June 11, Czartoryski heard
his ominous words about the priority of his obligations towards
France (*que je me dois à la France avant tout*).[56]

The French Emperor had in mind the chance of making peace
after the prospective fall of Sebastopol, and he intended to demand at the peace conference the return to the arrangements of
Vienna; but he still considered the alternative of a full-scale
offensive war. He was greatly impressed by the British government's offer of taking over a Polish formation, and ready to
promote the idea of a Polish legion sponsored by both France
and Britain. He was also visibly struck by Prince Adam's remark
that until Polish soil had been attained, the main resources for
the Polish forces would be found in the enemy's ranks (prisoners
and deserters) and he understood very well that in order to have

[54] Harrowby to Czartoryski, June 13, quot. Handelsman, III, 487.
[55] Handelsman, III, 453-468, 488-492 et passim.
[56] See Handelsman, III, 470-474, 479-482.

the cooperation of the Poles, they must be given some hope.

There was one way left for Czartoryski, to preserve and to build up the Cossack nucleus of the future national army. In July and August the Hôtel Lambert had to face a peace feeler from the Russian side through the medium of Bärensprung, the Police Director in Poznań, who managed to induce Count Titus Działyński to assume the role of intermediary. The latter tried to win over Chrzanowski, Morawski, and Mickiewicz by promises of concessions for the Kingdom. Mickiewicz retorted that "the Pole could be united with the Russian, but only under the condition of remaining a Pole and not only in a part of Poland, but in the whole of the old Poland." Prince Adam was later approached; he gave a considered and tactful but negative reply. He rightly suspected that the idea was to undermine his political position in the West and in Turkey as well, by discrediting him, and thus to neutralize him for the time of final negotiations. Działyński was encouraged to try to obtain as much as possible for his country, but he had to act in his own name only. Walewski's suggestion to Działyński was a similar one.[57]

In August Zamoyski was summoned to London, where his and Harrowby's exertions to bring the business of the Polish formations to an end lasted longer than expected. There was after the fall of Sebastopol more hope for peace in Paris and in London as well, so decisions were delayed. At last it was decided in October that a Polish division was to be formed by Zamoyski on British pay, equipped by Great Britain and France, but still disguised under the name of the Sultan's Cossacks. The undertaking was signed by Zamoyski on November 16.[58] Neither Prince Adam nor Zamoyski abandoned the hope that the Polish division would become a national force *de iure* as it was *de facto* and its organization was continued to the very end of the war; many officers and men of other ranks came from the west, and more Poles from prisoners' camps were enlisted. As Zamoyski was to be too long away from his post in Constantinople, Prince Ladislas

---

[57] Handelsman, III, 497-501; and his *Czartoryski, Nicholas I et la question du Proche Orient*, pp. 145-146.

[58] See Clarendon's and Zamoyski's letters to Harrowby, Aug.-Nov. 1855 (H.Mss., XXVIII), Zamoyski's to Sadyk Pasha and Panmure's to Zamoyski (*Zamoyski*, VI, 156-159, 165-167, 174-176). Handelsman, III, 514-518, 541-549.

was dispatched there in September as emissary to the emerging forces. He was accompanied by Mickiewicz, now more than ever an affectionate friend of Prince Adam and his enthusiastic supporter. Unfortunately, discrepancies arose between Sadyk Pasha, who was jealous of his monopoly of Cossack formations in Turkey, and Zamoyski, who was anxious to create a genuine Polish and Christian force. No better solution was found but to leave Sadyk with his first regiment in the Turkish army outside the new formation and to secure for him some French and British supplies. This action provoked Sadyk's indignant protestations and a violent campaign of slander and abuse. Mickiewicz paid a visit to Sadyk's regiment of Ottoman Cossacks at Burgas and was enchanted when he saw that force commanded by Poles and partly composed of Poles; he thoroughly enjoyed a few days of military life. He changed his mind about Zamoyski's division and advocated that every effort be made to help Sadyk's Cossacks and increase their number, and he argued about it with the young Prince, who adhered to his instructions. Inevitable frictions arose around that matter and embittered the last weeks of the poet's life. He fell on November 26 a victim of cholera in Constantinople, and the 1st Polish Infantry Regiment escorted him in deep mourning on his last journey.[59]

In the meantime, the Polish cause was unexpectedly raised by French diplomatic initiative and dropped as the result of an exchange of views with the British government. In a note of September 15 Walewski suggested, that if peace negotiations started, the restitution of the Kingdom of Poland as stipulated in the Vienna Treaty should be one of the principal conditions, and he proposed a formal accord of both Western allies for demanding the restoration of a Polish state. The British government declared itself much in favor of Poland's liberation, but they declined any commitments which might extend and prolong the war; they thought an accord on Polish affairs premature, preached moderation and the need of not humiliating Russia. Walewski hastily

[59] For Mickiewicz's journey to the East and his death, see Handelsman, III, Ch. 24, and his *Mickiewicz 1853-55*. He disposed of the nonsensical rumors of the poet's death by poisoning. Reports of his companions who attended him in his last hours are given in full.

agreed with the British suggestion to postpone the matter to a proper moment, which was never to come. As he was "dying for peace" at that moment, the whole episode was interpreted as an attempt to frighten the British government by the prospect of extending the war and so to soften its attitude with regard to the problem of the Black Sea. A less hazardous interpretation is possible. As Walewski had just discussed with his Emperor the necessity of making peace, he certainly found him reluctant to end the war without having made a gesture in the Polish cause; and he drafted his note in order to placate his master's scruples, as he was satisfied about the prospective answer. When he received it, Czartoryski could safely be told that France had been ready to prolong the war only for the sake of the independence of Poland, but Britain declined the proposal.[60]

The drama was nearing its close. In November the peace conditions were discussed in long letters by Napoleon III and Queen Victoria, and they agreed upon concluding peace on reasonable terms without making the restoration of Poland or other far-reaching changes a condition.[61] Thus the Polish cause as an obstacle for peace-making was eliminated. The final conditions were presented on December 28 in St. Petersburg and accepted on January 15, 1856 by Alexander II. They were hard and humiliating, and certainly it was for the Tsar a terrible experience. Prince Adam from his Hôtel Lambert clearly discerned the motives of the decision as they were expressed at the conference at the Winter Palace on January 15: The Russians were afraid that if a third campaign were fought, Poland would become one of the principal aims of the war.[62] In fact they discussed the probability of the loss of Volhynia, Podolia, Finland, and of the Kingdom of Poland; those provinces were, as Kisselev emphasized, just liabilities; if invaded, they would join the enemy, and their later recovery would be very uncertain. When compared with such a

[60] See Handelsman, "Stanowisko Francji w sprawie polskiej we wrześniu 1855" (The Attitude of France with Regard to the Polish Question in September 1855), in *Studia ku czci Kutrzeby*, 1938, II, 305-311; and Handelsman, III, 517. For Walewski's real intention, see Granville's letter to Clarendon, Chantilly, Oct. 7, 1855, E. Fitzmaurice, *The Life of Granville*, 1905, I, 120-123.

[61] Martin, *The Life of the Prince Consort*, III, 524-531.

[62] Handelsman, III, 578.

prospect, the conditions of the ultimatum seemed moderate.[63] On February 1 the preliminary peace was signed. The day before, Lord Stratford wrote to Harrowby: "Poor Poland! Her revival is a regular flying Dutchman. Never is—always to be. We played a wretched game in 1830, when Nicholas incorporated the Duchy of Warsaw [sic!] which was an European creation and ought to have been so treated by the Powers of Europe. . . . Is it too late for that? I mean for restoring the European position of the Duchy of Warsaw as connected with Russia, but not identified with her?"[64]

Prince Adam's efforts were now concentrated on two objectives: the raising of the Polish problem at the conference and the preservation of the Polish force in Turkey.[65] Neither of the two was to be achieved.

In his first talk with Orlov, on March 2, Napoleon III alluded to the necessity of reconstructing Europe; he mentioned Poland and Italy and announced that Russia's approach to those problems would determine his own to her interests in still unsettled matters. The discussion of the Polish question with the French Emperor was accepted by Orlov, and he gave some vague promises in the name of his sovereign. Napoleon III demanded (on April 7 or 8) more precise pledges. He was ready to abstain from raising the matter on the conference table if he had the promise of an amnesty, of home rule for the Kingdom under a Grand Duke, of concessions for the Polish language and religion elsewhere. Orlov's answer was that all this would be granted, and Napoleon assured Czartoryski that he had got a pledge from the Tsar.

There was a parallel action taken by Britain. Palmerston recommended the Polish cause to Clarendon on March 3: something must be done to satisfy "the Parliament, the Press, the public opinion, the London Polish Association and old Czartoryski." Clarendon had on April 9 a long talk with Orlov, and he was well prepared. He told the Russian plenipotentiary that the

---

[63] Jomini, *Etudes diplomatiques*, ii, 394-395.
[64] Stratford de Redcliffe to Harrowby, Jan. 31, 1856 (H.Mss., xxviii, 179-180).
[65] See Czartoryski's and Zamoyski's letters to Harrowby, 1856 (*ibidem*); and Handelsman, iii, 380-381.

Congress could not keep silent with regard to the stipulations of Vienna; he insisted upon national constitution, religion, and language, and demanded a statement on the intended concessions for Poland, either a spontaneous one, or as answer to a question. Orlov declared that his Emperor was ready to return to his Polish subjects all that had been suggested, but he could not give such a declaration to the Congress, as it would be misrepresented in Russia; he could not appear as yielding to foreign pressure, for this would spoil the spontaneous acts which he was preparing. In a further talk, on April 14, he reaffirmed that such were his emperor's decisions and announced that those acts would be connected with the forthcoming coronation.[66] Now Clarendon was himself satisfied that it was preferable to leave the initiative with the Tsar, than to offend him by exerting diplomatic pressure on him.[67]

Prince Adam took a more realistic view when he wrote to Harrowby: "I have seen Lord Clarendon ready to take the initiative on behalf of Poland. But he thought that it could be prejudiciable to Russian concessions. I am afraid that Emperor Alexander will do neither less nor more, but just what he thinks convenient. I am afraid that it will be neither sincere nor very substantial, and the dead silence over Poland after mentioning other countries which had no more direct rights for being mentioned by the Congress, will deeply afflict my countrymen. . . ."

Thus the stipulations of the Treaty were strictly limited to the Eastern problems. As to the Polish question, the only result was a verbal assurance of Alexander II's good intentions, which were presented to Prince Adam as *un engagement d'honneur*. The Tsar himself immediately disavowed such an interpretation of Orlov's utterances by a warning he gave on May 23 and 26 to

[66] Handelsman, III, 585-586, 614-617. Boutenko, *Revue Historique*, V, 155, pp. 219-292; Clarendon to Palmerston, Apr. 15, 1856 (Filipowicz, *Confidential Correspondence*, 210-212).

[67] See *Zamoyski*, VI, 195, 206, 214-217 et passim; Czartoryski to Harrowby, May 1, May 25, 1856 (H.Mss., XXVIII, 149-150, 159-160, and n.d., April, *ibid.*, pp. 171-172); Cz.M.(E), II, 358. Illuminating was Clarendon's explanation in the House of Lords on Ld. Lyndhurst's question, July 11, 1856 (*Hansard*, 3rd Ser., CXLIII, 632-641).

Polish delegations with the fateful words: *Point de reveries!* and *Tout ce que mon père a fait est bien fait.*

The news of the peace was a terrible blow to the emigration; once more the old Prince had to resist pressure from different quarters not to expose himself and his sons any more, as an amnesty was expected, and the possibility arose that the Emperor would give him back his estates. He asked the young Valerian Kalinka, the future historian, to write an article on amnesty, and wanted to know what would be its principal idea; Kalinka suggested saying that there had once been a rule in Japan that no European was permitted to land there but by treading a cross under his feet; the emigration by returning to Poland under foreign domination would trample its past with their own feet. Prince Adam approved of his idea.[68] He decided to continue to live and to act in exile.

The fate of the Polish division was sealed before long. The troops were disbanded by the British government's orders and recommended to the good will of the Turks; some of them remained in the Turkish army—one regiment of Ottoman Cossacks, and another of Ottoman Dragoons; a handful went to the Caucasus to join the Circassian insurgents, Czartoryski's fighting allies.

When the liquidation of the Polish division was nearly completed and Zamoyski's sojourn in Turkey was ending, Lady Stratford invited him and Countess Zamoyska at Terapia. Lord Stratford was rather gloomy; the savior of Turkish independence and old friend of Czartoryski felt uneasy about Poland's fate, as nothing has been done for her liberation. He expressed pessimistic views on the future and preached resignation. There was no remedy, the Poles—the coming generation at least—must become Russians or Germans. Countess Zamoyska asked: "And what about my son [a little boy]?" "He must become either German or Russian, it depends upon where he will settle." She retorted with vehemence: "I would prefer to strangle him with

[68] V. Kalinka to Zamoyski, Mar. 29, 1856 (*Zamoyski*, VI, 214). On May 27 the Act of Amnesty was signed, but it was neither general nor generous, the condition was in fact trampling one's own past with one's own feet. See Angeberg, *Recueil . . . Pologne*, pp. 1119-1121.

my own hands." Painful silence followed. A few days later, Lady Stratford wrote to the General to tell him that her husband had been extremely excited and he spent a sleepless night, he walked for some hours around his room and then sat at his desk and wrote a poem, which she sequestrated and enclosed in her letter. It had as motto the words of the Gospel (Mark 5): "She is not dead but sleepeth" and paid an eloquent tribute to Poland's unconquerable spirit and to the man "whose sturdy brand high-flashing o'er his native land keeps hearth and altar pure"; "*His* lot is to endure . . . to prove, *She is not dead*." The poem ended with a glorious vision of a new struggle. "Hurrah! for Poland! Oh! She lives, she combats, vanquishes, forgives! How sweet, how bright the *dream*."

When meeting Lord Stratford, Zamoyski thanked him for his poem; it expressed the feelings of a noble friend, but for the last word, which was suggested by the diplomat.[69]

In any case, Lord Stratford proved once more how right was Burke when stating, that "an Englishman is the unfittest person on earth to argue another into slavery."

Prince Adam benefited from his poem; he used the words of the Gospel in his speech on November 29, 1857: "She is not dead, she is asleep. Thus even a mighty Monarch cannot forbid her to dream."

[69] See Viscount Stratford de Redcliffe, *Shadows of the Past. In verse*, 1866, pp. 281-284 and "Notes." The circumstances in which it was written are told by Countess Zamoyska in a letter to her sisters, Nov. 25, 1856. *Zamoyski*, VI, 236-237.

CHAPTER 20

BRIGHTNESS IN THE DUSK

THE WAR WAS OVER, as was the period of Czartoryski's semi-official friendly relations with both Western governments as a recognized spokesman of his nation. He realized once more that "hesitation, uncertainty, difficulty in taking decision were not exclusively symptoms of our [Polish] weakness, but they hampered the best intentions on the highest level of others as well, and their decisions, in spite of their powerful means."[1]

The old man endured the terrible disappointment of 1856 with his usual imperturbability, with "patient, obstinate and always active self-sacrifice," free from both "delusions and despondency."[2] He watched with a vigilant eye the developments in Poland and denounced the discrepancies between the pledges of April 1856 and the subsequent deeds. He carried on the routine work with the support of his younger son, Ladislas. The diplomatic service of the Hôtel Lambert not only survived the new crisis, but it became increasingly efficient. It seemed that Prince Adam, when nearing the end of his laborious life, concentrated on that part of his work with the object of leaving it fully prepared for the service of renascent Poland. He did not neglect during the last five years of his life any occasion for intervening on behalf of his country, or for provoking and inspiring interventions, recalling promises and pledges, or for interceding for other oppressed peoples, such as the Bulgarians, or the Circassian insurgents, and to promote the cause of Rumanian unity.[3]

Intimate relations with the Tuileries survived the war and its aftermath. Empress Eugénie used to "conspire" with Prince Ladislas about European politics and the annual balls at the

---

[1] See his *Discours prononcé en séance de la Société Littéraire et Historique Polonaise de Paris, le 3 mai, 1855* (1855).

[2] So C. de Mazade in the preface to Cz.M.(F), I, p. xvii.

[3] For his policy of the last period see Handelsman, III, Ch. 26.

Hôtel Lambert were attended by the imperial court, the aristocracy, and many foreign diplomats—as even the Austrian envoy came in 1859 and recorded it as an *événement*.

The Prince was assisted now by a council or circle for discussing problems and preparing decisions and there was a bureau as executive body. The network of his contacts with the homeland was not only maintained, but even extended and improved. Correspondents were designated among his most energetic and influential followers in all parts of Poland, and a close liaison was established not only with the leaders of the gentry, but also with those of the Polish bourgeoisie and of the Jewish as well. Two of his confidential emissaries emerged before long as national leaders: Count Andrew Zamoyski in the Kingdom, and Prince Adam Sapieha in Galicia.[4]

In 1858 he stayed for a short time on Polish soil, at Gołuchów in Poznania, the residence of his daughter Isabella, the Princess of the Revolution, now Countess Działyńska, and he was moved and surprised by the enthusiastic welcome of his countrymen. On his way there he paid a visit to his brother Constantine, living in Vienna, with whom he indulged in recollections of their early days. He was received by the Emperor; the conversation was at first neither friendly nor animated since Francis Joseph felt somewhat uneasy at this meeting with the old rebel. But he seemed moved by the Prince's appeal on behalf of Galicia and his suggestion that the Poles would prove grateful and repay generous deeds.[5] Two years later, after the Italian war and the defeats of Magenta and Solferino, in 1860, Prince Adam received from Vienna two overtures made to Prince Ladislas by Gołuchowski in the name of the Emperor. Prince Adam was invited to persuade Napoleon III of the possibility of a durable agreement with Francis Joseph. An independent Poland was to be restored under a Hapsburg archduke or even under a British prince, Galicia restored to Poland, Venezia to Italy, and Bosnia given as compensation to Austria. These overtures were rejected by Napoleon

---

[4] Handelsman, iii, 634-641.

[5] Notes from Vienna in Czartoryski's notebook. The audience took place on Aug. 30, 1858. Czartoryski's account (in Cz.Mss., Nr.5734, pp. 211-213), quoted by S. Kieniewicz, *Adam Sapieha*, 1939, pp. 43-44.

III with disdain; he was still in hostile mood towards Austria and in most friendly relations with Alexander II. But for Prince Adam and the Hôtel Lambert they were indications of new possibilities for Poland's restoration, and their policy once more slowly evolved towards what was later to be called the Austro-Polish solution.[6]

In the same year, when a meeting of the partitioning sovereigns was to be held in Warsaw, Prince Adam recommended to the Polish leaders in all parts of Poland to submit jointly to the three monarchs petitions on behalf of the Polish nation, to state her rights and her claims. There were divergences of views among them about the common action to be taken; but much was done later separately according to the Prince's suggestions.[7]

At the end of 1860 he inspired a petition of Galicia to the Emperor Francis Joseph, demanding provincial self-government and shortly before his death he once more recommended to the Galician Polish leaders a conciliatory approach to the problem of the Ruthenes.

Some hopes were aroused by the new Russian Emperor's repeatedly reported liberal tendencies and his *rapprochement* with Napoleon III; the "Spring of Sebastopol" lasted in Russia, and even Poland experienced at last a warmer spell. An Agricultural Association was allowed in 1857, and it became a powerful organization of landowners and farmers, presided over by Count Andrew Zamoyski, Ladislas' brother, and Prince Adam's nephew and devoted friend. He enjoyed immense popularity in the country. The society was in full control of the public opinion of the upper and middle classes in the Kingdom, and Prince Adam rightly discerned that it amounted *de facto* to a national representation.

The great work of land reform and emancipation of the peasants was inaugurated in Russia. Prince Adam instructed Andrew Zamoyski to speed up the work of reform in Poland and to make the landowners realize the necessity of granting to the people

[6] Short information from Czartoryski's papers in *Polski Słownik Biograficzny* sub voce *Czartoryski Władysław*. See also Cz.M.(E), II, 359; and Handelsman, III, 677-680.

[7] Handelsman, III, 661-663, 691.

of their own free will the ownership of lands. His instructions for the Committees for the Peasant Problem which were appointed by the Russian government in the Lithuanian and Ruthenian provinces were along the same lines, insisting upon a solution being reached by freely contracted agreements with the peasants. The most important result for Poland ought to be secured, namely "mutual good will, gratitude of the people and unity between them and the landowners."[8]

Early in 1861 the situation in Poland was growing tense. The agrarian problem had become acute, as the enfranchisement of the Russian peasants had already been decided upon; there was much unrest among Polish peasants; the Polish Reds from the Underground, which was once more growing strong, strove for a solution by preparing a popular insurrection, and Andrew Zamoyski's "Whites" of the Agricultural Association were at last inclined to agree on the principle of peasant ownership of lands.

Patriotic feelings had become excited by years of expectation, and once more the youth and the people of Warsaw were eager to risk everything in order to demonstrate for the unity, freedom, and independence of Poland.

Prince Adam sounded Napoleon III on the possibility of raising the Polish question; but the French Emperor was anxious to consolidate his new friendship with Russia, and he preached restraint and moderation in the hope of a better future resulting from the permanent influence of France in St. Petersburg. So Czartoryski instructed Count Andrew in February 1861 to seize any opportunity for submitting a petition to the Tsar; it was to be sponsored by representatives of all classes of the population and to demand home rule for the Kingdom and invoke the Treaty of Vienna, as establishing legal bonds between the Kingdom and Russia.[9] At the same time he insisted upon the need for a proclamation by the Agricultural Association, that they stood for the granting of land to the peasants.

Unexpected events occurred a few days later. On February 27

[8] For Czartoryski's last exertions to enforce a solution of the peasant problem, see Handelsman, III, 664-673.

[9] Czartoryski to A. Zamoyski, Feb. 20, 1861 (M. Handelsman, *Książe Adam Czartoryski*, 1938, pp. 46-47).

there was a patriotic manifestation in Warsaw: clashes with the police occurred, the troops intervened, firing started, and a few men were killed. The old General Gorchakov, Lieutenant of the Realm, hesitated to use force to break the growing spirit of revolt, preferring rather to placate public opinion. He therefore appealed to Andrew Zamoyski and other Polish notables for their support in appeasing the city and the country. A Polish delegation was formed—an embryo of a national representation, and a Polish security guard was improvised for maintaining order. There was something like an abdication of the conqueror, who gave up his powers to the conquered; a "moral revolution" in an atmosphere of exaltation of patriotic and religious feelings.

Gorchakov was anxious to secure Polish proposals for a settlement that would be acceptable to his sovereign. But Zamoyski's advice was too far-reaching; when he was asked what ought to be done to appease the country, he bluntly retorted: "Vous en aller" (get out). And the long-debated address proposed by the delegation and signed by several thousand people was more an act of protest denouncing the wrong done by the military rulers of the country, than a move towards a settlement of the internal situation of the Kingdom.

For Prince Adam the news from Warsaw was like a bright glow suddenly spreading in the dusk. He greeted it as the beginning of liberation; and he repeated with tears old Simeon's words: "Lord, now lettest thou thy servant depart in peace, for my own eyes have seen thy salvation." He hastened to recognize the Warsaw delegation as an emerging national authority and put himself and his organization at their disposal.[10]

He consulted the French Emperor, who seemed much impressed by the news and encouraged the demand for concessions. Then Prince Adam drafted his last instruction for his countrymen in the homeland.[11] It was an enthusiastic acknowledgment of their dignified and unyielding attitude; he compared them with the early Christians "who had only the palm of martyrdom for a weapon and vanquished the world." He quoted Napoleon III's warnings against riots and his half-promises of discreet and

---

[10] Letter to A. Zamoyski, Mar. 20, 1861 (Handelsman, *op.cit.*, p. 47).
[11] Mar. 22, 1861 (*loc.cit.*, pp. 48-50).

friendly intercession. He declared: "I and all my collaborators regard ourselves as delegated by the homeland, and bound to fulfill its wishes and support its efforts. The decision of continuing, notwithstanding any concessions, to strive for the complete liberation of Poland, entire and independent, always was and will be the leading idea of the emigration." He demanded national discipline and unity.

In his last speech on May 3, 1861, he repeated some sentences of the instruction, especially that moving appeal: "Do not descend, O my Nation, from the elevation where nations and sovereigns must respect you. By firmly remaining there you will be safer and more certain in seeing your goal and continually approaching it. Though racked by bitter suffering, though driven to despair by treason and violence, resist the temptation to fight your oppressors by meaner weapons. You shine above them by your virtue and goodness: these are the indomitable forces of Poland, and in them is her hope for the future."[12]

The political developments in Poland reached a crucial stage in the month of April, as the result of Marquess Wielopolski's independent action. He had been for a long time an opponent of the policy of the Hôtel Lambert; he had suggested a compromise with the three partitioning powers and securing provincial self-government and possibly a home rule at the price of abandoning separatism. He hated Zamoyski and the Agricultural Association; he was violently opposed to giving the peasants the ownership of their lands; he despised the land reform in Russia as revolutionary and socialist; and he was the most unpopular man in the country. Strongly supported by Polish civil servants in Warsaw and St. Petersburg, he came to terms with Gorchakov on his taking a post in the administration. He secured important concessions: the creation of a Council of State, the restoration of local self-government, the reorganization of the educational department under his own direction, the reform of the schools and the foundation of a university. He was entrusted with all the preparatory work for further reforms, as well as for land reform. He started by attempting to crush potential opposition, he suppressed the Agricultural Association and bullied the Church for supporting the principle of granting the ownership of land to the peasants. Mass demonstrations followed and many salvos were fired by Russian infantry in applying Wielopolski's own regulation for military interventions in case of riots. There was a massacre; the Marquess was regarded as responsible for it and, in spite of his bitter struggle againts the Russian bureaucracy for the rule of law and Polish administration of the country, he became in fact one more obstacle to any understanding between the Tsar and the Poles.[13]

Notwithstanding the Marquess' ruthless dealing with the Agricultural Association, the reaction of the Hôtel Lambert and of Andrew Zamoyski was rather moderate, their attitude was non-committal but expectant, and they did not intend to impede his work.

The "Whites" in the Kingdom regarded themselves as a party of opposition; they were ready to serve the country and to take part in the work of reform, and even to give Wielopolski descreet support without renouncing their claim for a free and reunited Poland. But neither the Tsar nor Wielopolski himself were willing to suffer any political opposition; on the other side, revolutionary feelings were increasing and violent reprisals provoked despair and favored the growth of the Party of Movement—the revolutionary Reds.

Prince Adam was still following the dramatic course of events in Poland with unshaken faith. He tried to give support to his countrymen in the homeland by once more mobilizing public opinion in the West. There had been a protracted silence in the British Parliament over Poland. In 1856 he had in vain implored the British Ministers to mention the Polish cause in the House. Now a new wave of pro-Polish feelings rose in Britain; an address of "certain noblemen and gentlemen of this country to that venerable representative of the Polish nation" expressed their concern over Poland's fate. In his reply he said: "It has given me pleasure to perceive that you have so thoroughly grasped the character of the movement which at this moment agitates Poland. You have

---

[13] For the history of the first two weeks of the Marquess' public functions, see his most recent biography: A. Skałkowski, *Aleksander Wielopolski*, 1947, iii, Ch. 2. (an apology). Cf. Handelsman, iii, 674-676.

appreciated fully the spirit of order and moderation which marks it. . . . The contest is entirely on the field of right and entirely pacific and moral. What Poland demands, what she expects, is support of the same character. The morality of Europe is now the point in question. . . ."

On July 2 Pope Henessy brought forward a motion on Poland in the House of Commons; he mentioned the address, quoted Czartoryski's reply, and exposed the indifference of the British government with regard to Poland in 1854-1856; he even affirmed that Austria had been prepared and anxious to re-establish Poland, that France approved, and that only British reluctance prevented the Polish problem from being raised. Palmerston dismissed the allegation of Austria's pro-Polish attitude with visible dismay; but even if she had been willing to act on those lines, "we had not the means, even if this country had the will, to embark on such an operation." Both he and Russell expressed their hope of seeing the national institutions in Poland restored and of full moral support being given by Britain for such a peaceful solution of the problem.[14] Zamoyski was delighted with the statements of both ministers and sent an enthusiastic report to Paris.

Prince Adam's life was visibly nearing its end. He still dictated new pages of his Memoirs, addenda to his "Essai," and his remarks on the government of Poland. But his physical strength was slowly waning. He moved in summer to a country house at Montfermeil. He felt that his end was nearing. He met his death with cheerful calmness, and received the last sacraments praying together with the clergyman. The day before his death, July 14, he gathered round him the members of his family, his friends and collaborators and gave orders for the reading of his political testament. There it was stated that the homeland had now taken the direction of its destinies into its own hands; the task of the emigration was now to serve the homeland, and particularly to inform governments and public opinion abroad on the situation in Poland. In order to ensure the continuity of the political service in emigration he recommended that his younger son, Ladislas, should continue his work, and warmly invited both his older son Witold and General Zamoyski to assist him.

[14] *Hansard*, 3rd Ser., CLXIV, 210-234.

"With the deepest feeling of humility and emotion" he thanked the Lord for allowing him to live to the moment "when the future of the Polish nation was emerging from a secular eclipse." When hearing those words, he sobbed and those around him wept. He preached confidence in divine mercifulness, striving more for eternal triumph than for temporary success and ended: "Thy Will be done, Almighty Lord." Almost blind he asked for a pen, and signed the will with his full name.[15]

Next morning, July 15, Ladislas Zamoyski arrived from London to see for the last time the man whom he had adored and served with self-sacrifice and boundless devotion.[16] Prince Adam, now completely blind but conscious, questioned him about news from Britain and was told of the cause of Poland having been once more raised in the Parliament and of the ministerial declarations.

In the afternoon he was dying. When hearing the name of Poland, a last smile illuminated his face, and he uttered his last words: "Oh! I bless her. . . ."

―――――――

"Factus est magnus in conspectu populi, a die illa et deinceps." These words pronounced by Father Alexander Jełowicki in Prince Adam's funeral sermon were more than mere rhetoric. The Poles in the homeland and abroad suddenly became aware that they had lost the greatest among them. In most churches in all parts of Poland services were celebrated. In Warsaw, Wielopolski allowed a solemn service to be held, and on July 22 the Holy Cross Church was packed with people, while many thousand people stood outside in mournful silence; they escorted the celebrating Archbishop to his palace and an immense crowd knelt when he gave them blessings from the balcony. Silently they then dispersed.

In London, in the House of Lords, on July 19, 1861, Lord Brougham, when presenting a petition on the situation of Poland, mentioned the death of the man with whom he had once worked,

―――――――

[15] For the last moments of his life, see *Zamoyski*, vi, 356-365; H. Kajsiewicz, *Mowa pogrzebowa po ś. p. Księciu Czartoryskim*, 1862, pp. 23-27; Charles de Montalembert, *Une nation en deuil. La Pologne en 1861* (1861), p. 24-25; P. Félix, *Le Prince Adam Czartoryski*, 1862, pp. 98-103.

[16] See the entry relating to him in Czartoryski's will.

and paid tribute to his memory in some carefully elaborated sentences marked by visible restraint: "Prince Czartoryski, when he lived in Paris, not alone upheld the spirit of Poland, but was the friend and the adviser of all who bore relationship or interest to that country. In no particular was the loss of this eminent, accomplished, and virtuous man more to be lamented than on account of the sound and moderate advice, which he had constantly given to Polish emigrants, counselling them always to take the course which would most benefit Poland, without giving offence to the country in which they have taken refuge. The only consolation remaining to his friends was that, although at an unusually advanced age, he retained to the last his faculties unimpaired, his feelings as warm as ever, the love of his country and hope for her restoration as strong. This closing scene affords the only consolation of his countrymen and his friends."[17]

In France, Montalembert—a devoted friend, supporter and admirer—paid tribute to Prince Adam in his pamphlet *A Nation in Mourning*.[18] "Nobody understood and represented better that alliance of Catholicism and modern Freedom of which Poland gives a most accomplished example, than the illustrious and venerable Prince Adam Czartoryski. . . . We have observed him during thirty years kind, calm, fearless . . . a living incarnation of the disregarded Right; his mere presence used to be to monarchs a reproach of their outrages and to his countrymen a lesson of perseverance and unshaken hope. . . . How inspiring was that long life, which reached the last limits assigned to human existence through so many different vicissitudes, without having at any time deviated from the path of honor, of duty and of self-sacrifice."

Both these eloquent voices of Czartoryski's contemporaries exalted his moral grandeur, and so did in 1862, on the occasion of the annual Polish celebration at Montmorency, the Jesuit Père Félix, whose sermon was a study in the nature of the greatness of "the great patriot who also was a great Christian." The conclusion read: "He is dead as a patriarch of the Emigration, as an

---

[17] *Hansard*, 3rd Ser., CLXIV, 1143-1145, Ld. Stratford de Redcliffe supported the petition.
[18] Ch. de Montalembert, *Une nation en deuil. La Pologne en 1861* (1861).

Angel guiding you in your pilgrimages on foreign soil; and, I can say it on his grave, he is dead as your king in exile. . . ."[19] Much earlier Mickiewicz had regarded Prince Adam as the only real king of Europe.

The portrait of Prince Adam given by Père Félix seems to be the most impressive among the few left by his contemporaries, as none equals it in the deep insight into his spiritual life in the last decades. "Intelligence illuminated his mild visage and radiated from his physiognomy, and his speech, when necessary, made it burst out in lightnings; but he used to veil it with reticence and modesty. He ignored the art—modern par excellence—of putting oneself forward; not only did he never pose, he used to efface himself. His writings will reveal that feature of him and they will reveal what he concealed too much: a great mind grown by a great knowledge, a splendid talent adorned by a rare instruction. . . . He reveals there in the first instance something, which when elevated, may even be more valuable than genius, and when reaching a certain height is nearing genius itself, common sense. He had the gift of a deep insight, of perceiving the truth, and discerning realities from the imaginary and the positive from dreams of idealism.

"Being a man of intelligence and common sense, he was even more a man of integrity and virtue: *Testimonium consecutus est esse iustus.* His life rendered a glorious testimony to his rectitude. . . . *Erat vir ille simplex et rectus.* . . . When thrown by his life into most complex and often most delicate situations, his mind was animated by a passion for justice and honor and never deviated for one minute from its eternal line. Even when engaged in the tortuous paths of the labyrinth of politics, where his destiny forced him to travel, he did not choose any other way, but the right one; and at the time when diplomacy all around him from one corner of Europe to the other was often lie arguing against lie, he invariably maintained his standard, a very rare one in politics: he never belied either others or himself. He was convinced that the real ability of a statesman consists in the application of the principles of truth, justice, and honor to the gov-

---

[19] Similar allusions are to be found in Montalembert's book and Kajsiewicz's sermon.

ernment of people. His great soul vigorously rejected any policy
of expediency, of violence and betrayal; and his work on diplomacy stigmatizes with proud indignation that immoral art of
governing, which makes politics not a balance of justice but an
equilibrium of interests, not a triumph of rights, but a glorifica-
tion of success. He understood, like a poet of his nation, that
nothing can be built with mud, and that even in politics, even in
diplomacy, 'virtue is the supreme wisdom.' "[20]

The orator paid a special tribute to one of the Prince's virtues,
which dominated his moral physiognomy: his goodness. "It was
not only the essence of his nature; it could be said that it *was*
his nature itself; it shone in his mild regard and radiated in his
smile, mixed with the melancholy of an exile, a melancholy long
as the exile was, but always serene and kind. And it was not
an ordinary and sterile kindness, but a generous one: generous
in giving, generous in forgiving. He had in a high degree the
gift, the rarest perhaps in politicians, to forget injury. The missiles
of malevolence seemed not to penetrate to his heart; and even
if he felt injured, his goodness, like a blessed dittany, shed itself
over his wound to soothe and to heal. His soul, as Bossuet had
said, was entirely directed to love and eager to give itself; magnanimous in forgetting the wrong, it was generous in accomplishing the good. . . . But the most exquisite fruit of his goodness,
its sweetest scent, was his disinterestedness. . . . Those who had
a different opinion about this, did not know him. His was not
only the purest disinterestedness, but also its charity, may I say,
its virginity. Like a virgin, afraid of a shadow on her heart, he
feared in his public life any appearance of selfishness. . . ."[21]

There was in Père Félix's moving eulogy some restraint, when
he spoke of Prince Adam as of a man of action, and even some
doubt if his power and promptitude of decision, which allowed
the events to dominate, were equal to his virtues: The orator
tried to explain the cases of indecision in Prince Adam's actions
by his superior intelligence and acute consciousness of obstacles
and difficulties. He praised Prince Adam's perseverance, as he

[20] The "Poète Anonyme," as Sigismund Krasiński was still referred to.
[21] So he explained Prince Adam's reluctance to impose his dictatorship in 1830-
1831: "It was his virtue which fettered his will." See pp. 64-65.

was pursuing the same great aim during more than seventy years.

Père Félix echoed in his remarks the judgments of many Poles, even of Father Kajsiewicz in a previous funeral sermon. Prince Adam's contemporaries were often impressed by his reverses and the confidence in his statesmanship was not always unshaken even among those who cherished him.

Julius Słowacki, when alluding to him in one of his poems (1846), had called him greater for his intentions than for their results, and mentioned the melancholy fame of his misfortunes. Certainly his intentions were sublime, and his setbacks and disappointments severe. The Grand Design of a free and united Europe which he tried to promote under the auspices of the idealistic and liberal Russian autocrat was to be turned years later into the Holy Alliance of Alexander and Metternich. He thought that his conceptions of collective security with a code of positive international law, of a natural balance between free and contented nations, or between their federations and free unions, and of an European League of Nations, were in conformity with the spirit of the British institutions and with the trends of British public opinion. He hoped for British understanding and support; in fact they sharply collided with Pitt's and later with Castlereagh's conceptions of security based on a material balance of power and the building up of "barriers" against the aggressive power of the day, without any regard for the rights or claims of nationalities. But his great universalist ideas still met with some response in the first decades of the 19th century; later they seemed to a new generation of statesmen rather immature and fantastic, and fell into oblivion; and President Wilson, when putting forward kindred political conceptions in 1917-1919, appears not to have been aware of the striking antecedent.

Prince Adam's program for a free union of a liberated and liberal Poland with a liberal Russia met with hostile opposition both in Europe and in Russia. In Vienna he succeeded in obtaining a recognition of the rights of the Poles in all the provinces of the former Commonwealth to national institutions and representations, and the creation of a small Kingdom of Poland— which, it was expected, would be extended to the East—under the Russian Emperor's crown and with a constitution. But before long the Kingdom became the ground of a protracted duelling between an oppressive and arbitrary regime and underground revolutionary movements. His efforts to restore the rule of law by means of peaceful opposition were interrupted by the outbreak of the revolution of 1830.

The great work he had done as curator of the Vilna University in the eastern provinces of the old Commonwealth for preserving and developing Polish culture and national consciousness, was brought to an abrupt end during his imperial friend's lifetime, and almost completely destroyed by his successor some years later. The November Revolution of 1830, which he had tried in vain to prevent, elevated him to the post of President of the National Government; his name—as many contemporaries agreed—had greatly contributed to rally Poles from all provinces under the national banner. His attitude was that of a devoted and disinterested servant of his country and he did not decline responsibilities even when the necessary powers were refused him. This did not prevent his being suspected of contending for the royal crown. He was determined to continue fighting to the end; nevertheless he was overthrown before the end of the struggle by a revolt of extremists.

He was one of the Polish leaders who did not underestimate the importance of the peasant problem and the expediency of a generous gesture. Nevertheless he was attacked later as an enemy of the peasantry and a representative of its social oppressors.

What still remained of his cherished "republican delusions" and his firm liberal creed was confronted in 1831 with all the perils besetting an immature parliamentary regime in the midst of hostile invasion and domestic revolution. It was certainly a mental sacrifice for him, when, by thinking over his experiences of 1831, he became a convinced partisan of constitutional monarchy, laying the emphasis upon the monarchical principle, the responsibilities and powers of the sovereign.

When he became an outlaw and exile, he overcame his habitual reluctance to impose himself or to strive for power: he assumed responsibilities and duties when they could be carried only with self-denial and sacrifice. But he failed to rally the majority of his countrymen, to pacify party feuds and restore national unity. His

continuous efforts to win over parliaments and liberal governments for the defense of his work of 1815, of those clauses of the
Treaty which contained precarious guarantees of his nation's
rights, were in vain, and the protracted struggle was finally lost
in 1846, when the West allowed the three partitioning powers to
destroy the Republic of Cracow.

His policy linked the Polish cause with the much larger conflict between the liberal West and the absolutist powers. He strove
to build up a union of free Europe, of which the alliance of Britain
and France was to be the cornerstone; but inveterate animosity
and petty quarrels repeatedly disintegrated the Western bloc. He
thought of a grand alliance with the active concurrence of the
subjugated peoples of Central and Eastern Europe, in which his
own nation would play an important part; but he repeatedly
perceived that for the Western statesmen a free Europe meant
Western Europe, and that even when at war with Russia they
would abstain from raising the Polish problem; and his apprehensions were fully confirmed by the political and military developments of the Crimean War.

Nor was his long and patient work in settling the discords of
the peoples of Eastern Europe and paving the way for their
future free association more successful. In spite of his efforts,
sanguinary national feuds tore Hungary asunder at the very
time of her struggle against Austrian and Russian invasion; and
he did not succeed in securing a lasting agreement between his
own countrymen and the Ruthenians in Galicia. He worked for
the liberation of Greece, of Rumania, of Serbia, for a united
Italy; he welcomed the national revival of Czechs, Slovaks, Croats,
and Slovenes; he kindled the first sparks of the awakening Bulgarian nationality and was ready to support a Ukrainian national
movement; but this policy of paving the way for the future
triumph of the principle of nationality proved of no avail for the
immediate future of his own country.

Such was the long sequel of his setbacks, failures, and disasters.
But his achievements were by no means negligible. As Alexander's
friend, minister, and curator of the University of Vilna, he secured
invaluable and durable benefits for his country by strengthening
and fostering Polish culture and Polish national consciousness in

the Russian-annexed part of the former Polish Commonwealth; and many times, in 1831, 1863-1864, and again in 1917-1920 Czartoryski's legacy manifested itself by vigorous and self-sacrificing action on the part of the strong and patriotic Polish element in those territories, and by its allegiance to the cause of an independent and united Poland. By founding the Kingdom of Poland he secured for his country the survival of political existence in a national state; and in spite of its ordeals, the fifteen years of its separate existence were of immense value for the future of the Polish nation; some, at least, of its institutions survived for several decades, and not all of its legacy disappeared even during the time of systematic Russification. As an exile he revived abroad some of the functions of a Polish independent state and, although he did not succeed in his efforts to form a permanent nucleus of a Polish armed force, he created a unique phenomenon—a Polish diplomatic service which was tacitly recognized by France and Britain, by the Porte and the Vatican, by Brussels, Turin, Belgrade, etc., which came out into the open at some crucial moments, survived disasters, and lasted more than thirty years. He left it as a legacy to his nation. He did not achieve Poland's restoration; but he succeeded in keeping the Polish problem alive for thirty years, and Poland's rights "inscribed on the walls of Parliaments." One of his achievements was a durable reconciliation of the Polish patriotism with the Catholic Church. It proved of paramount importance for the national survival in the forthcoming period of deadly perils.[22]

All this would never have been achieved without great will power, strenuous exertions, indefatigable activity and bold decisions. His early French biographer, Baron Louis de Viel-Castel, when analyzing with much insight his political career, rightly emphasized that "he was not one of those politicians . . . who regard the success as the only criterion of the value of a cause, and who consider any protracted resistance against what they presumptuously call the ultimate decree as nearly criminal, because a revolt against Providence, and who prostrate themselves before the *faits accomplis*.[23] No wonder that in his obstinate

---

[22] Cf. P. Félix, pp. 68-70, 89-93.
[23] *Le Correspondant*, 1862, XIX, 679.

struggling against political evils, as resulting from acts of outrageous violence, he mostly met overwhelming odds and found rather seldom fullhearted support. The reverses which he experienced in his political endeavors were partly due to one important feature of his political thinking: namely, that it was mostly in advance of that of his contemporaries and sometimes outran the conditions of his time in anticipating developments, which were realized only in the lifetime of the present generation. His name, long forgotten outside his own country, became familiar after the First World War to historians of different nations, as the name of the statesman who had worked long ago for an independent Poland, for an independent Greece, a united Italy, a united Rumania, a united Yugoslavia, for the emancipation of other Slav peoples of the Balkans or under the Hapsburg crown, for the solving by peaceful means of their mutual dissensions and their relations with the Hungarians, Italians, and Turks. French, Russian, and German historians became aware of the striking analogies between his and Woodrow Wilson's conceptions; and the legacy of his ideas seems not to have been exhausted at Versailles and Geneva; his conceptions were even closer to the more recent ones of a European Union. His shadow which during his lifetime embarrassed sovereigns and statesmen at Kalisz, Reichenbach, Chaumont, or Vienna, would feel more at home at Geneva, or Strasbourg, or Lake Success. Many a time his voice was heard crying in the wilderness; his destiny was to prepare the way for history, by straightening out its paths. *Defunctus adhuc loquitur.*

SOURCES AND SELECTED BIBLIOGRAPHY

A. *BIOGRAPHIC MATERIAL*

I. *Manuscripts*

Family documents, correspondence, and writings of Cz.'s[1] parents, brothers, sisters, his sons and daughter in Czartoryski Family Records (Archiwum Domowe), Cracow.

Cz.'s personal correspondence with his parents, family, friends (incl. Alexander I), *ibidem.*

Cz.'s writings in drafts or (and) copies, fragments of memoirs and diaries, notebooks with biographic entries, *ibidem.*

Cz.'s political correspondence, notes, memoranda, minutes of conversations, in the Mss. Coll. of the Czartoryski Museum, Cracow.

Princess Isabella's (Cz.'s mother's) correspondence with him and other members of the family, and the original Ms. of his Diary, 1813-1817, were in the Podzamcze Mss. of the National Library in Warsaw (destroyed in 1939).

A collection of Cz.'s letters to many Polish and foreign persons, 1821-1859 in the Bibliothèque Polonaise in Paris, Mss. Coll. 54.

Archives of the Vilna University Curator's Office in the Czartoryski Museum, Cracow. See Archiwum Kuratorii Wileńskiej, Wilno 1926 (a catalogue).

Ladislas Zamoyski's papers containing his correspondence with Cz. and others, incl. Lord Dudley Coutts Stuart, Lord Harrowby, Sigismund Krasiński, in the Zamoyski Library, Warsaw (probably destroyed in 1939). A scanty selection was published, *Jenerał Zamoyski,* Kórnik 1910-1930, 6 vols.

Lord Dudley Coutts Stuart's "Polish letters" in the Harrowby Mss. Coll. at Sandon Hall, vols. xxv-xxviii; a few samples: J. A. Teslar, "Unpublished letters of Cz. and Zamoyski," *Slavonic and East Eur. Review,* xxix, 1950.

II. *Czartoryski's Works*

"Bard polski," in J. U. Niemcewicz's *Skarbiec historii polskiej,* vol. i, Paris 1840; then separately, Paris 1860.

---

[1] Cz. = Adam (Adam George, Adam Jerzy) Czartoryski.

Bibliography

Essai sur la diplomatie, par un Philhelléne, Marseilles 1830 (and a posthumous edition, Paris 1864).

Le dernier mot sur le Statut Organique imposé à la Pologne, Paris 1833.

Mémoires du Prince Cz. et sa correspondance avec l'Empereur Alexandre I. Publiés par Charles de Mazade. Paris 1887. 2 vols.

Memoirs of Prince Cz. and his Correspondence with Alexandre I, with Documents relative to the Prince's Negotiations with Pitt, Fox, Brougham and an account of his Conversations with Lord Palmerston and other English statesmen. Edited by Adam Gielgud, London 1888, 2 vols.

A Polish version of the first part of Cz.'s memoirs was published by B. Zaleski, *Żywot Cz.* in large extracts from the original Ms.

Extracts of the Diary 1813-1817 (destroyed in 1939) inserted in S. Askenazy's "Polska i Europa," *Biblioteka Warszawska* 1909, and *Uwagi,* Warsaw 1924. A copy was in the Family Records.

Zbiór mów mianych 1838-1847 (Speeches, ed. by T. Olizarowski), Paris 1847. A German edition by F. C. Biederman, *see* A.II. Many speeches published separately, 1830-1861, also in English and French.

Żywot J. U. Niemcewicza, Paris 1860.

Several literary works: poetry, a novel, essays, philosophical treaties, hitherto unpublished, in Cz. Family Records. A list of them in J. Bieliński's *Żywot Cz.,* vol. II. See extracts in L. Dębicki, *Puławy.*

III. *Other Original Sources*

Alexandre I et le Prince Cz. Correspondance particulière et conversations 1801-1803. Publiés par Prince Ladislas Czartoryski.

Mémoires du P-ce Cz. et sa correspondance, and *Memoirs of P-ce Cz., see* A.II.

Speeches, see A.II.

Nicholas Mikhailovich, Grand Duke, *L'Empereur Alexandre I,* St. Petersburg 1912, 2 vols. Further letters from Alexander I's correspondence with Cz.

———, *Le Comte Paul Stroganov,* St. Pet. 1905, 3 vols. Stroganov's correspondence with Cz., Novosiltsov, and Kochubey.

Archiv Vorontsova, Moscow 1870 ff., 40 vols., esp. vols. XI, XII, XIV, XV, XVIII. Corr. with Cz., Novosiltsov, Stroganov, Kochubey and others relating to Cz.

Several letters of Cz. in *Russkiy Archiv,* 1875, 1876, 1884, 1908.

Książę Cz. i Józef Twardowski. Korespondencja 1822-24, Poznań 1899.

Bibliography

Album Muzeum Narodowego w Rapperswilu, 1872, vol. I, Cz.'s correspondence with Louis Plater.

[Zamoyski Ladislas], *Jenerał Zamoyski,* Kórnik 1910-1930, 6 vols. Memoirs, notes, correspondence, mostly with Cz. or relating to him, covering years 1830-1861.

Czartoryska, Isabella, *Listy do starszego syna, księcia Adama.* Ed. S. Duchinska, Cracow 1891.

Dębicki, Ludwik, *Puławy,* Cracow 1887 ff., 4 vols. large extracts from the writings and letters of the Cz. family.

Gawroński, Franciszek Rawita, *Materiały do historii polskiej XIX w.,* Cracow 1909. Czaykowski's correspondence with Cz. and Zamoyski.

Memoirs

Cz.'s memoirs, *see* A.II.

Barante, baron de, *Souvenirs,* Paris 1892, vol. II.

Golovin, Countess, *Memoirs,* London 1910.

Niemcewicz, Julian Ursyn, *Pamiętnik 1807-1809,* Warsaw 1903. *Pamiętniki 1809-1820,* Poznań 1871, 2 vols. *Pamiętnik 1830-1831,* Cracow 1909. *Pamiętniki. Dziennik pobytu zagranicą.* Poznań 1876-1877. 2 vols.

Potocka (Anne), *Mémoires de la Comtesse . . . ,* Paris 1897.

Rzewuska, Rosalie, *Mémoires,* Rome 1939, vol. I.

IV. *General Biographies, Biographic Essays and Studies*

Askenazy, Szymon, "Książę Cz.," *Szkice i Portrety,* Warsaw 1937.

———, "Rozmowy w Belwederze," *Nowe Wczasy,* Warsaw 1910.

———, "Nauka wielkoksiążęca," *Uwagi,* Warsaw 1924.

Biedermann, Friedrich Carl, "Fürst Cz. und seine Reden an die polnische Emigration," in *Unsre Gegenwart und Zukunft,* vols. VIII, IX, Leipzig 1847.

Bieliński, Józef *Żywot księcia Cz.,* Warsaw 1905, 2 vols.

Dębicki, L., *Puławy,* Cracow 1887, 4 vols.

Felix, C. J., *Le Prince Cz.,* Paris 1862.

Gadon, Lubomir, *Książę Cz. podczas powstania listopadowego,* Cracow 1900.

Handelsman Marceli, "Książę Cz.," *Przegląd Współczesny,* 1938 enlarged version of his article in Polski Słownik Biograficzny, vol. IV.

———, *Adam Cz.,* Warsaw 1948-1950, 3 vols. (in four).

Jełowicki Aleksander, *Mowa pogrzebowa na cześć X. Cz.,* Paris 1861.

Kajsiewicz, Hieronim, *Mowa pogrzebowa po ś.p.Księciu Cz.,* Paris 1862.

Bibliography

Kukiel, M., "Banicja księcia Adama i katastrofa Puław," *Kwartalnik Historyczny*, 1930.

——, *Książę Adam*, Paris 1950.

Montalembert, Charles de, *Une nation en deuil. La Pologne en 1861*, Paris 1861.

Nagórska-Rudzka, Walentyna, "Książę Cz. w dobie powstania listopadowego," *Przegląd Historyczny*, 1930.

Viel Castel, Louis de, "*Le Prince Cz.*," in Le Correspondant, vol. XIX, Paris 1862, and a Polish translation by L. Siemieński, *Dyplomata polski XIX w.*, Cracow 1863.

Zaleski, Bronisław, *Żywot księcia Cz.*, Poznań 1881, vol. 1 (to 1801).

Żmigrodzki, M., "Książę Cz. jako pedagog," *Przewodnik Naukowy i Literacki*, 1885.

B. MATERIAL RELATING TO CZARTORYSKI'S POLITICAL ACTIVITIES

I. Years 1801-1815

1. Manuscripts

Cz.'s papers and correspondence, *see* A.I. Particularly notes, memorandas, projects 1803-1815, the treatise "Sur le système politique que devrait suivre la Russie," 1803 (Ms. 5226), correspondence with Stroganov, Novosiltsov, Ypsilanti, Capo d'Istrias, Wintzingerode, d'Antraigues, Piattoli, Stanislas and J. U. Niemcewicz, Kropiński, Linowski, Matuszewic, Louis Plater.

Archives of the Vilna Curator's office, *see* A.I.

Public Record Office, F. O. Russia, esp. 1803-1807.

2. Published Original Sources

Angeberg, Comte de (Chodźko, Leonard), *Recueil des traités, conventions . . . concernant la Pologne*, Paris 1862.

——, *Le Congrès de Vienne*, Paris 1863, 2 vols. (documents).

Cz.'s correspondence and memoirs, *see* A.I.

Nicholas Mikhailovich, *see* A.III.

Archiv Vorontsova, see A.III.

Martens, Theodor, *Recueil des traités conclus par la Russie*, St. Petersburg, 1874 ff., esp. vols. I, XI, XII, XIII, XIV.

Sbornik Russk. Istoricheskago Obshchestva, vols. VI and LXXXII.

Sbornik materialov dla istorii prosveshchenia v Rossii, St. Petersburg 1897, vol. II.

Bibliography

French diplomatic correspondence with Russia published in *Sbornik R. Istor. Obsh.*, vols. LXX, LXXV, LXXXII, LXXXIII, LXXXVIII-IX, CXII, and by Nicholas Mikhailovich, *Rélations dipl. de la Russie avec la France*, St. Petersburg, 1905 ff., 5 vols.

French correspondence with the Duchy of Warsaw: Handelsman M., *Instructions et dépêches des residents de France à Varsovie, 1807-1813*, Cracow 1914, 2 vols.

Maistre, Joseph de, *Mémoires politiques et correspondance diplomatique*, Paris 1858, 2 vols.

———, *Correspondance diplomatique 1811-1817*, Paris 1860-1861, 2 vols.

Rose, John Holland, *Despatches relating to the Third Coalition*, London 1901.

Talleyrand, Charles Maurice de, *Correspondance de . . . et du roi Louis XVIII pendant le Congrès de Vienne*, Paris 1887.

Webster, Sir Charles, *British Diplomacy 1813-1815*, London 1921.

Wellington's Selected Dispatches, vol. IX.

[Brougham, Henry], *An Appeal to the Allies and the English Nation on behalf of Poland*, London 1814.

The Edinburgh Review, 1814.

Mémoires

Bignon, Louis de, *Souvenirs d'un diplomate*, Paris 1864.

Dembowski, Leon, *Moje wspomnienia*, St. Petersburg 1898, 2 vols.

Niemcewicz, J. U., *Pamiętnik 1807-1809*, Warsaw 1903.

———, *Pamiętniki 1809-1820*, Poznań 1872, vol. I.

Ogiński, Michel, *Mémoires*, Paris 1826, vols. III, IV.

Talleyrand, C. M. de, *Mémoires*, Paris 1891, vol. II.

3. Secondary Works

Askenazy, Szymon, *Napoleon a Polska*, Warsaw 1919, vol. III.

———, "Cz. ministrem rosyjskim," *Wczasy Historyczne*, Warsaw 1902.

———, "Na rozdrożu," *Biblioteka Warszawska*, 1911.

———, "Polska i Europa," *Biblioteka Warszawska*, 1909.

———, "Z przeszłości Czarnogórza," "O sprawie polskiej 1812," "Zjazd w Puławach," *Szkice i portrety*, Warsaw 1937.

Bartoszewicz, Kazimierz, *Utworzenie Królestwa Kongresowego*, Cracow 1916.

Batowski, Henryk, "Un précurseur polonais de l'Union Balcanique," *Revue Internationale des Etudes Balcaniques*, 1936.

Bibliography

Bignon, Louis de, *Histoire de France sous Napoleon*, Bruxelles 1842, 1846, vols. II, III.

Dupuis, Charles, "Les antécédents de la Société des Nations. Le plan de Czartoryski et d'Alexandre I, "*Séances et Travaux de l'Academie des Sciences Morales et Polit.*, 92ᵉ Année, 1929.

Handelsman, Marceli, *Napoléon et la Pologne*, Paris 1909.

———, *Rezydenci napoleońscy w Warszawie*, Cracow 1915.

———, *Pomiędzy Prusami a Rosją*, Warsaw 1922.

Iwaszkiewicz, Janusz, *Litwa 1812*, Warsaw 1912.

Krotoska, J., *Stosunek Talleyranda do sprawy polskiej 1806-14*, Warsaw 1936.

Kukiel, Marian, "Ligue des Nations, Union Européenne et la 3ᵉ Coalition," *Teki Historyczne* (Historical Papers), 1950.

———, "Plan Polityczny cz. 1803," *Rocznik Polskiego Towarzystwa Naukowego*, London 1951.

———, "Vues sur le trône de Pologne en 1812," *Revue des Etudes Napoléoniennes*, 1932.

———, "*Wojna 1812 roku*," Cracow 1937, 2 vols.

Loret, Maciej, *Między Jeną a Tylżą*, Warsaw 1902.

Morley, Charles, "Alexander I and Czartoryski," *Slavonic and East Eur. Review*, 1947.

———, "Cz.'s Attempts at a new Foreign Policy under Alexander I," *American Slavic and East European Review*, 1953.

Nagórska-Rudzka, W., "Opinia publiczna w Księstwie Warszawskiem w roku 1813," *Przegląd Historyczny*, 1928.

Nicholas Mikhailovich, *see* A.III, and *Kniazia Dolgorukie*, St. Petersburg 1901.

Rain, Pierre, *Un Tsar idéologue. Alexandre I*, Paris 1913.

Schiemann, Theodor, *Geschichte Russlands unter Nikolaus I*, Berlin 1904, I.

Schilder, Nicholay Karlovich, *Imperator Alexandr I*, St. Petersburg 1897, vols. I-III.

Smolka, Stanisław, *Polityka Lubeckiego*, Cracow 1907, 2 vols.

Vernadsky, G., "Alexandre I et la probleme Slave," *Revue des Etudes Slaves*, 1927, vol. VII.

Waliszewski, Casimir, *Le règne d'Alexandre I*, Paris 1923, 3 vols.

Wawrzkowicz, Eugeniusz, "Anglia i Rosja przed wojną 1812," *Biblioteka Warszawska*, 1912.

———, "Aleksander I i Cz. w Londynie 1814," *Biblioteka Warszawska*, 1910.

———, "Anglik, przyjaciel Polski" (R. T. Wilson), *Biblioteka Warszawska*, 1912.

Bibliography

——, "Anglia a sprawa polska 1813-1815" Warsaw 1917.

Webster, Sir Charles, *The Congress of Vienna*, London 1919.

——, *The Foreign Policy of Castlereagh, 1812-1815*, London 1831.

Zaleski, Bronisław, "Księcia Cz. ministerstwo spraw zagranicznych," *Przegląd Polski*, 1878-1879.

II. Years 1815-1831

1. Manuscripts

Cz.'s papers, *see* A.I, esp. volumes relating to the Senate of the Kingdom, to the High Court, to the National Government 1830-1831, correspondence with representatives abroad and with Skrzynecki.

Papers of the Polish Foreign Office 1831 and of several dipl. agencies, *ibidem*.

Skrzynecki's papers, *ibidem*.

Horodyski's papers relating to the Polish diplomacy 1830-1833, in the Mss. Coll. of the Polish Acad., Cracow.

Archives of the Polish Legation 1830-1832 in the Mss. Coll. of the Bibliothèque Polonaise, Paris.

Public Record Office, F. O., Russia 1830-1833, 1848-1849, and Austria 1830-1831, 1846, 1853-1856.

Arch. des Affaires Etrangères, Paris, Corr. Russie, 1830-1832, 1848-1849, 1856, Corr. Autriche, 1846, 1853-1856.

Papers of the Criminal High Court 1831-1834, Archiwum Akt Dawnych (State Archiv), Warsaw.

2. Published Original Sources

Angeberg, *Recueil des traités, see* B.I, 2.

Cz. i Józef Twardowski, korespondencja 1822-24, Poznań 1899.

Bieczyński, Tadeusz, *Sąd Sejmowy 1827-29*, Cracow 1873.

Lewak, Adam, *Le Général Lafayette et la cause polonaise*, Warsaw 1934 (doc. and speeches).

Lisicki, Alexander, *Margrabia Wielopolski*, Cracow 1878, vol. IV (Papers of the London Mission, 1830-1831).

Pomarański, Stefan, "Diariusz Senatu 1830-31," *Archiwum Komisji Hist. Polskiej Akademii Um.*, Cracow 1930.

Rostworowski, Michał, *Diariusz Sejmu 1830-31*, Cracow 1907-1912, 6 vols.

Sbornik Russk. Istor, Obshchestva, vols. CXXXI, CXXXII (Correspondence of Nicholas I and Grand Duke Constantine).

Bibliography

Smolka, Stanislas, *Korespondencja Lubeckiego*, Cracow 1909, 4 vols.
Talleyrand, Ch. M. de, *Correspondance diplomatique. Ambassade à Londres*, Paris 1891.

Memoirs

Niemcewicz, J. U., *Pamiętnik 1830-31*, Cracow 1909.
Sapieha, L., *Wspomnienia*, Lwów 1913.
Talleyrand, Ch. M. de, *Mémoires*, Paris 1891-1892, vol. iv.
Zamoyski, Ladislas, *Jeneral Zamoyski*, Kórnik 1910 ff., vols. i, ii.
Zamoyski, Andrzej, *Moje przeprawy*, Cracow 1906.

3. Secondary Works

(a) Written by Contemporaries

Barzykowski, Stanisław, *Historia powstania listopadowego*, Poznań 1883-1888, 5 vols.
Forster, Karol, *Powstanie narodu polskiego, 1831*, Berlin 1873.
Hoffman, Karol, *Rzut oka na stan polityczny Królestwa Polskiego pod panowaniem rosyjskiem*, Warsaw 1831.
Mochnacki, Maurycy, *Powstanie narodu polskiego*, Paris 1834, 2 vols.
Morawski, Teodor, *Dzieje narodu polskiego*, Poznań 1876-78, vols. v, vi.

(b) Written by Later Historians

Askenazy, Szymon, *Łukasiński*, 2nd ed., Warsaw 1929, 2 vols.
———, *Rosja-Polska 1815-30*, Lwów 1907.
———, "Polskie zabiegi dyplomatyczne 1831," *Biblioteka Warszawska*, 1902, 1903.
Dutkiewicz, Józef, *Austria wobec powstania listopadowego*, Cracow 1933.
———, *Francja a Polska 1831*, Łódź 1950.
Gadon, Lubomir, see A.IV.
Guyot, Raymond, *La première Entente Cordiale*, Paris 1926.
Handelsman, M., *Francja i Polska*, Warsaw 1920.
———, *Les idées françaises et la mentalité politique en Pologne*, Paris 1927.
Kallenbach, Józef, "Kuratoria Wileńskie," *Czasy i Ludzie*, Warsaw 1905.
Karnovich, Eugeni P., *Tsesarevich Constantine Pawlovich*, St. Petersburg 1899.
Kukiel, Marian, "Banicja księcia Cz.," see A.IV.

Bibliography

————, "La Révolution de 1830 et la Pologne," *Revue Internationale d'Histoire Polit. et Constitutionelle*, No. 11, 1953.

Łopaciński, Wincenty, "Strategiczne pomysły Cz.," *Biblioteka Warszawska*. 1914.

Morley, Charles, "The European Significance of the November Uprising," *Journal of Central European Affairs*, 1952.

Mościcki, Henryk, *Wilno i Warszawa w "Dziadach" Mickiewicza*, Warsaw 1908.

Nagórska-Rudzka, W., *see* A.IV.

Schiemann, Teodor, *Geschichte Russlands unter Nikolaus I*, Berlin 1904-1919, vols. II and III.

Schilder, N. V., *Imperator Alexandr I*, St. Petersburg 1897, vol. IV.

————, *Imperator Nicholay I*, St. Petersburg 1903, vols. I, II.

Sliwiński, Artur, *Joachim Lelewel*, Warsaw 1902.

Webster, Sir Charles, *The Foreign Policy of Palmerston 1830-1841*, London 1951.

Więckowska, Helena, *Opozycja liberalna w Królestwie Polskiem*, Warsaw 1925.

III. Years 1831-1861

1. Manuscripts

Cz.'s papers in Czartoryski Mss., esp. his diplomatic memoranda and projects, minutes of his conversations with European statesmen, esp. with Palmerston, Napoleon III, Drouyn de Lhuys, Persigny, Walewski; his correspondence with S. Barzykowski, J. Bem, F. Breański, L. Bystrzonowski, W. Chrzanowski, M. Czaykowski, H. Dembiński, T. Działyński, K. Hoffman, K. Kniaziewicz, G. Małachowski, A. Mickiewicz, Charles de Montalembert, T. Morawski, J. U. Niemcewicz, L. Orpiszewski, L. Sapieha, J. Skrzynecki, Lord Dudley Coutts Stuart, F. Zach, Ladislas Zamoyski, L. Zwierkowski (Lenoir).

Papers of the political leagues, "Związek Jedności Narodowej" and "Trzeci Maj."

Papers of Cz.'s political office, "Bureau." The correspondence with agencies and emissaries.

Papers of Bem, Breański, Bystrzonowski, Chrzanowski, Dembiński, *ibidem.*

Papers relating to Polish institutions in exile, *ibid.* and in Bibliothèque Polonaise.

Archives of the Polish Legation in Paris 1831-1833 and records of the Polish Diet in exile, in Bibliothèque Polonaise in Paris.

Bibliography

Cz.'s letters and documents relating to the seizure of Sieniawa in 1846, *ibidem*, Ms. Coll. 54.

Papers of Bem, Breański, Adam Mickiewicz, Karol Sienkiewicz, Bystrzonowski, Kniaziewicz, Peter Łagowski, *ibidem*.

Woronicz, Janusz, "Moje wspomnienia" (unpublished memoirs), *ibid.*

Lord Dudley Stuart's correspondence with Cz. and others relating to Polish questions, *see* A.I.

Czaykowski's papers, *see* A.I.

2. Published Original Sources

Angeberg, *Recueil*, *see* B.I, 2.

Extracts from Cz.'s papers in his *Memoirs*, vol. II.

Album Muzeum Narodowego w Rapperswilu, 1872, vol. I, *see* A.III.

Benis, Adam, *Une mission militaire polonaise en Egypte*. Le Caire 1938, 2 vols. (Contains large extracts from Cz.'s political correspondence, 1832-34.)

[Zamoyski, Ladislas], *Jenerał Zamoyski*, *see* A.III, vols. III-VI.

Gawroński, Franciszek Rawita, *Materiały do historii polskiej XIX w.*, *see* A.III.

Talleyrand, Ch. M., *Correspondance diplomatique*, *see* B.II, 2.

Hansard, *Parliamentary Debates*, esp. years 1832-1833, 1836, 1846, 1856, 1861.

Periodicals

Polonia, or Monthly Reports on Polish Affairs. Published by the Literary Society of the Friends of Poland, London 1832.

The British and Foreign Review, London 1835-1844, 18 vols.

The Portfolio, ed. by D. Urquhart, London 1836-1837 and 1843-1845, 12 vols. French translation, Paris 1837.

Kraj i Emigracja. Zbiór pism politycznych i wojskowych, ed. by L. Bystrzonowski, Paris 1835-1843, 2 vols.

Trzeci Maj, ed. by J. Woronicz and L. Orpiszewski, Paris 1839-1846.

Wiadomości Polskie, ed. by W. Kalinka and J. Klaczko, Paris 1857-1861.

Roczniki Polskie z lat 1857-1861, ed. by W. Kalinka and J. Klaczko, Poznań 1865.

Political Treatises and Pamphlets

Bystrzonowski, Louis, *Sur la Serbie*, Paris 1845.

Bibliography

Hoffman, Karol, *Cztery powstania*, Paris 1837.

Klaczko, Julian, *Zapomniane pisma (1850-1866)*, Cracow 1912.

Lelewel, Joachim, *La couronne de Pologne et la royauté*, Paris 1837.

Ostrowski, Józefat Bolesław, *Rewolucja 1830 i jej kierownicy*, Paris 1844 (libellous).

——, *Adam George Prince Cz.*, Paris 1845 (libellous).

Woronicz, Janusz, "Rzecz o dynastii w Polsce," *Kraj i Emigracja*, 1839, vol. ii.

Memoirs

Breański, Felix, "Autobiografia," *Przewodnik Naukowy i Literacki*, 1913.

Budzyński, M., "Zapiski," *Russkaya Starina*, 1895, 1896, 1897, 1898, 1900, 1904.

Jełowicki, A., *Moje wspomnienia*, Paris 1839, 2 vols.

Koźmian, Stanisław E., *Anglia i Polska*, Poznań 1862, vol. i.

Miłkowski, Zygmunt, "Mehmed Sadyk Pasza," *Sylwetki emigracyjne*, Lwów 1904.

Pulszky, Franz v., *Meine Zeit, mein Leben*, Pressburg 1880-1883, 4 vols.

3. Secondary Works

Batowski, Henryk, *Państwa bałkańskie 1800-1923*, Cracow 1938 (extensive bibliography).

Bell, Herbert G. F., *Lord Palmerston*, London 1936, 2 vols.

Bolsover, G. H., "David Urquhart and the Eastern Question," *Journal of Modern History*, 1936.

Czapska, Maria, *Ludwika Śniadecka*, Warsaw 1938.

Feldman, Józef, *Sprawa polska 1848*, Cracow 1933.

——, "U podstaw stosunków polsko-angielskich," *Polityka Narodów*, 1933.

Frejlich, Józef, *Legion Jenerała Bema*, Warsaw 1912.

Friedjung, Heinrich, *Der Krimkrieg und die Oesterreichische Politik*, Stuttgart 1907.

Gadon, Lubomir, *Emigracja polska*, Cracow 1901-1902, 3 vols.

Gleason, John H., *The Genesis of Russophobia in Great Britain*, Cambridge 1950.

Guichen, Eugene de, *La guerre de Crimée et l'attitude des puissances*, Paris 1936.

Handelsman, M., *A. Cz.*, see A.IV, esp. vols. ii, iii.

——, *Francja i Polska*, and is a link to the French version of the same book: *Les idées . . .* etc.

——, *Les idées françaises*, see B.II, 3.

{ 333 }

Bibliography

————, *Czartoryski, Nicholas I et la question du Proche Orient,* Paris 1934.

————, *Rok 1848 we Włoszech i polityka Cz.,* Cracow 1936.

————, *Ukraińska polityka księcia Cz.,* Warsaw 1937.

————, *Mickiewicz 1853-1855,* Warsaw 1933.

————, "Stanowisko Francji w sprawie polskiej," *Studia hist. ku czci S. Kutrzeby,* Cracow 1938, vol. II.

Kieniewicz, Stefan, *Społeczeństwo polskie w powstaniu poznańskiem,* Warsaw 1935.

————, *Adam Sapieha,* Lwów 1939.

Kukiel, M., "Koncepcje powstania narodowego," *Teki Historyczne,* 1948.

Lewak, Adam, *Dzieje emigracji polskiej w Turcji (1831-1878),* Warsaw 1935.

Mickiewicz, Władysław, *Żywot Adama Mickiewicza,* Poznań 1890-1895, 4 vols.

Morawski, K., *Polacy i sprawa polska w dziejach Italii,* Warsaw 1937.

Pawlicowa, Maria, "O niektórych pomysłach monarchicznych," *Kwartalnik Historyczny,* 1927.

————, "Ze starań o legię, 1853-54," *Kwartalnik Historyczny,* 1932.

Pawłowski, Bronisław, "Przeprawa księcia Cz. przez ziemie austriackie," *Kwartalnik Historyczny,* 1909.

Rusjan, Ludwik, *Polacy i sprawa polska na Węgrzech 1848-49,* Warsaw 1934.

Shcherbatov, Prince, *General-Feldmarshal Kniaz Paskevich,* St. Petersburg 1888-1904, vols. IV-VII.

Schiemann, Teodor, *see* B.II, 3, vols. III and IV.

Serejski, M. H., *Karol B. Hoffman,* Łódź 1953.

Temperley, Harold, *England and the Near East. The Crimea,* London 1936.

Webster, Sir Charles, *The Foreign Policy of Palmerston,* London 1951.

————, "Urquhart, Ponsonby and Palmerston," *English Hist. Review,* 1947.

Wereszycki, Henryk, "O sprawę polską 1854 i 1855," *Kwartalnik Historyczny,* 1927.

Widerszal, Ludwik, *Sprawy kaukaskie 1831-1864,* Warsaw 1934.

————, *Bułgarski ruch narodowy,* Warsaw 1937.

Żywczyński, Mieczysław, *Geneza i następstwa encykliki "Cum Primum,"* Warsaw 1935.

INDEX

Index

197, 212, 225, 241, 251-257, 285; and Cracow, 240, 257-258; and Polish national movement 1846, Galician massacres, 253-257; and the revolution of 1848-1849, 261-265, 271-274; and Crimean war, 278-281, 283, 285-291, 294, 298; and Polish question revived, 285-291, 293-294, 296; and soundings of Czartoryski, 290-291, 307-308

Azeglio, Massimo d', Italian political writer and statesman, 260

Baden, revolution of, 268
Baden, Markgraf, then Grand Duke Frederick of, 28, 42
Badeni, Stanislas, Count, Polish diplomatic emissary, 225
Bakunin, Michael, Russian revolutionary leader, 270
Balkan peoples, 33-36, 39-41, 70-81, 225-226, 232, 245-248, 275, 281, 320, 322
Baltic Sea, 32-33, 197, 262, 264, 284, 288
Bar, town in Podolia, Confederation of, 6
Baraguey d'Hilliers, Achille, French general and diplomat, 285
Barante, Amable-Guillaume-Prosper-Brugière, Baron de, French politician and diplomat, 21-22
Bärensprung, Prussian police director, 299
Bartenstein, town in Eastern Prussia, agreement of, 77, 84
Barzykowski, Stanislas, member of the Polish National Government 1831, politician and historical writer, 217, 227, 262, 298
Batignolles (Paris suburb), Polish school at, 216
Bavaria, 89
Beaumont, Miles Thomas Stapleton, Lord, 247
Beaumont, Thomas Wentworth, British member of Parliament and political writer, 200-201, 203, 236, 238, 240 n
Belgium, 53, 67, 166, 174-175, 181, 184, 203 n, 211-212, 229, 240; and Poles in Belgian army, 211-212, 240
Belgrade, 247-248, 262, 270
Bell, George, British politician, skipper of the *Vixen*, 237, 243
Bell, Stanley, British writer and politician, skipper of the *Vixen*, 237

Belvedere, palais in Warsaw, 23, 236
Bem, Joseph, Polish and Hungarian general, 211-212, 216-217, 272-274
Benckendorff, Alexander T., Count, Russian general and chief of political police, 149 n, 164, 174
Bentham, Jeremy, British philosopher, 117 n
Berg, Grand Duchy of, 80
Berlin, 58-59, 61-62, 64-66, 69-70, 116, 166, 179, 250, 258, 261-263, 266-268, 286-287
Bernadotte, Jean Baptiste, Prince of Ponte Corvo, then Prince Regent of Sweden, then Charles XIV, King of Sweden, 65, 292. *See* Oscar I, Charles XV, Oscar, Prince of Sweden
Białystok, district of, 86
Bieliński, Peter, Polish senator, 146-147, 159
Biernacki, Felix, librarian and Czartoryski's political agent, 110-113, 133 n
Bignon, Louis, Baron, French diplomat, 98, 180, 204, 206
Birmingham, 206
Bismarck, Otto, Prince, German Chancellor, 122, 298
Blacas, Pierre Louis, Comte de (afterwards Duke), French Minister of Foreign Affairs, 125 n
Black Prince (Edward, Prince of Wales), 222
Black Sea, 262, 282, 284, 288
Błotnicki, Hipolit, tutor of young Czartoryskis, 168
Blum, Robert, German republican leader, 268
Bochnia, town in Galicia and district of, 253
Bohemia, 106, 156, 264
Bonaparte (or Buonaparte), *see* Napoleon I
Bonaparte, Jerôme (Jerôme Napoleon), King of Westphalia, 85, 98-99, 288
Bonaparte, Joseph (Joseph Napoleon), King of Naples, then King of Spain, 56
Bonaparte, Louis Napoleon, Prince, President of the French Republic, then Emperor, *see* Napoleon III
Bonaparte, Napoleon, Prince, 283
Bosnia, 248, 307
Bosphorus, 229, 239, 248, 282

Index

Index

Chłopicki, Joseph, Polish general, 168, 172-173, 176-179, 186

Chodźko, Leonard, Polish historian and politician, 165

Chopin, Frederick, 215

Chrzanowski, Adalbert (Wojciech), Polish general, 187, 216, 227, 234-235, 239-240, 244-245, 260, 262, 271, 281, 283, 298-299

Cintrat, Pierre, political director of the French Ministry of Foreign Affairs, 231, 284-285

Circassians, 235-238, 240, 243, 248, 256, 296, 304

Circourt, Adolphe de, French diplomat, 265

Clarendon, George William Frederick Villiers, 4th Earl of, British statesman, 237, 279, 286, 297, 302-303

Cobenzl, Louis, Count, Austrian diplomat, 64

Cologne, 273

Confederations of Radom, 5; of Bar, 6; General Confederation of the Kingdom of Poland 1812, 9, 98-106

Constantine Olgerdovich, Duke of Czernichow and Czartorysk, 3

Constantine Pavlovich, Grand Duke Tsesarevich, 21 n, 22-23, 33, 96, 102, 125-126, 132, 150, 161, 164-173, 236; and Nicholas I, 140-150, 164-170, 172, 178, 186; and Czartoryski, 22-23, 33, 132-139, 145-146, 148, 178; and the Insurrection 1830, 169-173, 186

Constantinople, 39, 52, 88, 207, 229, 237-238, 244-245, 247, 262, 276, 281-283, 285-286, 299-300, 304-305

Constitution of May 3, 1791, 9, 12-13, 37, 94, 98

Corfu, island of, 41

coronation plot (against Nicholas I), 159-161

Cossacks, 248-249, 270, 284; Polish formations, 281, 287, 294-300, 304-305

Courland, 284

Courland, Anna, Princess Biren-Sagan, Duchess of, 88

Courtenay, Thomas Peregrine, British politician and author, 199

Cowper, Lady Amelie, then Lady Palmerston, 197 n

Cracow (and Republic of), 104, 114, 126, 130, 192, 194, 240, 242-243, 253-254, 257-258, 265, 267, 290

Crimea and Crimean war, 284-302, 320

Croatia, Croats, 34, 245, 272, 273, 320

Currie, English doctor, 12-13

Custozza, battle of, 271

Czacki, Thaddeus, Polish politician, scholar and bibliophile, 137

Czartorysk, ducal fief in Volhynia, 3 n

Czartoryska, Anna, Princess, née Princess Sapieha, 136-137, 209, 215-216, 255-256

Czartoryska, Isabella, née Flemming, 5, 9, 10-15, 21, 88-90, 98-99, 107-108, 136

Czartoryska, Izabella, Princess, née Morstin, 3

Czartoryska, Maria, see Württemberg, Princess Maria of

Czartoryska, Maria Amparo, Princess, née Countess of Vista Allegre, 249, 297

Czartoryska, Sophie, née Sieniawska, 3

Czartoryski, Princes, descent, 3; part in Polish history, 3; the Family, 3-4, and their coup d'état, 4-5; and Russia, 4-6, 13-17; and Constitution of 1791, 13; and Kościuszko, 14-15; and Napoleon, 98-99; and Enlightenment, 144; and attitude in 1830, 170, 193; and "kingship de facto," 220-221, 227-228

Czartoryski, Adam Casimir, Prince, general of Podolia, 4-6, 8-15, 30, 89-90, 98-99; personality, 4, 6, 8-9; marshal of the convocational Diet 1764, 5; Commander of the Cadet Corps, 6; and the Committee for National Education, 6; and Stanislas Augustus, 8-9; and the Constitution of 3rd May, 9; and Napoleonic Poland, 89-90; and marshal of the General Confederation 1812, 9, 98-99

CZARTORYSKI, ADAM GEORGE, Prince, descent, spiritual inheritance, education, 9-15; and personality, 12-13, 15, 19-22, 26-28, 68, 72, 88-89, 143-144, 159, 193-194, 214-215, 222-223, 228, 255-256, 278-279, 316-320; and first struggles for freedom, 13-16; and Russian Court, 16-22; and mission to Italy, 22-23; Secret Committee, 25-26, 29, 35, 69-77, 79, 81; assistant then acting minister of Foreign Affairs in Russia, 26-77, 232, 320;

Index

curator of the Vilna University, 26, 29-30, 37-38, 79, 138-139, 318-319

Planning Russia's foreign policy, 28-40; conceptions of a united Europe, 30-35, 43-49, 151-158, 320; principle of nationality, 46-47, 49, 151-156; Society of States, and League of Nations and safeguards of peace, 31, 35, 46-50, 151, 155-156; and Sully's Grand Design, 35, 129, 151, 156-157; and Saint-Pierre, 31; and Kant, 31, 153; and Woodrow Wilson, 47, 49, 318, 322

Plans of Poland's restoration in union with Russia, 33-39, 61, 67, 74, 78-81, 83-85, 91-101, 106-130, 155-158, 318; and Eastern Polish provinces, 36-38, 83-84, 89-98, 108, 224, 318, 320-321; and planning new maps of Europe, 30-35, 43-48, 79-81, 156; and Third Coalition, 59-67; plans of action against Prussia, 61-67, 72-76; Austerlitz, 68-71, 73-74; leaving Russian governmental duties, 74-77; crisis in policy and friendship, 77-101; and Russian friends, 25-26, 29, 35, 44-56, 86, 93, 99, 105

Facing a Napoleonic Poland, 86-100; and refusing to elevate "altar against altar," 92-98; and trying to rescue a Polish State, 102-129; and making of the Kingdom of Poland, 129-135; and breakdown of his policy, 134-138

Marriage, 136-137; Puławy and Vilna, 137-139, 143; and Geneva and Florence, 142-143; trial of the Patriotic Society, 145-150; leader of the opposition, 151-170; and the "coronation plot," 159-160; and the November Revolution, 167-178, 319; president of the National Government, 178-193, 210-211, 221-222, 319; his diplomacy, 178-185; his strategy, 178-179, 185-192; outlaw, 193, 214; exile, 193-320

Emigration, 194, 209-320; vindication of Poland's rights, 194-208, 301-304, 308-310, 319-320; national leadership, 217-228, 261-271, 281-299, 307-313, 319-321; "kingship de facto," 219-221, 227-228, 254-255, 261, 315-316; and the Hôtel Lambert, 227-228; and leading political ideas, 217-219, 221-224; and rebuilding of a national armed force, 194-195, 211-212, 219, 235, 264, 281-301; and diplomatic activities in exile, 210-314; and the problem of peasants, 163-164, 217-218, 223-224, 252-253, 309-310; relations with the Holy See, 152, 157, 225-227; working for an Anglo-French alliance and integration of a free Europe, 229-231, 242-246, 249, 257-258, 277-286, 320; and the Eastern question, 33-36, 39-41, 70-81, 225-226, 245-249, 270, 274-301

Insurrection of 1846 and consequences, 251-259; revolution of 1848-1849, 260-273; Crimean war, war aims and strategic conceptions, 278-288; recognized by the Allies as spokesman of the Polish Emigration, 284-285; his conditions of an insurrection, 291, 294-295, 297; vindication of the Polish cause at the Congress of Paris, 301-304; and the aftermath, 304-306; and possibilities of an "Austro-Polish" solution, 307-308

Events in Poland in 1861 and his last instructions and will, 310-314

RELATIONS WITH OTHER COUNTRIES

Czartoryski and Austria, 33-34, 41-43, 45, 49, 51, 53-54, 56, 58-69, 102, 109, 152-158, 179-180, 240, 245, 255, 256, 263-264, 269, 278-291; and Balkan peoples, 33-36, 39-41, 70-81, 225-226, 245-248, 275; and Belgium, 184, 211, 230, 240; and Bohemia (Czechs), 157, 245, 264, 269, 270, 320; and Bulgaria, 226-227, 275, 306, 320; and Circassians, 235-240, 243, 248, 256, 296, 304, 306; and Cossacks, 248-249; and Egypt, 212-233; and France, 32-35, 40-42, 44-53, 81, 155-158, 176-185, 194-211, 223, 231, 241-245, 251-258, 261-262, 274-275, 277-303, 320; and Germany, 34, 45, 81, 230-231, 260-268; and Great Britain, 12-13, 28, 32, 34-36, 38-41, 52-59, 66-70, 74-75, 80-81, 84-87, 109-131, 151, 195-210, 222, 229-232, 240-245, 257-260, 271, 274-275, 277-304, 312-314, 318, 320; and Greece, 36, 39-41, 70, 143, 155, 232; and Holland, 45, 56, 81; and Hungary, 157, 264, 320; and Italy, 34, 45, 152, 157, 229, 259-261, 320; and Lithuanians, 224; and Portugal, 211,

Index

231-232; and Prussia, 29, 33, 35, 39, 56, 61-78, 80-81, 85, 102, 106, 109, 157-158, 249-250, 261-269, 278, 290; and Rumania, 36, 239, 272-273, 278-279, 320, 322; and Serbia, 36, 272-275, 320; and Slavs, 33-36, 40, 245-249, 260-276, 320-321; and Spain, 212, 231-232, 249; and Sweden, 54, 157, 292-293; and Switzerland, 34, 41, 45; and Turkey, 3-36, 39-41, 70, 81, 156-157, 232-235, 239-240, 245-249, 274-304; and Ukrainians (Ruthenians), 224, 248-249, 269-270

RELATIONS WITH PEOPLE

Czartoryski and Alexander I, 17, 19-30, 35, 38-40, 54, 63-81, 83-85, 88-109, 114-116, 118, 124, 132-135, 137, 139, 140, 143, 221-222, 318, 320; and Elisabeth, 21-23, 132, 134-135, 143, 146; and Constantine Pavlovich, 22-23, 33, 39, 133-139, 145-148, 150, 167-169, 230; and Napoleon I, 33-35, 42, 44, 73, 79-82, 85-88, 91-101, 154-158, 275; and Pitt, 12-13, 43, 50-54, 56-59, 120; and Castlereagh, 14, 17, 121-130; and Nicholas I, 140, 145-150, 157-164, 193-194, 198-199, 225-227, 235-237, 245-247, 261-264; and Grey, 12, 14, 113, 116, 126, 176, 197-198, 236, 258; and Palmerston, 181-182, 184-185, 198, 205, 207, 229-232, 236-237, 239, 240-243, 257-258, 265-266, 271, 279, 295-298, 302; and Talleyrand, 42, 88, 120-121, 127-128, 131, 154, 176, 181, 184-185, 195-197, 204-205; and Napoleon III, 275, 277-304, 306; and Alexander II, 301-306, 309; and Francis Joseph I, 289-290, 307-308

PHILOSOPHICAL ATTITUDE

Czartoryski and Christianity, 144, 152, 224-228, 311-314; and Freemasonry, 107, 144, 224-225; and literary, philosophical, and political writings and speeches, 15-16, 144, 151-158, 204 n, 221-225, 311-313

Czartoryski, Augustus, Prince, Voyvode of Ruthenia, 3-4, 110

Czartoryski, Casimir, Prince, Vice Chancellor of Lithuania, 3

Czartoryski, Constantine, Prince, Polish general, 14-15, 17, 21, 90, 98, 119, 183, 255-256, 307

Czartoryski, Ladislas, Prince, Polish statesman, 209, 221, 228, 249, 297, 299-300, 306-307, 313

Czartoryski, Leon, 143

Czartoryski, Vitold, Prince, soldier and politician, 209, 221, 228, 249, 270, 313

Czaykowski, Michael, then Mehemet Sadyk Effendi, then Sadyk Pasha, Polish diplomatic agent, then Turkish general, 245-248, 273-276, 281-282, 294, 299-300

Czechs, national revival of, 245, 269-270, 320

Czernichov, province in Ukraine, 3

Dąbrowski, Jan Henry, Polish general, 84

Danube, river, 60, 83, 273, 281, 284, 286, 297

Danubian principalities, see Moldavia and Wallachia

Danzig, 29

Decembrist conspiracy and insurrection, 144-147, 205

Delavigne, Charles, French poet, 209 n

Delbrück, Hans, German historian, 184

Dembe Wielkie, battle of, 187

Dembiński, Henry, Polish general, 179, 191, 212, 217, 233-234, 272-274

Democratic Society (Polish Democratic Party), 217, 219, 251-255

Désages, Émile, political director of the French Ministry of Foreign Affairs, 231

Diebitsch, Ivan, Count Zabalkansky, Russian field marshal, 166-169, 174, 185-190

Dino, Dorothy, née Princess Biren-Sagan, Duchess of, 21-22, 88, 91, 204

Disraeli, Benjamin, British statesman, 279

Dnieper river, 87, 95, 115, 248, 270, 284

Dniester river, 39

Dobrudja, 248, 281

Dolgoruki, Michael Petrovich, Prince, aide-de-camp to Alexander I, 26, 54

Dolgoruki, Peter Petrovich, Prince, aide-de-camp to Alexander I and diplomatic emissary, 26, 54, 64-68, 70

Don river, 248-249

Dresden, 8, 97, 145, 165

Index

Index

Frederick Augustus, Elector then King of Saxony and Duke of Warsaw, 8, 84, 105, 127-128

Frederick William III, King of Prussia, 29, 53, 62, 64-67, 78, 84, 96, 104, 106-107, 114, 120, 125, 129, 165-166

Frederick William IV, King of Prussia; and Nicholas I, 249-250; and Poland, 249-250, 258-259, 261-266

Freemasonry, 107, 116, 144, 224-225

Freiligrath, Ferdinand, German poet, 213 n

Friedland, battle of, 77, 81

Gadon, Lubomir, Polish historical writer, 219

Gagarin, Nicholas S., Prince, Russian diplomat, 225

Galicia, 36, 65, 89-91, 115, 117, 183, 192, 278; and insurrection 1809, 89-91; and insurrection 1846, 251-256; and peasant problem, 251-254, 263-264; and massacres, 253-254, 257; and revolution 1848, 262-270; and problems of its future 1854-1859, 278, 290-292, 307-308

Galitzin, Serge, Prince, Russian general, 90

Garashanin, Elias, Serbian statesman, 247-248

Garlike, B., British diplomat, 39 n

Gatchina, Russian imperial residence, 19

Gedymin, Grand Duke of Lithuania, 3

Geneva, 143, 322

Genoa, 59

Gentz, Frederick, political writer and Austrian diplomat, 112

George III, King of Great Britain, 39, 54, 67

George IV, King of Great Britain (former Prince of Wales and Prince Regent), 54, 116, 125

Georgia, 235

Germany (German Empire, German Confederation), 32, 34, 42-43, 45, 49, 53, 67, 70, 81, 106, 113, 120, 156, 209, 213, 227, 229-230, 244, 257-259, 261-268, 286, 288

Gervinus, Georg Gottfried, German historian and politician, 259

Gibraltar, 58

Gielgud, Adam, Anglo-Polish journalist, 25

Gladstone, William Ewart, British statesman, 287

Glasgow, petition on behalf of Poland, 206

Gloucester, William, Duke of, 28

Gneisenau, Neidhardt Augustus, Prussian general, 110

Golovine, Varvara N., Countess, 21

Gołuchów, Działyńskis' residence in Poznania, 307

Gołuchowski, Agenor, Count, Austro-Polish statesman, 290, 307

Gorchakov, Alexander, Prince, Russian statesman, 298

Gorchakov, Michael, Russian general, Lieutenant of the Realm in Warsaw, 310-311

Görgei, Arthur, Hungarian general, 110

Gower, Lord Leveson, afterwards 1st Earl Granville, British envoy to Russia, 53 n, 55, 58, 59, 69-70, 84-85, 116

Gower, Lord Leveson, afterwards 2nd Earl Granville, British diplomat, 231 n, 301 n

Graham, Sir James, British minister, 279

Great Britain, 12, 14, 32, 34-35, 38-42, 51-53, 63, 65, 67, 74-75, 79, 81, 84-85, 116, 155-156

    Policy of a balance of power (just equilibrium), 39, 50-53, 109-114, 116-130, 181-182; and conceptions of safeguarding peace, 52-53; principle of nationality, 111-112, 113, 259-260; "principle of partition," 114, 120-125, 155; "bastion of European liberalism," 32, 34, 44-46, 86-87, 181, 229-230, 259-260, 273-274; India and colonialism, 153; public opinion and parliament, 112-113, 116, 124-125, 128-130, 197-203, 205-207, 232; policies towards Russia, 12-13, 39-42, 50-53, 59-60, 65, 67, 74-75, 109-114, 116-130, 181-182, 184, 195-207, 209-210, 227-230, 234-235, 244-245, 265-266, 279, 294-296, 300-301

    and Polish cause, 109-114, 116-130, 181-182, 184, 195-207, 209-210, 227, 240-245, 257-258, 262-266, 272, 294-296, 300-301; and Polish force under British command, 296-300

Great Diet (Great Seym), (1788-1792), 8, 12, 84, 261

Greece, Greeks, 36, 39, 41, 143, 155, 232, 320, 322

Index

Index

Index

Lazarists, religious order, cooperating with Czartoryski in Turkey, 248

League of National Unity (right wing independentist), 217-219, 252

Lebzeltern, Louis, Austrian general and diplomat, 104

Leipzig, 194, battle of, 107

Lelewel, Joachim, historian, Polish underground leader and member of the National Government 1831, 168-169, 172, 183, 205, 210

Leopold I, King of Belgium, 185 n, 211, 240, 243 n

Leuchtenberg, Maria-Eugene-Joseph-Napoleon, Duke of, 266

Leveson, Lord, see Gower

Leypuny, town in Lithuania, 103

Libelt, Charles, Polish philosopher and democratic leader, 266

Lieven, Christoph, Count, then Prince, Russian diplomat, 127 n, 230

Lieven, Dorothy, née Benckendorff, Countess, then Princess, 21, 184 n, 197, 200, 201 n, 202 n, 205, 236

Linowski, Alexander, Polish politician, 119

Literary Association of the Friends of Poland, 250, 302

Lithuania, 10, 13-15, 36-37, 62, 83-84, 89, 96-100, 103, 108, 112, 119, 121 n, 133-134, 138-143, 146, 165, 189, 200, 202, 224, 249, 254, 262, 284

Lithuanian Army Corps, 142, 149-150, 165-166, 186

Liverpool, Charles Jenkinson, Baron Hawkesbury, then the 2nd Earl of, British statesman, 39 n, 122-129

Lobkovitz, Augustus Longinus, Prince, Governor of Galicia, 183

Loftus, Lord, 241

Lombardy, Lombardians, 260, 270-271

Łomża, town in Central Poland and province of, 188

London, 12, 40, 43, 44, 49, 55-56, 59, 61, 63, 67, 76, 110, 116, 127-128, 179, 181, 184, 195, 208-209, 230-231, 237, 242-244, 250, 266, 279, 289, 291, 299, 314

Londonderry, 3rd Marquis of, see Stuart, Charles William

Lord, Robert Howard, American historian, 36

Lorraine, 115

Louis XVIII, 120 n

Louis Philippe, Duke d'Orléans, then King of the French, 166, 175-176, 180-181, 199, 203-204, 231, 239, 261

Louise, Queen of Prussia, 29, 35, 65-67

Low Countries, see Netherlands

Lubecki, Xavier Drucki-L, Prince, Polish statesman, 97, 150, 161, 172-173

Lublin, town in Central Poland and province of, 189-190, 192

Lubomirski, Casimir, Prince, 97

Lubomirski, George, Prince, Polish statesman in Galicia, 269-270

Łukasiński, Valerian, major, Grand Master of the Polish National Freemasonry, 138, 144-145, 161

Lushington, Stephen, British lawyer and politician, 199

Lyndhurst, John S. Copley, Baron, British statesman, 303 n

Maas river, 53

Mackintosh, Sir James, British politician, 117

McGregor, British diplomat, 140

McNeill, Sir John, British diplomat and political writer, 236-237

Magenta, battle of, 307

Magyars, see Hungarians

Mahmud II, Sultan, 242

Maistre, Joseph de, political and philosophical writer, Sardinian diplomat, 27

Małachowski, Gustave, Count, Polish statesman, 177, 181 n, 209, 217

Małachowski, Stanislas, marshal of the Great Diet, 13, 84

Malta, 41, 56-59

Mansfield, Sir James, Lord Chief Justice, 12

Maret Hugues, Duke of Bassano, French statesman, 100

Marcinkowski, Charles, doctor, Polish politician, 219, 250

Maria II, Queen of Portugal, 211, 214

Maria Alexandrovna, Grand Duchess, 21

Maria Christina, Queen of Spain, 249, 297

Maria Teodorovna, née Princess Sophie Dorothy Augusta of Würtemberg, Grand Duchess then Empress of Russia, 18, 22, 26, 29, 39, 71, 76, 140

Maria Theresia, Empress, 36

Index

Index

Index

afterwards Duke of, Portuguese statesman, 211

Palmerston, Henry John Temple, Viscount, British statesman, 176, 179 n, 182, 184-185, 196-198, 200-207, 229-230, 236-245, 257-260, 265-266, 274-275, 279, 283, 289, 294-298; and European liberalism, 197-198, 229-230, 241, 257-259; and Russia, 182, 197-198, 201-204, 229-230, 234-238, 257-258, 265-266, 274, 283-284, 287, 301-302; and Poland, 182, 197-198, 201-204, 207, 257-258, 265-266, 271, 274, 279, 289, 292, 296, 301-303, 313; and Czartoryski, 230, 234, 236-245, 247, 256, 275, 279, 302-303

Panmure, Fox Maule, 2nd Baron, British war secretary, 299 n

Paris, 51, 59, 75, 97, 114-115, 165, 168, 175-177, 179, 194-195, 205, 210, 215-217, 231, 242, 243, 249, 252, 256, 261-262, 265, 268, 279, 282, 289, 299, 313, 315

Paskievich, Ivan, Count Eryvansky, then Prince of Warsaw, Russian field marshal, 190-192, 246, 251, 273

Patriotic Society, Polish underground league, 144, 159, 165, 213, 220

Paul I, Emperor of Russia, 10, 17, 18, 20-24, 26, 28, 42, 44, 50, 54, 64, 136, 142; and Alexander, 17, 19, 20-21, 23; and Elisabeth, 21-22; and Czartoryski, 21-22; and his death, 23-24, 26, 42, 44

Pedro I, Emperor of Brazil, Regent of Portugal, 211

Peel, Sir Robert, British statesman, 201, 207, 233, 234, 243-244

Périer, Casimir, French statesman, 184, 206

Persia, 107, 229

Persigny, Jean-Gilbert-Victor-Fialin, Duke of, French statesman, 285

Peterswalde (Peterswaldau), borough in Silesia, 109

Petronevich, Abraham, Serbian leader, 247-248

Philaretes, secret society of, 138-139

Philomates, secret society of, 138-139

Phull, Karl Ludwig August, Prussian and Russian general, 84

Piattoli, Scipione, Abbé, Italian, Polish and Russian diplomat, 12, 30 n, 44 n

Piedmont, 34, 56, 213, 260-261, 270

Pigott, Sir Robert, British member of Parliament, 201

Pilica, river in Central Poland, 65, 104

Pitt, William, British Prime Minister, 12-13, 39, 43, 49-55, 57, 70, 84, 120; and Czartoryski's policy, 49-63, 70, 81, 111, 129, 318

Pius IX, Pope, 226, 259-260

Plater, Louis, Count, Polish politician, 97, 177, 180-181, 194, 217

Płock, town in Central Poland and province of, 190-192

Plutyński, Antoni, Polish historian, 89 n

Po river, 257

Podolia, 89, 103, 133, 207, 304

Poitiers, center of the Polish Democratic Society, 251

Poland, the Commonwealth and partitions, 3-9, 13-15, 36-38, 132, 152, 157, 197, 261, 299; and Czartoryski's plans of her restoration, 33-39, 61-66, 74, 79-81, 83-84, 87, 91-92, 96, 102-103, 110-117, 124, 127-128, 178-183, 211, 218-219, 230-231, 234-235, 245-246, 250, 261-271, 278, 284, 288, 320, 321; and her eastern provinces, 10, 13-15, 36-37, 62, 83-84, 89-101, 103, 108, 114-115, 119-121, 126-134, 140-143, 146, 161, 189, 200, 224-225, 319, 321; and Alexander I, 28, 61-67, 74, 78-81, 83-85, 89-102, 105, 107-142; and Napoleon, 78-81, 83-85, 89-106; and after his defeat, 103-118; and in Vienna, 119-131; and safeguards of her rights, 128-131, 194-202, 297; and the Kingdom of, 130-150, 155-170, 199, 244-245, 251, 256, 269, 290-292, 299, 301-303, 308-314, 319-321

Revolutions in France and Belgium and the November revolution, 164-169, 176, 179; and war of 1831, 178-192; and fate after, 193-194, 198, 200-201, 223; and Great Emigration, 193-194, 209-311; and the Polish state in exile, 216-228, 319-321; and the Underground movement, 251-254; and the peasant problem, 163-164, 217-219, 251-254, 263, 308-312; and the Catholic Church, 225-226, 321; and the attempted revolution of 1846, 251-255; and its conse-

Index

quences, 256-259; and revolutions 1848-1849, 260-278; and her cause in the Crimean war, 278-304; and the "moral revolution," 308-313
See also Warsaw, Duchy of; Galicia; and Poznania
Polish National Lodge (Masonic in London), 224-225
Polish People's Association, revolutionary underground league, 223
Połock, town and province of, 37
Pomerania, Polish (Royal Prussia, West Prussia), 29, 81 n, 86, 117
Pomerania, Swedish, 58, 61-62
Poniatowski, Joseph, Prince, Polish Commander-in-chief and war minister, 63, 84, 89, 90, 95, 97, 103, 105-107
Poniatowski, Stanislas, Castellan of Cracow, 3
Poniatowski, Stanislas Anthony, *see* Stanislas, Augustus
Ponsonby, George, British politician, 117
Ponsonby, John, Viscount, British diplomat, 237, 238, 239
Pope Henessy, John, Irish and Roman Catholic politician, member of Parliament, 289 n, 312-313
Portfolio, David Urquhart's political periodical, and Czartoryski, 236-237
Portugal, 211, 213, 229-232
Potemkin, Gregory, Prince, Russian general and statesman, 18
Potocka, Anne, Countess, 2do voto Wąsowicz, 136
Potocki, Ignatius, Count, Grand Marshal of the Grand Duchy of Lithuania, 13
Potocki, Stanislas, Count, Polish general, 168
Potocki, Stanislas Kostka, Count, Polish statesman, 132
Potsdam, 10, 61, 66-67, 78; and Treaty of, 61, 66-68, 74
Pourtalès, Steiger Louis, Count, friend to Prince William of Prussia, 266 n
Poznań (Posen), 29, 104, 117, 120, 254, 267, 299
Poznania (Grand Duchy of Posen, Prussian Poland), 227, 249-255, 258-259, 263-269, 291-292, 299, 307; and insurrection of, 264-268; and Czartoryski's leadership, 292, 307

Pozzo di Borgo, Charles Andrew, Count, Russian diplomat, 112, 175 n, 204
Pradt, Dominique de, Archbishop of Malines, French diplomat and political writer, 153
Prądzyński, Ignatius, Polish general, 187-189
Praga, suburb of Warsaw, 186-187
Prague and Slav Congress of, 269-270
Pressburg, treaty of, 80-81
Prussia, 33-34, 42-43, 45, 49-54, 56-89, 94, 96, 102, 104-106, 109, 113-115, 117, 120-132, 157, 165-167, 175, 179; and Poland, 13-14, 33-34, 61-66, 74, 78-85, 104-106, 110, 114, 117, 122, 125, 128, 130, 131, 157, 183-184, 196-197, 207, 209-210, 212, 240, 248-249, 252, 254, 257-259, 294, 299; and Grand Duchy of Posen, 227, 249-250, 254, 257-259, 261-269, 299; and "South Prussia," 62, 65; and Eastern Prussia, 62, 104; and West (Royal) Prussia, 81 n, 86
Puławy, residence of the Princes Czartoryskis, 10, 20-24, 65, 78, 119-120, 132, 137, 168, 173, 193, 203, 230 n
Pulszky, Francis, Count, Hungarian diplomat, 272
Pyrenees mountains, 56

Racine, 11
Racławice, battle of, 99
Radiants, students' association in Lithuania, 138
Radom, town in Poland; and Confederation of, 5
Radowitz, Joseph Maria von, Prussian aide-de-camp to the King and politician, 250
Radziwiłł, Antony, Prince, 106, 114, 259
Radziwiłł, Michael, Prince, Polish general, 179, 186
Ramorino, Jerôme, French colonel, then Polish general, 191-192, 213
Razumovsky, Andrew, Prince, Russian diplomat, 65, 70
"Reds" or "Party of Movement" in Poland, 309-311
Reeve, Henry, British political writer, 236-237, 240, 243
Reichenbach, town in Silesia and agreement of, 108-110, 122, 322

Index

Index

Index

Index

Index